The Law and Economics of the Environment

Edited by

Anthony Heyes

Professor of Economics, Royal Holloway College, University of London, UK

Edward Elgar

Cheltenham, UK • Northampton, MA, USA

Published by
Edward Elgar Publishing Limited
Glensanda House
Montpellier Parade
Cheltenham
Glos GL50 1UA
UK

Edward Elgar Publishing, Inc.
136 West Street
Suite 202
Northampton
Massachusetts 01060
USA

A catalogue record for this book is available from the British Library

Library of Congress Cataloging in Publication Data
The law and economics of the environment / edited by Anthony Heyes.
    p. cm.
  Includes bibliographical references and index.
  1. Environmental law—Economic aspects. 2. Law and economics. I. Heyes,
Anthony, 1967–

  K3585 .L39 2001
  333.7—dc21
                                                                    00–067689

ISBN 1 84064 339 0
Printed and bound in Great Britain by MPG Books Ltd, Bodmin, Cornwall

Contents

Figures

Tables

Contributors

Anna Alberini is Assistant Professor in the Department of Agricultural and Resource Economics, University of Maryland, College Park. She is an Associate Editor of the *Journal of Environmental Economics and Management*. Her publications include: 'Air quality and episodes of acute respiratory illness in Taiwanese cities' (with Alan Krupnick), *Journal of Urban Economics* (1998), 44(1): 68–92; and 'Estimating an emissions supply function from accelerated vehicle retirement programs' (with Winston Harrington and Virginia McConnell), *Review of Economics and Statistics* (1996), 78(2): 251–6.

David Austin is Research Fellow in the Quality of Environment Division at Resources for the Future, Washington, DC. His publications include: 'On and off the liability bandwagon: explaining state adoptions of strict liability in hazardous waste programs' (with Anna Alberini), *Journal of Regulatory Economics* (1999), 15(1): 41–63; and 'An event-study approach to measuring innovative output: the case of biotechnology', *American Economic Review* (1993), 83(2): 253–8.

James Boyd is a Research Fellow in the Energy and Natural Resources Division at Resources for the Future, Washington, DC. His publications include: 'Should relative safety be a test of product liability?' (with Daniel Ingberman), *Journal of Legal Studies* (1997), 26(2): 433–73; and 'Non-compensatory damages and potential insolvency' (with Daniel Ingberman), *Journal of Legal Studies* (1994), 23(2): 895–910.

Marcel Boyer is Jarislowsky Professor of Economics at the University of Montreal and President of CIRANO. His publications include: 'Toward a political theory of the emergence of environmental incentive regulation' (with Jean-Jacques Laffont), *RAND Journal of Economics* (1999), 30(1): 1427–59; and 'Environmental risks and bank liability' (with Jean-Jacques Laffont), *European Economic Review* (1997), 41(8): 1427–59.

Richard T. Carson is a Professor of Economics at the University of California, San Diego. He is Director for International Environmental Policy, Institute for Global Conflict and Cooperation, University of California. His publications include: 'The impact of "no opinion" response options on data quality in a CV survey' (with co-authors), *Review of Economics and Statistics* (1998), 80(1): 335–8; and 'Property rights, protest and the siting of hazardous waste facilities' (with Richard Carson), *American Economic Review* (1986), 76(2): 285–90.

David J. Chapman is a specialist in the evaluation of natural resource damages at the US National Oceanic and Atmospheric Administration (NOAA). His publications include: *Tampa Bay Oil Spill, Damage Assessment and Restoration Plan*, Vol. II: *Human Use Losses* (with others), Silver Springs, MD: NOAA, 1999; and 'The role of natural resource economics in natural resource damage assessments', in *Proceedings of the Yosemite Law Institute*, Yosemite, CA (1998).

Mark A. Cohen is Associate Professor of Economics and Strategy in the Owen Graduate School of Business, Vanderbilt University, where he is also Director of the Vanderbilt Center for Environmental Management Studies. His publications include: 'Regulating corporate criminal sanctions: federal guidelines and the sentencing of public firms' (with Cindy Alexander and Jennifer Arlen), *Journal of Law and Economics* (1999), 42(1): 393–422; and 'Information as regulation: the effect of community right to know laws on toxic emissions' (with Shameek Konar), *Journal of Environmental Economics and Management* (1997), 32(1): 109–24.

Paul K. Freeman is Project Manager of the Natural Catastrophes and Developing Countries Project at the International Institute of Applied Systems Analysis (IIASA) in Laxenberg, Austria. He was founder and Chief Executive of the specialty environmental insurance company, ERIC, and is a member of the Corporate Advisory Board of the Wharton School of the University of Pennsylvania. His publications include: 'Gambling on global catastrophes', in *Investing in Prevention: A Special Report on Disaster Risk Management*, Washington, DC: World Bank, 1999; and 'Environmental insurance as a policy enforcement tool in developing countries', *Journal of International Economic Law* (1997), 18(3): 422–86.

Michael Hanemann is a Professor in the Department of Agricultural and Resource Economics at the University of California, Berkeley. His publications include: 'Valuing the environment through contingent valuation', *Journal of Economic Perspectives* (1994), 8(4): 19–43; and 'Willingness to pay and willingness to accept: how much can they differ?', *American Economic Review* (1991), 81(3): 635–47.

Winston Harrington is a Senior Research Fellow in the Quality of the Environment Division at Resources for the Future, Washington, DC. He currently serves on the Editorial Council of the *Journal of Environmental Economics and Management*. His publications include: 'Fuel economy and motor vehicle emissions', *Journal of Environmental Economics and Management* (1997), 33(3): 240–52; and 'Determinants of participation in accelerated vehicle retirement programs' (with Anna Alberini and Virginia McConnell), *RAND Journal of Economics* (1995), 26(1): 93–112.

Anthony Heyes is a Professor of Economics at the Royal Holloway College, London University. His publications include: 'Environmental regulation by private contest', *Journal of Public Economics* (1997), 63(3): 407–28; and 'Towards an efficiency interpretation of regulatory intervention lags', *Journal of Regulatory Economics* (1996), 10(2): 81–98.

Terrance M. Hurley is Assistant Professor of Economics at the University of Minnesota. His publications include: 'Effort levels in Cournot Nash contests with asymmetric information' (with Jason Shogren), *Journal of Public Economics* (1998), 69(2): 195–210; and 'Rent dissipation and efficiency in a contest with asymmetric valuations', *Public Choice* (1998), 94(3): 289–98.

Daniel Ingberman is a Principal at the Law and Economics Consulting Group (LECG) in Emoryville, California. His publications include: 'Siting noxious facilities: are markets efficient?', *Journal of Environmental Economics and Management* (1995), 29(3): 20–33; and 'An experimental investigation of multi-defendant bargaining in joint-and-several and proportionate liability regimes' (with co-authors), *Journal of Accounting and Economics* (1997), 23(2): 189–221.

Robert Innes is a Professor in the Department of Agricultural and Resource Economics at the University of Arizona. His research has won a number of notable awards, including the Hicks–Tinbergen Prize in 1994. His publications include: 'Self-policing and optimal law enforcement', *Journal of Political Economy* (1999), 107(6): 1305–25; and 'Takings, compensation, and unequal treatment for owners of developed and undeveloped property', *Journal of Law and Economics* (1997), 40(2): 403–32.

Howard C. Kunreuther is the Cecilia Yen Koo Professor of Decision Sciences and Public Policy, Wharton School, University of Pennsylvania. He is Co-director of the Wharton Risk Management and Decision Processes Center, a Fellow of the US National Bureau of Economic Research (NBER), and is on the editorial boards of the *Journal of Regulatory Economics* and the *Journal of*

Risk and Uncertainty. His publications include: 'Retroactive liability or the public purse?' (with Jim Boyd), *Journal of Regulatory Economics* (1997), 11(1): 79–90; and 'Are risk-benefit trade-offs possible in siting hazardous facilities?' (with Douglas Easterling), *American Economic Review* (1990), 80(2): 252–6.

Tracy R. Lewis is the James Walter Professor of Economics at the University of Florida, Gainesville, where he is also Director of Energy Policy in the Public Utility Research Center, Co-editor of the *Journal of Law, Economics and Organisation*, and on the editorial board of the *American Economic Review*. His publications include: 'Protecting the environment when costs and benefits are privately known', *RAND Journal of Economics* (1996), 27(4): 819–47; and 'Inflexible rules in incentive problems' (with David E.M. Sappington), *American Economic Review* (1989), 79(1): 69–84.

Robert Cameron Mitchell is Professor of Geography at Clark University, MA. He is an expert on survey methods. His publications include: 'Property rights, protest and the siting of hazardous waste facilities' (with Richard Carson), *American Economic Review* (1986), 76(2): 285–90; and *Using Surveys to Value Public Goods: The Contingent Valuation Method* (with Richard Carson), Washington, DC: RFF/Johns Hopkins University Press, 1989.

Carl V. Phillips recently obtained his PhD from Harvard University and is now a visiting fellow at the Center for the Philosophy of Science, University of Minnesota. His publications include: 'Restoring natural resources with destination-driven costs' (with Richard Zeckhauser), *Journal of Environmental Economics and Management* (1998), 36(3): 225–42; and 'Communicating the health effects of consumer products: the case of moderate alcohol consumption and coronary heart disease', *Managerial and Decision Economics* (1996), 17(5): 459–70.

Donatella Porrini is Assistant Professor in Political Economy at the Institute of Economic and Statistical Science at the University of Milan. Her publications include: 'Labour market regulation in Italy, employment and welfare' (with Gianandrea Goisis), in Mario Baldassari, Luigi Paganetto and Edmund S. Phelps (eds), *Equity, Efficiency and Growth: The Future of the Welfare State*, New York: St. Martins Press, 1996, pp. 193–211; and 'Scope economies and the Italian banking system: a theoretical contribution and exploratory empirical analysis' [in Italian], *Economia Internazionale* (1994), 47(2): 218–37.

Richard A. Posner is Senior Lecturer at the University of Chicago Law School (where he was formerly the Lee and Bren Freeman Professor of Law) and Chief Judge in the US Court of Appeals (7th Circuit). He is widely acknowledged as a founding father in the field of law and economics. He is author of the celebrated *Economic Analysis of Law*, now in its fifth edition. His journal publications include: 'Social norms and law: an economic approach', *American Economic Review* (1997), 87(2): 365–9; and 'The law and economics movement', *American Economic Review* (1987), 77(2): 1–13.

Thomas A. Rhoads is Assistant Professor in the Department of Economics, Towson University. His publications include: 'On Coasean bargaining with transactions costs' (with Jason Shogren), *Applied Economics Letters* (1999), 6(12): 779–83; and 'Educational contributions, academic quality, and athletic success' (with Shelby Gerking), *Contemporary Economic Policy* (2000), 18(2): 248–58.

David E.M. Sappington holds the Lanzillotti–McKethan Eminent Scholar Chair in the Department of Economics at the University of Florida, Gainesville, where he is also Director of the Public Policy Research Center. He is on the editorial boards of a number of journals, including the *American Economic Review* and the *Journal of Regulatory Economics*. His publications include: 'Information management in incentive problems' (with Tracy Lewis), *Journal of Political Economy* (1997), 104(4): 796–821; and 'Penalizing success in dynamic incentive contracts: no good deed goes unpunished?', *RAND Journal of Economics* (1997), 28(2): 346–58.

Chad Settle recently completed his PhD at the University of Wyoming, and is now an Assistant Professor of Economics at Tulsa University. His working papers include: 'Rational valuation in the Yellowstone interactive web experiment' (with Todd Cherry and Jason Shogren) (2000); and 'An integrated model of wildlife at risk from exotic invaders' (with others) (2000).

Jason F. Shogren is Stroock Distinguished Professor of Natural Resource Conservation and Management in the Department of Economics and Finance, University of Wyoming. His publications include: 'Resolving differences in willingness to pay and willingness to accept' (with others), *American Economic Review* (1994), 84(1): 255–70; and 'Economics of the Endangered Species Act' (with Gardner Brown), *Journal of Economic Perspectives* (1998), 12(2): 3–20.

Hilary Sigman is Associate Professor of Environmental Economics at Yale University, having previously held faculty positions at Rutgers University and the University of California, Los Angeles (UCLA). She is a Faculty Research Fellow at the National Bureau of Economic Research (NBER) and serves on the Editorial Council of the *Journal of Environmental Economics and Management*. Her publications include: 'Midnight dumping: public policies and illegal disposal of used oil', *RAND Journal of Economics* (1998), 29(1): 157–78; and 'A comparison of public policies for lead recycling', *RAND Journal of Economics* (1995), 26(3): 452–78.

R. Todd Smith is an Associate Professor of Economics at the University of Alberta. He is on the Editorial Board of the *Canadian Journal of Economics*. His publications include: 'Banking competition and macroeconomic performance', *Journal of Money, Credit and Banking* (1998), 30(4): 793–815; and 'Market risk and asset prices', *Journal of Economic Dynamics and Control* (1993), 17(4): 555–69.

Henry van Egteren is an Associate Professor of Economics at the University of Alberta. He currently serves on the Editorial Council of the *Journal of Environmental Economics and Management*. His publications include: 'Regulating an externality-generating public utility: a multi-dimensional screening approach', *European Economic Review* (1996), 40(9): 1773–97; and 'Marketable permits, market power and cheating' (with Marian Weber), *Journal of Environmental Economics and Management* (1996), 30(2): 161–73.

Richard J. Zeckhauser is Frank P. Ramsey Professor of Political Economy at the Kennedy School of Government, Harvard University. He is, amongst other things, a Fellow of the Econometric Society and of the National Bureau of Economic Research (NBER). He is Editor or Associate Editor of several journals including the *Review of Economics and Statistics* and the *Journal of Risk and Uncertainty*. His publications include: 'Willingness to pay and the distribution of risk and wealth' (with John Pratt), *Journal of Political Economy* (1996), 104(4): 747–63; and 'Risks to selves, risks to others' (with Christopher Avery and Jody Heymann), *American Economic Review* (1995), 85(2): 61–6.

Preface

Richard A. Posner*

Environmental law has played an important role in economic thinking about law, indeed in economic thinking generally. Pollution and congestion were central examples of externalities in important contributions to economics by Pigou, Knight and, of course, Coase; Coase's essay 'The problem of social cost', a key document in the economic analysis of law, is about external costs and uses examples from the English common law of nuisance. These great economists and the early work of the lawyer-economists that followed them focused on the law of nuisance at a time when statutory regulation of pollution and other externalities was far less extensive than it has become. The exploration of the basic economics of externalities and the basic common law doctrines and institutions for dealing with externalities constitute a 'first generation' of economic analysis of environmental law.

The present book of essays illustrates the 'second generation' of economic analysis of environmental law. The fundamental economic issues, and the common law, are no longer the focus. The lessons of the 'first generation' have been absorbed and transcended. The focus has shifted to the level of application, which is the level at which the economist and the lawyer-economist can best hope to influence policy. The essays take up issues of public choice, statutory detail, liability rules (strict liability versus negligence), and remedies (both civil and criminal) with specific reference to insolvency and agency problems. The basic economic framework is assumed, and the discussion proceeds to the concrete methods of implementing the economic approach. The authors are all well-regarded experts, and their essays exhibit a high degree of theoretical rigour. Although international in scope, the focus is on the United States, and the Superfund statute, which regulates clean-up of toxic waste sites, receives particular attention consistent with its importance especially in the litigation of environmental disputes.

US public policy today (and, to a lesser extent, that of other countries – but the gap is narrowing) is highly receptive to economic analysis. Just as populism has receded as a point of resistance to an economic approach to antitrust policy, so hostility to 'commodification', and the belief that to discuss environmental values in economic terms is inevitably to disparage and depreciate those values, have receded in the environmental area. The opportunity for economic analysis to influence policy is therefore very great, as we have seen already in the adoption of the 'bubble' concept and in tradable-emissions schemes for sulphur dioxide. These are ingenious economic approaches to problems of environmental regulation that would have been unthinkable a generation ago. We are making progress – and the essays in this volume will do much to assure that progress continues.

NOTE

* Judge, United States Court of Appeals for the Seventh Circuit; Senior Lecturer, University of Chicago Law School.

1. Law and economics of the environment: an overview

Anthony Heyes

'Law' – in its various shapes and forms – has always been central in society's protection and management of its natural environment. The boundaries between legal, regulatory and other approaches to environmental policy are blurred. For current purposes a watertight definition or boundary of what constitutes 'law and economics' isn't needed, and we don't venture one: the book contains a set of chapters that fall within any reasonable definition.[1] The coverage is not, of course, exhaustive. The discipline of economics has incentives as one of its central organizing principles, and this is arguably the defining feature of 'the economic approach' to thinking about law. This tradition is reflected in the chapters here.

PROPERTY RIGHTS AND COASE

The celebrated Coase Theorem dictates that under a particular set of assumptions – in particular in a world without transactions costs – decentralized bargaining will lead to the efficient use of resources. Provided there is a well-defined initial allocation of property rights in place, disputing parties will bargain until such efficiency is achieved *regardless of what that initial allocation looks like*. The logic is pleasing in its simplicity, and second nature to economists trained since the 1960s. Consider a world populated by a single polluting factory and a single household. If the factory owner has the right to pollute, the household will 'bribe' him to reduce his emissions down to the point at which the marginal private benefit to the householder of cleaner air just equals the factory owner's marginal cost of abatement (to that point there is a surplus to be generated from trade – and in a world of zero transactions costs it is reasonable to think that that surplus will be reaped). If, on the other hand, the householder has a right to clean air, the factory owner will 'bribe' him to waive that right and allow emissions up to the point at which the householder's marginal disutility from pollution just equals the marginal benefit to the factory owner of being allowed to emit (which is the same thing, of course, as the marginal cost of abatement).

The theorem is an optimistic one. Under either allocation of property rights, the same pattern of economic activity – the uniquely productively efficient one – emerges as the end point of the decentralized process of bargaining between the two interested parties. The government doesn't need to involve itself in that decentralized trading or regulate activity in any way (indeed such intervention could only reduce aggregate surplus). In so far as the benchmark it represents is deemed an applicable one, it points to the central role of an efficiency-motivated government being to establish, through legal and other instruments, a set of well-defined and enforceable property rights. For sure that allocation of property rights will affect the distribution of surplus – and distributional decisions are typically the sorts of decisions for which political processes are thought to be well-suited – but not the efficiency of the pattern of economic activity which emerges.

The requirements for the Coase Theorem to 'work' are, of course, not ones that will be met in any real world setting. The primary service performed by Coase is to provide a benchmark of how things *would* work in a hypothetical world without transactions costs. The implications of throwing 'grit' (im-perfectly competitive markets, costly enforcement of property rights, non-profit-maximizing producers and so on) into the works can then be thought of in terms of departures from that benchmark.

Thomas Rhoads and Jason Shogren examine the devolutionary trend in environmental policy in the United States, with particular reference to *Enlibra* – the US Western Governors Association's new doctrine for environmental management through decentralized, collaborative decision-making – in Coasean terms. They compare the evolving system with the Coasean benchmark and assess its likely efficiency. The principles could equally be thought about in any other setting where control over key features of the natural environment has been handed to local people who live and work in that environment.

In any real world setting transactions costs or bargaining frictions arise and have the potential to cause bargained outcomes to depart from efficient outcomes. The empirical questions are: (a) how big are those frictions; and (b) how far will the *potential* for inefficiency be translated into *actual* inefficiency? There is no easy answer to questions of this sort. They require a model of how agents bargain over surplus, and how that behaviour depends upon the bargaining environment. The attempt to understand and model the way in which individuals behave when asked to divide a cake, or to cooperate in non-zero sum settings, has exercised some of the most powerful minds that economics has ever attracted (John Nash, Ariel Rubenstein *et al.*).[2]

In the environmental context the question of local cooperation over resources has been advanced by observation in the field and in the laboratory.[3] The experimental literature in this area is a rich one, and Rhoads and Shogren provide a selective chronological review. Results from the laboratory have, in the main, corroborated Coase. As Rhoads and Shogren note:

> With an experimental design now firmly in place, further investigations probed the boundaries of the Coase Theorem. Generally these papers suggested that the Coase Theorem was robust in its assumptions and ... the evidence strongly supported the key behavioural outcomes implied by the Coase Theorem.

In all of these things, of course, institutional arrangements – the design of the arena within which collaborative agreements are to be forged – can matter. Rhoads and Shogren point to the important role that test-bedding experimental research can play in helping to shape 'sensible' institutions for dispute resolution. The original experimental results of their own work, which they present, provide further empirical support for the proposition that collaborative processes lead to (reasonably) efficient and equitable results in both individual and 'team' bargaining contexts.[4]

THE BASICS OF LIABILITY

Perhaps the most obvious way in which law has been used in the environmental sphere is in the attribution of liability.

A variety of different allocations can be made. The versions most commonly employed (and studied) are those of strict liability and negligence-based liability. In its simplest form strict liability dictates that if A damages B then A is liable for that damage, and corresponds most closely with the 'polluter pays principle' that many policy-makers espouse. In order to secure compensation, someone damaged by the firm's activities need only show causation. Under a negligence-based regime the polluter is only liable for damage inflicted if s/he has failed to exercise an appropriate degree of care in carrying out his/her business. To be successful the plaintiff needs to show both causation and negligence. In a 'perfect' world – absent of informational asymmetries, enforcement problems and so on – either regime can be used to achieve efficiency.[5]

In settings in which more than one entity (firm or individual) can be said to have contributed to some damage, liability may be joint (or 'proportionate', where the total is shared in proportion to contribution) or joint-and-several (where any single contributor can be held liable for the whole lot). In the context of contaminated land in the United States, for example, the Comprehensive Environmental Response, Compensation, and Liability Act (CERCLA) famously assigned retroactive, strict joint-and-several liability upon a range of potentially responsible parties (PRPs).

Liability has been used as a primary instrument of policy in a variety of environmental settings, but particularly in the context of contaminated land. A liability regime establishes, at least in theory, a configuration of property rights. Distinctions are not as clean as previous outline may have suggested: a variety of hybrids can be constructed. Thus a strict regime may be augmented by allowing for a 'state of the art' defence (which, analytically, reduces to a negligence-based system with the required standard of care being set to correspond with the state-of-the-art level).

A variety of complications arise in the application of theory to practice. Some of the most studied are those that arise under 'judgment proofness'. Judgment proofness refers to the case in which a polluter faces a binding bankruptcy constraint and so is unable to meet legitimate claims for damages against it. Its deleterious impact upon incentives have long been known (Shavell 1986 provides a good statement). In many environmental settings, such as those involving industries in which firms are comparatively small yet have the potential to inflict substantial or even catastrophic environmental damage, the potential for judgment proofness can be pervasive. The problem has been exacerbated by the 'strategic subsidiarization' whereby firms hive off some of their high-risk operations into separately incorporated subsidiaries, shielding the assets of the parent from liabilities arising out of those activities (Ringleb and Wiggins 1990).

It is clear that judgment proofness – or the potential for judgment proofness – might significantly reduce the efficacy of any sort of liability regime (though see Beard 1990 for an alternative view). Even a fully enforced regime of strict liability would no longer serve to internalize completely the externalities of interest. When those responsible cannot pay, this reduces both the source of funding for remediation and compensation and, in so far as that inability to pay would be anticipated by would-be polluters, reduces the incentives for *ex ante* care.

In a number of countries, growing frustrations about shallow-pocketed polluters being unable to honour their responsibilities has led to governments, courts and agencies going 'in search of deep pockets'. Vicarious liability involves extending the family of potentially liable parties beyond those most directly adjacent to the damage.

There are two directions in which it is natural to extend liability: vertically (backwards or forwards along the supply chain) and horizontally (to others engaged in the same activity). Policy-makers have experimented with both. Increasing the number of pockets from which damaged parties might seek redress not only increases (other things being equal) the chance of finding a solvent 'pocket' to fund remediation and compensation, but might also be expected to create incentives for those vicariously liable to bring pressure to bear on the actual polluter to be more responsible in the first place. Provided the targets of the extension of liability are chosen carefully – not just to have deep pockets, but also to have some scope to influence the polluter – such a policy could be effective

In their chapter **Jim Boyd and Daniel Ingberman** provide a clear and insightful analysis of the incentive effects of *vertical* extension of environmental liability. Vertical extension involves passing liability through chains of contracts: from the polluter to suppliers, lenders, transport contractors, customers and so on, or through chains of ownership.

They illuminate the rationale for extending environmental liability in these ways (in terms of increasing the degree of cost internalization and deterrence), but caution that it is by no means obvious that such extensions will enhance welfare; they can distort production and contracting decisions in undesirable ways. The authors provide three examples of such distortions (downward bias in capital-intensity of production; avoidance of otherwise welfare-improving contracts due to fear of exposure to liability of partners; premature dissolution of firms where liabilities are 'long tail' or latent), though others can certainly be identified. They point to the role that 'bonding', or financial responsibility requirements more generally, can play as an alternative to the extension of liability. As with all 'real' policy analysis, the results are not clear-cut: good policy will depend upon setting and local circumstances.

In the quest for deep pockets it is not surprising that banks have proven a popular candidate, and the economic and political-economic implications of extending environmental liability to those who lend to polluters are analysed by **Marcel Boyer and Donatella Porrini** in their chapter (to which we shall return below). The high-water mark of environmental liability for contaminated land in the US was the immediate aftermath of the *United States* v. *Fleet Factors* case in 1991, in which a District Court ruled that a lender would be regarded as a potentially responsible party wherever it had the capacity to be involved in management (until that point it had been required that the lender actually exercise that control). The precise specification of contexts in which a lender might be required to fund clean-up and compensation was the subject of a series of judicial and administrative interpretations during the early to mid-1990s (in 1992 the US Environmental Protection Agency (EPA) published its *Final Rule* – which turned out not to be). Broadly, though, the threat of lender liability, in all but very particular sets of contexts, has abated since that time. This trend has been paralleled in policy debate in Europe.

Tracy Lewis and David Sappington draw insights from their recent and more generally applicable work on designing contracts to motivate wealth-constrained agents. They propose a particular *horizontal* extension of liability. Horizontal vicarious liability might take the form of holding chemical companies as a group liable for damage done by any one of them (there is already an element of this implicit in the sort of industry-wide levies that contribute to Superfund in the United States, for example). In addition to increasing the number of pockets from which damaged parties could seek redress, such horizontal extensions might be expected to create incentives for industry members to police one another (Kraakman 1986).

The authors propose a liability rule, the essence of which is that all potential producers who wish to have the opportunity to engage in some risky activity (say transporting oil across a body of water) would be required to post a non-refundable bond with the government The government would then select a single producer to operate, and deliver all the posted bonds to the selected producer if and only if he avoids a socially damaging accident. If the accident occurs, the bonds that have been posted would be used to compensate victims. This is an ingenious proposal, ensuring as it does that at the point at which it makes its safety decisions the operator has a great deal to lose (a much greater amount than his initial wealth).

A great deal of theoretical work has been done on the relative merits of strict and negligence-based approaches to environmental liability. The approaches taken vary both between and within jurisdictions. Within the EU, for example, Germany and the Netherlands favour strict liability for most types of environmental damage, whereas the tradition in the United Kingdom is for a negligence basis. Within the European Union, single market and other considerations have motivated a push towards harmonization. The EU published a White Paper in February 2000 proposing harmonization on the basis of a strict system. An important distinction between the European proposals and the experience of CERCLA – and the key thing that will make it 'fly' politically – however, is that it will it will not be applied retroactively. Whilst it will not, therefore, make life easier for Environment Agencies trying to find money to repair the cumulative damage of the past, it is to be hoped that it will enhance incentives for the prevention of future damage.

In the United States effective environmental liability is, in some circumstances, determined by individual states. In their contribution, **Anna Alberini and David Austin** exploit the fact that liability structures vary across states (in particular in the liability structure imposed by their so-called 'mini-Superfund' programmes) to explore the effects of strict liability upon uncontrolled releases of pollutants into the environment.[6]

The history of strict liability in the context of contaminated land varies substantially across the US. In some states (for example, New Jersey) it was adopted as early as the 1970s. In the industrial Midwest some states adopted comparatively early (Missouri) and some comparatively late (Michigan). Ohio reverted from a strict to a negligence-based approach in the 1990s, before switching back. Illinois repealed strict liability in 1995. A handful of states (Colorado, Virginia, North Dakota) have never adopted.

Alberini and Austin provide convincing evidence (a) that states adopted strict liability in response to their suffering a greater-than-average rate of spill events, and (b) that the adoption 'worked', in the sense of reducing the rate of occurrence of such events. They also provide evidence (reminiscent of Ringleb and Wiggins 1990, already mentioned) that firms have developed behavioural responses to avoid liability, when they are strictly liable for the releases. In states with strict liability, greater spill severity and frequency are associated with smaller production units (their proxy for firms with fewer assets), whereas this association is not present in states operating a negligence-based regime. The authors provide some interesting and insightful interpretation of their results.

CLEANING THINGS UP

Whilst the mind-set of many economists is forward-looking – bygones are bygones, and in a world of non-distortionary taxes it doesn't really matter who pays for cleaning up damage done in the past – the focus of a lot of policy discussion is retrospective. It is unarguably the case that the primary political motivation for many of the decisions taken in the design and implementation of CERCLA (in particular the use of joint and several liability) was the desire to have a system that would actually deliver clean-up. In its deliberations in the context of contaminated land the focus of successive governments in the United Kingdom has similarly been backward-looking: focused much more on damage already done than on the incentives that any particular regime might be likely to create for patterns of care and activity in the future.

More generally, in thinking about legal design and how the legal system deals with remediation, it is interesting to think more fundamentally about the economics of clean-up. The standard economic model of the environment assumes that the cost and benefit functions are 'well behaved'; that is, with quality as the independent variable, the marginal cost of additional quality (that is, of 'clean-up') is assumed everywhere increasing and marginal benefit falling. The former follows from the supposition of diminishing marginal physical product of clean-up effort, the latter from assumption of diminishing marginal utility from consumption of the 'good' called environmental quality.

In a most readable and significant contribution **Carl Phillips and Richard Zeckhauser** take a step back to reconsider the standard approach, based as it is on two of the most deeply ingrained 'retained assumptions' in microeconomics. They present a compelling argument that the mechanics of restoring an injured resource (such as cleaning a tarred beach) will very often be such that the primary determinant of the cost of restoration will be the final level of restored quality, not the 'distance' between pre- and post-restoration quality as standard theory supposes.[7] The starting point may have very little impact on the cost. In so far as the model is indeed a picture of the reality of clean-up, and this depends upon context, we can no longer expect cost functions to be convex in the amount cleaned up, and the standard economic prescription – that remediation should be mandated up to the point at which marginal benefit equals marginal cost – must be thrown out of the window. Employing the standard 'well-behaved' model when clean-up costs are destination driven will create the wrong incentives for environmental protection *ex ante* and for remediation *ex post*. Phillips and Zeckhauser go on to consider in some detail the implications – sometimes fundamental – of destination-driven costs for various aspects of the design of legal institutions.

As we have already noted, a primary rationale for the approach taken to contaminated land in the United States (most particularly the imposition of joint and several liability) was driven by a real political desire to get things done: to provide the EPA with the tools it needed actually to effect a significant programme of remediation. So how has it worked in practice? What has been cleaned up, how well, and who has paid for it? These are the questions motivating the authoritative survey chapter contributed by **Hilary Sigman**.

The contributions extracted from responsible parties to fund clean-up under CERCLA have indeed been substantial, though the flow remains significantly smaller than the money being spent by the EPA out of taxes and general revenues. A number of empirical relationships are identified. The joint and several nature of liability promotes (or does not deter) out-of-court settlement, particularly when trial outcomes are highly correlated. This is important as the legal costs and delays associated with litigation can be substantial: there is evidence that transactions costs can account for up to a third of realized clean-up expenditures when the latter are extracted by litigation.[8] The way in which clean-up is going to be funded influences the chosen remedy (the EPA chooses less extensive remedies when clean-up is to be funded by a PRP rather than out of public funds), how much a given remedy costs, and the rate at which clean-up progresses (though there is some ambiguity over the sign of that impact). Sigman also goes on to consider the other possible impacts of liability (incentives for precaution, the possible 'chilling' effect on the incentives for brownfield redevelopment, the cost of capital and so on).

LEGAL ENFORCEMENT

In regulatory contexts, enforcement efforts will typically be underpinned by the threat of legal sanction of one sort or another. Though a great deal of the literature on the design of regulatory (and, indeed, liability-based) regimes has proceeded on the assumption of full enforcement, putting in place an effective and efficient robust enforcement regime is a critical part of any environmental policy-maker's task.[9] The analysis of compliance and enforcement – and how that analysis leads us to rethink the conduct of policy – has become a topic of great interest in the field in recent years.[10]

Without providing a survey of the compliance literature, **Winston Harrington and Anthony Heyes** consider some recent developments in 'penalty theory'. One interesting strand of recent research uses 'event study' methods to estimate the 'market' (sometimes referred to as reputational) penalties which are implied by stock market responses to 'news' that a firm has violated an environmental law, is to be pursued by a regulatory agency, or simply has a bad (though not necessarily illegal) environmental record according to some other measure. Pioneering event studies were conducted in the context of prosecution for corporate fraud (Karpoff and Lott 1993) and airline safety (Borenstein and Zimmerman 1988), and a variety of applications are collected in a special issue of the *Journal of Law and Economics* edited by John Lott and published in 1999. These penalties can be substantial. Badrinath and Bolster (1996), in a study fairly typical of the genre, examine the stock market reaction to EPA judicial actions on a sample of publicly traded firms between 1972 and 1991. They show that a firm's valuation declines 0.43 per cent in the week of settlement (implying that 86 per cent of the effective penalty for prosecutions for environmental violations in the US is reputational – only 14 per cent is the effective penalty is the actual fine levied by the agency). Mark Cohen returns to this issue – and in particular the 'stigma effect' of criminal prosecution – in a later chapter.

Most conventional ideas on the relationship between penalties and compliance – for example, that maximal compliance will be induced by setting penalties at their highest feasible level – stem from quite simple (and predominantly static) models of the compliance decision. Harrington and Heyes concern themselves, in particular, with what the optimal approach to the levying of penalties might look like in settings where the enforcement agency and the regulated firm interact repeatedly and/or in more than one context. These are realistic premises. It is realistic to think that Dow Chemical, or almost any other significant polluter, interacts with the EPA not just today, but in a repeated and ongoing way. In addition, they interact in a variety of settings: at different plants or in different geographical regions, and in the context not just of clean air regulation, but also of clean water, toxic waste, contaminated land and so on. This gives the agency a lot of scope to link issues, both through time and across settings. In particular, optimality will require that the agency let many known violators 'off-the-hook' in order to generate both 'penalty leverage' and 'penalty dealing' (in neither case are maximal fines compatible with maximal enforcement).

It is traditional to think of 'enforcement' of environmental laws and regula-tions as being the exclusive territory of public agencies (the EPA, Department of Justice or whoever). In a number of jurisdictions, however, there is a long tradition of private citizens using the courts to help enforce federal environmental policy.[11] Naysnerski and Tietenberg (1992) provide some evidence of the significance of citizen suits in the United States. A recent Supreme Court decision (in *Friends of the Earth* v. *Laidlaw Environmental Services (TOC) Inc.*) upheld the ability of private citizens to access the courts to 'help' in enforcing federal environmental policy.

So what are the implications of this sort of involvement (or potential involvement) of citizens or non-governmental organizations (NGOs) in the implementation of policy? After a brief outline of the current state of play and analysis of some of the most significant cases, **Chad Settle, Terry Hurley and Jason Shogren** develop a formal framework within which such questions can be explored. The basic framework is that of the contest or lottery-auction – now in common use in the rent-seeking literature – in which two sides in a dispute (here a polluting firm and a green NGO) exert 'effort' to bring about a legal, regulatory or political decision in their favour. They investigate the efficiency of the decisions that flow out of a contest-based system, and the implications of things such as the way in which legal costs are apportioned, and strategic lawsuits against public participation (SLAPPs). The generality of the analysis makes it difficult to draw specific policy conclusions without imposing further restrictions on the model, and in their conclusions the authors point to the need to provide some underpinning to conflict models of this sort. The 'privatization' of environmental law remains a most ripe area for research.

In his contribution **Robert Innes** does a most excellent and valuable job of bringing together a lot of the issues that arise in the design of policies aimed at inducing firms to self-audit, self-report and self-police their infringements of legal and regulatory requirements (three activities for which he uses the collective term 'self-enforcement'). All environmental policy programmes incorporate, to a greater or lesser extent, an element of one or more of these self-enforcement elements, and Innes considers how governments can design policy programmes which will provide polluters with appropriate incentives to (a) keep tabs on what they are doing (auditing); (b) let the relevant authorities know (reporting); and (c) initiate appropriate and prompt polluters' remedial actions (policing).

After some formal analysis, drawing upon some recent and important work in this area, he compares the prescriptions of the model with the practice of US environmental law, and reaches some mixed conclusions. It is worth noting that, in addition to the explicit requirements and sanctions contained in many federal statutes, and the inducements implicit in the business practices of both the EPA and Department of Justice, over 20 states have recently enacted laws that encourage self-enforcement.[12] A parallel trend can be found in the development of policy in the European Union, Canada and elsewhere.

CRIMINAL LAW

Mark Cohen considers the role that the criminal law does play – and should play – as a tool of environmental policy. There has been a dramatic growth in the use of criminal law in this field over the past two decades or so. In the United States, at the federal level there were only 25 criminal environmental prosecutions during the whole of the 1970s. During the 1990s this number leaped to about 180 per year.[13] Russell (1992: table 7.8) documents the growth during the 1980s of both the number of criminal prosecutions initiated by the EPA and the resulting sentences. Despite the growth, the numbers of corporate executives serving time in American prisons remains very small.

This is an area in which the differing mind-sets of legal scholars and economists can become particularly apparent. Whilst there is no single definition of what constitutes a crime, lawyers look to define 'crime' in inherent terms. Many legal scholars maintain that the single distinguishing characteristic of a crime is 'moral culpability'. Traditional legal theory defines crimes by the notion of *mens rea* or criminal intent, but this view has been all but discarded in the case of modern regulatory crime.[14] Economists tend to focus on the role that the criminal law can play in providing a further set of sanctions (incarceration, probation and so on) with which environmental incentives might be reinforced. In this sense Cohen 'shows his colours' as an economist. As he notes in his conclusions: 'Throughout, I have taken a pure economic efficiency approach in analysing the usefulness of criminal law. Thus, I have not considered the possibility that society values "fairness" or "retribution", for example' – omissions which many legal scholars might find puzzling.

Cohen provides a most useful summary of the current state of play with regards to environmental crime; the incentive role of monetary and non-monetary sanctions; the role that criminal law might play as a cost-saving device; substitutability between corporate and individual penalties. The chapter also provides an illuminating summary of the empirical evidence available (in some places scant, in many places flowing from the author's own work in this area).

PLANNING LAW AND THE LOCATION OF POLLUTION

In environmental economics, space matters. For many classes of environmental externality the key determinant of who suffers what is location: those people living in the immediate vicinity of an industrial plant, for example, can be expected to bear the greatest disamenity from that plant's activities. Because of this, planning law – the body of law which controls who can do what, and where – can have a considerable impact upon the productive and distributional efficiency of patterns of economic activity. Whilst we tend to think in terms of decisions to site large, discrete noxious entities, such as nuclear power stations, landfills and airports, planning decisions will affect the patterns of land use much more generally, and can have a more widely pervasive influence on our lives.

Countries vary significantly in the channels through which law (as opposed to, say, political input) operate in the land-use process, and the extent to which planning decisions are devolved. In a paper entitled 'Siting noxious facilities: are markets efficient?', Ingberman (1995) develops a formal model of the non-cooperative location of noxious sites in a world without central planning. It is not surprising that any unregulated system of location is likely to generate highly inefficient patterns of land use.

Academic economists – and policy-makers – have devised a number of ways to encourage more efficient siting decisions, and there is a growing literature in this field.

Robert Cameron Mitchell and Richard Carson highlight some of the most important aspects of the problem. Their central contention is that hazardous waste siting has a history of being so contentious and so difficult – subject to such intensive protest, quasi-political activity and rent-seeking – because of the ambiguity of property rights. They make a proposal for the allocation of community property rights and review some recent siting decisions, noting the successful role played by referendums in a number of cases.

RISK AND ENVIRONMENTAL LAW

Throughout legal and policy discussion in the sphere of environmental problems – and in particular when thinking about potential catastrophes – scholars and practitioners refer to the role that insurance might play as all or part of a sensible solution. In their contribution, **Howard Kunreuther and Paul Freeman** make a convincing case for using an insurance-based rather than a liability-based system to provide social protection against both chronic and sudden environmental risks. They envisage a set of enforceable insurance contracts, in combination with a programme of third-party inspections and/or well-specified performance standards, as an alternative to existing legal and regulatory programmes. The legal system would not, of course, be removed from the frame – its role would be shifted (from assessing liabilities to interpreting and enforcing insurance contracts, for example). Potential polluters would be obliged to carry insurance for damage they might do. In a competitive and well-functioning insurance market, premiums would reflect expected firm-specific pay-outs, internalizing the gains to the firm from risk-reducing actions and so generating the market incentives for firms to behave 'correctly'.

The authors illustrate their ideas by working through four case studies: (a) health damage due to asbestos; (b) liability for contaminated land; (c) environmental damage due to leaking underground storage tanks; (d) sudden accidents such as explosions at chemical plants.

The precise specification of insurance-based programmes – and the extent to which they would work – depends upon context, and Kunreuther and Freeman identify the characteristics required for them to work well. The ideas raised by the author offer exciting policy prospects.

POLITICAL ECONOMY

Throughout economics, the political-economic questions are amongst the most important of all. What policies will be politically sustainable, as opposed to economically sensible? How must policy design be adjusted to take account of the political and bureaucratic environment in which they are to be implemented? There is a long tradition of interest in such questions (Buchanan and Tullock 1975 is a well-known early contribution). In recent years, however, there has been a rapid growth in the application of increasingly complex modelling techniques in political economy.

In their chapter, 'Law versus regulation: a political economy model of instrument choice in environmental policy', **Marcel Boyer and Donatella Porrini** analyse some of the political-economic considerations that might lead to preference between instruments. They develop a formal incomplete information model in which the regulatory agency may be subject to capture, to contemplate the relative merits of extended (strict, joint and several) lender liability versus an incentive regulation framework. Capture is introduced in a reduced-form fashion by an overvaluation of the informational rents accruing to firms. They show (perhaps not surprisingly) that the regulatory option may perform better or worse than the legal option depending upon the importance of that overvaluation.

As we have already noted, the application in the chapter remains a topical one. Though the issue of lender liability was, to a great extent, 'put to bed' in the United States during the 1990s, it remains a significant issue in the European Union. The lessons to be learned from the analysis – that prudent choice of policy instrument must take account of the incentives of political actors, not just standard 'textbook' economic considerations – is of much broader significance.

Much of the modern debate regarding environmental policy emphasizes the international political arena and the need for concerted action to be taken at the supranational level. This reflects not just the significance of trans-boundary environmental damage and the problems that they create – acid rain, global warming, damage to the high seas and so on – but an increasing recognition of the intricate codependence of the environment and trade.[15] Even when the environmental damage associated with production is borne entirely within national borders, individual governments may have an incentive to set domestic environmental requirements too low in order to give domestic producers a competitive advantage, or to attract mobile producers from other jurisdictions (leading to a 'race-to-the-bottom'). Alternatively, they may set domestic environmental requirements too high in order to 'export' the production of dirty goods abroad (leading to a 'race-to-the-top'). In either case there are almost certain to be gains from a coordinated solution.

Whilst a lot has been written about the inefficiencies that can arise when individual national governments set their domestic environmental standards non-cooperatively – and the desirability of internationally coordinated and/or harmonized policies – there is something of a hole in the formal economics literature on the implications of harmonizing environmental law. **Henry van Egteren and Todd Smith** make a start on filling that hole. They apply their discussion to the ongoing debate over harmonization of environmental law in the European Union.

They argue that harmonization based on strict liability – which is modelled as being unfettered by considerations such as a state-of-the art defence – can implement a socially optimal outcome. Though not necessarily surprising – strict liability modelled in this way equates with application of the polluter pays principle, such that all externalities are fully internalized – the formal demonstration is useful. When all countries have a negligence-based system, the crucial issue then becomes who sets the negligence standard. If it is set by individual governments then the well-known problems associated with the non-cooperative setting of standards (sketched in the preceding paragraph) resurface, and social optimality will not be achieved. As expected, social optimality will require that standards are set centrally.

ENVIRONMENTAL VALUATION IN COURT

Much of the theoretical discussion of the comparative properties of different liability regimes, regulatory programmes and so on, proceeds on the implicit or explicit assumption that courts can assess, with some degree of surety, environmental damage.[16] The sensible operation of any programme of environmental management will require that the costs and benefits of environmental protection can be expressed in the same metric (money).[17]

The major techniques of environmental valuation (the travel cost method, contingent valuation and so on) are well known, and the validity of use of the alternative approaches in various contexts has been the subject of hot contention and feverish academic research activity in recent years. **David Chapman and Michael Hanemann** offer a fascinating 'inside' view of the way in which the academic discipline of environmental valuation articulates with the US legal system. They recount their experiences as expert witnesses in the high profile *American Trader* oil-spill case.

One of their key conclusions is simple: details matter. The case involved, in particular, the valuation of loss of recreational beach use. Chapman and Hanemann note that, in contrast to many academic debates, in this case both sides were agreed on the theory (that consumer surplus was the appropriate measure of value), and the appropriate valuation methods (that either CV or the travel cost method were appropriate). The contested issues related predominantly to the facts of the case. The authors provide a detailed chronology of how the case unfolded, and draw some general lessons about the role of academic economics in the courtroom.

CONCLUDING REMARKS

The issues that might sensibly be addressed in a book with the title *Law and Economics of the Environment* are, it hardly needs saying, many and various. Only a subset of those that we consider the most interesting and significant feature here. As with much good research in the social sciences, the contributions pose more questions than they answer.

NOTES

1. The stated aim of the *Journal of Law and Economics* – whose editors might be seen as arbiters of the boundaries of the discipline – is to 'explore the complex relationships between law and economics, focusing on the influence of regulation and legal institutions on the operation of economic systems'.
2. Coase, of course, told us where the bargaining process should end up – with all of the available surplus extracted – but had little to say about the mechanics of how it would get there.
3. Field observation in this area is particularly associated with the fascinating work of Elinor Ostrom and collaborators. Ostrom *et al.* (1994) provides a good overview.
4. They extend earlier work by designing an 'expensive' collaborative design in which citizen groups are provided in advance with information about how a particular collaborative framework might or might not meet their needs.
5. Under a fully enforced system of strict liability environmental costs are fully internalized such that efficiency would follow naturally from the optimizing behaviour of the polluter. Under a negligence-based system the required standard of care would have to be set at its efficient level.
6. The NPL only contains around 1400 sites across the whole of the US. Further liability is often imposed on polluters by state 'mini-Superfund' laws, the aim of which is to deal with the very large number of non-priority contaminated sites that do not qualify for the Federal Superfund programme.

7. They cite engineering and other literature in which the cost of a remediation project can depend upon dozens of factors, but where the initial concentration of the contaminant plays little or no role, at least within certain bounds. Replacement, for example, will sometimes be more efficient than trying to salvage a damaged site. When the dioxin contamination of Times Beach, Missouri was discovered in 1982, the immediate solution was for the Superfund to pay $33 million to relocate all residents and businesses to a safer location, a cost that was independent of the quantity of the pollutant.
8. There is growing evidence of a substantial transactions cost burden with all forms of regulation – including environmental. See Crews (1998) for some provocative anecdotal evidence, and Dixon (1995) for a particular application to Superfund.
9. For an up-to-date and thorough survey of the enforcement literature, see Heyes (2000).
10. A totally unscientific sequence of abstract searches using EconLit/WedSPIRS suggests that of papers about environmental regulation published during the decade of the 1980s, the word 'enforcement' appeared in the abstract of only about 2 per cent of them. For papers published in the 1990s (of which there were, note, about twice as many) that proportion rises to about 9 per cent.
11. Note that we are not talking here about situations where individuals sue firms to gain compensation for damage inflicted against them personally – a type of action familiar in civil law – but rather where individuals or private groups move to enforce a piece of regulation more generally.
12. The encouragement can take different forms, but usually entails some combination of liability protections and privilege for information generated by self-reports and/or contained in self-reports. The precise boundaries of such protections and privileges are submerged, in places, in murky legal waters, and remain to be tested.
13. No comparable figures exist for criminal prosecutions under state law.
14. It surprises many that it is not just individuals who can be charged with a crime, but also corporations.
15. 'Environment and trade' has, in the past few years, become a sizeable subfield in its own right.
16. Notice that we are not talking here about something hypothetical, like forecasting the damage that might flow from a given regulatory programme. Rather this is the problem of attaching a monetary value to actual and experienced damage.
17. The exception to this type of statement is systems, as envisaged by Coase and examined by Rhoads and Shogren in their chapter, in which decision-making is completely decentralized.

BIBLIOGRAPHY

Badrinath S. and P.J. Bolster (1996), 'The role of market forces in EPA enforcement activity', *Journal of Regulatory Economics* 10(2): 165–81.
Beard, R.T. (1990), 'Bankruptcy and care choice', *RAND Journal of Economics* 21(4): 626–34.
Borenstein, S. and M.B. Zimmerman (1988), 'Market incentives for safety of commercial airline operation', *American Economic Review* 78(5): 913–35.
Buchanan, J.M. and G. Tullock (1975), 'Polluter's profits and political response: direct controls vs. taxes', *American Economic Review* 65(1): 139–47.
Crews, C. (1998), 'Ten thousand commandments: towards accountability and disclosure in the regulatory state', *Public Manager* 26(3): 5–9.
Dixon, L.S. (1995), 'The transactions costs generated by Superfund liability', Chapter 7 in R. Revesz and R.B. Stewart (eds), *Analyzing Superfund: Economics, Science and Law*, Washington, DC: Resources for the Future.

Heyes, A.G. (2000), 'Implementing environmental regulation: enforcement and compliance', *Journal of Regulatory Economics* 17(2): 102–29.

Ingberman, D. (1995), 'Siting noxious facilities: are markets efficient?', *Journal of Environmental Economics and Management* 29(3): 520–33.

Karpoff, J. and J.R. Lott (1993), 'The reputational penalty firms bear after committing criminal fraud', *Journal of Law and Economics* 36(2): 757–62.

Kraakman, R.H. (1986), 'Gatekeepers: the anatomy of a third party enforcement strategy', *Journal of Law, Economics and Organisation* 2(1): 53–104.

Naysnerski, W. and T. Tietenberg (1992), 'Private enforcement of federal environmental law', *Land Economics* 68(1): 28–48.

Ostrom, E., R. Gardner and J. Walker (1994), *Rules, Games and Common Pool Resources*, Anne Arbor, MI: University of Michigan Press.

Ringleb, A.H. and S. Wiggins (1990), 'Liability and large-scale, long-term hazards', *Journal of Political Economy* 98(3): 574–95.

Russell, C.S. (1992), 'Monitoring and enforcement', in P. Portney (ed.), *Public Policies for Environmental Protection*, Washington, DC: Resources for the Future.

Shavell, S. (1986), 'The judgement-proof problem', *International Review of Law and Economics*, 6(1): 45–58.

2. Coasean bargaining in collaborative environmental policy

Thomas A. Rhoads and Jason F. Shogren*

INTRODUCTION

Prophets and pragmatists have seen the future of environmental policy, and it is local control through consensus with added accountability (for example, Sabel *et al*. 1999). Many people would like this view of the future, especially those in rural settings. Local resource control is an old idea that they have long advocated to the central powers that have long dominated environmental policy. Those who live near the land believe they know the land, and have a vested interest in its care. Just as they are accountable to the land, they see themselves as accountable to each other, and to the nation. Working together to find common ground just makes common sense, which is why collaborative decision-making has begun to flourish in rural settings like the western United States. Collaboration groups now number in the hundreds, ranging from informal grassroots gatherings to government-mandated advisory councils.

A good example of this decentralized, collaborative decision-making vision is *Enlibra*, the US Western Governors Association's new doctrine for environmental management.[1] The governors want less remote control and more local control over western resources. *Enlibra* outlines their push for strong local leadership to balance development and conservation goals, and resolve environmental conflicts. The first *Enlibra* principle is: 'national standards, neighborhood solutions – assign responsibilities at the right level'. Locals understand local conditions. In contrast to unimaginative bureaucratic responses, the federal government should help local people and policy-makers develop their own plans to achieve binding targets and to provide accountability.

The second *Enlibra* principle is 'collaboration, not polarization – use collaborative processes to break down barriers and find solutions'. The western governors believe that community-based collaboration can help produce creative solutions with political momentum. As more attention is given to alternative decision-making processes like *Enlibra*, such as cooperative negotiation and mediation, opportunities increase for local stakeholders to initiate natural resource management plans and resolve environmental disputes. This development points to a future of environmental and natural resource policy-making that increasingly rests on the use of localized Coasean bargaining among private citizens (Coase 1960).

Coasean bargaining emerged from the *Coase Theorem* (see Cooter 1989). Recall the Coase Theorem says that disputing parties will bargain until they reach an efficient private agreement, regardless of which party is initially assigned to hold the unilateral property rights. As long as these legal entitlements can be freely exchanged, government intervention is relegated to designating and enforcing well-defined property rights. An abundance of experimental evidence already confirms that rules matter in generating efficient outcomes in Coasean bargaining.[2] The evidence suggests that experimental testbeds can generate experience and data on the efficiency of bargaining rules and protocol to share with policy-makers interested in how applications of environmental decision-making processes affect outcomes and behaviour.

This chapter begins by briefly examining the devolution of environmental policy and how it closely resembles Coase's world. We then demonstrate how laboratory experiments have explored Coasean bargaining to probe the design and analysis of decision-making systems in environmental policy. This approach allows for the opportunity to provide appropriate incentives in the environmental decision-making process.

DEVOLUTION AND COASEAN BARGAINING

The design of natural resource management plans and the resolution of environmental disputes by local stakeholders is largely attributed to opportunities recently afforded in the regulatory process.[3] Alternative dispute resolution techniques are now widely promoted and used to resolve the environmental disputes that were once dominated by litigation (for example, Crowfoot and Wondolleck 1990; Fiorino 1995; Snow 1997). Much change has occurred within the environmental policy arena over the past three decades in the United States. Driven by increasing social demands for a clean and safe environment, the federal government has been largely responsible for actively regulating polluting activities and for otherwise taking a leading role in protecting the environment. Generally, this has resulted in significant gains in environmental quality in the United States. Recently, however, local participation in the environmental regulatory process has become more common as environmental protection is no longer exclusively a federal government activity. A significant degree of authority in environmental policy-making is moving to the local level, and with it a greater reliance on Coasean bargaining procedures.

As the federal government pushes many environmental policy issues to states and communities because of increasingly scarce federal funds that are available for environmental protection and regulation, there is now a higher degree of regional, state and local involvement in environmental policy. This development allows increased local involvement in creating environmental policy that can be expected to generate efficiency gains as policies are designed and implemented for strictly local issues. These local policies can often eliminate the welfare losses that can occur when applying a national standard of environmental quality in which a cost-effective solution may not be possible. Devolution of environmental protection and regulation efforts away from the federal government allows states and communities to use alternative decision-making processes to develop environmental management plans and enforce environmental policies while adopting specific policies that complement current federal legislation.

The push away from traditional decision-making strategies has also intensified as more policy-makers and affected parties involved in solving environmental problems recognize some shortcomings of command-and-control approaches (Renn *et al.* 1995). In 1990, the Congress passed the Administrative Dispute Resolution Act in response to the success experienced in the private sector with using negotiation, mediation, arbitration and other similar dispute resolution techniques. The Congress found that alternative means of dispute resolution have 'yielded decisions that are faster, less expensive, and less contentious' than existing dispute resolution procedures such as litigation (Public Law 101–552, sec. 2). This legislation authorized and encouraged federal agencies to use alternative dispute resolution techniques for the prompt and informal resolution of disputes, and recognized the benefits of negotiation methods.

Two reasons help explain why the traditional decision-making process may generate inefficient solutions in the environmental arena. First, local net benefits are sometimes underweighed relative to the net benefits accruing to a more broadly defined population.[4] This tends to discourage local support of the traditional decision-making process. Second, traditional methods can foster a general neglect of local and anecdotal knowledge of those people most familiar with specific environmental problems and suggests that substantial benefits may not be captured if local stakeholders are excluded from the negotiation process. Now let's consider the Coase Theorem and explore what role economics can play to refine environmental decision-making processes.

The Coase Theorem

With environmental management practices moving from a centralized to a relatively more decentralized mode of operation and implementation in the

United States, the relatively informal mechanisms through which environmental negotiations are taking place and the prevalence of locally derived solutions to environmental management problems contrast with the more structured and institutional nature that was standard in the 1970s and 1980s (Amy 1987). This creates an arena where centralized and decentralized approaches to environmental management are interwoven. As such, economic evaluations of current environmental negotiation processes and management planning initiatives rest on the insight and analytic foundation provided by the Coase Theorem (Coase 1960).

Many commentators state that the central tenet of the Coase Theorem is that two parties bargaining in a world of zero transaction costs will arrive at a mutually advantageous agreement that is both private and socially optimal.[5] A simple example illustrates. Riley and Ole disagree about the appropriate level of species protection in the Medicine Bow National Forest. Riley logs, and removes habitat that puts some species such as the lynx at extra risk. Ole wants to protect the habitat given his preferences for conservation. Both have rights to the forest, but Ole fears that Riley's logging will increase the risk that lynx will disappear from the forest. Figure 2.1 shows the net marginal cost (MC) to Ole from logging-induced species risk, and the net marginal benefit (MB) to Riley from logging. The socially efficient level of logging, L*, is when the

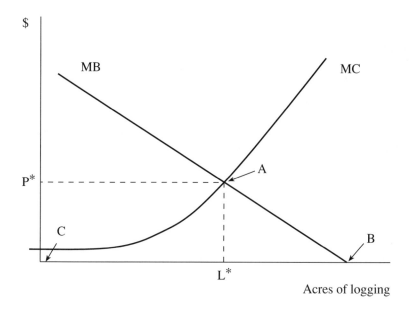

Figure 2.1   Coasean bargaining

incremental gain to Riley equals the incremental cost to Ole, MB = MC (point A). But if Riley is allowed to log, he will do so until his net marginal benefits hit zero (point B). And if Ole is allowed to stop the logging, he will set the level of logging at the level in which his net marginal costs are zero (point C). No decentralized system exists to secure the socially optimal level even though both Riley and Ole would be better off.

The Coase Theorem now takes centre stage. The government can create a market by assigning the property rights to either Riley or Ole. Suppose Ole is given the rights. The MC curve in Figure 2.1 is Ole's supply of acres to log, the MB curve is Riley's demand for logging acres. Riley pays Ole P* for each logging acre, until the market clears and the demand for logging equals the supply at the efficient level, L*. Now if Riley was given the property rights, the MC curve is now Ole's demand for lynx habitat, and the MB curve is Riley's supply of habitat. Ole now pays Riley P* for each acre of habitat until the market again clears at the point in which the demand for habitat equals the supply at the efficient level, L*. The Coase Theorem works: the market price, P*, sets the acres of logging at the efficient level, regardless of the initial assignment of property rights.

This interpretation, however, fails to convey fully the essence of what Coase intended. Coase did not simply envisage a zero transaction costs world. Instead, he argued that the institutional constraints on assigning property rights have no impact on economic efficiency only when transaction costs are non-existent. Precisely because the prevailing theoretical system downplays the existence of transaction costs, economists have been less successful than they could be in explaining the impact of a change in the law on the allocation of resources (Coase 1988).

The importance that the Coase Theorem commands in the debate over efficient environmental policy makes it imperative to establish what Coase meant. Coase (1988) argues he has been misunderstood. He did not champion a zero transactions costs world; rather he argued that the institutional constraints on defining property rights are immaterial to economics from an efficiency standpoint only when transaction costs are zero. Since this world does not exist, efficiency is affected by the assignment of property rights. Coase (1988: 15) states that '[what my argument does suggest is the need to introduce positive transactions costs explicitly into economic analysis so that we can study the world that does exist'. This is the world of incomplete markets, and is pervasive in many different forms throughout the economy.

If a Pigovian tax can be imposed on a polluter then transaction costs must be low enough to enable bargaining until a private and socially optimal agreement is achieved. In this case, regulatory policy would therefore be concerned exclusively with the assignment of unambiguous property rights. But this situation does not exist; it is not costless for a regulator to collect information regarding the most efficient level at which to set a Pigovian tax. Transaction costs matter, so the rules of negotiating also matter. Thus, research probing the boundaries of the assumptions in the Coase Theorem becomes necessary to design institutional frameworks that minimize the impact of real-world friction on efficiency. This will help in designing environmental policies to implement those measures that can generate the improvements in efficiency envisaged by economists. Now let's consider how laboratory evaluations established the predictive strength of the Coase Theorem. From that early affirmation, Coasean bargaining experiments are now used to suggest refinements of actual decision-making processes in the environmental arena.

Coasean Bargaining Experiments

Beginning with the independent work of Prudencio (1982) and Hoffman and Spitzer (1982), and for almost two decades, a line of researchers has taken advantage of the experimental economics laboratory to investigate carefully the boundaries of the axioms that characterize the Coase Theorem. The assumptions required for the Coase Theorem to hold include:

1. two parties to an externality;
2. perfect information regarding each agent's production or utility functions;
3. competitive markets;
4. no transaction costs;
5. costless court system;
6. profit-maximizing producers and expected utility-maximizing consumers;
7. absence of wealth effects; and
8. parties will arrive at mutually advantageous bargains when no transaction costs are present.

Regan (1972) stated that the presence of assumption (8) alone is needed to prove the Coase Theorem.

Regan (1972) maintained that the assumptions of the Coase Theorem imply that parties to an externality will agree on a Pareto optimal level for an externality-generating activity, and that the attainment of this agreement will be generated through a mutually advantageous bargain between the parties. This assertion has largely framed the analytical structure by which the results derived in Coasean bargaining experiments are interpreted and presented; this framework is expected to generate efficient agreements in which the parties to the bargain achieve a mutually advantageous distribution of wealth. First, a review of the existing Coasean bargaining experiments is warranted.

Numerous experiments in the psychology arena throughout the 1970s investigated two- and three-person bargaining games, producing a literature that is arguably richer than the Coasean bargaining literature of today. Many of these experiments incorporated one or more of the axioms that typify Coasean bargaining.[6] Although Pareto optimal choices were generally more prevalent as conditions lined up more closely with the Coase axioms, no consensus emerged on how the gains from trade were to be divided among the parties to a bargain in these pre-Coasean experiments.[7] Because the predicted mutually advantageous distributions of wealth did not occur in many of these bargaining experiments, the notion of rationality was challenged in theoretical and experimental economics.

Economic experiments probing the boundaries of Coasean bargaining began to emerge when an outside option became available for bargainers. An initial series of papers investigating the Coase bargaining problem in the laboratory was concerned primarily with relaxing certain axioms of the Coase Theorem in an effort to better understand the impact on efficiency and distribution of wealth. Prudencio (1982) and Hoffman and Spitzer (1982) established the framework for these earliest experiments. The first result, and one that is generally seen throughout subsequent Coasean bargaining experiments, is that parties to a bargain can often develop a negotiated agreement that is efficient. This singular feature of these first Coasean bargaining experiments lent initial support to the first of two key behavioural outcomes implied by Coasean bargaining – namely, that two parties will agree on a Pareto optimal level of an externality. Efficiency was the typical outcome in almost all of these agreements.

The second result differed considerably between the two original Coase bargaining experiments. Bargainers in the Hoffman and Spitzer (1982) experiment were characterized by settling on a distribution of wealth that was equal between the parties, while the bargainers in the Prudencio (1982) experiment focused more on giving the available gains from trade to the party that did not hold the property right. These results are different from each other largely because subjects in the Prudencio (1982) design only had knowledge of their own payoffs while the Hoffman and Spitzer (1982) design allowed each player to have complete information about the payoffs of both players. The Hoffman and Spitzer (1982) design suggested that the distribution of wealth was equitable (that is, 50/50 split) while the Prudencio (1982) design was characterized by constrained self-interest (that is, 80/20 split). That is to say, the player with unilateral property rights took for him/herself what was available from the outside option and gave the rest to the other player. These results are consistent with Croson (1996) and Straub and Murnighan (1995) in ultimatum games.

The results of those first experiments had significant implications regarding the experimental validity of the distribution and rationality implications of the Coase Theorem. As such, Hoffman and Spitzer (1982) conceded that, while their results did not support the precise implications of Coase's hypothesis regarding the distribution of wealth in almost all of the bargaining agreements, these discrepancies were not significant enough to detract from support of the Coase Theorem. But the fact remained that ambiguous results existed regarding the ability of bargainers to reach mutually advantageous bargaining agreements in a Coase setting. By providing subjects with a more complete understanding of the meaning of unilateral property rights, Harrison and McKee (1985) generated strong support for both behavioural implications of the Coase Theorem. Additionally, Hoffman and Spitzer (1985) determined that moral authority and allocation mechanisms had no adverse impact on efficiency, but provided more mutually advantageous bargaining agreements. Thus, a general experimental design for assessing the robustness of the most important axioms of the Coase Theorem in terms of efficiency and distribution was established.

With an experimental design now firmly in place, further investigations probed the boundaries of the Coase Theorem. Generally, these papers suggested that the Coase Theorem was robust in its assumptions: efficiency was not dampened by large bargaining groups (Hoffman and Spitzer 1986), asymmetric payoffs (Coursey *et al.* 1987), or requiring contractual consent from the other player (Schwab 1988). Additionally, a Coasean bargaining setting generated efficient solutions to externalities in experimental markets (Harrison *et al.* 1987). While the distribution of wealth could be manipulated by relaxing some of Coase's axioms (see Hoffman and Spitzer 1986; Schwab 1988), the evidence strongly supported the two key behavioural outcomes implied by the Coase Theorem.

These experiments affirmed the importance of the laboratory approach to support the axioms of the Coase Theorem; Shogren (1989), following Roth and Malouf (1979) refined the general design of the Coasean bargaining experiment to include a binary lottery to control for subjects' risk preferences. This refinement allowed for greater precision in studying the robustness of Coase's axioms by relaxing key underlying assumptions. Uncertain payoff streams had no impact on predicted efficiency (Shogren 1992), while imperfect contract enforcement did (Shogren and Kask 1992). Further, institutional structure played a key role in predicting the distribution of wealth among bargainers. Mutually advantageous distributions became more common with membership on a team directing loyalty (Shogren 1989) and in a tournament setting with non-linearly increasing payoffs (Shogren 1997).

These first Coasean bargaining experiments directed the flow of research from the laboratory to the real world. But research is now motivated and framed in more direct reference to the resulting policy implications. Conflicts in the environmental arena are now the focus of current Coasean bargaining experimental efforts. Reflecting the real world concern that delay can erode bargaining gains in an environmental conflict, Shogren (1998) determined that efficiency was hindered by non-increasing marginal delay costs. Some types of bargaining rules can further enhance efficiency of the private resolution of environmental conflict by serving as a substitute for bargaining experience (Spencer and Shogren 2000).

Testbedding research holds the most immediate promise for Coasean bargaining experiments in shaping dispute resolution in the environmental arena. By providing a source of experience and data about how various rules might work in a collaborative setting, testbed research offers an initial evaluation of the performance properties of the rules to be examined in this Coasean bargaining setting and becomes necessary to design and refine institutional collaborative frameworks (see Plott and Porter 1996; Plott 1997). With a focus on the impact of specific rules on efficiency and distribution in resolving environmental conflicts among private citizens, Coasean bargaining experiments can suggest efficient policy mechanisms in this arena. Just as the experimental laboratory is being used to study feasibility, limitations, incentives and performance of proposed markets designs for deregulation in natural gas and electric power systems (see McCabe *et al.* 1989, 1990, 1991; Rassenti *et al.* 1994), the experiment presented in this chapter is intended to further refine alternative decision-making processes currently in use in the environmental arena using efficiency as the evaluation tool.

The remainder of this chapter focuses on a specific lab examination of how Coasean bargaining relates to collaborative decision-making processes – the alternative decision-making process increasingly used in environmental policy. This examination provides a useful example of how Coasean bargaining can work as a method that can influence how we think about the design and analysis of decision-making systems at work in the environmental arena.

THE COLLABORATIVE DECISION-MAKING PROCESS

People have turned to the collaborative decision-making process more and more to resolve environmental disputes and develop natural resource management plans at the local level. The collaborative decision-making process places an emphasis on achieving consensus decisions outside the courtroom by seeking solutions based on mutual gain. Allowing voluntary participation of all concerned stakeholders and providing for assistance from facilitators or mediators gives government, business, and citizen groups the opportunity to develop jointly environment and natural resource management strategies.

Attention to the workings of the collaborative process as an institutional framework used in the environmental arena has focused on documenting the structure of this decision-making process (see Bacow and Wheeler 1984; Bingham 1986; Crowfoot and Wondolleck 1990; Johnston and Krupin 1991; Melling 1995; Porter and Salvesen 1995; and Bernard and Young 1997). Researchers using the case study approach have identified a number of key elements that are likely to help produce successful dispute resolution processes. But a prescription for success according to one researcher studying one case can be different from that of another researcher examining another case. As the number of key elements of success required in each design varies considerably (and the probability of generating a successful outcome), the resources required to implement these designs can also be expected to vary.[8] This poses a unique challenge for the environmental decision-maker with an opportunity to select an appropriate and cost-effective collaborative process for a particular environmental issue but with only limited resources to dedicate to the design and implementation of a decision-making process (Manring *et al.* 1990).

Using a laboratory experiment, we probe the efficiency and distribution aspects of a bargaining process that incorporates the major elements of collaborative decision-making. Proposed as such, this 'expensive' collaborative process suggests an upper limit on efficiency levels that can be realized in a collaborative decision-making process in which implementation costs are not constrained by a budget.[9] That is, the concern with this examination does not rest on the costs of implementation, but rather is focused on the upper limit of benefits that a typical collaborative effort can generate.[10] The Coasean bargaining experiment produces baseline measures of efficiency and distribution for generating consensus decisions in this setting. This analysis provides information to help local community groups and public officials think about which process is most appropriate for resolving a specific environmental dispute or developing a local natural resource management plan. This can fill the current gap in knowledge of these topics by taking advantage of the economic analysis provided in Coasean bargaining experiments to further develop and refine environmental decision-making processes.

The Collaborative Process

We use economic bargaining theory and the experimental laboratory to determine the maximum level of benefits we can expect from implementing an 'expensive' collaborative process. Target measures of efficiency and the distribution of wealth can provide helpful information to policy-makers, but the existing literature ignores these more general economic issues, and as yet guidelines for implementing the collaborative decision-making process based on economics do not exist. The experiment herein fills this gap and provides an economic foundation that can provide a more complete description of the collaborative process.

The collaborative decision-making process became a widely used policy-making instrument in the environmental arena once environmental protection was established as a high priority within the American political scene (see Gray and Hay 1986). The collaborative decision-making process can be characterized as a subset of the more general techniques of alternative dispute resolution, including methods such as regulated negotiation, facilitation and mediation. The most essential element of the collaborative decision-making process is the reliance on all stakeholders forming consensus decisions. In its most fundamental form, we define the collaborative process as one that permits voluntary participation of all concerned stakeholders. The process is voluntary so stakeholders are not forced into an arena that may have the appearance of a regulatory process. The collaborative decision-making process, defined in this manner, is generally applied in many areas across the United States and throughout the world (see Western 1994; Poffenberger 1994; and Statham 1994). As such, the collaborative decision-making process that we examine in the laboratory is described in the following subsection.

Experimental Design

The experimental design here closely follows that of previous Coasean bargaining experiments. A total of 27 undergraduate students from the University of Wyoming were recruited and served as subjects. Each subject was inexperienced in face-to-face Coasean bargaining. As the subjects entered the lab, each was randomly assigned an identification number, placed on a bargaining team with two other players and given an identical set of instructions. A monitor read the instructions aloud, and then asked subjects to answer a series of questions to ensure they clearly understood their role in the experiment. In all, three identical treatments were rendered, in which each treatment included six bargaining sessions. Each subject participated in two sets of bargaining sessions and was paired with a different player from each of the other two teams in that treatment for each bargaining set.[11]

A three-player (A, B and C) Coasean bargaining framework is modelled in which forming consensus decisions can provide greater expected rewards for players than the expected rewards available from always taking the outside option.[12] Each bargain involves two perfectly enforced contracts – a number and a transfer contract. The number contract specifies the initial chances of winning a reward, expressed in terms of lottery tickets allotted to each player. This decision requires the bargaining triad to select one of six numbers from a 'lottery schedule' (see Table 2.1) in which each number corresponds with a different initial distribution of lottery tickets. The players then use the transfer contract to redistribute the lottery tickets.

In keeping with the design of prior Coasean bargaining experiments, unilateral property rights are assigned to one of the players in each bargaining triad: the controller. While this design feature may not replicate the precise workings of every collaborative process, it provides a setting in which one stakeholder is given a relatively larger endowment than the other stakeholders. The controller has the right to select a number unilaterally, representing the chance to win the lottery, and inform the monitor, who will then stop the bargaining session. This is called the controller's right. The two non-controllers can attempt to influence the controller to reach a consensus decision, and thus have a chance at winning the reward by offering to give part or all of their lottery tickets to the controller. The controller has the opportunity to exercise the controller's right at any time during a bargaining session without agreement from the two non-controllers. A dice game determines the controller before each set of bargaining sessions. Unilateral property rights are given to the player who wins this dice game. Winning the dice game is intended to instil a sense that the controller has earned the property rights in the ensuing bargaining sessions.[13]

In addition, players were members of a bargaining team. Cash awards were given to each subject based on how many lottery tickets their team captured during the bargaining sessions. First ($7), second ($5) and third place ($3) prizes were given following each set of bargains. Each member on the team with the most accumulated lottery tickets for the two bargaining sets received an additional $20. Shogren (1989) demonstrates that membership on a bargaining team results in subjects making relatively more mutually advantageous agreements because individuals are forced to be responsible to some entity other than themselves.[14] Each player is given a non-transferable initial endowment of M = $5 before each set of bargaining sessions. A $1 entrance fee is required from each player to enter each bargaining session, representing the real commitment of resources required of participants in an actual collaborative process.

If a bargaining triad arrives at a consensus decision – defined as an agreement garnering approval of all three subjects in the triad – in selecting the number and transfer contracts three times in at most five bargaining sessions, the reward for each of the three consensus lotteries is Y = $10. The experiment is designed in this fashion since the collaborative decision-making process is one in which solutions are often derived through a series of negotiation sessions with the same group of stakeholders over a period of time. The bargaining triad is permitted to take up to five bargaining sessions to reach three consensus decisions, reflecting the concern that participants in a collaborative process sometimes agree to disagree on a particular issue, committing instead to attempt to reach consensus on the controversial issue at a later time (Crowfoot and Wondolleck 1990). For those bargaining triads not making consensus decisions in the manner described above, the reward for each lottery is Z = $2. If the bargaining triad fails to come to an agreement on the distribution of lottery tickets within the allotted five-minute bargaining time, each player receives no lottery tickets. This particular feature of the experimental design models those collaborative processes in which the collaborative benefits generated can be significantly greater than individual benefits (see Snow 1997).

The law and economics of the environment

Table 2.1   Lottery ticket distribution schedules

Number	A's lottery tickets (%)	B's lottery tickets (%)	C's lottery tickets (%)	Number	A's lottery tickets (%)	B's lottery tickets (%)	C's lottery tickets (%)
Schedule 1				Schedule 6			
1	0	0	70	1	70	0	0
2	25	15	30	2	20	35	15
3	40	55	5	3	30	20	20
4	0	70	0	4	0	70	0
5	5	25	40	5	0	0	70
6	70	0	0	6	30	10	30
Schedule 2				Schedule 7			
1	0	70	0	1	70	0	0
2	30	30	10	2	30	30	10
3	70	0	0	3	0	70	0
4	0	0	70	4	0	0	70
5	50	5	45	5	45	50	5
6	35	10	25	6	10	20	40
Schedule 3				Schedule 8			
1	5	35	60	1	30	20	20
2	40	20	10	2	60	30	10
3	0	0	70	3	0	70	0
4	0	70	0	4	70	0	0
5	20	25	25	5	15	15	40
6	70	0	0	6	0	0	70
Schedule 4				Schedule 9			
1	70	0	0	1	0	70	0
2	0	70	0	2	10	15	45
3	20	35	15	3	40	50	10
4	25	15	30	4	70	0	0
5	55	5	40	5	25	10	35
6	0	0	70	6	0	0	70
Schedule 5				Schedule 10			
1	50	40	10	1	20	30	20
2	0	70	0	2	0	0	70
3	30	20	20	3	30	25	15
4	0	0	70	4	15	25	60
5	70	0	0	5	0	70	0
6	35	10	25	6	70	0	0

The Coasean Bargaining Model

To form baseline measures of efficiency and distribution, a consensus equilibrium and a 'bookend' outcome for a three-player Coasean bargain are defined. While the consensus equilibrium is not unique, together with the bookend outcome, they are benchmarks to make subsequent comparisons. In his seminal work, Schelling (1960) noted that an appropriate theory of behaviour in games with multiple equilibria should indicate which equilibrium would be observed. An equilibrium becomes focal when a group of people come to expect behaviour consistent with this equilibrium. Rationality is predicated on the belief that each player expects the other players in the group to expect play consistent with this focal point equilibrium and to act on that expectation (Ochs 1995). The most obvious focal point equilibrium in this experiment is the consensus equilibrium since that is the agreement that provides the reward with the highest expected value. This is the equilibrium in which consensus decisions are formed in each of the first three bargaining sessions of each bargaining set, thus minimizing entrance fees and maximizing the expected reward. It is further assumed that each of these consensus decisions results in a Pareto efficient distribution of lottery tickets; all the available lottery tickets are distributed.[15]

We also examine the 'bookend' outcome. This is the outcome in which consensus is never achieved and the controller takes the outside option in each of the five bargaining sessions – not one of these decisions results in a Pareto efficient distribution of lottery tickets.[16] This reflects a lower limit to the efficiency that can be achieved in a collaborative setting primarily because none of the high value rewards is captured and is provided as a proxy for the efficiency that could be generated from a lengthy litigation proceeding.[17] The 'bookend' outcome suggests a comparison of the efficiency generated from the collaborative framework to the efficiency expected through litigation.

Let player A be the controller; players B and C are the non-controllers. All players are risk-neutral. Define $p_A \in [0,1]$ and $(1 - p_A)$ as the probabilities that the controller wins the large or small reward, $Z > z = 0$. The cost of entering each bargaining session for the controller is c_A. Finally, define p_A^0 as the probability that the controller wins Z given he/she takes the outside option. Then player A's expected utility from a negotiated agreement in this bargain is given by $Eu_A = p_A u(Z - c_A) + (1 - p_A)u(z - c_A) + u(c_A)$ and $Eu^{c-0} = p_A^0 u(z) + u(c_A)$ is the controller's expected utility from taking the outside option.

We define $p_B \in [0,1]$ and $(1 - p_B)$ as the probabilities that this non-controller wins the large or small reward, $Z > z = 0$. The cost of entering each bargaining session for this non-controller is c_B. Player C is also a risk-neutral player. Likewise, define $p_C \in [0,1]$ and $(1 - p_C)$ as the probabilities that this non-controller wins the large or small reward, $Z > z = 0$. The cost of entering each bargaining session for player C is c_C. Then player B's expected utility from a negotiated agreement is given by $Eu_B = p_B u(Z) + (1 - p_B)u(z) + u(c_B)$. Similarly, player C's expected utility from a negotiated agreement is given as $Eu_C = p_C u(Z) + (1 - p_C)u(z) + u(c_C)$. Now define the probability that none of the three players in the bargaining group wins the large reward as $p_H = 1 - p_A - p_B - p_C$. Then $Eu_B^{nc-0} = (1 - p_A^0 - p_H - p_C)u(z) + u(c_B) = u(c_B)$ and $Eu_C^{nc-0} = (1 - p_A^0 - p_H - p_B)u(z) + u(c_C) = u(c_C)$ are the measures of expected utility for players B and C given that the controller takes the outside option.

The Nash bargaining problem for the collaborative decision-making process in a one-shot game is given by:

$$\underset{p_A, p_B, p_C, \hat{p}_H}{\text{Max}} \left[\left(Eu_A - Eu^{c-0} \right) \left(Eu_B - Eu^{nc-0} \right) \left(Eu_C - Eu^{nc-0} \right) \right]. \quad (2.1)$$

The solution to this maximization problem yields:

$$p_A = p_A^0 + \frac{p_H}{3}, \text{ and} \quad (2.2)$$

$$p_B = p_C = \frac{1 - p_A^0 - \dfrac{p_H}{3}}{2}. \quad (2.3)$$

That is, the controller and the two non-controllers should distribute the available house lottery tickets evenly among themselves, while the controller retains rights to the lottery tickets specified by the outside option. Given that the outside option is 70 lottery tickets for the controller and that 30 lottery tickets remain undistributed, the predicted distribution is $p_A = 80$ and $p_B = p_C = 10$.

Since equal splits are often associated with repeated, face-to-face negotiations (see Greenberg 1979; Shapiro 1975), equation (2.2) serves as an upper bound on the number of lottery tickets the controller should capture. In addition, an incentive exists for the controller to try to prevent breakdown since s/he has a higher expected reward associated with consensus agreements than with breakdown.[18] This further suggests that the one-shot Nash bargaining solution provides an upper bound on the number of lottery tickets the controller can capture. We can therefore expect to see relatively more constrained self-interest (see Shogren 1997) and equity in the distribution of wealth in the present design than in a one-shot game that does not include an incentive for the controller to give away lottery tickets.

Two indications of efficiency are examined. The first measure is reward efficiency and is measured for the bookend outcome and the consensus equilibrium. Reward efficiency is the improvement in actual expected gain as a percentage of the potential gain due to bargaining. Let E indicate either a bookend (B) outcome or a consensus (C) equilibrium. Define r as the number of bargaining sessions in the bargaining set. D is a dummy variable that takes a value of 1 if the consensus reward was awarded three times in the bargaining group and is 0 otherwise. Finally, X_E is the maximum expected gain that can be achieved in the bookend outcome (E = B) or consensus equilibrium (E = C); $-0.38 \leq R_C \leq 1$ and $1 < R_B \leq 5.14$.[19] Then reward efficiency is defined as:

$$R_E = \frac{\sum_{i=1}^{r}\left[(p_A + p_B + p_C)Z - (c_A + c_B + c_C)\right] + 3D(Y - Z) + \left[M_A + M_B + M_C\right]}{X_E}.$$

(2.4)

Finally, probability efficiency is measured as:

$$\Gamma = \{[p_A + p_B + p_C] - p_A^0\}/(1 - p_A^0)$$

(2.5)

to determine the extent to which subjects maximize the joint probability of winning the reward. For example, if the subjects distribute all 100 lottery tickets among themselves, $\Gamma = 1$. Alternatively, if the controller exercises the controller's right, $\Gamma = 0$. Most bargaining groups are able to achieve $\Gamma = 1$.

Results and Discussion

Table 2.2 shows the payoff distribution of each of the bargains, broken down by efficiency levels. Of the 18 bargaining groups that were formed through the experiment, only two groups (11 per cent) did not generate three consensus agreements within the five allotted bargaining sessions. Of the other groups, nine (50 per cent) reached the consensus equilibrium by generating three consensus agreements in the first three bargaining sessions, three groups (17 per cent) took four bargaining sessions to form three consensus agreements and four (22 per cent) took all five bargaining sessions to generate three consensus agreements. Only one negotiated outcome of the agreements in the experiment that distributed all 100 lottery tickets gave the controller at least his/her outside option. The experiment was characterized by equity; this is discussed later in this subsection.

The average number of offers made in reaching a negotiated agreement increased significantly with rounds ($F = 2.231, p = 0.075$). The average number of offers per negotiated agreement increased from 2.06 in the first round to 3.67 in the fifth round and the structure of negotiating agreements changed with increasing rounds. A majority of bargains ended with two or fewer offers made per round in the first two rounds of bargaining. Beginning in the third round, a majority of the negotiated agreements involved three or more offers among the players. This is expected and can most likely be attributed to players becoming more familiar with the experiment and the specific rules of the game. The players become more precise in their demands.

Table 2.2   Experimental results: distribution

Round	n	Pareto efficient	Payoff distribution				
			Equal split[a]	Controller earns outside option	Controller earns more than outside option	Disagree	Other
1	18	14	12	3	0	0	3
2	18	16	15	1	0	0	2
3	18	14	13	4	0	0	1
4	9	4	5	3	0	1	0
5	6	4	4	2	0	0	0
Total	69	53	49	13	0	1	6

Note: [a] As in Harrison and McKee (1985), an essentially equal split is defined as an agreement with an equal split or a split within 10 per cent of an equal split of lottery tickets.

The average number of lottery tickets received from bargaining by the controller ($F = 0.747$, $p = 0.564$) and the total received for the two non-controllers ($F = 1.526$, $p = 0.206$) did not change with bargaining rounds. Finally, average probability efficiency, which measures the ability of the bargaining group to capture more of the available lottery tickets, does not significantly change with bargaining rounds ($F = 1.898$, $p = 0.122$). Average probability efficiency was 0.78 in the first round and decreased to 0.67 in the final round. The drop in probability efficiency from round one to round four, while not significant ($F = 2.724$, $p = 0.111$), is interesting and suggests a potential impact as half of the bargaining groups were no longer in the sample after having reached the three consensus decisions in the first three rounds. The subsequent rise in probability efficiency in the last round may have been due in part to some players wanting to form one last consensus decision to ensure a higher value of the money chips they had attained in previous bargaining rounds. A larger sample may indicate significant differences in average probability efficiency across rounds.

Result 1: Efficiency is relatively high in the expensive collaborative decision-making process. On average, collaborative groups captured almost 90 per cent of the expected gains to be made in the consensus equilibrium; an average of over 450 per cent of the expected gains in the bookend outcome were captured.

Table 2.3 shows that the collaborative decision-making process is as efficient as earlier Coasean bargaining experiments.[20] Mean and median values for consensus equilibrium reward efficiency, R_C, are 0.89 and 0.99. On average, bargainers were able to capture almost 90 per cent of the expected gains to be made in the consensus equilibrium setting.[21] Note the consensus equilibrium represents the upper bound on the expected gains that can be made from bargaining in the collaborative framework. So even in a setting that implemented the most costly elements of the collaborative process – such as face-to-face bargaining, maintaining participant continuity and providing for the involvement of all stakeholders – and emphasized consensus, bargainers still left 10 per cent of the potential gains from trade on the table. Because this result is in line with results of other Coasean bargaining experiments, it suggests a realistic upper limit to the level of efficiency that can be generated in a Coasean setting – regardless of implementation costs.

Table 2.3 Experimental results: efficiency and rationality

	Mean	Median	Standard deviation
Efficiency			
Reward efficiency ($n = 18$)			
Consensus equilibrium	0.89	0.99	0.24
Bookend equilibrium	4.56	5.07	1.25
Probability efficiency ($n = 69$)	0.73	1.00	0.56
Rationality			
% of risk-neutral Nash solution of one-shot bookend game			
Controller	52	44	19
Sum of non-controllers	253	310	127

Mean and median values for reward efficiency in the bookend outcome case, R_B, representing the lower bound in the level of expected gains to be made in the collaborative process, are 4.56 and 5.07. On average, bargainers captured about 4.5 times the potential gains available in a minimally effective negotiation process. This suggests that groups can reach highly efficient outcomes when the situation provides for five times greater rewards through consensus versus litigation. Further, 77 per cent of the bargains resulted in Pareto efficient agreements. The evidence here suggests that the collaborative process can generate efficient bargaining outcomes in strongly win–win situations; bargainers appear to focus on making consensus decisions in prompt fashion when the gains to consensus are large and obvious, recognizing the increased resource costs of prolonged bargaining.[22]

Equation (2.6) tests whether learning and subject effects or some combination created differences in reward efficiency:

$$R = \beta_0 + \sum_{i=2}^{5}\beta_i r_i + \sum_{k=2}^{3}\omega_{1k}A_{1k} + \sum_{l=1}^{3}\omega_{2l}A_{2l} + \sum_{m=1}^{3}\omega_{3m}A_{3m}, \qquad (2.6)$$

where r_i are the (T − 1) rounds and A_{zk} are the (N − 1) A players from the three treatments, z = 1,2,3. The restriction that reward efficiency was independent of both round and player, $\beta_{Round2} = \beta_{Round3} = ... = \omega_{12} = \omega_{13} = ... = \omega_{33} = 0$, is not rejected at the 5 per cent level ($F = 1.14$). These results suggest that efficiency in the collaborative decision-making process can be expected regardless of the number of times a group meets and the stakeholders who participate.

Result 2: The distribution of wealth is best characterized by equity. The controller only received about 50 per cent of the expected wealth predicted by the Nash bargaining solution in the one-shot game, while the non-controllers together captured over 250 per cent of the expected wealth. Over 70 per cent of the agreements were equitable splits.

Evidence from Table 2.3 lends support to the claim that the distribution of wealth is dominated by equity. In total, equitable splits were the result in 71 per cent (49 of 69) of all agreements. Just 19 per cent (13 of 69) of all agreements were mutually advantageous, a relatively low indicator of behaviour that is consistent with self-interest or constrained self-interest (see Shogren 1997). Data from Table 2.3 tell us that the controller received, on average, 52 per cent of the expected wealth predicted by the Nash bargaining solution in the one-shot game. The non-controllers together received 253 per cent of the expected wealth. This again suggests that equity dominates bargaining agreements in the collaborative process.

Because the experiment was designed such that subjects were members of a bargaining team, it was expected that there would be less incentive for equitable splits.[23] Shogren (1989) suggests that providing a context for loyalty in face-to-face bargaining experiments is essential to generating the mutually advantageous agreements predicted by bargaining theory. The team structure incorporated herein, however, produced a large portion of equitable splits.[24] One possibility for this behaviour is that free-riding dominated bargaining; that is, winning the team competition did not provide the subject with a large enough incentive to maximize their share of lottery tickets since subjects relied heavily on their team-mates (and not themselves) to secure a relatively large portion of the team's lottery tickets. The presence of equitable splits may have been further enhanced by the incentive for subjects to avoid offending the players in their bargaining group. Subjects who did not want to be perceived by those in their bargaining group as being 'tough' negotiators (see Roth 1995) thus left the task of capturing a large portion of lottery tickets to the other members of their team. Finally, altruism cannot generally be ignored in bargaining experiments. While fairness is often not an explanation for all observed equal splits, some of the subjects can be expected to be primarily motivated by considerations of fairness (see Forsythe *et al.* 1994). And intuition suggests this is a real factor in face-to-face collaboration; but the countervailing forces are what is missing from this experiment.

CONCLUSIONS AND EXTENSIONS

Coase suggested over 40 years ago that decentralized environmental policy deserves more attention, at the very least as a benchmark, to judge the effectiveness of the rules and protocol that define how people can work together to resolve conflicts and disputes. Today we see that such collaborative decision-making processes are flourishing in environmental management because more local control in exchange for stricter accountability is a tradeoff many people are willing to make.

This chapter has explored how we can use Coasean bargaining to understand better the effectiveness of these collaborative decision-making processes. We extend the earlier work that examined the collaborative decision-making process on a strictly case-by-case basis, providing citizen groups with the appropriate information about how a particular collaborative framework may or may not meet their specific needs. Emphasizing the benefit of forming consensus decisions in the collaborative decision-making process, a Coasean bargaining experiment is introduced, generating baseline measures of efficiency and distribution for an 'expensive' collaborative design.

The evidence presented here suggests that equity along with a level of efficiency comparable to previous Coase experiments dominate this 'expensive' collaborative process. With bargainers already at the table with facilitators enabling full information sharing about payoffs (providing a power balance among stakeholders), prepared to negotiate and given that stakeholders hold final authority in implementing consensus decisions, the collaborative decision-making process appears to be effective. As such, under the conditions provided in the experiment, the results provide empirical support of the collaborative process as an efficient and equitable process. This suggests that when large and obvious payoffs are available to stakeholders through collaboration, efficiency and equity can be expected. It still remains unclear why equity dominated the agreements in this setting even though a team structure was present. Free-riding may have been pervasive and in this context remains an open research question.

This framework generates results comparable to simpler negotiation frameworks already tested in the lab. This suggests that the extra features incorporated in the present experimental design, such as forming consensus decisions in a team structure that is maintained over a prolonged period of time, add little of significant value to Coasean bargaining. Natural extensions of the current research abound. The results presented here serve as a source of experience about how an expensive collaborative process works. As such, future studies should investigate which rules of the collaborative decision-making process can be dropped without efficiency loss. Empirically testing the effects of these procedural issues will go a long way towards developing a more complete understanding of the collaborative decision-making process as it relates to using alternative dispute resolution methods to settle environmental disputes and developing natural resource management programmes.

NOTES

*   We thank Tom Crocker, Rob Godby, Chuck Mason and Deb Paulson for their valuable comments. We also gratefully acknowledge the financial support of the Institute for Environment and Natural Resources at the University of Wyoming. All errors remain our own.
1.   For more on *Enlibra* go to http://www.westgov.org/wga/initiatives/enlibra/default.htm.
2.   See, for example, Hoffman and Spitzer (1982, 1985, 1986); Harrison and McKee (1985); Shogren and Kask (1992); and Shogren (1992, 1997, 1998).
3.   The Alternative Dispute Resolution Act of 1990 has moved environmental protection activities away from an extensive reliance on the federal government to a more balanced approach that includes local citizen groups and others. Prior to this, the private sector was already using negotiation, mediation, facilitation and other alternative methods to resolve disputes in the environmental arena.
4.   While winners could hypothetically compensate losers in this scenario, this prospect often is not attractive at the local level. In fact, local groups have an incentive to organize and compete for a transfer of wealth from other groups to themselves (that is, engage in rent-seeking activities), which can explain why local groups became discouraged with traditional decision-making procedures.
5.   Some have argued that the Coase Theorem, expressed in this manner, is tautological (Bromley 1989).
6.   Hoffman and Spitzer (1982) provide an excellent review of the literature of these early bargaining experiments and their link to modern boundary experiments that investigate Coasean bargaining.
7.   See Shogren (1989, 1997) for an examination of this issue in Coasean bargaining experiments.

8. Bingham (1986: 145) notes costs of environmental dispute resolution methods ranging from $1000 for a case with two parties and one mediator to $40 000 for a case with 12 parties and two mediators.

9. Typically, collaborative groups are limited in the level of funding that can be directed to the operation of the negotiation efforts.

10. We assume this collaborative process tested in the laboratory includes costly features suggested by researchers.

11. Each set of bargaining sessions included multiple rounds of bargaining with the same players. Sets of bargaining rounds were included to incorporate reality – the repeated nature of meeting with the same group of stakeholders for a particular environmental or natural resource concern typifies collaborative decision-making (see Keystone Center 1996; and Porter and Salvesen 1995). However, it should be noted that this is not completely adequate to simulate real social or interpersonal relationships.

12. The outside option is the term applied to the assets the property owner can rightfully take if the collaborative process breaks down at any point.

13. As we shall later note, axiomatic bargaining theory predicts that as a result of bargaining, the controller should receive more lottery tickets than the two non-controllers as well as more lottery tickets than the outside option. We shall also see that Coasean bargaining experiments do not typically generate these predicted results. Moral authority can be attached to the notion of the controller's right if capturing that right involves some degree of skill in a game (Harrison and McKee 1985).

14. Pilot experiments revealed that subjects were not arriving at mutually advantageous agreements in the experimental lab as predicted by theory. The team structure was incorporated in the design of the experiment in an attempt to move away from equitable splits of available lottery tickets and in the direction of predicted behaviour.

15. The earliest Coasean bargaining experiments referred to this situation as joint-profit maximization (see Hoffman and Spitzer 1982, 1985, 1986; and Harrison and McKee 1985). In a collaborative process, a Pareto efficient distribution indicates that the gains from bargaining will be distributed across the stakeholders. In nuclear incinerator siting issues, for example, location of the incinerator will generate different levels of utility for the stakeholders in the area assuming that proximity to the incinerator is inversely related to the general level of utility for each stakeholder. A solution to this siting problem must account for the different levels of utility of each stakeholder.

16. It is implied that at least one of the stakeholders prefers litigation to collaboration.

17. Assume a lengthy litigation proceeding forces a judge to select one of the numbers from the lottery schedule (see Table 2.1) and involves the same cost as a collaborative process. Litigation and the collaborative process are assumed to be substitutes.

18. The controller's expected reward from taking the outside option in all five rounds – and thus never forming a consensus decision – equals his/her certain reward from giving all the tickets to the other two players in that bargaining group in the first three rounds. This suggests that a risk-neutral controller has an incentive to give a portion of his/her lottery tickets to the non-controllers to achieve consensus, and thus avoid breakdown, and capture a higher expected reward from agreement.

19. X_B is calculated as the value of the numerator in (2.4) when $r = 5$ and $D = 0$; X_C is the value of the numerator in (2.4) when $r = 3$ and $D = 1$.

20. While efficiency is measured in a somewhat different manner in the present experiment because of the entry fee required of subjects, a similar proportion of agreements that maximized joint payoffs characterized earlier experiments.

21. Of the 18 collaborative groups that were examined, 16 groups distributed all three of the available consensus rewards within five bargaining sessions.

22. Mean and median values for probability efficiency, Γ, equal 0.73 and 1.00. These values are comparable to those determined in other Coasean bargaining experiments.

23. In general, equitable splits are more common in experimental designs that feature: (a) repeated, face-to-face negotiations (see Greenberg 1979; Shapiro 1975); (b) the ability to choose a Pareto optimal allocation which is an equal split (see Fouraker and Seigel 1963; Michener *et al.* 1979; Siegel and Fouraker 1960); (c) public payoffs (see Leventhal *et al.* 1972; Reis and Grunzen

1976); and (d) full information about each player's payoffs (see Roth and Malouf 1979; Nydegger 1977). Roth (1995) notes that results from sequential bargaining games point to a general preference by bargainers to be partly concerned with their relative share of the reward.

24. Many times stakeholders have developed strong animosity towards one another in the years preceding participation in a collaborative process. Future research should test how this impacts equity in the collaborative decision-making process.

REFERENCES

Amy, D. (1987), *The Politics of Environmental Mediation*, New York: Columbia University Press.

Bacow, L. and M. Wheeler (1984), *Environmental Dispute Resolution*, New York: Plenum Press.

Bernard, T. and J. Young (1997), *The Ecology of Hope: Communities Collaborate for Sustainability*, Gabriola Island, BC: New Society Publishers.

Bingham, G. (1986), *Resolving Environmental Disputes: A Decade of Experience*, Washington, DC: Conservation Foundation.

Bromley, D. (1989), 'Entitlements, missing markets and environmental uncertainty', *Journal of Environmental Economics and Management* 17(1): 181–94.

Coase, R. (1960), 'The problem of social cost', *Journal of Law and Economics* 3: 1–44.

Coase, R. (1988), *The Firm, the Market and the Law*, Chicago: University of Chicago Press.

Cooter, R. (1989), 'The Coase Theorem', in J. Eatwell, M. Milgate and P. Newman (eds), *The New Palgrave: Allocation, Information and Markets*, New York: W.W. Norton, pp. 64–70.

Coursey, D., E. Hoffman and M. Spitzer (1987), 'Fear and loathing in the Coase Theorem: experimental tests involving physical discomfort', *Journal of Legal Studies* 16: 217–48.

Croson, R. (1996), 'Information in ultimatum games: an experimental study', *Journal of Economic Behavior and Organization* 30: 197–213.

Crowfoot, J. and J. Wondolleck (1990), *Environmental Disputes: Community Involvement in Conflict Resolution*, Washington, DC: Island Press.

Fiorino, D. (1988), 'Regulatory negotiation as a policy process', *Public Administration Review* July/August: 764–72.

Fiorino, D. (1995), 'Regulatory negotiation as a form of public participation', in O. Renn, T. Webler and P. Wiedemann (eds), *Fairness and Competence in Citizen Participation: Evaluating Models for Environmental Discourse*, Dordrecht: Kluwer Academic.

Forsythe, R., J. Horowitz, N. Savin and M. Sefton (1994), 'Fairness in simple bargaining experiments', *Games and Economic Behavior* 6: 347–69.

Fouraker, L. and S. Siegel (1963), *Bargaining Behavior*, New York: McGraw-Hill.

Gray, B. and T. Hay (1986), 'Political limits to interorganizational consensus and change', *Journal of Applied Behavioral Science* 22: 95–112.

Greenberg, J. (1979), 'Group vs. individual equity judgments: is there a polarization effect?', *Journal of Experimental Psychology* 15: 504–20.

Harrison, G. and M. McKee (1985), 'Experimental evaluation of the Coase Theorem', *Journal of Law and Economics* 28: 653–70.

Harrison, G., E. Hoffman, E. Rutström and M. Spitzer (1987), 'Coasian solutions to the externality problem in experimental markets', *Economic Journal* 97: 388–402.

Hoffman, E. and M. Spitzer (1982), 'The Coase Theorem: some experimental tests', *Journal of Law and Economics* 25: 73–98.

Hoffman, E. and M. Spitzer (1985), 'Entitlements, rights, and fairness: an experimental examination of subjects' concepts of distributive justice', *Journal of Legal Studies* 14: 259–97.

Hoffman, E. and M. Spitzer (1986), 'Experimental tests of the Coase Theorem with large bargaining groups', *Journal of Legal Studies* 15: 149–71.

Johnston, B. and P. Krupin (1991), 'The 1989 Pacific Northwest Timber compromise: an environmental dispute resolution case study of a successful battle that may have lost the war', *Willamette Law Review* 27: 613–43.

Keystone Center (1996), *The Keystone Center National Policy Dialogue on Ecosystem Management: Final Report*, Keystone, CO: Keystone Center.

Leventhal, G., J. Michaels and C. Sanford (1972), 'Inequity and interpersonal conflict: reward allocation and secrecy about reward as methods of preventing conflict', *Journal of Personality and Social Psychology* 23: 88–101.

Manring, N., K. Nelson and J. Wondolleck (1990), 'Structuring an effective environmental dispute settlement process', in J. Crowfoot and J. Wondolleck (eds), *Environmental Disputes: Community Involvement in Conflict Resolution*, Washington, DC: Island Press.

McCabe, K., S. Rassenti and V. Smith (1989), 'Designing smart computer assisted markets: an experimental auction for gas networks', *European Journal of Political Economy* 5: 259–75.

McCabe, K., S. Rassenti and V. Smith (1990), 'Auction design for composite goods: the natural gas industry', *Journal of Economic Behavior and Organization* 14: 127–49.

McCabe, K., S. Rassenti and V. Smith (1991) 'Smart computer-assisted markets', *Science* 254: 534–8.

Melling, T. (1995), 'Bruce Babbitt's use of governmental dispute resolution: a midterm report card', *Land and Water Law Review* 30: 56–90.

Michener, H.A., I. Ginsberg and K. Yuen (1979) 'Effects of core properties in four-person games with side payments', *Behavioral Science* 24: 263–80.

Nydegger, R. (1977), 'Independent utility scaling and the Nash bargaining model', *Behavioral Science* 22: 283–302.

Ochs, J. (1995), 'Coordination problems', in J. Kagel and A. Roth (eds), *The Handbook of Experimental Economics*, Princeton, NJ: Princeton University Press.

Plott, C. (1997), 'Laboratory experimental testbeds: application to the PCS auction', *Journal of Economics and Management Strategy* 6(3): 605–38.

Plott, C. and D. Porter (1996), 'Market architectures and institutional testbedding: an experiment with space station pricing policies', *Journal of Economic Behavior and Organization* 31: 237–72.

Poffenberger, M. (1994), 'The resurgence of community forest management in eastern India', in D. Western, R.M. Wright and S. Strum (eds), *Natural Connections: Perspectives in Community-based Conservation*, Washington, DC: Island Press.

Porter, D. and D. Salvesen (1995), *Collaborative Planning for Wetlands and Wildlife: Issues and Examples*, Washington, DC: Island Press.

Prudencio, Y. (1982), 'The voluntary approach to externality problems: an experimental test', *Journal of Environmental Economics and Management* 9: 213–28.

Rassenti, S., S. Reynolds and V. Smith (1994), 'Countenancy and competition in an experimental auction market for natural gas pipeline networks', *Economic Theory* 4: 41–65.

Regan, D. (1972), 'The problem of social cost revisited', *Journal of Law and Economics* 15: 427–37.

Reis, H. and J. Grunzen (1976), 'On mediating equity, equality and self-interest: the role of self-preservation in social exchange', *Journal of Experimental Social Psychology* 12: 478–92.

Renn, O., T. Webler and P. Wiedemann (1995), 'A need for discourse on citizen participation: objectives and structure of the book', in O. Renn, T. Webler and P. Wiedemann (eds), *Fairness and Competence in Citizen Participation: Evaluating Models for Environmental Discourse*, Dordrecht: Kluwer Academic.

Rhoads, T. and J. Shogren (1998), 'Current issues in Superfund reauthorization and amendment: how is the Clinton administration handling hazardous waste?', *Duke Environmental Law and Policy Forum* 8(2): 245–71.

Rhoads, T. and J. Shogren (1999), 'On Coasean bargaining with transaction costs', *Applied Economics Letters* 6: 779–83.

Roth, A. (1995), 'Bargaining experiments', in J. Kagel and A. Roth (eds), *The Handbook of Experimental Economics*, Princeton, NJ: Princeton University Press.

Roth, A. and M. Malouf (1979), 'Game-theoretic models and the role of information in bargaining', *Psychological Review* 86: 574–94.

Sabel, C., A. Fung and B. Karkkainen (1999), 'Beyond backyard environmentalism', *Boston Review* 24: 4–53.

Schelling, T. (1960), *The Strategy of Conflict*, London: Oxford University Press.

Schwab, S. (1988), 'A Coasean experiment on contract presumptions', *Journal of Legal Studies* 17: 237–68.

Selten, R. (1991), 'Properties of a measure of predictive success', *Mathematical Social Sciences* 21: 153–67.

Shapiro, E.G. (1975), 'Effect of expectations of future interaction on reward allocations in dyads: equity or equality', *Journal of Personality and Psychology* 31: 873–90.

Shogren, J. (1989), 'Fairness in bargaining requires a context: an experimental examination of loyalty', *Economics Letters* 31: 319–23.

Shogren, J. (1992), 'An experiment on Coasian bargaining over *ex ante* lotteries and *ex post* rewards', *Journal of Economic Behavior and Organization* 17: 153–69.

Shogren, J. (1997), 'Self-interest and equity in a bargaining tournament with non-linear payoffs', *Journal of Economic Behavior and Organization* 32: 383–94.

Shogren, J. (1998), 'Coasean bargaining with symmetric delay costs', *Resource and Energy Economics* 20: 309–26.

Shogren, J. and S. Kask (1992), 'Exploring the boundaries of the Coase Theorem: efficiency and rationality given imperfect contract enforcement', *Economics Letters* 39: 155–61.

Siegel, S. and L. Fouraker (1960), *Bargaining and Group Decision Making: Experiments in Bilateral Monopoly*, New York: McGraw-Hill.

Snow, D. (1997), 'Empire or homelands? A revival of Jeffersonian democracy in the American West', in J. Baden and D. Snow (eds), *The Next West: Public Lands, Community, and Economy in the American West*, Washington, DC: Island Press.

Spencer, M. and J. Shogren (2000), 'Protocol for inexperienced Coasean bargainers confronting delay costs', *Resource and Energy Economics* 22: 79–90.

Statham, D. (1994), 'The farm scheme of North York Moors National Park, United Kingdom', in D. Western, R.M. Wright and S. Strum (eds), *Natural Connections: Perspectives in Community-based Conservation*, Washington, DC: Island Press.

Straub, P. and K. Murnighan (1995), 'An experimental investigation of ultimatum games: information, fairness, expectations, and lowest acceptable offers', *Journal of Economic Behavior and Organization* 27: 343–64.

Western, D. (1994), 'Ecosystem conservation and rural development: the case of Amboseli', in D. Western, R.M. Wright and S. Strum (eds), *Natural Connections: Perspectives in Community-based Conservation*, Washington, DC: Island Press.

3. The vertical extension of environmental liability through chains of ownership, contract and supply

James Boyd and Daniel Ingberman

INTRODUCTION

When pollution creates a social loss, who should be liable? Common sense, standard legal doctrine and notions of economic efficiency agree that liabilities should be assigned to the polluters. But what if the polluter is unable to pay? When the polluter's wealth is insufficient to internalize damages, liability is often extended to its business partners, even if the business partners are substantially removed from involvement with the polluting activity. This chapter describes the rationale for extended liability and its use in environmental law. Extended liability improves incentives for precaution. But while extended liability improves cost internalization and deterrence, it need not improve welfare. The ways in which extended liability can reduce welfare are the focus of this analysis.[1]

Extended liability can lead to a set of liability avoidance strategies that distort production decisions. In this chapter we describe three such strategies. First, potentially liable firms can minimize the capital intensity of production, in order to expose less capital to future tort claims. Second, firms may avoid otherwise desirable contractual relationships in order to avoid exposure to liabilities externalized by their business partners. Third, when liabilities are long-tailed (that is, latent), firms can dissolve prematurely in order to avoid future liability. These strategies may be privately rational when liability is extended. They are distorting, however, since they lead to social production costs that are higher than they would otherwise be.

The chapter is organized as follows. First, we describe the rationale for extended liability and the conditions under which it is most common. Second, we give a brief overview of extended liability in US environmental liability law. This includes a description of how liability may be extended jointly and severally to contractually affiliated firms, the way in which corporate parents may be liable for the actions of subsidiaries, and the liability of suppliers for pollution created by retail operations. Third, we describe, in turn, the three liability-avoidance strategies noted above. In all three cases, the production distortions created by extended liability can outweigh its deterrence-related benefits. We conclude with a discussion of alternative policies to promote cost internalization.

WHY SHOULD LIABILITY BE EXTENDED?

The motivation for extended liability is cost internalization. Extended liability expands the pool of capital available to compensate victims and, by forcing greater joint cost, internalization can be expected to induce more efficient investments in precaution. Business partners, if jointly liable, have both the motive and the opportunity to monitor the safety of the firms with whom they choose to do business. Accordingly, extended liability ideally generates private sector self-monitoring and ostracism of firms that cannot produce or signal adequate safety.

There are two important conditions necessary for this benefit to arise, however. First, for there to be an incentive problem at all, the primary risk generator must itself be unable to fully internalize social injury costs. This state of affairs is referred to as the judgment-proof problem. The judgment-proof problem can arise when firms lack the wealth necessary to internalize liabilities and have those liabilities discharged in bankruptcy.[2] A defendant will also be judgment-proof if it has legally dissolved prior to the realization of tort claims.[3] Note that the judgment-proof problem thwarts the cost-internalizing aims of tort law. In particular, judgment-proof firms will be insufficiently deterred by liability and consequently will underinvest in safety.[4]

For extended liability to improve welfare, there must be this cost externalization brought about by judgment-proof defendants. One other condition must also be satisfied, namely, that injury costs not be internalized by the market itself. If the consumer of a product bears the injury cost, this can be foreseen and incorporated in the initial transaction. Prices will reflect the risks borne by the consumer and the producer will thereby internalize the full benefits of risk reduction. Thus, for extending liability to have a benefit, defendants must be judgment-proof and victims must be external to the market transactions giving rise to the injury. These conditions are commonly satisfied in environmental torts.

When satisfied, these conditions motivate the extension of liability to promote the benefits of improved cost internalization: improved deterrence, compensation, and prices that more closely reflect the full social costs of production.[5]

EXTENDED ENVIRONMENTAL LIABILITY

In order to explore the effects of extended liability our analysis features *producers*, *contractors* and *victims*. Consider Figure 3.1, which describes the general relationships between these parties. Producers control the safety of a product or service. Contractors – whom we may also term 'business partners' – are contractually tied to the producer in some way. They may be customers, suppliers or owners. The production or consumption of the product involves a risk of injury. Upon injury, victims seek compensation via liability.

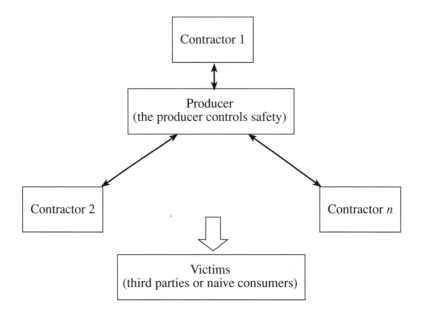

Figure 3.1   Relationships between producers, contractors and victims

Producer-only liability shields contractors from liability, even if the producer is insolvent. In the event of insolvency, residual damages – the difference between assessed damages and the producer's capital value – are externalized to third parties. In contrast, *extended liability* makes contractors liable for residual damages.

In an environmental context the producer is the polluter, typically the operator of a polluting facility or other operation, such as a transport business. In the United States, liability can be extended from this polluter to a wide variety of entities including subsequent owners of real estate on which the facility is, or was, located; businesses that disposed of waste at the facility; business partners in a chain of retail distribution relationships; and parent corporations. The scope of these extensions is broad and serves the so-called 'remedial purpose' interpretation of liability under the Comprehensive Environmental Response, Compensation, and Liability Act (CERCLA). Under this interpretation, the net of liability is cast widely in order to promote speedy, private sector financed clean-up of polluted sites.

Proportional vs. Joint and Several Liability

Not only are a wide set of entities subject to potential liability under CERCLA, but damages, if applied, are typically not limited by notions such as proportional contribution. To illustrate, consider two forms of extended liability, *proportional* and *joint and several*. Under proportional extended liability, damages externalized by a judgment-proof producer are assigned to contractors on a proportional basis.[6] Consider a landfill operator that disposed of waste brought to it in equal amount by q firms (contractors). If the landfill operator is judgment-proof, proportional liability caps the contractors' liability at $(1/q)$th of the producer's externalized damages.[7] That is, contractors' liabilities are limited to their proportional share of the residual damages; if this bankrupts some contractors, any remaining residual damages are externalized. By contrast, under joint and several liability, each contractor can be held liable for the full amount of the residual damages. The latter rule is most characteristic of environmental liability law in the US.[8]

When litigation and business relationships involve multiple parties, as illustrated on pp. 59–61, this distinction between proportional and joint and several liability is important to understanding the normative properties of extended liability. The classic example of this kind of 'horizontal' liability extension relates to clean-up of sites such as landfills, where pollution was due to disposal of wastes contributed by many firms. The horizontal reach of liability is quite broad under US environmental law.

Extensions of Liability within the Chains of Ownership and Supply

In other types of environmental cases, the extension of liability takes on a 'vertical' form. Examples include the extension of liability from a subsidiary to a parent corporation, or from a retailer to a sole supplier.

Consider the extension of liability from a subsidiary to a corporate parent. In this type of situation two broad, and opposing, strands of appellate thinking have emerged. The first corresponds to the remedial purpose perspective described above, in which the overarching goal is cost recovery. Accordingly, this perspective favours parent corporation liability, as in *United States* v. *Kayser-Roth Corp*.[9] This case adopted a very broad definition of facility 'operation'. In effect, the court ruled that the corporate owner of a polluting subsidiary is a CERCLA operator, due to the parent's management of the subsidiary. This definition of operator (the responsible party) is not explicitly identified in the statute. It is also in direct opposition to common law principles which explicitly protect the owners of a corporation from the liabilities created by it.[10]

Some of this conflict has been resolved by *United States* v. *Bestfoods*, a recent case decided by the Supreme Court.[11] *Bestfoods* affirms the applicability of limited liability in the CERCLA context – holding that the parent was not liable for the actions of the subsidiary. However, *Bestfoods* clarifies the conditions under which liability could be extended to the parent. The parent can be liable if it was in fact the operator. This requires a finding that the parent actively directed the workings of, managed and conducted the affairs of the facility. Alternatively, the parent can be found indirectly liable if the subsidiary was found to be an abuse of the corporate form, designed, for example, expressly to shield the parent from liability.[12]

The common law principle of limited corporate liability thus serves as an important limitation on vertical extensions of environmental liability where ownership is concerned. When the relationship is not one of ownership, however, but of supply, this limitation does not exist.

In some cases, but not all, suppliers may be liable for damages associated with independent retail operations. As an illustration, consider *Shell Oil* v. *Meyer*, a case resolved under Indiana state law.[13] The case involved contamination due to leakage of an underground gasoline storage tank. As in *Bestfoods*, the extension of liability question hinged in large part of the definition of 'operator'. Plaintiffs sought recovery from Shell Oil, the supplier of gasoline, arguing that the refiner's brand creates leverage over the operators of a branded gasoline station. The court rejected the notion that Shell, or oil refiners in general, is liable on this basis. However, Shell was the employer of an independent contractor who filled the tanks and their measured contents. This independent contractor was found to be an 'operator' and Shell vicariously liable as the operator's employer. Shell's ability to influence the actions of this independent contractor was deemed sufficient to justify the extension of liability.[14]

These cases illustrate the extension of liability in environmental cases, and the limits imposed on such extensions. From a legal standpoint, the key determinants of whether liability should be extended or not relate to the degree of control exercised by business partners over the actions of polluters and a desire to preserve the limited liability nature of the corporation. In the sections that follow we describe an additional set of factors that speak to the normative desirability of extended liability.

LIABILITY AVOIDANCE THROUGH REDUCED CAPITAL INTENSITY

The endogeneity of capital investments and transactions plays a central role in our analysis. A polluter's capital investment defines the scale of liabilities extended to contractors and serves as a signal to contractors of the polluter's safety incentives. The endogeneity of the terms of, and decision to participate in, a transaction with a liability-generating trading partner is an issue that most studies of extended liability ignore.[15] Moreover, the social costs of liability-driven distortions in production are underappreciated in economic analyses of tort law. An exception is Ringleb and Wiggins (1990) who demonstrate an empirical relationship between enterprise scale and the threat of liability.

In this chapter, we demonstrate the way in which the threat of liability can distort both producer and contractor capital investment decisions. When liability is extended, contractors' capital choices can be distorted by their incentives to limit the wealth they expose to liability. As a consequence, extended liability's search for deep pockets can lead to shallower-pocketed contractors. Distorted contractor capital investments increase production costs and thereby reduce welfare.[16]

We derive these results using a model that extends liability to contractors proportionally. A different set of distortions is possible when liability is extended jointly and severally, as will be shown on pp. 59–61.

An Overview of the Model

In this analysis welfare maximization, or the *first-best*, requires (a) minimization of unit *production costs* through input (here capital) and output choices, and (b) the balancing of marginal *safety expenditures* against the marginal reduction in expected *social costs* they produce. Production costs are the total cost of producing and selling a product, excluding safety expenditures. Expected social costs result when the product or service in question fails and creates social costs. As we show, liability creates private incentives that can lead firms to minimize neither production costs nor the sum of safety expenditures and social costs.

In particular, potentially liable firms may seek to reduce those liabilities by reducing their capital exposure, rather than by increasing safety. This has two important consequences. First, welfare maximization requires the minimization of production costs. If firms make capital production decisions to limit their liabilities, production costs will not be minimized. As we shall show, liability can distort firms' capital–output ratios and thereby lead to inefficiencies in production and greater externalization of costs. Second, as more social costs are externalized, deterrence is weakened. Thus, we shall show that explicitly considering the impact of liability on capital production decisions is central to understanding the relative desirability of alternative liability rules.

The analysis employs a simple one-period model in which capital investment incentives reflect both liability costs as well as the productive benefits of capital investment. All capital investment takes place at the beginning of the period in the form of equity investment. For simplicity we assume that once productive capital is invested in a firm, the capital is immobile until all tort claims are realized at the end of the period. Any within-period earnings are distributed to shareholders before the realization of tort claims.[17] Our qualitative conclusions continue to hold, however, even if firms are allowed to substitute debt financing for equity.[18] More specifically, let:

K   = a producer's capital investment;
w = the social marginal cost of capital;
q = a producer's output; and
$C(q,K)$ = its direct costs of production, not including its capital costs.

Assume that markets are competitive, and that the timing of the firm's investment and returns is as follows. Imagine that at the beginning of the period, a firm is contemplating an investment of K in order to reduce production costs. The firm is risk-neutral, and capital earns a market rate of return of w per period.

During the period, the firm's productive activities produce value, but also generate a liability risk. Let:

s = the producer's expenditure on safety;
$L(s,K)$ = a producer's expected liability as a function of its safety investment
             s and legally recoverable capital value K.

The firm's liabilities are realized at the end of the period. The firm invests in safety to reduce its expected liabilities. Also, liability is limited. Therefore, the firm's liability costs are capped by its capital value K.

Liability and Capital Investment

If a capital investment is subject to tort claims, the private cost of capital exceeds its social, or 'riskless' cost. This liability-driven capital cost premium can distort capital investment and result in a failure to minimize production costs.

Consider the way in which financial markets price the capital used by potentially liable firms. Whenever capital may be lost to future liability claims, the capital's implicit price to the firm includes a premium to compensate for the risk of loss. As shown in the model, this risk premium is equal to the probability that the firm's liabilities will exceed its capital value. The derivation of the premium can be conveyed simply. Consider a firm contemplating a marginal increase, ΔK, to its total capital value, K. The firm expects a future liability L that is of uncertain magnitude. In the event that the realized loss does not exceed the firm's wealth ($L \leq K$), the marginal increase in capital ΔK is not lost to liability claims, since the firm's existing capital is sufficient to internalize all claims. However, when damages exceed the firm's wealth ($L > K$) a marginal increase

ΔK is lost to liability claims. Thus, the liability-based premium to the marginal cost of capital is simply the probability that the firm is made insolvent by its tort liabilities, that is, the probability that L > K.

When does the risk premium attached to capital create welfare-reducing distortions? Clearly, firms' capital investment decisions are a function of capital's benefits as well as its costs. Investment in capital reduces the costs of developing, manufacturing, distributing and servicing products and services. In this model we capture these benefits of capital investment through the effects of K in reducing production costs C(q,K).

The incentive to externalize liability costs can also manifest itself in a desire to increase output. By increasing output, producers can spread their capital exposure over a larger number of units. Note that holding wealth fixed, a firm's per-unit expected liability costs fall as output increases. Irrespective of whether the output-increasing or capital-reducing effect dominates, potentially liable firms can have an incentive to reduce their products' expected liability per unit.

A Formal Model and the Welfare Optimum

This subsection presents the remainder of the model and defines the welfare maximum.

Producers' production costs are a function of their capital investments and output choices. We have already defined output q and direct production costs net of capital costs C(q,k). The analysis is facilitated by also defining average costs. Let:

ac(q,K) = the average cost of producing output, not including liabilities, safety expenditures, or capital costs. Average costs are U-shaped in q, for every K. The minimized value of ac(·) is decreasing in K, and the q that minimizes ac(·) is increasing in K.

Production can also create social costs that are reduced, in expectation, by investment in safety. Let:

m = the social cost of a unit of output that causes injury. In the absence of liability, all injury costs would be borne by third parties (who transact with neither producers nor contractors);

s = expenditure on safety, per unit of output;

$R(b, s)$ = the probability that a fraction b or less of a producer's output fails and causes a social loss of m per failed unit;

$r(b, s)$ = the probability density function associated with $R(b, s)$;

$F(s)$ = the per-unit expected social cost of a producers' production
$$= \int_0^1 m \cdot b \cdot r(b,s)db.$$

Contractors do not generate risks of their own. However, they require capital for the production of their own good or service. For simplicity, each contractor in the market makes a single unit of output. Each contractor requires one unit of a producer's output as an essential input to the contractor's own activities. Let:

j = a contractor's capital investment;
$c(j)$ = the cost to a contractor of producing a unit of its product, not including the cost of the input purchased from producers, capital costs or liability costs. This cost is decreasing in j at a decreasing rate.

Both producer and contractor markets are assumed to be competitive.

N = the total number of producers;
Q = Nq = aggregate producer output = aggregate contractor output;
$P(Q)$ = consumers' inverse aggregate demand for the joint producer–contractor product.

The welfare function is:

$$W(j,K,q,s,Q) = \int_0^Q P(x)dx - Q \cdot \left[ac(q,K) + s + \frac{wK}{q} + F(s) + c(j) + wj \right].$$

(3.1)

The first term denotes the social benefits of the joint good. The second term denotes producer, contractor and social costs. The necessary conditions for a solution to this problem are given in equation (3.2):

$$\frac{\partial W}{\partial Q} = 0 \Rightarrow P(Q) = \left[ac(q,K) + s + \frac{wK}{q} + F(s) + c(j) + wj \right] \quad (3.2N)$$

$$\frac{\partial W}{\partial q} = 0 \Rightarrow \frac{\partial ac}{\partial q} = \frac{wK}{q^2} \quad (3.2q)$$

$$\frac{\partial W}{\partial K} = 0 \Rightarrow -q\frac{\partial ac}{\partial K} = w \quad (3.2K)$$

$$\frac{\partial W}{\partial s} = 0 \Rightarrow -\frac{\partial F}{\partial s} = 1 \qquad (3.2s)$$

$$\frac{\partial W}{\partial j} = 0 \Rightarrow -\frac{\partial c}{\partial j} = w. \qquad (3.2j)$$

Denote the simultaneous solution of equations (3.2) as $\{N^*, q^*, K^*, s^*, j^*\}$. The interpretation of these conditions is standard: (3.2N) says that the market's aggregate output is that which equates supply and demand at the minimized value of average cost; (3.2q) says that the first-best output choice equates the marginal increase in unit production cost from producing an additional unit of output (beyond the minimum of ac($\cdot$)) to the decrease in the unit capital cost obtained by increasing output; (3.2K and 3.2j) say that efficient contractor and producer capital investments equate the respective marginal benefits of increased capital (in the form of reduced production costs) to the social marginal cost of capital; (3.2s) says that the marginal social benefit of increased safety – in terms of the reduction in expected injury costs – should equal its marginal cost, which is normalized to one.

Producer-only Liability

The social costs internalized by a producer are a function of the producer's capital value K. Realizations of damages that exceed K cost the producer K, due to limited liability; the remainder of the loss is externalized. Let $L(s,q,K)$ denote the expected liability per unit of output of a producer with capital K, output q and safety s. Specifically:

$$L(s,q,K) = \int_0^{K/mq} m \cdot b \cdot r(b,s)db + \int_{K/mq}^1 \frac{K}{q} r(b,s)db. \qquad (3.3)$$

The first integral represents the expected cost of liabilities that do not bankrupt the firm ($bqm < K$). The second integral represents the firm's expected liability costs for realizations that exceed its wealth. Note that when a firm's maximum possible damage assessment, mq, exceeds its capital K, then for any safety expenditure, the firm's expected liabilities $L(s,q,K)$ are strictly less than expected social costs $F(s)$.

Given perfect competition, the long-run equilibrium leads to production decisions that maximize the joint surplus of producers, contractors and consumers. The joint surplus is equal to:

$$V(j,K,q,s,Q) = \int_0^Q P(x)dx - Q.\left[ac(q,K) + s + \frac{wK}{q} + L(s,q,K) + c(j) + wj \right].$$

(3.4)

Note that the only difference between (3.1) and (3.4) is that F(s) has been replaced with L(s,q,K). This reflects producers' ability to externalize social costs that exceed their wealth.

The first-order necessary conditions for the maximization of market surplus (3.4) are:

$$\frac{\partial V}{\partial Q} = 0 \Rightarrow P(Q) = \left[ac(q,K) + s + \frac{wK}{q} + L(s,q,K) + c(j) + wj \right] \quad (3.5N)$$

$$\frac{\partial V}{\partial q} = 0 \Rightarrow q\frac{\partial ac}{\partial q} + q\frac{\partial L}{\partial q} = \frac{wK}{q} \quad (3.5q)$$

$$\frac{\partial V}{\partial K} = 0 \Rightarrow q\frac{\partial ac}{\partial K} - q\frac{\partial L}{\partial K} = w \quad (3.5K)$$

$$\frac{\partial V}{\partial s} = 0 \Rightarrow -\frac{\partial L}{\partial s} = 1 \quad (3.5s)$$

$$\frac{\partial V}{\partial j} = 0 \Rightarrow -\frac{\partial c}{\partial j} = w. \quad (3.5j)$$

Denote the simultaneous solution of equations (3.5N–j) as $\{\hat{N}, \hat{q}, \hat{K}, \hat{s}, \hat{j}\}$.
By way of definition, when

$$K^* \geq mq^*, \quad (3.6)$$

we say that a producer is *fully capitalized at the first-best*. Otherwise, the producer is *undercapitalized at the first-best*.

We now characterize the distortions in producer capital investment and output choice created by producer-only liability. Note that (3.5*j*) and (3.2*j*) are equivalent. This reflects the fact that since contractors have no liability, producer-only liability does not distort their capital investments. As for liability's effect on producer choices:

Proposition 1: (a) As long as the producer is fully capitalized at the first-best, producer-only liability leads to first-best safety and does not distort producer capital investments and output choices; (b) otherwise, producers underinvest in safety and choose a suboptimal capital–output ratio.

The proof of this result appears in the appendix. When the producer is fully capitalized at the first-best, the welfare maximum – including the first-best safety choice – is privately optimal for the producer. This follows because a firm that is fully capitalized at the first-best has a zero probability of bankruptcy when it chooses that first-best capital investment. By contrast, when the firm is undercapitalized at the first-best, it has a strictly positive probability of insolvency when it makes first-best output and capital choices. In that case, liability distorts the firm's productive decisions, and it underinvests in safety. Specifically, recall that the first-best safety investment equates the marginal cost of safety to its marginal benefit in terms of reduced expected social losses. By contrast, the producer only internalizes losses up to K. Whenever the firm is undercapitalized, some realizations of loss leave it insolvent. This truncates the firm's benefits of safety, relative to the social benefits. As a result, the firm undercapitalized at the first-best will choose suboptimal safety expenditures as well as a suboptimal capital investment.

The first-order conditions of the producer's choice problem allows liability's effects on capital and output to be seen more clearly. First consider the effect of liability on capital investment. Differentiating equation (3.3), the definition of $L(s,q,K)$, shows that:

$$q\frac{\partial L(s,q,K)}{\partial K} = \int_{K/mq}^{1} r(b,s)db. \qquad (3.7)$$

Equation (3.7) says that the increase in the producer's expected liabilities from an increase in K simply equals the probability that a producer is made insolvent by liability. Substituting (3.7) into (3.5K) and rearranging yields:

$$-q\frac{dac}{dK} = w + \int_{K/mq}^{1} r(b,s)db. \qquad (3.8)$$

Recall that equation (3.2K) says that the first-best capital investment equates the price of capital (w) to the reduction in total costs that result from an increase in K. Comparing equation (3.2K) to (3.8) shows that the possibility of liability-induced insolvency raises the marginal cost of capital by an amount equal to the probability of insolvency.

Additionally, the probability of insolvency distorts the firm's output choice in a way analogous to the capital distortion.[19] The producer's output choice equates the marginal increase in average production cost from producing an additional unit of output to the decrease in average capital costs obtained by spreading capital costs across additional units of output. When there is no threat of liability, the first-best output (defined in (3.2q)) occurs when capital is priced at its social marginal cost w. The threat of insolvency, however, raises the producer's private cost of capital to w plus the probability of insolvency. The result is an increase in output. By increasing output, the firm reduces the per-unit level of capital it exposes to liability.

Thus, holding capital fixed, liability causes the producer to expand output beyond the level that minimizes production costs. As shown in the proof of the proposition, when the capital and output effects are combined, together they imply that liability leads producers to choose an inefficiently small capital–output ratio.

Extended Liability

For the analysis of extended liability, assume that contractors can observe and directly condition on producer's safety investments. Given the extension of liability to contractors, total market surplus is given by:

$$V(j,K,q,s,Q) = \left(\int_0^Q P(x)dx - Q \cdot \left[ac(q,K) + s + \frac{wK}{q} + L(s,q,K+jq) + c(j) + wj \right] \right),$$

(3.9)

where:

$$L(s,q,K+jq) = \int_0^{\frac{K+jq}{mq}} m \cdot b \cdot r(b,s)db + \int_{\frac{K+jq}{mq}}^1 \left(\frac{K}{q} + j \right) \cdot r(b,s)db.$$

(3.10)

To understand this expression, note that producer and contractor capital values are insufficient to pay all possible realizations of social costs when $K + jq < mq$.

As above, we maximize total market surplus (3.9) to find the long-run competitive equilibrium. The first-order conditions of this problem are given in equation (3.11) below:

$$\frac{\partial V}{\partial Q} = 0 \Rightarrow P(Q) = \left[ac(q, K) + s + \frac{wK}{q} + L(s, q, K + jq) + c(j) + wj \right]$$

(3.11*N*)

$$\frac{\partial V}{\partial q} = 0 \Rightarrow q \frac{\partial ac}{\partial q} + q \frac{\partial L}{\partial q} = \frac{wK}{q}$$

(3.11*q*)

$$\frac{\partial V}{\partial K} = 0 \Rightarrow -q \frac{\partial ac}{\partial K} - q \frac{\partial L}{\partial K} = w$$

(3.11*K*)

$$\frac{\partial V}{\partial s} = 0 \Rightarrow -\frac{\partial L}{\partial s} = 1$$

(3.11*s*)

$$\frac{\partial V}{\partial j} = 0 \Rightarrow -\frac{\partial c}{\partial j} - \frac{\partial L}{\partial j} = w.$$

(3.11*j*)

Note that the first-order conditions under extended liability have the same form as under producer-only liability, except for the contractor's capital choice and the definition of L(·). Denote the simultaneous solution to equations (3.11*N*–*j*) as $\{N^e, q^e, K^e, s^e, j^e\}$.

Equations (3.11) and (3.5) allow for a comparison of production decisions under the two liability rules. As in the case of producer-only liability, the analysis is facilitated by defining what it means to be fully capitalized. A producer and its associated contractors are *jointly fully capitalized at the first-best* when:

$$K^* + j^*q^* \geq mq^*.$$

(3.12)

Thus, the producer and its contractors are jointly fully capitalized at the first-best when, at their efficient capital and output choices, a producer and its contractors together have enough capital to internalize all possible liabilities.

Otherwise, the producer and its contractors are jointly undercapitalized at the first-best.

Proposition 2: (a) Extended liability leads to the first-best only when a producer and its associated contractors are jointly fully capitalized at the first-best. (b) Otherwise, extended liability distorts contractor capital investments. (c) However, compared to producer-only liability, extended liability leads to greater safety and more efficient producer capital and output choices.

The proof of this result appears in the appendix. The proposition says that when the producer and contractors are jointly undercapitalized at the first-best, then first-best capital inputs and producer outputs will not be chosen. When liability is extended, contractors underinvest in capital since their effective marginal cost of capital is higher than the social opportunity cost. This leads to excessively costly contractor production and, all else equal, reduces welfare.

Summary

Whenever liability distorts capital investment or output, firms fail to minimize production costs. Extended liability, however, can improve deterrence by expanding the pool of capital available for the internalization of social costs. In practice, this improvement arises because contractors' demand producer safety in order to reduce their expected, residual liabilities. By contrast, under producer-only liability, there is no contractor demand for safety. Thus, improved deterrence is an unambiguous benefit of extended liability.

Overall, however, extended liability need not improve welfare. Because liability can distort production, extending liability to contractors expands the potential scope of these distortions. When liability is limited to producers, contractors make efficient production decisions. When liability is extended, contractors' incentives to externalize damages may distort their capital investments and other productive decisions.

This concern is somewhat tempered by the fact that extended liability improves the efficiency of producer capital and output decisions, relative to the decisions made when liability is producer-only. Under extended liability, a contractor's benefit from transacting with a producer is a function of the contractor's residual liability. This means that contractors value larger producer capital–output ratios, since higher capital–output ratios mean smaller residual liabilities for contractors. Thus, contractors demand, and producers will 'supply' more capital-intensive output when liability is extended. Also, increased producer capitalization, by limiting residual contractor liabilities, reduces distortions in contractor production.

Nevertheless, the introduction of distortions in the capital and output decisions of contractors means that, on balance, extended liability can reduce welfare. Moreover, distorted contractor production is most likely in the class of cases where it is most desirable to extend liability to improve deterrence. That is, producers that place the least value on capital externalize the most social costs. This heightens the need to extend liability to improve deterrence. But, in turn, the large residual liabilities created by such producers are more likely to significantly distort contractor capital investments and output choices.

DISTORTED PRODUCER AND CONTRACTOR AFFILIATIONS

The previous section showed how extended liability can lead to capital investment and output decisions that do not minimize average costs. We turn now to a second type of distortion that can arise when liability is extended. In this section we describe situations in which heterogeneous contractors (contractors with different levels of wealth) avoid purchasing from a common producer. When liability is joint and several, deeper-pocketed contractors expose their wealth to the residual liabilities created by shallower-pocketed contractors. Accordingly, the market can 'separate,' with producers tailoring their services to contractors in different wealth categories. Under some circumstances, this separation can reduce welfare. For example, if markets are thin, specialized producers may be unable to sell sufficient output to minimize production costs.[20]

Consider the concept of *affiliation*. Contractors are affiliated when they contract with a common producer. Note that affiliations are not the bilateral contracts between individual contractors and a producer. The distinction between affiliation and explicit contracts is important because affiliation alone is sufficient to establish joint liability between two or more firms. Contractors who purchase from a common producer are affiliated, even though there is no bilateral contract explicitly joining them. Thus, different contractors may be liable for harms arising due to the activities of the other, even in the absence of a contract between them. When liability is extended jointly and severally contractors are implicitly bound – via liability exposure – to other contractors with whom they are affiliated.

Affiliations are fundamental to economic activity. Franchisees are affiliated via franchisers, distributors are affiliated via producers, polluters are affiliated via the firms that dispose of or transport pollutants, and limited partnerships are affiliations of otherwise independent contractors. Affiliations are economically ubiquitous because they are beneficial. For instance, whenever average costs are decreasing over some range, affiliations allow for production at a scale which minimizes costs.[21]

Joint and several liability creates an incentive to avoid affiliation when contractors differ in wealth. Consider an example of this kind of situation, one in which a land-filler disposes of the waste of both multinational corporations and the local general store. Waste disposal is an intermediate good essential to the production of a variety of products and services. Accordingly, both shallow- and deep-pocketed contractors are potential users of a common producer's product. Both wealthy and less-wealthy contractors may, absent liability concerns, choose to be affiliated.

When liability is limited to the producer, affiliation has no cost to contractors of different types. Contractors are indifferent to producers' safety and the characteristics of other contractors with whom they are affiliated. This has an advantage: producer-only liability does not inhibit the affiliation of varied contractor types. However, when liability is joint and several, contractors of different wealth types may avoid affiliation. This occurs for two reasons. First, contractors of different wealth demand different levels of producer safety. Deeper-pocketed contractors have a greater exposure to the producer's residual liability, and so prefer to purchase from safer (and more expensive) producers than do shallower-pocketed contractors. If contractors' preferences for safety are divergent enough, they may forgo affiliation in order to purchase from producers who are, from the contractors' private perspective, optimally safe.

Second, when liability is joint and several, deeper-pocketed contractors are liable for the liability shares of shallower-pocketed contractors. Deep-pocketed contractors' liability is not capped at their proportional share of the social loss. As a result, deeper-pocketed contractors subsidize liabilities generated by production serving shallower-pocketed contractors. This creates an incentive for deeper-pocketed contractors to not purchase from producers who also serve shallow-pocketed contractors.

To understand the nature of the subsidy, consider, for simplicity, two contractor types, Y and Z, with fixed capital investments $j_Y < j_Z$. Also, assume that each contractor demands one unit of a producer's product and there are q_Y and q_Z Y-type and Z-type firms, respectively. If both Y-types and Z-types purchase from the same producer, an individual contractor's 'proportionate share' of a producer's residual liability is:

$$\Phi = (L - \hat{K})/Q,$$

where $q_Y + q_Z = Q$. Whenever there is a realization of liability Φ for which:

$$j_Y < \Phi < j_Z,$$

the larger, Z-type contractors bear more than their share of the residual liability. This happens because the loss L leaves both the producer and Y-type contractors insolvent. When liability is joint and several, the liability remaining, over and above the Z-types' own share, can be imposed on them.[22] Note that as the difference in wealth between Y- and Z-types grows, so too does a Z-type firm's incentive to avoid affiliation with Y-type firms. The difference in wealth between types determines the implicit subsidy from the wealthier contractors to the less-wealthy contractors.

Because of differing demand for safety, and because of the subsidy from deep- to shallow-pocketed contractors, affiliation can be inhibited. There is a tendency for only similar types to affiliate under joint and several liability. In the extreme, the urge to separate can be so extreme that contractors vertically integrate with producers, or establish exclusive contracts, in order to guarantee that affiliation with other contractors will not occur.

Thus, extended liability can discourage affiliations that would otherwise allow for the minimization of production costs. Given a large number of contractors of a particular type this is not a cause for concern. However, if markets are thin, individual producers may be unable to sell and produce at a scale that minimizes production costs. For reasons akin to those in the previous section this means that extended liability can reduce welfare, even while it improves deterrence. For example, suppose extended liability induces particularly deep-pocketed contractors to vertically integrate and construct their own dedicated waste disposal facilities. Such deep-pocketed contractors may in fact operate very safe facilities. But if there is surplus capacity in the market for waste disposal, the construction of additional waste disposal facilities is unlikely to be efficient.

When the benefits of affiliation are small, extended, joint and several liability is preferable to producer-only liability. This follows, since extended liability improves deterrence and results in only a small increase in production costs. What if the benefits of affiliation are very large? Here, too, extended liability is preferable since the large benefits mean that affiliations will not be distorted. When the benefits of affiliation are of a more intermediate magnitude, however, welfare can be lower under joint and several liability.

If the benefits of affiliation are not great enough to sustain affiliation, this benefit will be lost. The corresponding increase in production costs must be weighed against the gain in deterrence from the extension of liability. On balance, welfare may be lower when liability is extended.

LIABILITY AND PREMATURE DISSOLUTION

This section extends the analysis of extended liability to consider cases where firms can *fly by night*, or exit the market, in order to avoid liability.[23] Flying by night is possible because firms, in a legal sense, can dissolve before the realization of injuries and liability. Premature dissolution is a kind of substitute for safety. Both reduce a firm's liability. Particularly when risks are long-tailed, dissolution may be a rational, if socially irresponsible, way to avoid future liability.

The ability to dissolve and escape liability begs the question of why potentially liable firms would ever *face the music*, that is, remain in the market to be liable. The answer is that premature dissolution entails costs of its own. The firm cannot simply be sold, since mere transfer of ownership triggers successor liability.[24] To effectively avoid liability, dissolution requires the piecemeal liquidation of assets. A firm's existence testifies to the value inherent in the collection of assets that form it. Piecemeal liquidation typically destroys that value. We refer to the loss in value when fly-by-night firms sell off their assets piecemeal as the *cost of premature dissolution*.

When liability is extended, contractors may choose to dissolve prematurely, rather than face liability. As in the earlier sections' analysis of distortions in capital investment and business affiliations, the possibility of premature dissolution as a liability-avoidance strategy creates costs. The costs of premature dissolution represent another way in which extended liability can reduce welfare.

A Simple Model of Liability and Premature Dissolution

To illustrate liability's interaction with a firm's dissolution decision let $L^p(s,k)$ denote a producer's expected liability given, as on p. 50, its safety investment s and capital k. Similarly, let $L^c(j,s,k,)$ denote a contractor's expected residual liability when liability is extended. Note that this expected liability is a function of the contractor's capital j, as well as the producer's capital and safety.[25]

When firms dissolve prematurely and liquidate their capital values before the realization of liability, value is dissipated. To denote this premature dissolution cost, let:

$(1 - \tau^p)k$ = the amount of value that can be salvaged by a fly-by-night producer, where $0 < \tau^p < 1$;

$(1 - \tau^c)j$ = the amount of value that can be salvaged by a fly-by-night contractor, where $0 < \tau^c < 1$.

Thus, τ^p and τ^c index producers' and contractors' premature dissolution costs. All other assumptions are identical to those used on p. 50.

When Will Firms Fly by Night?

A producer that plans to fly by night spends nothing on safety, since it does not expect to be liable. However, a firm that remains potentially liable has capital exposed to liability. Therefore, a potentially liable producer will invest in safety to reduce risk. Since contractors have no capital at risk under a producer-only liability rule, the producer's safety incentive reflects only the capital it has at risk, k. Following the notation on p. 50, let $\hat{s}$ denote the privately optimal safety choice of a potentially liable producer and let s^* denote the socially optimal (first-best) safety expenditure.

Now consider a producer's decision to fly by night or face the music. Observe that fly-by-night producers have costs $k\tau^p$. By contrast, a potentially liable producer has costs equal to $L^p(\hat{s},k) + \hat{s}$. Therefore, fly-by-night producers can undercut potentially liable producers whenever:

$$L^p(\hat{s},k) + \hat{s} > k\tau^p, \tag{3.13}$$

that is, only when the combined safety expenditures and expected liabilities of a potentially liable producer exceed the early dissolution cost of flying by night. When only producers are liable, equation (3.13) is a necessary and sufficient condition for producers to fly by night.

Suppose that there is no cost to premature dissolution ($\tau^p = 0$). Then equation (3.13) always holds and producers always fly by night. In this situation, the private benefits of liability avoidance strictly dominate the costs of market exit. There is no reason *not* to fly by night. As the cost of premature dissolution rises, however, flying by night becomes less attractive. In the extreme, when dissolution costs would consume all of a fly-by-night producer's capital ($\tau^p = 1$), it is best to remain potentially liable. In this case, early exit guarantees the firm the largest possible cost – its entire capital value. As long as there is a chance that remaining liable will not bankrupt the firm, facing the music yields lower expected costs. In general, there will be some level of τ below which firms will fly by night, and above which they will face the music.

In analyses of liability that do not permit exit, fully capitalized firms always make first-best decisions, since they internalize all social benefits and costs. Permitting exit adds richness to the description of liability's effects. Note that even a fully capitalized firm may choose to fly by night in this model, when the costs of premature dissolution are low. In other words, full capitalization is necessary, but not sufficient, for liability to generate optimal deterrence and cost internalization. Firms also must find it privately optimal to remain in the market.

No Liability Versus Producer-only Liability

We begin the analysis of extended liability by first comparing producer-only liability to a *no liability* rule. When there is no liability, producers do not invest in safety, since there is no benefit to themselves or contractors from doing so.

Moreover, producers and contractors always remain in the market, to avoid the costs associated with premature dissolution. The welfare implications of imposing liability on producers can now be easily summarized. Compared to having no liability at all, imposing liability need not increase welfare.

Note that if producer-only liability leads producers to fly by night, then imposing liability reduces welfare. The proof is straightforward. When there is no liability, producers fail to invest in safety. But this is also true when otherwise liable producers fly by night. Accordingly no liability and producer-only liability are in this case equivalently poor in terms of their effect on deterrence. Moreover, producer-only liability is strictly less preferable since it leads to the costs associated with premature exit. Early dissolution has no social value. Thus, if liability leads to exit, no liability is preferable. On the other hand, when liable firms do not fly by night, liability is strictly preferable. In this case, liability creates no dissolution cost but does lead to investment in safety.

The comparison between no liability and producer-only liability highlights the way in which the application of liability can reduce welfare. The desire to avoid liability can lead to premature, and socially costly, exit. The comparison also highlights the way in which firms can externalize costs. Producers will be underdeterred when they are undercapitalized *or* when they choose to fly by night. In either case, there is a rationale for extending liability to other firms, both to internalize costs and to promote greater investments in safety. Of course, extending liability to a larger set of firms may in turn lead them to fly by night. This tension is at the heart of the next subsection, which explores incentives to invest in safety and fly by night when liability is extended.

Extended Liability

When liability is extended, producers externalize their residual liabilities to contractors. Contractors know this, of course. How, then, does extended liability affect their decisions? In some cases, contractors themselves will fly by night in order to avoid liability. In others, when contractors face the music, they will be led to do business only with producers who do not fly by night, and who produce the appropriate amount of safety.

When extended liability does not drive contractors to exit, welfare is improved – for two reasons. First, liable contractors internalize some injury costs, and those costs are reflected in the market price of their final output. Second, liable contractors value producers who face the music and invest in safety. In fact, because contractors' capital is also exposed to liability, the safety demanded by a jointly liable producer–contractor pair is greater than when liability is limited to the producer alone. When both producer and contractor face the music the producer's safety choice will reflect the exposure of $k + j$ units of capital to liability risk. Because more capital is at risk, investment in safety will be greater when the producer and contractor are jointly liable – greater than $\hat{s}$. In turn, both expected social injury costs and private liability costs will be lower.

However, when extended liability leads contractors to fly by night, welfare suffers. Since contractors exit before their capital is exposed to liability, a potentially liable producer's safety choice will reflect only the capital it has at risk, k. Thus, the producer's safety choice under either producer-only liability, or extended liability is $\hat{s}$. There is no improvement in cost internalization or deterrence, only the cost of premature dissolution expended in order to avoid liability. Extended liability is likely to be most needed when firms find it relatively attractive to exit the market, rather than face liability. It is in just these circumstances (when τs are small), however, that extended liability can make matters worse by leading contractors to fly by night as well.

CONCLUSION

Extended liability is not a cure-all for the inefficiencies generated by judgment-proof polluters. Under certain conditions, it will promote cost internalization and greater investments in precaution, as intended. But extended liability can also lead to distortions in capital and output decisions, thwart desirable contractual affiliations, and promote premature corporate dissolution. These liability avoidance strategies mean that the cure of extended liability can be worse than the disease of insufficient producer deterrence. This is particularly true since extended liability has additional drawbacks, such as the large litigation costs associated with litigation among jointly liable defendants.

Since incomplete cost internalization is the root problem that recommends extended liability, it is worth asking whether there is not a more direct means to internalize externalities due to undercapitalization or early dissolution. In fact, there is: forced bonding. Also known as 'financial responsibility', bonding requirements foster cost internalization by mandating the existence of capital reserves dedicated to the satisfaction of liabilities, even after corporate dissolution. Bonding guarantees the existence of capital or coverage adequate to internalize even large injury costs. Bonding is increasingly common in environmental law, particularly in the US.[26]

Bonding has a decided advantage relative to extensions of liability to business partners. Namely, it shifts the burden of recovery from victims to the risk-generator. With extensions of liability victims must pursue compensation, sometimes years later, from former business partners or owners who are understandably reluctant to honour those claims. In contrast, bonding leaves the potential injurer as the residual claimant to the bond fund. This creates an unambiguous incentive for the producer to minimize its liabilities. Clearly, bonding requirements create implementation costs of their own. For instance, evidence of the financial instrument and the soundness of its provider must be monitored. On balance, however, their virtues argue for consideration as an alternative to other legal approaches to cost internalization.

APPENDIX

Proof of Proposition 1

For part (a): If $K^* \geq q^*m$, then $L(q,s,K) = F(s)$ and therefore K^*, q^* and s^* satisfy the first-order conditions in equation (3.5). For part (b): If $K^* < mq^*$, $L(q^*,s^*,K^*) < F(s)$ and therefore K^*, q^* and s^* cannot satisfy the first-order conditions in equation (3.5). Comparing (3.2s) and (3.5s) and using (3.3) shows that $\hat{s}(q^*,K^*) < s^*$ and that $\hat{s}(\hat{q},\hat{K}) < s^*$ if $\hat{K}/\hat{q} < K^*/q^*$. We now show that $\hat{K}/\hat{q} < K^*/q^*$ if $K^* < mq^*$.

Proof by contradiction: If $\hat{K}/\hat{q} < K^*/q^*$, then $L(\hat{s},\hat{q},\hat{K}) = F(s)$ from (3.3) and $\hat{s}(\hat{q},\hat{K}) = s^*$ from (3.5s). Also, by construction

$$\left[ac(\hat{q},\hat{K}) + \frac{w\hat{K}}{\hat{q}} \right] > \left[ac(q^*,K^*) + \frac{wK^*}{q^*} \right].$$

Thus, if $\hat{K}/\hat{q} < K^*/q^*$:

$$\left[ac(\hat{q},\hat{K}) + \hat{s} + + \frac{w\hat{K}}{\hat{q}} + L(\hat{s},\hat{q},\hat{K}) \right] > \left[ac(q^*,K^*) + s^* + \frac{wK^*}{q^*} + F(s^*) \right],$$

which is a contradiction given equation (3.5). Thus, when $K^* < mq^*$, liability leads to distorted capital and output decisions and the firm is underdeterred.

Proof of Proposition 2

For part (a): If $K^* + j^*q^* \geq mq^*$, then $L(s,q,K + jq) = F(s)$ and therefore K^*, q^*, s^*, and j^* satisfy the first-order conditions in (3.11). For part (b): If $K^* + j^*q^* < mq^*$, then $L(s,q,K + jq) < F(s)$ and $\partial L/\partial j > 0$. From (3.11j), it follows that $j^0 < j^*$. For part (c): Producer capital investments under the two rules are evaluated by noting that:

$$q\frac{\partial L(s,q,K+jq)}{\partial K} = \int_{\frac{K+jq}{mq}}^{1} r(b,s)db. \tag{3.13}$$

Comparing equations (3.7) and (3.13), the marginal cost of capital is lower when liability is extended. Thus, if q were to remain fixed at $\hat{q}$, then $K^e > \hat{K}$. Similarly, (3.11q) can be rewritten as:

$$q\frac{dac}{dq} = \frac{K}{q}\left(w + \int_{\frac{K+jq}{mq}}^{1} r(b,s)db\right). \tag{3.14}$$

Note that (3.5q) can be rewritten[27] as:

$$q\frac{dac}{dq} = \frac{K}{q}\left(w + \int_{K/mq}^{1} r(b,s)db\right). \tag{3.15}$$

Comparison of (3.14) and (3.15) shows that producers' output distortion is less under extended liability, so that if K were to remain at $\hat{K}$, $q^e < \hat{q}$. Following the same kind of argument used in Proposition 1 then shows that $K^e/q^e > \hat{K}/\hat{q}$, whenever producer-only liability does not achieve the first-best. Since $K^e/q^e > \hat{K}/\hat{q}$ and $j^e \geq 0$, $L(s,q,K+jq) > L(s,q,K)$, and the marginal decrease in expected liability is greater when liability is extended than when it is producer-only. In turn, this means that $s^e > \hat{s}$.

NOTES

1. Costs associated with multi-party litigation are important and, in themselves, reduce the desirability of extended liability. Empirical studies find that legal costs account for 32 per cent of all private sector expenditures under CERCLA (see Dixon 1995). We do not consider litigation costs in this analysis, however.
2. Tort claims are generally considered debts that can be discharged in bankruptcy proceedings. Some of the more celebrated examples of liabilities that have led to bankruptcy include the drug DES, the Dalkon Shield, and Johns Manville's asbestos products. For discussion of such cases see Roe (1984).
3. There are limits to firms' ability to avoid liability in this way. For example, dissolution requires more than a simple change in ownership. Assets acquired more or less intact trigger successor liability, wherein the acquiring firm inherits the purchased firm's liabilities. Piecemeal liquidation of assets is typically required.

4. The intuition behind this result is straightforward: insolvency truncates the penalties that are borne by tort defendants, thus creating an externalized social production cost. For analyses which have explored or employ this reasoning, see Schwartz (1985), Shavell (1986), Landes and Posner (1987), Kornhauser and Revesz (1990), and Boyd and Ingberman (1994).

5. Using this rationale, Hansmann and Kraakman (1991) have argued that there should be unlimited shareholder liability for corporate torts. The rationale has also been put forward in the literature on vicarious liability (the liability of principles for the actions of their agents), as in Sykes (1984) and Kornhauser (1982).

6. This is not to be confused with proportional liability rules that apportion damages based on relative fault. Fault implies an ability to exert precaution or contribute directly to safety. We assume that contractors can indirectly demand safety from producers, but not provide it directly themselves.

7. The proportional rule is descriptive of rules governing retailer liability for product defects. In that kind of application, extended liability would be limited to the proportion of sales made by a given retailer. No retailer would be held liable for sales made by a competing retailer. In general, it is worth noting that liability is extended in a variety of legal settings, in addition to product and environmental torts. In commercial law, liability may be to parent firms from subsidiaries and in employment law from employees to employers.

8. The joint and several nature of liability is perhaps the most notorious characteristic of the US environmental liability system, due to its unfairness and the vast amount of litigation stemming from the efforts of multiple defendants to minimize their share of liability. The remedial purpose doctrine is the typical defence. This defence may be invoked with some justification when there is difficulty in apportioning responsibility, as when the causal connection between one firm's (contractor's) actions and damages is difficult to establish.

9. 910 F.2d 1032 (1st Cir 1990).

10. See *Joslyn Manufacturing Co.* v. *T.L. James & Co.*, 893 F.2d 80 (5th Cir. 1990): 'Joslyn asks this court to rewrite the language of [CERCLA] significantly and hold parents liable for their subsidiaries' activities. To do so would dramatically alter traditional concepts of corporation law' (idem at 82).

11. 118 S. Ct. 1876, 1884–85 (1998). See also Hopkins (1999).

12. Allied Signal's divestiture of a facility for handling Kepone, a highly carcinogenic solvent, to a thinly capitalized firm is a classic example. See Goldfarb (1978). In such cases, when incorporation is found to serve a fraudulent or deceptive end, the common law will 'pierce the corporate veil' and extend liability to owners.

13. Ind., 79S04–9801-CV-43, 12/30/98. Depending on the cause of action, the conditions under which liability can be extended may be a function of state environmental laws, not the major federal statutes.

14. Key to Shell's liability was its use of an independent contractor. If instead the tanks had been filled and monitored by a separate firm (middleman), Shell would not have been vicariously liable.

15. Kornhauser and Revesz (1990) and Tietenberg (1989), for instance, consider models where multiple defendants jointly dispose of pollution. Significantly, however, these authors assume that the firms cannot refuse to be contractually associated with their subsequent codefendants or condition contracts on their solvencies or levels of safety.

16. The analysis in this chapter is based on Boyd and Ingberman (1997).

17. This is a simplifying, but reasonable, assumption given the incentives highlighted by our analysis. If a firm has cash on hand that is not used for productive purposes but is exposed to liability, then shareholders want that cash distributed immediately, unless there is a more profitable alternative investment. In other words, liability creates an incentive to remove all mobile non-productive capital from the firm.

18. When (a) torts have priority over secured credit in bankruptcy and (b) debt and equity have similar tax treatment, firms strictly prefer equity over debt financing. Even in the case where debt has priority over torts, since debt introduces moral hazard and monitoring costs, the substitution of debt for equity implies the same kind of inefficiency that our model highlights (the substitution of other inputs for capital). See Ingberman (1994) for an analysis of capital and

safety investments in non-joint liability settings as a function of the treatment of debt vs. equity in bankruptcy proceedings.

19. For a more detailed explication of this result, see Boyd and Ingberman (1997).
20. A more extensive discussion of this issue can be found in Boyd and Ingberman (1996).
21. Investments that can be used by more than one firm can be made without duplication by affiliated firms. And benefits of scope, such as the benefits of extensive retail and marketing networks, can be captured when producers are able to sell to a large number of contractors.
22. Consider a numerical example. The producer has wealth $K = 100$, a set of 10 contractors have wealth $j_Y = 10$ and another set of 10 contractors have wealth $j_Z = 20$. If $L = 340$, $\Phi = 12$. In this case, the producer bears 100 of the total liability and is left insolvent. The 10 smaller contractors each bear 10 and are also left insolvent. The larger contractors bear 140, 14 each. Note that 14 is greater than Φ, meaning that by being contractually affiliated via a common producer, Z-types are bearing liabilities due to production that serves Y-types.
23. The fact that exit can create inefficiencies through risk-externalization is discussed extensively in Hansmann and Kraakman (1991) who argue that '[a factor creating] inefficient incentives under limited liability is the shareholder's option to liquidate the corporation and distribute its assets before tort liability attaches. Since products and manufacturing processes often create long-term hazards that become visible only after many years, firms can – and often do – liquidate long before they can be sued by their tort victims'.
24. Assets acquired more or less intact trigger successor liability, so the acquiring firm inherits the purchased firm's liabilities. Thus, dissolution to avoid liability requires a more drastic dismantling and sale of the firm's assets.
25. Recall that contractors will expect less residual liability the more heavily capitalized and safe is the producer.
26. For an overview of environmental financial responsibility requirements, see Boyd (1997). Under the US Resource Conservation and Recovery Act, owners and operators must demonstrate financial responsibility for closure and post-closure of treatment, storage and disposal facilities, liabilities due to leaking underground petroleum storage tanks, and closure and post-closure municipal landfill costs. Offshore oil facilities and oil transport vessels must demonstrate financial responsibility under the Oil Pollution Act, and the Surface Mining Control and Reclamation Act requires bonds to cover the costs of post-closure mine reclamation activities.
27. This uses the identity:

$$\frac{dL}{dq} = \frac{1}{q^2}\left(-K \int_{K/mq}^{1} r(b,s)db\right) < 0,$$

which can be interpreted as follows. If the producer does not internalize all social costs then on average the firm pays F(s) for each unit of failed output when failures do not lead to bankruptcy and K/q for each failed unit when failure does lead to bankruptcy. Since the average cost of product failure depends on q only when insolvency occurs, as q increases, the expected costs of product failure fall by K/q^2 times the probability of insolvency.

REFERENCES

Boyd, James (1997), '"Green money" in the bank: firm responses to environmental financial responsibility rules', *Managerial and Decision Economics* 18: 491–506.

Boyd James, and Daniel Ingberman (1994), 'Non-compensatory damages and potential insolvency', *Journal of Legal Studies* 23: 895–910.

Boyd, James and Daniel Ingberman (1996), 'The polluter pays principle: should liability be extended when the polluter cannot pay?', *Geneva Papers on Risk and Insurance* 21: 180–97.

Boyd, James and Daniel Ingberman (1997), 'The search for deep pockets: is "extended liability" expensive liability?', *Journal of Law, Economics, and Organization* 13: 232–58.

Dixon, Lloyd (1995), 'The transaction costs generated by Superfund's liability approach', in Richard Revesz and Richard Stewart (eds), *Analyzing Superfund: Economics, Science, and Law*, Washington, DC: Resources for the Future.

Goldfarb, William (1978), 'Kepone: a case study', *Environmental Law* 8: 658.

Hansmann, Henry and Reinier Kraakman (1991), 'Toward unlimited shareholder liability for corporate torts', *Yale Law Journal* 100: 1879.

Hopkins, George (1999), '*United States* v. *Bestfoods*: the US Supreme Court sets new limits on the direct liability of parent corporations for polluting acts of subsidiaries', *ELR News and Analysis*, ELR 29: 10545.

Ingberman, Daniel (1994), 'Triggers and priority: an integrated model of the effects of bankruptcy on overinvestment and underinvestment', *Washington University Law Quarterly* 72: 1341–72.

Kornhauser, Lewis (1982), 'An economic analysis of the choice between enterprise and personal liability for accidents', *California Law Review* 70: 1345–85.

Kornhauser, Lewis and Richard Revesz (1990), 'Apportioning damages among potentially insolvent actors', *Journal of Legal Studies* 19: 617–51.

Landes, William and Richard Posner (1980), 'Joint and multiple tortfeasors: an economic analysis', *Journal of Legal Studies* 9: 517–55.

Ringleb, Al and Steven Wiggins (1990), 'Liability and large-scale, long-term hazards', *Journal of Political Economy* 98: 574–95.

Roe, Mark (1984), 'Bankruptcy and mass tort', *Columbia Law Review* 84: 846.

Schwartz, Alan (1985), 'Products liability, corporate structure, and bankruptcy: toxic substances and the remote risk relationship', *Journal of Legal Studies* 14: 689.

Shavell, Steven (1986), 'The judgment-proof problem', *International Review of Law and Economics* 6: 45.

Sykes, Alan (1984), 'The economics of vicarious liability', *Yale Law Journal* 93: 1231–80.

Tietenberg, Tom (1989), 'Indivisible toxic torts: the economics of joint and several liability', *Land Economics* 65: 305–19.

4. Horizontal vicarious liability

Tracy R. Lewis and David E.M. Sappington

INTRODUCTION

The judgment-proof problem has long been recognized as one with serious practical implications, particularly in the areas of environmental protection and product safety. A judgment-proof problem arises when the total resources that a producer commands are small relative to the social damages that its activities may cause. The producer's limited wealth makes it judgment-proof in the sense that it cannot be forced to compensate victims fully for the losses they suffer because of the producer's activities. Consequently, the producer takes too little care to limit the social damages that can arise from its activities (for example, losses from environmental contamination or unsafe products).[1]

Numerous solutions to the judgment-proof problem have been proposed. One potential solution is to ban completely activities that may result in severe environmental damage. Another possible solution is to impose stringent government oversight and control on the activities in question. A third alternative, which relies less on government intervention and more on providing direct incentives to producers, is to increase the loss that a producer experiences when its activities result in social damages, even though the producer's initial resources are limited. The purpose of this research is to propose a liability rule that serves exactly this purpose.

Under the liability rule that we propose (called *horizontal vicarious liability*), all potential producers that wish to have the opportunity to engage in a risky activity are required to post a non-refundable bond with the government. The government subsequently selects a single producer to operate, and delivers all posted bonds to the selected producer if it avoids a socially damaging accident. However, if an accident occurs, the bonds that have been posted are employed to compensate victims. Thus, as long as potential producers can be induced to post significant resources as non-refundable bonds, the selected operator stands to forfeit considerable wealth if its activities give rise to an accident. Consequently, the selected operator will take considerable care to avoid an accident. Furthermore, as we demonstrate below, the government can induce potential producers to deliver all of their wealth as non-refundable bonds simply by selecting a potential producer to undertake the risky, but now potentially very lucrative, activity with greater frequency the larger the bond it posts.

The essence of our proposal can be illustrated with a very simple example. Suppose there are two risk-neutral firms, A and B, that are equally qualified to ship oil across a body of water. Any oil spill on this environmentally sensitive body of water would cause $10 million in social damages. If firm A had $10 million in assets and firm B had no assets, a judgment-proof problem could be avoided simply by authorizing firm A to transport the oil and precluding firm B from doing so. Firm A could be motivated to take the ideal level of precaution against an oil spill in this instance simply by placing its $10 million at risk if a spill occurs.

Suppose, instead, that the total industry assets of $10 million are divided equally between firms A and B. In this case, if one of the shippers is selected at random to transport the oil, a judgment-proof problem will arise. Since any shipper would put only $5 million of its own resources at stake but could cause $10 million in social damages, the shipper cannot be forced to internalize the full impact of its actions. Consequently, the authorized shipper will take too little care to avert an oil spill.

Now suppose that in an attempt to resolve this judgment-proof problem, firm A is authorized to ship the oil and firm B, or some other financier with assets of at least $5 million, is designated to serve as firm A's creditor. In particular, firm A is instructed to secure access to an additional $5 million at fair market rates and, in the event of an oil spill, compensate victims for the full $10 million in damages that they suffer. Firm A's creditor will require compensation for the $5 million it puts at risk. If the creditor cannot monitor the level of care that firm A takes to avoid an oil spill,[2] the creditor can only secure this compensation in the form of a payment from firm A when no accident occurs, which is when firm A has the resources to deliver the promised payment. Suppose this payment amounts to $1 million. We refer to a policy of this sort, which effectively holds a producer's creditors liable for environmental damages that the producer causes, as *vertical vicarious liability*.[3]

Although vertical vicarious liability may appear initially to constitute sensible policy,[4] it can actually work contrary to the social interest. Indeed, in the present setting, vertical vicarious liability reduces, rather than increases, firm A's incentive to avoid a socially damaging accident.[5] Before firm A was required to secure financing, it stood to lose $5 million if an accident occurred. After it secures financing, firm A's net loss from an accident is only $4 million (because of the additional $1 million that firm A must pay to the creditor if no accident occurs). Consequently, firm A will rationally undertake less preventive care when vertical vicarious liability is imposed than when firm A alone is held liable for the damages from its activities. The net result is a decline in social welfare.[6]

Now consider the merits of horizontal vicarious liability in this setting. Suppose that firms A and B are both required to post their initial $5 million endowments as bonds. In return, each firm is afforded a 50 per cent chance of being selected to transport the oil. If the selected shipper transports the oil and avoids a socially damaging accident, it is awarded the entire $10 million bond.[7] In contrast, if an accident occurs, the entire bond is employed to pay for the social damages, and the shipper receives no payment.

This form of horizontal vicarious liability resolves the critical judgment-proof problem. The selected shipper now stands to lose $10 million (the magnitude of the total bond) if its activities cause an accident. Consequently, the selected shipper will be motivated to undertake the ideal level of precautionary effort. Furthermore, both firms find it profitable to participate in the venture because the prospect of receiving the $10 million prize with probability one-half justifies the initial $5 million investment.

This simple example merely illustrates the basic nature and the potential merits of horizontal vicarious liability. The example abstracts from a number of important practical concerns, such as the possibility that potential producers may benefit from hiding some or all of their initial assets when horizontal vicarious liability is implemented. To explore this and related issues in detail, we develop a formal model of horizontal vicarious liability in the following section. We also show there how horizontal vicarious liability can effectively enable the government to combine the observable assets of potential producers in order to mitigate the judgment-proof problem. In the third section, we show that the performance of a horizontal vicarious liability system need not be diminished when potential producers can hide or understate their initial assets. Our analysis concludes with an assessment of some of the practical difficulties in implementing horizontal vicarious liability; this final section also reviews the key differences between the horizontal vicarious liability rule that we propose and other related liability rules and incentive schemes.[8]

FULL-INFORMATION SETTING

We begin with a particularly simple setting in which the total assets controlled by each potential operator are observable and contractible. We shall consider the complications introduced by private knowledge of these assets (or wealth) in the next section.

Concentrated-wealth Setting

Initially, consider the hypothetical setting where there is only one potential operator who controls the entire industry wealth, denoted $W > 0$. With the entire industry wealth concentrated in the hands of this single operator, the operator will stand to forfeit considerable resources if its activities give rise to social damages. Consequently, the operator in this *concentrated-wealth setting* can be motivated to take considerable care to avoid a socially damaging accident.

To describe the concentrated-wealth setting formally,[9] let $V > 0$ denote the profit (or private value) that is generated by the operator's project. The project also causes social damages $D > 0$ if an accident occurs. An accident occurs with probability $p \in [0, 1]$. The operator can reduce the likelihood of an accident by exerting unobservable effort. This effort might involve undertaking extra precautions to guard against the spill of oil during its transport, for example. $C(p)$ will denote the operator's private, unobservable cost of securing accident probability p. Lower accident probabilities are more costly to secure, and there are diminishing returns to the efforts designed to reduce p. Formally, $C'(p) < 0$ and $C''(p) > 0$.[10]

The accident probability that the operator implements is influenced by the reward structure it faces. The government designs a simple reward structure for the operator. The operator is asked initially to deliver a bond, B, to the government. This bond cannot exceed the operator's wealth, $W \geq 0$. The government promises to return this bond and the profit from the project to the operator if no accident occurs. If an accident occurs, the government employs the bond and profit to compensate those who are injured by the accident. In this event, the operator receives no payment.[11]

In choosing the bond that it requires of the operator, the government seeks to maximize total expected surplus, which is the difference between expected industry profit ($\pi (p) = [1 - p]\,[B + V] - C(p) - B$) and uncompensated social losses due to accidents ($L(p) = p\,[D - (B + V)]$).[12] Formally, given accident probability p, total expected surplus, $S(p)$, can be represented as:

$$S(p) = \pi(p) - L(p) = V - pD - C(p). \tag{4.1}$$

In turn, the government's problem (GP) in this concentrated-wealth setting can be written formally as:

$$\underset{p,B}{\text{Maximize}} \quad V - pD - C(p)$$

subject to:

$$\pi(p) \equiv [1 - p][B + V] - C(p) - B \geq \bar{\pi}; \tag{4.2}$$

$$\tilde{p} = \arg\max_{\tilde{p}} \pi(\tilde{p}); \text{ and} \qquad (4.3)$$

$$B \le W. \qquad (4.4)$$

Expressions (4.2)–(4.4) summarize the three constraints that the government faces. First, to ensure that the operator is willing to operate, the government must promise the operator at least its reservation level of expected profit ($\bar{\pi} \ge 0$).[13] Second, as expression (4.3) indicates, the operator chooses the equilibrium accident probability, p, to maximize its own expected profit.[14] Third, expression (4.4) reflects the fact that the bond the government collects from the operator cannot exceed his wealth. G(W) will denote the expected value of the government's objective function at the solution to (GP) when industry wealth, and thus the single operator's wealth, is W.

Unless otherwise noted, a judgment-proof problem is assumed to exist in this concentrated-wealth setting. In other words, total industry wealth is assumed to be small relative to the social damages from an accident. Consequently, even when a single operator controls the entire industry wealth, it cannot be induced to implement the socially preferred accident probability, $p^* \equiv \mathrm{argmin}_p \{pD + C(p)\}$, simply by requiring it to bear the full cost of an accident (D) whenever it occurs. Formally, we assume:

$$W + V < D. \qquad (4.5)$$

We further assume that the government does not need to restrict the bond that it collects from the operator in order to ensure its participation. Thus, as expression (4.6) indicates, if the operator were to post its entire wealth as a bond that it forfeits in the event of an accident, the operator would anticipate rent from the operation:

$$\mathrm{Max}_p \{[1 - p][W + V] - C(p) - W\} > \bar{\pi}. \qquad (4.6)$$

Expression (4.6) will hold, for example, when industry wealth is limited, the profit from the project is large, and the equilibrium probability of an accident is small.

Two conclusions follow immediately in this setting. First, the government will always collect the entire industry wealth from the operator (that is, B = W at the solution to (GP)). The more the operator stands to lose when an accident occurs, the more care it will take to avoid an accident. Therefore, the government induces the smallest possible accident probability by requiring the operator to post its entire wealth as a bond. Second, because the operator implements a smaller accident probability the more it stands to lose when an accident occurs, total expected surplus increases as industry wealth increases. This latter conclusion is recorded formally as Lemma 1:

> **Lemma 1** The government's expected welfare in the concentrated-wealth setting increases as the operator's wealth increases. (Formally, $G'(W) > 0$.)[15]

Lemma 1 implies that the concentration of industry wealth presumed in the concentrated-wealth setting is ideal for the government. A question that arises now is whether horizontal vicarious liability can enable the government to achieve this ideal outcome even when industry resources are widely dispersed among potential producers. To address this question, we turn to the dispersed-wealth setting.

Dispersed-wealth Setting

The dispersed-wealth setting is analogous to the concentrated-wealth setting except that there are $n \geq 2$ potential operators. For simplicity, the potential operators are assumed to be identical in all respects, except possibly for their wealth levels. $W_i > 0$ will denote the wealth of the ith potential operator. Total industry wealth is W in the dispersed-wealth setting, just as it is in the concentrated-wealth setting, so

$$\sum_{i=1}^{n} W_i = W.$$

Lemma 1 implies that the government will be disadvantaged by any dispersion of wealth if it simply selects one potential operator to operate the project. The reduced wealth of the selected operator renders the judgment-proof problem more constraining, and thereby reduces the government's welfare. Also, as Pitchford (1995) has shown, the losses that arise from dispersed wealth are not alleviated by vertical vicarious liability. In particular, the government would not gain if it selected one potential operator to operate the project and required the other potential operators and/or outside financiers to provide credit to the selected operator. As noted in the introduction, creditors who are held (vertically) vicariously liable for the damages caused by the operator will require some payment from the operator when no accident occurs in order to offset their losses when an accident occurs. Consequently, the operator's net financial gain from avoiding an accident is reduced, which leads it to select a higher accident probability. The net result is a reduction in the government's welfare.

(As we explain on pp. 82–3, this conclusion is sensitive to the assumption that the creditors' monitoring technology is identical to the government's technology.)

In contrast, horizontal vicarious liability can eliminate any potential social losses due to wealth dispersion. It can do so in the following manner. Under horizontal vicarious liability, each potential operator is required to post its wealth as a non-refundable bond with the government. In return, the potential operator is awarded a chance of being selected to operate the project. The probability (q_i) that potential operator i is selected to operate the project is $q_i = W_i/W$. Thus, the more wealth a potential operator posts as a bond, the greater are its chances of being selected to operate the project. Potential operators who are not selected forfeit their bonds and receive no additional payments.

This reward structure serves two important purposes. First, it induces each potential operator to participate and to voluntarily deliver all of its wealth to the government. To see why, notice that as it posts additional wealth as a bond, a potential operator's probability of being selected to operate the project increases at the constant rate $1/W$. (This rate is constant because W is constant.) Also notice from expression (4.6) that the net expected return of the selected operator ($[1 - p] [W + V] - C(p)$) exceeds the sum of its reservation profit level ($\bar{\pi}$) and industry wealth (W). Consequently, the marginal expected return to posting an extra dollar of wealth exceeds $(W + \bar{\pi})/W$, which, in turn, exceeds unity. Since the marginal expected return from posting more wealth always exceeds the associated marginal cost, all potential operators will deliver all of their wealth to the government. Second, the reward structure provides pronounced incentive for the selected operator to avoid an accident. Indeed, since the operator is awarded the entire industry wealth (W) and the profit from the project (V) if no accident occurs but receives nothing if an accident does occur, the selected operator in the dispersed-wealth setting faces the same incentives that its counterpart in the concentrated-wealth setting faces. This fact underlies the conclusion reported in Proposition 1:

Proposition 1 Horizontal vicarious liability eliminates any potential social loss from wealth dispersion. In particular, through the use of horizontal vicarious liability, the government achieves the same level of welfare in the dispersed-wealth setting that it achieves in the concentrated-wealth setting.

The key difference between horizontal vicarious liability and vertical vicarious liability reflected in Proposition 1 merits emphasis. Under vertical vicarious liability, the selected operator delivers a portion of its profit to its creditors when no accident occurs in order to compensate them for the wealth that they forfeit when an accident occurs. Consequently, vertical vicarious liability reduces the differential reward that the operator enjoys when it avoids an accident, and thereby reduces its incentive to avoid an accident. In contrast, this differential reward for avoiding an accident is increased under horizontal vicarious liability. When the selected operator avoids an accident under horizontal vicarious liability, its differential reward is the sum of the profit from the project and the entire industry wealth. This differential reward exceeds the corresponding differential that is implemented in the absence of vicarious liability, and so horizontal vicarious liability mitigates the judgment-proof problem for the selected operator.[16] Furthermore, the prospect of being selected to operate the lucrative project is sufficient to ensure the participation of all potential operators, even though potential operators who are not selected to operate the project suffer a loss.

PRIVATE INFORMATION SETTING

The discussion to this point has presumed that the wealth of each potential operator is observable and contractible. In practice, assets that are readily observed may understate the resources that are, or could be, available to potential operators. As Ringleb and Wiggins (1990) point out, producers may intentionally limit their forfeitable assets in order to reduce their potential losses from liability claims.[17] Furthermore, when the government's ability to discover hidden assets is limited, a potential operator may simply understate its actual wealth level. Doing so reduces the bond that it puts at risk. However, it also reduces its chances of being selected to operate the lucrative project. Therefore, it is not immediately apparent whether a potential producer will, in fact, wish to conceal a portion of its actual wealth endowment when it can do so with impunity under a horizontal vicarious liability regime.

To explore this issue, consider the following setting, which we call the dispersed private-wealth setting. This setting is identical to the dispersed-wealth setting except that potential operators are privately informed about their individual wealth endowments. We shall denote by $W_i \in [0, \overline{W}]$ the wealth of potential operator i. The wealth of each potential operator is the realization of an independent and identically distributed random variable with distribution function $F(W_i)$. For concreteness, we assume that the wealth levels are generated by the uniform distribution, so that $F(W_i) = W_i/\overline{W}$.[18] We also assume that total expected industry wealth is the same in the dispersed private-wealth setting as in the dispersed-wealth setting. Therefore, the expected wealth of each potential operator in the former setting ($\hat{W}_i$) is the average wealth of the potential operators in the latter setting, that is:

$$\hat{W}_i = \int_0^W W_i dF(W_i) = \frac{1}{n} W.$$

The best the government can hope to do in the dispersed private-wealth setting is to replicate the outcome in the concentrated-wealth setting. This is because diminishing returns to motivating reductions in accident probabilities cause social welfare at the solution (GP) to to be a concave function of industry wealth. To attempt to replicate the performance of the concentrated-wealth setting, the government must promise the selected operator a fixed reward when it avoids an accident, rather than a reward that varies with realized industry wealth. This fixed reward will be the sum of the profit from the project (*V*) and the expected industry wealth (W). As in the concentrated-wealth setting, if an accident occurs, the selected operator receives nothing and the sum of W and *V* is employed to compensate the victims of the accident. Potential operators who are not selected to operate never receive any payments, and they forfeit the bonds they post with the government. Notice that under this policy, the government breaks even on average, but may experience a budget surplus or deficit in any particular instance.

The critical question is whether the government can induce all potential operators to deliver all of their wealth as a bond with such a reward structure in the dispersed private-wealth setting. Proposition 2 reports that the government can do so through careful choice of the rule that determines which potential operator is selected to operate the project. This rule is defined by $q_i(\cdot)$, which is the probability that potential operator *i* is selected to operate the project. This probability can vary with the bond (B_i) posted by potential operator *i* and with the bonds posted by all other potential operators. Of course, the bond that a potential operator can post is limited by its actual wealth (that is, $B_i \le W_i$ for all $i = 1, ..., n$).

Proposition 2 Horizontal vicarious liability can eliminate any potential social loss from wealth dispersion, even when potential operators are privately informed about their wealth levels. In particular, through the use of horizontal vicarious liability, the government can achieve the same level of expected welfare in the dispersed private-wealth setting that it achieves in the concentrated-wealth setting.

Proposition 2 indicates that the government can design a selection rule that induces potential operators to post all of their wealth as non-refundable bonds in the dispersed private-wealth setting. The selection rule promises each potential operator a higher probability of being selected to operate the project the more wealth that it posts. In the case where there are only two potential operators (labelled 1 and 2), the selection rule is relatively simple. In this case, potential operator 1 is selected to operate the project when he posts bond B_1 if and only if potential operator 2 posts a bond that is smaller than

$$\tilde{B}_2 \equiv \left[\frac{W}{R^c + W} \right]\left[\frac{1}{2} R^c + B_1 \right],$$

where $R^c = [1 - p^c][W + V] - C(p^c) - W - \bar{\pi}$ is the rent that accrues to the operator in the concentrated-wealth setting, and where p^c denotes the equilibrium probability of an accident in that setting.

This selection rule is illustrated in Figure 4.1. The bonds posted by potential operators 1 and 2 increase with movements in the horizontal and vertical directions, respectively. In the region above the straight line depicted in Figure 4.1, potential operator 2 posts a relatively large bond compared to operator 1, and so is selected to operate the project (so $q_2 = 1$ and $q_1 = 0$). Potential operator 1 is selected to operate the project in the complementary region, where it posts a relatively large bond compared to operator 2.

Notice that as R^c approaches zero, $\tilde{B}_2$ approaches B_1, so the operator that posts the most wealth is selected to operate the project. In terms of Figure 4.1, the critical boundary, $\tilde{B}_2(B_1)$, approaches the diagonal line segment connecting the points $(0, 0)$ and $\overline{W}, \overline{W}$ as R^c approaches zero. As R^c increases, the potential operators risk forfeiting a more lucrative opportunity by understating their

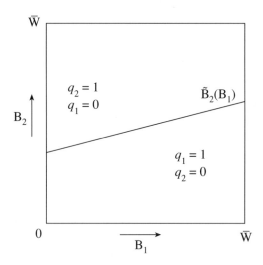

Figure 4.1   Selecting an operator

wealth. Consequently, they are less prone to do so. This allows the government to induce full revelation of wealth with a selection rule in which the probability that a potential operator is selected to operate the project varies more with the absolute amount of the bond that it posts and less with the amount of its bond relative to the bond delivered by the other potential operator. In terms of Figure 4.1, the vertical intercept of the $\tilde{B}_2(B_1)$ boundary increases and the slope of the boundary decreases as R^c increases.[19]

The selection rule that is implemented under horizontal vicarious liability more generally is similar. (The rule is characterized formally in equation (A4.7) in the appendix.) The key feature of the selection rule is the fact that a potential operator is selected to operate the project with greater frequency as the bond that it posts increases relative to the bonds posted by other potential operators. Consequently, understatement of wealth reduces one's chances of being selected to operate the lucrative project. When wealth levels are generated by the uniform distribution, there is always a relatively large probability that some other potential operator will report a higher wealth level than the potential operator that understates its wealth level. Consequently, the pronounced likelihood of forfeiting one's chance to operate the lucrative project deters understatement of wealth in this setting.

Full revelation of wealth is not guaranteed under all circumstances, but it will occur when wealth endowments are generated by many distributions other than the uniform distribution.[20] The essential requirement is that the higher wealth realizations be sufficiently likely that another potential supplier is relatively likely to (truthfully) report a higher wealth level than a potential supplier who understates its actual wealth level.

Notice that potential operators voluntarily reveal (and put at risk) the entirety of their wealth endowments in order to avoid losing the right to operate the lucrative project to a competitor who reveals a higher wealth level. For this reason, wealth dispersion is advantageous for the government when wealth endowments are not observed publicly. If it were common knowledge that a particular potential operator controlled the entire industry wealth, then the threat of losing the right to operate to a higher bidder could not be employed to motivate the wealthy operator to post all of its wealth as a bond. In this sense, wealth dispersion, which is a key cause of the judgment-proof problem, can actually help mitigate the adverse consequences of the judgment-proof problem under the identified horizontal vicarious liability regime.

CONCLUSIONS

We have illustrated how horizontal vicarious liability can help to resolve the concerns introduced by the judgment-proof problem in some settings. In particular, we have shown how the government can employ horizontal vicarious liability to secure the outcome it would implement if the resources of all potential operators were concentrated in the hands of a single operator, thereby rendering the judgment-proof problem less constraining. Furthermore, we have indicated that there are plausible conditions under which this outcome can be ensured even when each potential operator is privately informed about the magnitude of the resources at its disposal.[21]

Although our findings suggest that horizontal vicarious liability may be a more effective policy instrument than vertical vicarious liability in some settings, it is important to emphasize the limitations of horizontal vicarious liability. Most importantly, to implement horizontal vicarious liability, the government must:

1. be well aware of both the types of activities that give rise to accidents and the social damages that the accidents cause;
2. have a reasonable understanding of the technology of accident prevention;
3. be able both to identify potential operators in advance of their operation and to regulate their activities; and
4. be able to identify and measure the losses from accidents when they occur.

The information required to fulfil these four criteria may be available to the government in some settings. For instance, the government may be well informed about the potential dangers associated with transporting oil or hazardous waste material, or with operating nuclear power plants. The government may also be readily able to identify parties that undertake these activities and, in many cases, to measure the social damages that arise from these activities. However, in instances where the potential magnitude of the social damages from identified productive activities is not recognized until long after the activities have begun and/or where it is difficult to identify the activities (or actors) that produce social damages,[22] the form of horizontal vicarious liability that we have analysed is unlikely to serve as a useful policy instrument for the government.

It should also be noted that our formal analysis has presumed all parties to be risk neutral. If potential operators are, in fact, risk averse, they may be less anxious to put their entire wealth at risk in order to maximize their chances of being selected to operate under a reward structure that entails significant variation in potential payoffs. Consequently, at a minimum, the particular forms of horizontal vicarious liability analysed here are likely to warrant modification when potential operators are averse to risk.[23]

We also simplified our formal analysis by abstracting from the possibility that some parties might be better able than the government to monitor the actions that the operator undertakes to avoid an accident. When superior monitoring technologies are available, additional considerations emerge. For instance, if a creditor can better monitor an operator's efforts to avoid an accident than can the government, then vertical vicarious liability can enhance social welfare. This is the case because, by placing the creditor's resources at risk, the creditor can be induced to employ its superior monitoring ability to better motivate the operator to take care to avoid an accident.[24]

One implication of this finding is that a comparison of the performance of vertical and horizontal vicarious liability regimes is less straightforward when superior monitoring technologies are available. Indeed, the case for the particular horizontal vicarious liability rules proposed here may be strongest when superior monitoring technologies are not available. A second implication is that different horizontal vicarious liability rules may best promote social welfare when superior monitoring technologies are available.[25] In particular, it may be optimal for potential operators to be rewarded differentially according to whether the operator avoids or incurs an accident. Such a compensation structure, which bears some resemblance to joint liability arrangements, may best motivate potential operators to monitor the activities of the selected operator. A careful analysis of this issue merits additional investigation.[26]

Future research should also analyse appropriate modifications of horizontal vicarious liability rules in settings where potential operators differ in their ability to avoid socially damaging accidents.[27] It may be optimal, for example, to bias the selection procedure in favour of potential operators who are known to be best able to avoid accidents, even though their initial wealth endowments may be limited. The optimal design of a horizontal vicarious liability mechanism in a setting where potential operators are privately informed about both their wealth endowments and their innate abilities to avoid accidents would seem to be a particularly fertile area for future research.

Future research might also entertain the possibility that an operator's unobserved activities affect the magnitude of the social damages from an accident as well as the likelihood of an accident. Future investigations might also explore the optimal design of liability systems in settings where multiple projects can proceed simultaneously. Issues that are naturally addressed in assessments of joint liability rules arise in such settings.[28] In addition, such settings will facilitate an analysis of the optimal number of projects. When multiple projects are possible, the government might intentionally authorize fewer projects than would be socially optimal in the absence of a judgment-proof problem. With fewer authorized projects, potential bidders may bid particularly aggressively (via posting large bonds) for the right to operate one of the scarce projects. Consequently, the problem of motivating truthful revelation of wealth endowments may be mitigated at the same time that the judgment-proof problem is alleviated.[29]

In concluding, it may be instructive to emphasize the key differences between the horizontal vicarious liability mechanism that we have analysed and five other mechanisms that may appear to share some similar features or purpose. First, notice that horizontal vicarious liability is not simply a standard form of liability insurance. The distinguishing feature of horizontal vicarious liability is that it increases the loss suffered by an operator when its activities give rise to social damages. In contrast, standard forms of liability insurance do just the opposite.

Second, notice that horizontal vicarious liability is quite distinct from such popular financing institutions as time-sharing arrangements. Time-sharing arrangements allow multiple beneficiaries of a project (for example, a vacation residence) to share the fixed costs of the project. Although horizontal vicarious liability can serve this same purpose, it also serves to alleviate moral hazard concerns while limiting industry rent.

Third, although horizontal vicarious liability shares an important feature with all-pay auctions, it is not simply an all-pay auction.[30] Under both horizontal vicarious liability and all-pay auctions, all individuals make payments *ex ante*, but only one individual is awarded the 'prize' *ex post*. One key difference between the institutions is that, under horizontal vicarious liability, the prize (that is, the reward structure offered to the selected operator) is endogenous, and is linked to the payments made by the participating individuals. A second difference is that, under horizontal vicarious liability, the prize is explicitly designed to mitigate moral hazard concerns.

Fourth, as noted above, horizontal vicarious liability is distinct from joint liability. Joint liability arrangements which hold multiple producers liable for social damages can be beneficial when all of the producers undertake activities that may harm the environment. Horizontal vicarious liability, in contrast, provides social gains even when it is common knowledge that social damages result from the activities of a single, readily identifiable producer.

Finally, despite some superficial resemblances, horizontal vicarious liability differs in purpose and design from crime deterrence policies that impose very large penalties very infrequently.[31] These policies are designed to reduce the costs of detecting criminal activity, whereas horizontal vicarious liability need not influence the government's monitoring costs. (It did not do so in the simple setting analysed here.) Furthermore, the success of these deterrence policies depends on the absence of a judgment-proof problem, whereas horizontal vicarious liability rules are designed to overcome a binding judgment-proof problem.

APPENDIX

Proof of Lemma 1

Define the Lagrangian function associated with (GP) as follows:

$$\mathcal{L} = V - pD - C(p) + \lambda\,[(1-p)\,[B+V] - B - C(p) - \bar{\pi}] + \gamma\,[W - B]. \quad \text{(A4.1)}$$

The necessary conditions for a solution to (GP) include:

$$\mathcal{L}_B = -\gamma - p\lambda - \left[D + C'(p)\right]\frac{dp}{dB} \leq 0; \quad B[\cdot] = 0. \quad \text{(A4.2)}$$

If follows from (4.3) and (4.5) that:

$$D + C'(p) = D - [B + V] > 0. \quad \text{(A4.3)}$$

Since $dp/dB < 0$, (A4.2) and (A4.3) together imply that:

$$\gamma + p\,\lambda > 0. \quad \text{(A4.4)}$$

If $\gamma = 0$, then (A4.4) implies that $\lambda > 0$. Hence, $\pi(p) = \bar{\pi}$, which violates (4.6). Therefore, by contradiction, $\gamma > 0$. This completes the proof, because $G'(W) = (\partial\mathcal{L})/(\partial W) = \gamma > 0$. ∎

Proof of Proposition 1

Let p^c denote the equilibrium probability of an accident in the concentrated-wealth setting. Also, let R^c denote the operator's rent at the solution to (GP) when industry wealth is W. From (4.6):

$$R^c = [1 - p^c]\,[W + V] - C(p^c) - \bar{\pi} - W > 0. \quad \text{(A4.5)}$$

Finally, let $q_i = W_i/W$ denote the probability that potential operator i is selected to operate the project when it delivers its wealth W_i to the government. Notice that these $\{q_i\}_{i=1}^{n}$ constitute a well-defined probability structure.

The expected profit of the ith potential operator under this reward structure is:

$$\pi_i = \frac{W_i}{W}\left\{\underset{p}{\text{Max}}\ \left[(1-p)[W+V]-C(p)\right]\right\}+\left[\frac{W-W_i}{W}\right]\overline{\pi}-W_i$$

$$= \frac{1}{W}\left\{W_i\left[(1-p^c)[W+V]-C(p^c)+[W-W_i]\overline{\pi}\right]\right\}-W_i$$

$$= \frac{1}{W}\left\{W_i[R+W+\overline{\pi}]+[W-W_i]\overline{\pi}\right\}-W_i$$

$$= \overline{\pi}+\frac{W_i}{W}R > \overline{\pi}. \hspace{3cm} \text{(A4.6)}$$

The inequality in (A4.6) ensures that each potential operator is willing to participate under the specified reward structure. Furthermore, by construction, the accident probability (p^c) and rent (R^c) secured in the concentrated-wealth setting is implemented in the dispersed-wealth setting. ■

Proof of Proposition 2

Define R^c and p^c as in the proof of Proposition 1. (See (A4.5).) Also let $q_i(W)$ denote the probability that potential operator i is selected to produce when $W \equiv (W_1, ..., W_n)$ is the vector of wealth levels reported by potential operators $1, ..., n$, respectively. Suppose that for each $i = 1, ..., n$:

$$q_i(W) = \begin{cases} 1 \ \ \text{if}\ \ W_j \leq \overline{W}\left[\dfrac{\dfrac{R^c}{n}+W_i}{R^c+W}\right]^{\frac{1}{n-1}} & \text{for all}\ \ j \neq i \\[1.5em] 0 \ \ \text{otherwise.} \end{cases} \hspace{1cm} \text{(A4.7)}$$

Notice that $q_i(\cdot) \in [0, 1]$ for all $i = 1, ..., n$ and that $\sum_{i=1}^{n} q_i(\cdot) = 1$. Thus, it will suffice to show that when the government: (a) delivers $W + V$ to the selected operator when no accident occurs (and 0 otherwise); (b) requires all potential operators to post their announced wealth levels as non-refundable bonds; (c) makes no payments to potential operators who are not selected to operate the project; and (d) implements the probability structure in (A4.7), each potential operator will announce its actual wealth realization and choose to participate in the proposed contractual arrangement.

Let $W_{-i} \equiv (W_1, ..., W_{i-1}, W_{i+1}, ..., W_n)$ and let E_{-i} denote the expectation of potential operator i regarding W_{-i}. Then the expected profit of potential operator i when its wealth is W_i and it reports its wealth to be W_i' is:

$$W_i - W_i' + E_{-i}\left\{q_i\left(W_i', W_{-i}\right)\left[\left(1 - p^c\right)[W + V] - C\left(p^c\right)\right] + \left[1 - q_i(\cdot)\right]\overline{\pi}\right\}$$

$$= W_i - W_i' + F^{n-1}\left(\overline{W}\left[\frac{\dfrac{R^c}{n} + W_i'}{R^c + W}\right]^{\frac{1}{n-1}}\right)\left[R^c + \overline{\pi} + W\right] + \left[1 - F^{n-1}(\cdot)\right]\overline{\pi}$$

$$= W_i - W_i' + \left[\frac{\dfrac{R^c}{n} + W_i'}{R^c + W}\right]\left[R^c + W\right] + \overline{\pi} = W_i + \overline{\pi} + \frac{R_c}{n} > \overline{\pi}.$$

(A4.8)

The first equality in (A4.8) follows from (A4.7). The second equality follows from (A4.5) and from the fact that $F^{n-1}(W) = (W/\overline{W})^{n-1}$. The third equality in (A4.8) follows from rearranging terms. (A4.8) reveals that the potential operators have no strict incentive to misrepresent their actual wealth levels (and so, we assume, they report them truthfully) and that the potential operators will participate voluntarily in the proposed contractual arrangement. ∎

NOTES

1. Shavell (1987) provides an eloquent exposition of the judgment-proof problem.
2. We shall return to explore this important assumption on p. 82.
3. The word 'vertical' relates to different stages of the production process. The word 'horizontal' denotes different (actual or potential) producers at the same stage of the production process.
4. Such a policy was implemented in the United States via the Comprehensive Environmental Response, Compensation, and Liability Act (CERCLA) of 1980. CERCLA extends liability for environmental damages to certain creditors of the producers that cause the damages. For a discussion of CERCLA and its interpretation by the courts, see Barr (1990); Nation (1994); Singer (1995); and Jennings (1996), for example.
5. This important observation is due to Pitchford (1995).
6. As we explain in the Conclusion, this is sensitive to the assumption that the creditor is not better able than society at large to monitor firm A's efforts to avoid an accident.
7. In addition, the selected shipper is compensated directly for its transport costs and for its personal costs of delivering the ideal level of precautionary effort.
8. It is important to emphasize at the outset that liability is effectively extended to potential producers in our model, not to other actual producers. Consequently, our analysis differs from

others (for example, Watts 1998) that examine the merits of joint liability in settings where multiple producers may pollute the environment simultaneously.

9. The model described here is analogous to Pitchford's (1995) model.

10. To ensure an interior value for p, it is further assumed that $\lim_{p \to 1} C'(p) = 0$ and $\lim_{p \to 0} C'(p) = -\infty$. We also assume that $C'''(p) > 0$, to ensure concavity of the government's problem that is defined below.

11. This reward structure is without loss of generality in the present setting. Lewis and Sappington (2001) consider an extended setting in which social damages can take on any value between 0 and D. Notice that we consider only monetary reward and penalty structures. Segerson and Tietenberg (1992) examine the role that incarceration can play in motivating desired behaviour when monetary rewards and penalties are limited.

12. It can be shown that our main findings continue to hold if the government acts to maximize a weighted average of expected government net revenues and industry profit, where the weight on the former exceeds the weight on the latter. The higher weight on government net revenues might arise, for example, from the social costs of distortionary taxes employed to raise government revenues. (See, for example, Ballard *et al.* 1985.)

13. We assume throughout that, despite the judgment-proof problem, it is best for society to undertake the project, rather than preclude it.

14. All parties are assumed to be risk neutral here in order to focus on the effects of the judgment-proof problem. The effects of risk aversion are discussed in related models by Kornhauser (1982); Sykes (1981, 1984, 1988); and Newman and Wright (1990). We discuss the effects of risk aversion in the Conclusion.

15. The proof of Lemma 1 is presented in the appendix, along with the proofs of all other formal results.

16. See Lewis and Sappington (1999) for additional thoughts regarding the merits of imposing penalties for damages that differ from the magnitudes of the damages.

17. Ringleb and Wiggins (1990: 589) estimate that 'the incentive to evade liability has led to roughly a 20 percent increase in the number of small corporations in the U.S. economy'. See Boyd and Ingberman (1997) for related observations. Schwarcz (1999) questions whether firms are likely to act strategically to make themselves judgment-proof in practice.

18. The importance of this assumption will be discussed shortly.

19. Notice that as the $\tilde{B}_2$ (B_1) boundary in Figure 4.1 shifts upward and becomes flatter, operator 2 is more likely to be selected to operate the project when operator 1 posts a large bond ($B_1 > W/2$) but is less likely to be selected when operator 1 posts a small bond ($B_1 < W/2$). This is the sense in which the likelihood that operator 2 is selected becomes less sensitive to the bond that it posts relative to the bond that operator 1 posts as R^c increases.

20. For instance, full revelation will be ensured by the proposed form of horizontal vicarious liability whenever $F(W_i) = [W_i/\overline{W}]^\beta$ and $\beta \geq 1$. The analysis developed in Lewis and Sappington (2000a) can be employed to develop a more complete assessment of: (a) the conditions under which limited knowledge of wealth levels is not constraining for the government; and (b) the primary changes that arise when this limited knowledge is constraining. They examine how a principal should allocate productive opportunities to wealth-constrained agents, but do not address the judgment-proof problem directly. See Che and Gale (1998, 2000) and Lewis and Sappington (2000b, c) for related analyses.

21. Since potential operators have no incentive to hide their wealth under the prescribed conditions even when they can do so costlessly, more costly methods of hiding wealth would also be unprofitable. This is true, in particular, of the production distortions designed to limit financial exposure that Ringleb and Wiggins (1990) and Boyd and Ingberman (1997) identify.

22. Ringleb and Wiggins (1990: 575) cite 'radiation, DES, cigarette smoking, saccharin, occupational carcinogens, asbestos, dioxin, vinyl chloride, [and] PCB' as examples of substances and activities that entail latent health hazards whose long-term impacts took many years to recognize. See Teitenberg (1992: 512–16) for a discussion of the special problems associated with identifying and controlling latent health hazards.

23. As noted above, Kornhauser (1982), Sykes (1981, 1984, 1988), and Newman and Wright (1990) consider the effects of risk aversion in related models. Gobert and Poitevin (1998) allow for a risk-averse lender who may be held responsible for the actions of the operator.
24. See Chu and Qian (1995) and Boyer and Laffont (1997) for additional thoughts on this issue.
25. Another implication is that rules of the type embodied in CERCLA would seem to be most appropriate when creditors are better able than the government to monitor the activities of producers. The draughters of CERCLA may have been aware of this point, because CERCLA does not hold liable a creditor 'who, without participating in the management of a vessel or facility, holds indicia of ownership primarily to protect his security interest in the vessel or facility' (42 USC § 9601 (20)(A)).
26. See Varian (1990), Arnott and Stiglitz (1991), and Itoh (1991) for interesting analyses of settings where some agents are able to affect the performance of other agents.
27. Kornhauser (1982) analyses a model of vicarious liability in which one party (for example, the government or the creditor) can devote effort to identifying the potential operators who are best able to avoid socially damaging accidents.
28. See Tietenberg (1992: 533–4), Watts (1998), and Golbe and White (2000), for example.
29. Future research should also analyse settings in which different operators can operate in different time periods. See Che and Woo (1998) and Che (1999), for example.
30. See Baye *et al.* (1993, 1996) and Che and Gale (1998), for example, for useful analyses of all-pay auctions.
31. See Becker (1968), for example.

REFERENCES

Arnott, Richard and Joseph Stiglitz (1991), 'Moral hazard and non-market institutions: dysfunctional crowding out or peer monitoring?', *American Economic Review* 81(1): 179–90.
Ballard, Charles, John Shoven and John Whalley (1985), 'General equilibrium computations of the marginal welfare costs of taxes in the United States', *American Economic Review* 75(1): 128–38.
Barr, Lewis (1990), 'CERCLA made simple: an analysis of the cases under the Comprehensive Environmental Response, Compensation and Liability Act of 1980', *Business Lawyer* 45: 923–1001.
Baye, Michael, Dan Kovenock and Casper De Vries (1993), 'Rigging the lobbying process: an application of the all-pay auction', *American Economic Review* 83(1): 289–94.
Baye, Michael, Dan Kovenock and Casper De Vries (1996), 'The all-pay auction with complete information', *Economic Theory* 8: 291–305.
Becker, Gary (1968), 'Crime and punishment: an economic approach', *Journal of Political Economy* 76: 169–217.
Boyd, James and Daniel Ingberman (1997), 'The search for deep pockets: is "extended liability" expensive liability?', *Journal of Law, Economics, and Organization* 13(1): 232–58.
Boyer, Marcel and Jean-Jacques Laffont (1997), 'Environmental risks and bank liability', *European Economic Review* 41: 1427–59.
Che, Yeon-Koo (1999), 'Joint liability and peer sanctioning under group lending', University of Wisconsin – Madison, mimeo, March.
Che, Yeon-Koo and Ian Gale (1998), 'Standard auctions with financially constrained bidders', *Review of Economic Studies* 65(1): 1–22.

Che, Yeon-Koo and Ian Gale (2000), 'The optimal mechanism for selling to budget-constrained consumers', *Journal of Economic Theory* (forthcoming).

Che, Yeon-Koo and Seung-Weon Yoo (1998), 'Optimal incentives for teams', University of Wisconsin – Madison, mimeo, May.

Chu, C.Y. Cyrus and Yingyi Qian (1995), 'Vicarious liability under a negligence rule', *International Review of Law and Economics* 15: 305–22.

Gobert, Karine and Michel Poitevin (1998), 'Environmental risks: should banks be liable?', Université de Montréal CRDE, Working Paper 1198, December.

Golbe, Devra and Lawrence White (2000), 'Market share liability and its alternatives', New York University, mimeo, February.

Itoh, Hideshi (1991), 'Incentives to help in multi-agent situations', *Econometrica* 59(3): 611–36.

Jennings, Marianne (1996), 'Lender liability, CERCLA, and other things that go bump in the night', *Real Estate Law Journal* 24: 372–5.

Kornhauser, Lewis (1982), 'An economic analysis of the choice between enterprise and personal liability for accidents', *California Law Review* 70: 1345–92.

Lewis, Tracy and David Sappington (1999), 'Employing decoupling and deep pockets to mitigate judgment-proof problems', *International Review of Law and Economics* 19(2): 275–93.

Lewis, Tracy and David Sappington (2000a), 'Contracting with wealth-constrained agents', *International Economic Review* 41(3): 743–67.

Lewis, Tracy and David Sappington (2000b), 'Motivating wealth-constrained actors', *American Economic Review* 90(4): 944–61.

Lewis, Tracy and David Sappington (2000c), 'Optimal contracting with private knowledge of wealth and ability', *Review of Economic Studies* (forthcoming).

Lewis, Tracy and David Sappington (2001), 'Employing lenders' deep pockets to resolve judgment-proof problems', *American Economic Review* (forthcoming).

Nation, George (1994), 'Life without EPA's rule interpreting CERCLA's secured party exemption', *Banking Law Journal* 111(5): 499–506.

Newman, Harry and David Wright (1990), 'Strict liability in a principal–agent model', *International Review of Law and Economics* 10: 219–31.

Pitchford, Rohan (1995), 'How liable should a lender be? The case of judgement-proof firms and environmental risk', *American Economic Review* 85(5): 1171–86.

Ringleb, Al and Steven Wiggins (1990), 'Liability and large-scale, long-term hazards', *Journal of Political Economy* 98(3): 574–95.

Schwarcz, Steven (1999), 'The inherent irrationality of judgment proofing', *Stanford Law Review* 52(1): 1–53.

Segerson, Kathleen and Tom Teitenberg (1992), 'The structure of penalties in environmental enforcement: an economic analysis', *Journal of Environmental Economics and Management* 23: 179–200.

Shavell, Steven (1987), *Economic Analysis of Accident Law*, Cambridge, MA: Harvard University Press.

Singer, George (1995), 'Lender liability: evaluating risk under CERCLA and the security interest exemption', *Commercial Law Journal* 100(2): 156–90.

Sykes, Alan (1981), 'An efficiency analysis of vicarious liability under the law of agency', *Yale Law Journal* 91: 168–206.

Sykes, Alan (1984), 'The economics of vicarious liability', *Yale Law Journal* 93: 1231–80.

Sykes, Alan (1988), 'The boundaries of vicarious liability: an economic analysis of the scope of employment rule and related legal doctrines', *Harvard Law Review* 101(3): 563–609.

Tietenberg, Tom (1992), *Environmental and Natural Resource Economics*, New York: HarperCollins.

Varian, Hal (1990), 'Monitoring agents with other agents', *Journal of Institutional and Theoretical Economics* 146(1): 153–74.

Watts, Alison (1998), 'Insolvency and division of cleanup costs', *International Review of Law and Economics* 18(1): 61–76.

5. Liability policy and toxic pollution releases

Anna Alberini and David Austin

INTRODUCTION

This chapter examines whether imposing strict liability for the cost of cleaning up contaminated sites has increased the level of care taken by firms to avoid uncontrolled releases of pollutants into the environment and reduced the frequency and/or severity of such events.

Proponents of environmental policies based on strict liability contend that, faced with the prospect of disbursements over clean-up or to compensate third parties, firms will avoid improper disposal of pollution into the environment. In practice, a number of US environmental statutes incorporate strict liability for polluters. Under the Comprehensive Environmental Response, Compensation, and Liability Act (CERCLA, originally passed in 1980), parties that have contributed to badly contaminated sites may be forced to pay for clean-up. The full burden of environmental costs is placed on the responsible party (the polluter) and the Environmental Protection Agency (EPA) does not have to prove that the party failed to meet a standard of due care. Strict liability is often imposed on polluters by state 'mini-Superfund' laws, which address the numerous non-priority hazardous waste sites that do not qualify for the federal Superfund programme, and by the Offshore Continental Shelf Act (1974), which covers off-shore spills occurring during drilling operations.

Legal liability is one way in which firms can be made to internalize the pollution damages associated with their production activities. It is an *ex post* type of intervention, giving firms flexibility in how they wish to reduce the likelihood of uncontrolled releases of pollutants, while relieving the government of having to devise and prescribe safety standards and monitor firm compliance with regulations (Boyd 1996).

However, several factors may dilute the incentives of legal liability. Firms with relatively limited assets may be sheltered from the economic incentives created by strict liability (Shavell 1984; Tietenberg 1989). Firms may even select their asset level or corporate financial structure to minimize payment of damages in the event of an accident (Pitchford 1995; Ringleb and Wiggins 1990).[1]

In this chapter, we explore empirically the effects of strict liability on uncontrolled releases of pollutants into the environment, exploiting differences across the states in the liability structure imposed by their 'mini-Superfund' programmes. These programmes typically confer authority for the regulator to force responsible parties to conduct or pay for initial feasibility studies and remediation activities at non-priority sites, and establish financing mechanisms to pay for such activities when the responsible party is insolvent or no longer in existence (USEPA 1989). As of 1995, 45 states had passed statutes providing for enforcement authority and funding mechanisms.

Not all state programmes impose strict liability on responsible parties. As of 1987, 27 states had instituted strict liability provisions; by 1995 this number had climbed to 40. The remainder of the states relied on negligence-based liability.

Without data on firms' expenditures on care, this chapter uses data on accidents and spills involving hazardous substances to establish whether their frequency has been systematically affected by the introduction of strict liability. The spill data come from EPA's Emergency Response Notification System (ERNS) database. Because ERNS was begun in 1987, we are unable to establish how the previous passage of the federal Superfund law affected accidental releases. Instead, we examine whether the strict liability feature of state clean-up programmes has had any additional influence on accidental events, above and beyond that of the federal Superfund.

We estimate regressions relating the frequency of chemical spills to the extent of manufacturing activity and hazardous waste generation in the state, and to the liability structure of the state's mini-Superfund programme. Since state policies seeking to prevent contamination may well be endogenous with releases of pollutants into the environment and the formation of contaminated sites, we use instrumental-variable techniques, and allow for structural change across alternative liability regimes.

We find that states with more serious spills are more likely to adopt strict liability, and this policy does afford them a reduction in the frequency of spills. We also find evidence consistent with different behavioural responses by large and small firms, the latter being partially sheltered from liability.

The remainder of the chapter is organized as follows. In the second section, we present a simple model of state adoption of strict liability within its hazardous waste clean-up legislation. The third section presents the econometric model and the data, and the fourth the independent variables of the econometric model. The fifth section presents the results, and the sixth concludes.

A STATE'S CHOICE OF LIABILITY STRUCTURE

Economic theory suggests that firms can be expected to respond to the imposition of liability by changing their investment in accident prevention and safety equipment, but that the extent of this response depends on a number of factors.

Under ideal conditions, firms held strictly liable for pollution damages will undertake the socially efficient level of care (Shavell 1984). If the harm caused by a firm exceeds its assets or if the firm can escape legal judgment, the level of care chosen by the firm will be less than the efficient level. With damages of uncertain size, however, it remains unclear whether the level of care rises with the assets of the firm (Beard 1990). Whether strict liability or negligence-based liability is more effective in inducing efficient care against spills depends on how stringent the negligence standard is (at least when the firm's assets are sufficient to pay for the damages; Tietenberg 1989). The availability and cost of pollution insurance and the existence of safety devices and technologies can further influence care.

Although it will be difficult, in general, to predict both individual firms' and the aggregate level of pollution releases in a state, state legislatures may decide between strict liability and a negligence standard in the belief that their choice will influence the occurrence and/or severity of toxic releases. A rational state legislature should enact the liability regime that maximizes the net benefits of the state's hazardous waste clean-up programme.

We assume that benefits are the reduction in expected health damages for the population exposed to accidental toxic releases at contaminated sites where mitigation is subsequently undertaken. Formally:

$$B = \Delta r \cdot N(\mathbf{Z}) \cdot Q(E(S,\mathbf{A};\mathbf{Z});\mathbf{Z}) \cdot V(\mathbf{Z}) \qquad (5.1)$$

where Δr is the mitigation-induced change in the risk of developing health problems, such as cancer or acute symptoms, per person exposed, per unit of volume of the toxic substance. N is the number of exposed persons; Q is the quantity (volume) of toxic substance released; and V is the (dollar) value of a statistical life, or the average willingness to pay to avoid the symptoms of exposure to the toxic release.

Q should depend on the type and composition of economic activity in the state, $\mathbf{Z}$, reflecting the underlying propensity to release pollutants. It should also depend on the expenditure E incurred by firms to install safety equipment and monitor operations more closely to avoid pollution releases. E is assumed to depend on the presence of strict liability (S; $S = 0,1$), other liability and programme attributes (here summarized into the vector $\mathbf{A}$) and firm characteristics (contained in $\mathbf{Z}$).

The size of the exposed population should be influenced by residential patterns and population density, whereas the value of a statistical life used in the state's net benefit calculus should depend on socio-economic characteristics and residents' tastes. The vector $\mathbf{Z}$ therefore includes variables such as income and education (see Tolley *et al.* 1994) along with economic activity variables.

The costs of the programme include the litigation and administrative costs of forcing responsible parties to mitigate (here assumed to depend on pollution releases and state characteristics), plus any unrecoverable clean-up costs borne by the state:

$$C = C(Q(E(S;\mathbf{A};\mathbf{Z}));p(S,\mathbf{A};\mathbf{Z});\mathbf{Z}) \qquad (5.2)$$

where p denotes the fraction of all mitigation costs which the state must absorb. One would thus expect the administrative and litigation costs to depend on the type of liability adopted within the state programme.

By its choice of liability structure and other programme attributes, the agency can influence the probability p that the state will have to absorb unrecovered costs. However, its ability to control p may be affected by firm wealth: a state with a prevalence of small firms, for instance, may not find strict liability particularly useful, as such firms are more likely to have resources insufficient to handle the full costs of clean-up at their sites. By contrast, a state with an abundance of larger and wealthier firms may be able to keep p low by instituting strict and/or joint-and-several liability provisions. The state legislature may also opt for strict liability if it believes it is objectively difficult for the regulator to establish a standard of negligence and/or to determine when it has been breached.

The state will select the type of liability S and other liability and programme attributes, $\mathbf{A}$, to maximize the net benefits of the programme, $(B - C)$, subject to a resource constraint. The optimal levels of liability policy S and other programme attributes $\mathbf{A}$ should, therefore, depend on socio-economic characteristics $\mathbf{Z}$, as should net benefits, firms' expenditure on safety, E^*, and total releases, Q^*, anticipated by the state. In this model, E^* and Q^* are endogenous with the liability structure of the programme.

THE DATA AND THE ECONOMETRIC MODEL

Our theoretical model of state legislature behaviour presumes that the state chooses the liability structure to influence the precautions E taken by firms against pollution, and hence, Q, the uncontrolled releases of pollution into the environment. Actual releases, Q', may or may not be close to the level Q^* anticipated by the state, depending on the accuracy of the state's beliefs about the firms' behavioural responses and choices of E. Do states with strict liability have a lower level of Q', relative to states with comparable manufacturing, mining and population characteristics, but a different liability regime?

To answer this question, in this chapter we estimate econometric equations for pollution releases, which we measure as the frequency of spills and accidents involving toxic chemicals.

The Data

Our data come from EPA's Emergency Response Notification System (ERNS). Spills and releases of specified substances covered by certain environmental statutes must be reported to ERNS.[2] For each spill or release of a toxic substance, the ERNS database reports: (a) the date and place where each discharge occurred; (b) the substance spilled; (c) the affected medium (for example, air); (d) the number of fatalities, people injured and evacuated from a facility; and (e) the estimated damage to property (in dollars).

The ERNS database contains the quantity of chemicals released in each spill event, but because this variable has many missing values we prefer to work with spill frequencies, focusing on two alternative dependent variables in our econometric equations: (a) the number of spills of all CERCLA-listed chemicals per state per year (from 1987 to 1995); and (b) the (presumably more homogeneous) subset of those spills in (a) that caused at least one injury. We include in our counts only the spills and accidents occurring at a fixed facility to avoid the complexity of the federal, state and local regulations affecting chemical transport (Wentz 1989). We analyse aggregate counts per state per year because the information reported in ERNS is in most cases insufficient to identify the party responsible for the discharge, precluding individual-event or firm-level analyses.

The spills data were merged with manufacturing, mining and population variables (from assorted sources) and variables describing the liability structure in the state and its evolution over time (USEPA 1989, 1990, 1991; ELI 1993, 1995). This produced a panel data set following the 50 states plus the District of Columbia for nine years (1987–95).

Spill Equations

Spills of CERCLA substances are relatively common, and can be reasonably modelled using a regression equation where the dependent variable is log spill counts. The regression model is:

$$\ln y_{it} = \mathbf{x}_{it}\beta + S_{it}\gamma + \mathbf{A}_{it}\delta + \varepsilon_{it}, \tag{5.4}$$

where the vector $\mathbf{x}$ contains state-level socio-economic variables; β, γ and δ are vectors of parameters; S and $\mathbf{A}$ are a strict liability indicator and other associated policy variables, respectively; ε is the error term, and i and t denote the state and year, respectively.

Since chemical spills involving injuries are relatively rare events, for this variable we fit Poisson equations where state i's probability of experiencing y severe spills in year t is:

$$\Pr(Y_{it} = y_{it}) = \frac{e^{-\lambda_{it}}\lambda_{it}^{y_{it}}}{y_{it}!} \tag{5.5}$$

with $\lambda_{it} = \exp(\mathbf{x}_{it}\beta + S_{it}\gamma + \mathbf{A}_{it}\delta)$. When appropriate, equation (5.5) is amended to obtain a negative binomial model, which relaxes the Poisson model's assumption that mean and variances are both equal to λ_{it}.[3]

We initially run regressions that include the liability policy variables in the right-hand side of the model to see if they explain spills beyond what is predicted by the intensity of manufacturing and state socio-demographics. It is clear that these initial regressions assume that the presence of strict liability is exogenous to the dependent variable. We subsequently relax this assumption and allow the strict liability variable to be endogenous with the dependent variable, first in fixed-effects models and then by using instrumental-variable estimation techniques.

Liability Structure Equation

If the liability structure within a state is endogenous with the spill outcome, it is necessary to specify an additional equation expressing (the probability of) adoption of strict liability as a function of a set of instruments. Once this additional equation is estimated, a two-stage procedure yielding a consistent estimate of γ is obtained by replacing S in the right-hand side of equations (5.4) or (5.5) with a state's predicted probability of adopting strict liability.

To build the equation explaining the presence or absence of strict liability adoption, we assume that a state adopts the liability structure that maximizes the net benefits of its hazardous waste clean-up programme, defined as in the second section. The net benefits of regime k are expressed as:

$$NB_k = \mathbf{w}\alpha_k + \eta_k, \tag{5.6}$$

where the coefficients are allowed to vary with the liability structure ($k \in$ {S(trict), N(egligence)}), **w** is a set of variables influencing the state's benefit–cost calculus, and η is a standard normal error term.

Because the net benefits of adoption of a liability regime are not observed, we cannot estimate (5.6) directly. What we do observe is whether the state mini-Superfund programme imposes strict or negligence-based liability. A state's adoption of strict liability, therefore, implies that it deems its expected net benefits to be greater than the net benefits from a programme without that provision, leading to a probit equation.[4]

INDEPENDENT VARIABLES AND INSTRUMENTS

Determinants of Spill Severity

The vector **x** in equations (5.4) and (5.5) includes state socio-economic variables thought to influence aggregate spill rates and/or quantities released. Descriptive statistics for all variables are displayed in Table 5.1.

The number of toxic spills and/or the quantities released should depend on the extent of economic activity involving chemicals. We capture this using numbers of production units in the industrial and extractive sectors in the state, divided into 'large' and 'small' plants. Although both economic theory and actual examples emphasize that the incentives of liability may be diluted when firms' assets are limited, in our empirical work we are forced to proxy for firm size using numbers of employees to define small and large establishments. Data on the number of firms by asset size are not available at the state level. In this chapter, we report results obtained by defining small establishments as those with fewer than 20 employees.[5]

Smaller and larger firms may contribute to pollution releases at a different rate for various reasons. On the one hand, firms with limited assets, sheltered from liability, have less of an incentive to take precautions against pollution releases. On the other hand, larger firms or plants may use and store large amounts of chemicals or hazardous wastes, with the potential to accidentally discharge larger quantities. In addition, Occupational Safety and Health Administration (OSHA) requires large companies handling dangerous chemicals or hazardous wastes to prepare formal plans to handle emergencies, but waives this requirements for smaller plants (Wagner 1999).

To further capture the toxics riskiness of manufacturing processes in the state, we include among the regressors the amount of hazardous waste generated per capita in the state.

The key regressor STRICT is a dummy indicator for whether the state mini-Superfund programme prescribes strict liability in any given year. Figure 5.1

Table 5.1   Descriptive statistics

Label (if used in later tables)	Description	Mean	Std. dev.
	Spills of CERCLA substances per state per year	99.28	158.75
	Spills of CERCLA substances with injuries per state per year	3.03	5.35
	Number of mining establishments in the state	583.55	1091.20
	Number of manufacturing establishments in the state	7143.69	8456.48
	Number of manufacturing establishments in the state with fewer than 20 employees	4763.28	5747.49
	Number of mining establishments in the state with fewer than 20 employees	466.80	912.28
EXPEND	State expenditure per capita (1987 dollars)	10096.00	11701.00
ENVPROG	Percentage of state budget on environmental programmes	1.86	1.19
SITES	Suspected/actual hazardous waste sites in the state	1460.01	3821.68
LESSTHS	Percent of adults 25 years and older who lack high school diploma	23.77	5.54
HIGHSCH	Percent of adults 25 years and older whose highest educational attainment is completing high school	30.60	3.64
LPOPDENS	Log of population density ('000 residents per sq. mile)	0.43	0.08
ENVORG	Number of in-state members of three major environmental organizations per 1000 residents	8.49	3.54
HAZWASTE	Quantity of hazardous waste per capita generated in the state ('000 lb)	1.58	2.91
STRICT	State programme imposes strict liability	0.68	0.47
CITSUIT	State programme allows citizen suit	0.31	0.46
PUNDAMAG	Punitive damages charged to uncooperative firms	0.56	0.50
VICTCOMP	Firms required to compensate victims of release	0.24	0.43
CORTEFF	Percentage civil cases disposed of out of total civil cases filed	95.25	9.73
PCTDEMPR	Percentage votes for Democratic candidate in most recent presidential elections	48.04	9.14
LAWYERS	Number of lawyers working on state mini-Superfund cases per million state residents	1.38	1.73

shows that many, but not all, of the eastern states passed strict liability
provisions relatively early, shortly after the passage of CERCLA. In some states,
such as New Jersey and Rhode Island, strict liability has been in place since
the late 1970s. In the industrial Midwest, some states adopted liability relatively
early (Ohio, Missouri), others later (Michigan), and some repealed strict liability
in the mid-1990s.[6] Mountain states (presumably those where the mining
industry is politically powerful, or where the state legislature did not deem strict
liability appropriate to handle contaminated sites, many of which are associated
with past mining activities) generally have elected not to implement strict
liability, but there are some exceptions (such as Montana).

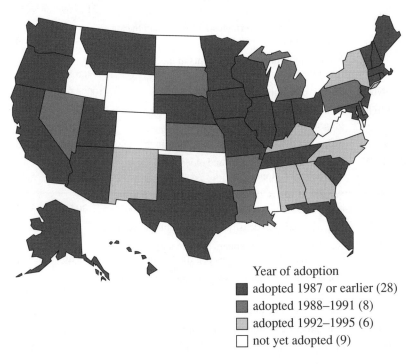

Year of adoption
■ adopted 1987 or earlier (28)
■ adopted 1988–1991 (8)
□ adopted 1992–1995 (6)
□ not yet adopted (9)

Figure 5.1   State adoption of strict liability

In most cases, liability standards are subject to interpretation by the state
courts, based on the statutory language and common law arguments advanced
by the state (ELI 1995). States upholding strict liability typically give enforcement authority to the state agency, making it possible for the agency to issue
unilateral orders to responsible parties and to refer cases with recalcitrant
responsible parties to the state general attorney. The burden of proof is placed
on the defendant, the firm alleged to be responsible for the release.

By contrast, under negligence-based liability the burden of proof is on the plaintiff (the state agency), which must show that the responsible party committed a negligent, reckless or intentionally wrongful act. The negligence standards are established by the courts on a case-by-case basis. It is generally argued that under negligence-based liability the state agency will have to spend more resources investigating the intent of parties involved at a contaminated site, and will face a smaller universe of parties to which liability may attach. This may lessen the incentive of firms to take care (ELI 1995).

While many responsible parties avoid litigation by reaching consent agreements with the state agency, under either liability regime the incentives faced by firms should be influenced by the expected outcome of litigation. This may depend on the aggressiveness of the state agency in prosecuting polluters; on the perceived efficiency of the state court system; and on the perception of whether the courts tend to rule in favour of the defendant or the plaintiff in toxic tort lawsuits.

We measure the prosecutorial aggressiveness of the state as the number of lawyers working on state Superfund cases per million residents. The state court efficiency is captured by the ratio of all civil cases disposed of to all civil cases filed in any given year (data from *Court Statistics Project*, National Center for Court Statistics, Williamsburg, VA). Lacking better statistics on state court rulings, we assume that state court preferences towards business activity and environmental quality are similar to the state's preferences. We proxy these preferences with the percentage of votes for the Democratic candidate in the most recent presidential elections (PCTDEMPR), a widely used political variable.

Additional explanatory variables include population density and membership, per 1000 residents, in any of three major environmental organizations. These factors may encourage firms to avoid releases for fear that they will cause more severe damages or be reported to authorities by community residents. They may also influence the reporting of spills to ERNS, implying that the sign of their coefficients is uncertain *a priori*.

How a firm responds to the imposition of liability should depend in part on its ability to deflect payment of some or all of the damages to its insurance companies. Unfortunately, data on pollution insurance purchased by firms and on claims paid to firms in relation to spills and contaminated sites are not available. This forces us to omit insurance variables from the right-hand side of the spills equation. In practice, we believe that such an omission will not make much difference: if firms with pollution insurance shirked from taking care to avoid releases of pollutants, the insurance providers would react by raising the standards of care required for firms to buy pollution insurance (see Gastel 1998).

Determinants of Liability Structure

The variables **w** influencing the liability policy and serving as instruments for it include predetermined economic and political characteristics of the state.

Specifically, we proxy uncontrolled toxics with the numbers of existing hazardous waste sites, past spills of CERCLA chemicals, and past injuries in spills of CERCLA chemicals. The numbers of small and large production units should capture both the toxics risk as well as the state's likely costs in running the remediation programme, and thus affect the state's choice of liability structure.

We proxy the size of the exposed population using the state's population density. We also include state residents' educational attainment levels, because they are likely to affect the public's perception of the hazardous waste problem in the state and the value of avoiding the illnesses associated with exposure to hazardous wastes (Tolley *et al.* 1994). Without information about the administrative costs of the state hazardous waste programmes, we assume that a programme's net benefits are influenced by the state resources available to the 'mini-Superfund' programme, here measured by state expenditures per capita and the percentage of state budgets dedicated to environmental programmes (from Hall and Kerr 1992).

Finally, the state legislature's net benefit calculus may be influenced by interest group pressure, attitudes of residents towards environmental quality, and attitudes of the state agencies towards the environment. These considerations suggest that political variables, such as the percentage of popular votes for the Democratic candidate in the most recent presidential election, be considered among the determinants of net benefits.

RESULTS

Preliminary Data Analyses

Our first order of business is to compare the incidence of spill events across states with and without strict liability in place. In states with strict liability, the average number of spills of CERCLA substances of any severity is 114.22 (standard error around the mean 10.69), and spills involving at least one injury average about 3.57 per year (s.e. 0.36). In states that uphold negligence-based liability, there is an average of 70 accidental releases per year (s.e. 4.55), with 1.97 involving injuries (s.e. 0.17). The differences are statistically significant.

When our observations are divided into three sets to reflect 'early adopters' (states that adopted strict liability prior to 1987), non-adopters and 'recent adopters' (states that adopted strict liability between 1987 and 1995), these findings are essentially confirmed. Early adopters typically have the most numerous spills, non-adopters the least, and recent adopters score in between. Interestingly, among recent adopters, the average frequencies and count of injuries are not statistically different before and after adoption of strict liability.

While it is tempting to interpret these results as linking strict liability with more numerous releases of pollutants, one needs to keep in mind that there are important differences across states with and without strict liability provisions: states that have adopted strict liability at some point over the 1987–95 period are typically more densely populated, participate more in environmental organizations and have a stronger manufacturing base.

Initial Regressions

The results of several variants of regressions (5.4) and (5.5), all of which include year dummies, are reported in Tables 5.2 and 5.3. Columns (A) of Tables 5.2 and 5.3 present our basic specification, in which the indicator for strict liability is included in the right-hand side and treated as exogenous.

In columns (B), we add three more dummy variables describing other features of the state mini-Superfund programmes. These indicate the presence of provisions for victim compensation in the programme; whether a state may impose punitive damages if it is forced itself to initiate the clean-up; and whether the statute allows private citizens to initiate actions against parties responsible for toxic releases lawsuits. The first two variables capture additional aspects of firms' exposure to liability. The citizen-suit provision is intended to help account for a firm's probability of being targeted by the state agency.

Treating strict liability as an exogenous regressor, we would conclude that the frequency of all CERCLA spills and that of CERCLA-listed substances with injuries increase with the number of small manufacturing units and are relatively insensitive to the number of large units.

Spill counts rise with the quantity of hazardous waste generated, whereas population density appears to be positively associated with the frequency of all CERCLA spills, and negatively associated with the incidence of the more severe spills. Perhaps this reflects the prevalence of reporting effects, in one case, and firms' efforts to avoid serious consequences, in the other.

The data also suggest a deterrent effect on the part of the lawyers working on state mini-Superfund cases and expeditiousness of the state courts. That the court efficiency effect is negative suggests that states are, on the whole, dominated by firms that associate lengthy litigation with increased costs, rather than with the opportunity to delay clean-up. The higher the fraction of votes for the Democratic candidate in the presidential elections, the lower the incidence of spills, although the coefficient of this regressor is significant only in the equations for spills with injuries.

Table 5.2　OLS regressions

	Base specif. (A)	Other liability features (B)	State fixed effects (C)	Endogenous liability[a] (A)	Switching regression model[a] (C) Strict liability	Negligence
Constant	−0.8021 (−1.572)	−0.6502 (−1.251)	−22.4239 (−2.283)	−1.3029 (−2.119)	−1.3994 (−2.179)	−4.3908 (−1.296)
Log manuf. firms 20+ emp.	0.0784 (0.576)	0.0595 (0.431)	0.8036 (1.496)	0.0443 (0.255)	0.0661 (0.415)	1.3662 (3.596)
Log manuf. firms 20 or fewer	0.4090 (2.755)	0.4259 (2.823)	1.1269 (1.145)	0.7341 (4.112)	0.7369 (4.350)	−0.6829 (−1.990)
Log mining firms 20+ employees	0.1203 (1.862)	0.1548 (2.313)	−0.0707 (−0.555)			
Log mining firms 20 or fewer	0.1900 (2.910)	0.1564 (2.310)	0.3630 (1.376)			
HAZWASTE	0.0316 (2.249)	0.0330 (2.333)		0.0617 (4.014)	0.0724 (2.669)	0.0750 (2.478)
LPOPDENS	0.0874 (2.105)	0.1001 (2.352)	−2.4850 (−2.109)	−0.0503 (−1.124)	0.0024 (0.047)	−0.4681 (−1.599)
ENVORG	−0.0490 (−3.648)	−0.0420 (−3.056)		−0.0699 (−4.243)	−0.0922 (−4.283)	0.0536 (1.629)
Strict liability dummy	0.1864 (2.523)	0.1778 (2.234)	−0.0356 (−0.393)			
Citizen suit allowed dummy		0.1509 (2.401)				
Punitive damages		0.1090 (1.277)				
Victim compensation		−0.1344 (−1.539)				
Predictor for strict liability				−0.2686 (−1.899)		
LAYWERS	−0.0059 (−0.304)	−0.0103 (−0.532)	0.0123 (0.689)	0.0071 (0.318)	−0.0304 (−1.190)	0.0401 (1.068)
CORTEFF	−0.1523 (−0.479)	−0.2525 (−0.792)	−0.0723 (−0.307)	−0.2330 (−0.595)	−0.0503 (−0.170)	0.9293 (1.177)
PCTDEMPR	−0.7049 (−1.097)	−0.7976 (−1.222)	−0.1289 (−0.107)	−0.7964 (−1.033)	−0.9432 (−1.243)	2.7289 (2.219)
Sample size	362	0.7394	362	313	313	
Adj. R square	0.7345	0.7394	0.9082	0.6563		

Notes:
[a]　Heteroscedasticity-corrected t statistics.
Dependent variable: Log CERCLA spills. T statistics in parentheses. All specifications include year dummies.

Table 5.3   Poisson regressions

	Base specif. (A)	Other liability features (B)	Negative binomial (C)	State fixed effects (D)	Endogenous liability[a] (E)	Switching regression model[a] (F)	
						Strict liability	Negligence
Constant	−6.8577 (−11.407)	−6.4044 (−9.581)	−5.8346 (−7.042)		−7.2083 (8.652)	−7.8248 (−9.050)	−6.4831 (−0.924)
Log manuf. firms 20+ employees	0.1079 (0.699)	0.2308 (1.351)	0.1195 (0.488)	−1.3679 (−0.978)	0.4369 (2.304)	0.2887 (1.421)	1.9901 (2.222)
Log manuf. firms 20 or fewer	0.6562 (4.104)	0.5387 (3.078)	0.5882 (2.321)	2.3522 (1.013)	0.7282 (3.898)	0.8734 (4.279)	−1.2042 (−1.491)
Log mining firms 20+ employees	0.3571 (3.884)	0.2514 (2.565)	0.1286 (1.332)	−0.3595 (−0.966)			
Log mining firms 20 or fewer	−0.0634 (−0.749)	0.0369 (0.411)	0.1134 (1.178)	−0.1901 (−0.296)			
HAZWASTE	0.0096 (0.596)	0.0139 (0.843)	0.0260 (1.047)		0.0567 (3.064)	0.0494 (2.195)	0.1117 (2.242)
LPOPDENS	−0.0751 (−1.406)	−0.0802 (−1.396)	−0.0049 (−0.065)	−1.1238 (−0.375)	−0.2403 (−3.260)	−0.1651 (−2.207)	−0.4978 (−0.699)
ENVORG	0.0477 (3.159)	0.0666 (3.771)	0.0142 (0.612)		0.0643 (2.531)	0.0746 (2.914)	0.0187 (0.333)
Strict liability dummy	0.3296 (4.179)	0.2302 (2.475)	0.2860 (2.600)	−0.2331 (−0.980)			
Citizen suit allowed dummy		0.0450 (0.592)					
Punitive damages		0.0749 (0.804)					
Victim compensation		0.0951 (0.976)					
Predictor for strict liability					−0.3155 (−1.645)		
LAYWERS	−0.0776 (−2.207)	−0.0964 (−2.685)	−0.0574 (−1.296)	0.0591 (0.597)	−0.0805 (−1.566)	−0.0902 (−1.305)	0.0888 (1.163)
CORTEFF	−0.0031 (−0.008)	0.0832 (0.202)	−0.1484 (−0.245)	1.2669 (1.880)	−0.2299 (−0.365)	0.3025 (0.482)	0.2320 (0.108)
PCTDEMPR	−1.5401 (−2.237)	−4.0194 (−4.405)	−1.3908 (−1.459)	−8.4698 (−2.039)	−4.0720 (−3.447)	−4.5019 (−3.522)	−0.0397 (−0.007)
Sample size	362	362	362	362	313	313	
Log likelihood	−703.58	−694.32	−669.64	−511.26	−637.89	−610.81	

Notes:
[a] Heteroscedasticity-consistent t statistics.
Dependent variable: number of spills with at least one injury. T statistics in parentheses. All specifications include year dummies.

Most importantly, the strict liability effect is positive and significant. All else remaining the same, a state with strict liability experiences 20 per cent more spills of CERCLA chemicals and 39 per cent more spills of the kind involving injuries than a comparable state maintaining negligence-based liability. Including the other three policy variables has little effect on this coefficient.

Estimating a negative binomial model to address the potential for overdispersion of severe spills does not change the strict liability result: the coefficient of the strict liability indicator remains positive and significant in column (C) of Table 5.3. A likelihood ratio test rejects the Poisson model in favour of the negative binomial,[7] but the two models remain relatively close in terms of estimated coefficients. The coefficient of the strict liability regressor is pegged at 0.2860, which is within 13 per cent of the coefficient in the comparable Poisson equation.

Interpreting Results

Why is strict liability positively associated with the frequency of chemical spills, even after controlling for economic activity, population characteristics and state agency and courts? We offer four possible explanations for this striking finding.

First, strict liability may have triggered behavioural responses in firms that result in less care and more severe accidents. A 1987 US General Accounting Office (GAO) study reports insurance industry assertions that 'CERCLA's standards of liability ... have reduced the availability of pollution insurance' and that '[strict] liability standards undermine incentives [of firms] to exercise due care to prevent pollution, because the standard of care is not related to the potential for liability'. This view is not unanimous, since elsewhere in the GAO study, industry representatives are quoted as saying that 'the standards of liability have in fact increased the standard of care taken by the industry'.

A second explanation is that strict liability *per se* is not responsible for the greater spill severity and injuries, but is correlated with omitted factors that are. We respecified our equations to include fixed effects to see whether omitted state-specific factors drive the result. Insignificant coefficients for the strict-liability dummy in the fixed-effects models provide evidence in favour of this explanation.

The fixed-effects regressions, reported in column (C) of Table 5.2 and column (D) of Table 5.3, indeed result in insignificant coefficients for the strict liability dummy. It is striking that these coefficients are negative and – at least in the equation for severe spills – sufficiently large in magnitude (–0.23) to prompt us to wonder by how much they would change were we to explicitly model strict liability as endogenous. The coefficients of most of the other variables are insignificant.[8]

In what follows, we investigate our two remaining explanations for the positive association between spill severity and strict liability, namely that the strict liability dummy may be (econometrically) endogenous with spill frequency, and, finally, that riskier industrial activities may have devolved, upon the institution of strict liability, to smaller firms that were sheltered from full liability and hence have little incentive to invest in care.

Endogenous Liability

As earlier explained, we estimate a model that explicitly allows for endogeneity of spill frequency and liability laws by using a two-stage procedure. Results for the first-stage probit equation for states' imposition of strict liability are reported in Table 5.4, where the dependent variable is the presence/absence of strict liability in state i in year t (with t ranging from 1988 to 1995)[9] and all independent variables are lagged one year.

Table 5.4 shows that the numbers of National Priorities List (NPL) sites and non-priority sites in the state are positively associated with the likelihood of imposing strict liability, although the respective coefficients are not statistically significant. Importantly, the past frequencies of spills of CERCLA chemicals and the past severity of such spills (the number of injuries) are positively and strongly associated with adoption of strict liability, confirming that strict liability provisions are passed in response to an underlying tendency to experience numerous and potentially severe releases of pollutants into the environment.

The more numerous a state's small manufacturing plants and its large mining establishments, the less likely it is to have strict liability laws. States with a preponderance of small firms may anticipate the difficulty of getting such firms to pay for clean-up under strict liability, and deem strict liability better suited to pollution problems arising from their manufacturing sector than from their mining activities.

Of the remaining variables, only education seems to have an effect: states with relatively low educational attainment levels appear less likely to impose strict liability. Although many variables are insignificant, probably because of collinearity between the independent variables, the model fits the data well, correctly predicting over 79 per cent of the observations.

When the predicted probability that strict liability is in place in state i in year t, $\hat{\Phi}_{it} = \Phi(\mathbf{w}_{it}\hat{\alpha})$, is entered in the equations for spill frequencies, replacing the strict liability dummy, the coefficients of strict liability become *negative* and significant at the 10 per cent level or better.[10,11]

Column (D) of Table 5.2, shows that $\hat{\gamma}$ is equal to -0.27 in the equation for all CERCLA spills, implying that, all else remaining the same, imposition of strict liability lowers the incidence of spills by 24 per cent.[12] The model predicts

Table 5.4   Probit equation of strict liability adoption

	Coefficient (t statistic)
Constant	1.1163 (0.44)
Log final NPL sites (lagged)	0.0946 (0.53)
Log state sites (lagged)	0.0486 (0.55)
Log spills of all CERCLA substances (lagged)	0.5050 (3.04)
Log total injuries in CERCLA spills (lagged)	0.2887 (3.35)
Log population density (lagged)	−0.0802 (−0.59)
Log manuf. firms 20+ employees (lagged)	0.5567 (1.24)
Log manuf. firms 20 or fewer employees (lagged)	−0.9879 (−1.68)
Log mining firms 20+ employees (lagged)	−1.1121 (−1.68)
Log mining firms 20 or fewer employees (lagged)	0.2948 (1.16)
HIGHSCH (lagged)	0.0448 (1.32)
LESSTHS (lagged)	−0.0636 (−2.89)
Log state expenditure per capita (lagged)	0.2996 (0.89)
% state budget for environmental programmes (lagged)	−0.0971 (−1.11)
% votes for Democratic candidate in presidential elections (lagged)	1.9228 (1.20)
Sample size	365
Log likelihood	−149.97

that a representative strict liability state can be expected to experience on average 98.30 spills per year (s.e. 5.67). Were strict liability removed, the number of spills would rise to 126.79.

Similarly, column (E) of Table 5.3 shows that the instrumental-variable procedure predicts that a state would experience 28 per cent fewer severe spills if strict liability were introduced.[13] We conclude that, rather than causing an increase in spill rates, strict liability was introduced by states *already* experiencing numerous chemical spills or having a substantial contaminated site problem, and has helped lessen such problems. This is confirmed by the results of a regression (not reported) limited to the subsample of states which at some point passed strict liability provisions. A regressor counting the 'years since strict liability was adopted' has a significant, negative effect, showing that spill figures slowly decline over time (at a rate of 4–5 per cent a year) once strict liability is in place.

At the same time, small manufacturing plants continue to contribute to spills incidence at a higher rate than larger plants, and are the main reason why spills remain more numerous in strict-liability states. One concern is that, despite the reasonable R^2 (0.65), the systems of equations slightly overpredict spills in negligence-based states and underpredict spills in strict-liability states. This prompted us to investigate structural changes across the two liability regimes.

Structural Changes

If the different liability structure triggers different behavioural responses in firms and alters the effects of state resident characteristics and of the variables measuring the likely outcome of litigation, a switching regression model with endogenous switching is intuitively appealing. For spills of all CERCLA substances, we assume that:

$$\ln y_{it} = \mathbf{x}_{it}\beta_N + \varepsilon_{it}^N \text{ if } S_{it} = 0 \text{ (under negligence)}, \tag{5.7}$$

$$\ln y_{it} = \mathbf{x}_{it}\beta_S + \varepsilon_{it}^S \text{ if } S_{it} = 1 \text{ (under strict liability)}, \tag{5.8}$$

with $S_{it} = 1$ if $S_{it}^* = \mathbf{w}_{it}\alpha + \eta_{it}$, and 0 otherwise, and η jointly normally distributed with ε^N and ε^S.

We estimate the model in two steps by limited-information maximum likelihood. In the first step, we fit a probit model of strict liability, using the estimated coefficients to form the inverse Mills' ratio, M_{it}, with $M_{it} = \phi(\mathbf{w}_{it}\hat{\alpha})/\Phi(\mathbf{w}_{it}\hat{\alpha})$ if $S_{it} = 1$, and $M_{it} = \phi(\mathbf{w}_{it}\hat{\alpha})/[1 - \Phi(\mathbf{w}_{it}\hat{\alpha})]$ if $S_{it} = 0$. In the second step, two separate OLS regressions are run, one for the observations with $S = 0$ and one for the sample with $S = 1$, each of which adds M_{it} from the first step to the list of original regressors.

For the count of severe spills, we fit the switching regime Poisson model suggested by Greene (1995). Without making any assumptions about the joint distribution of severe spill frequency and net benefits of the liability regime, we assume that (a) the marginal probability distribution of the liability regime is that of a Bernoulli variable with probability of strict liability equal to $\Phi(\mathbf{w}_{it}\alpha)$; and (b) the probability distribution of total injuries, conditional on the liability regime, is a Poisson with expected value (and variance) equal to:

$$\lambda_{it}^N = \exp(\mathbf{x}_{it}\beta_N + \theta_N \cdot M_{it}) \text{ if } S_{it} = 0 \text{ (under negligence), and} \qquad (5.9)$$

$$\lambda_{it}^S = \exp(\mathbf{x}_{it}\beta_S - \theta_S \cdot M_{it}) \text{ if } S_{it} = 1 \text{ (under strict liability)}, \qquad (5.10)$$

where M_{it} is defined as before, and estimation is carried out in two steps.[14]

Results for the switching regression models are reported in Tables 5.2 and 5.3, columns (E) and (F), respectively. For both the broader group and the narrower definition of spill events, in states with strict liability the number of spills is unrelated to the number of larger manufacturing establishments, while increasing with the number of small establishments. By contrast, in states imposing negligence-based liability, the numbers of larger manufacturing establishments is positively associated with chemical spill injuries.

The magnitude of these coefficients suggests that in strict-liability states, a 1 per cent rise (fall) in the number of small plants results in a 0.74 per cent rise (fall) in the number of accidents. This can be contrasted with the prediction that a 1 per cent change in the number of larger plants in a negligence-based state results in a 1.37 per cent change, of the same sign, in the number of spill events. No such large-firm effect is seen in strict liability states. The percentage change in *severe* spills is even larger, the elasticity with respect to small plants being 0.87 in the strict-liability regime, and that with respect to large plants being 1.99 in the negligence-based regime.

This provides support for the hypothesis that strict liability may have induced spin-offs or delegation of risky production activities from larger to smaller firms in hopes of avoiding liability. Strict liability may indeed carry some perverse effects with regard to firm behaviour, and these tendencies appear to be fairly widespread. We conjecture that the reason why severe spills are associated with larger plants in states maintaining negligence-based liability may be the scale on which chemicals are used in such plants. Among other things, the association between large plants and injuries in negligence-based liability states rules out worker safety requirements that vary with plant size as an explanation for our findings.

The models predict that a representative strict liability state has a total of 100 spills per year (s.e. 6.38), while a representative negligence-based state has 75.64 (s.e. 4.14). When attention is restricted to severe spills, the respective predictions (3.95, with a s.e. of 0.39, and 2.21, with a s.e. of 0.18) are even closer to the actual averages (3.97 and 2.22, respectively), suggesting that these models fit the data well.

Additional Checks

To check the robustness of the results, we also investigated the number of injuries associated with spills, a proxy for spill severity, since quantities released are often missing. The liability regime dummy was never significant, but injuries were found to increase at a higher rate with the number of small firms, especially under strict liability, whereas under negligence-based liability it is larger firms that appear to be associated with injury outcomes. This is consistent with our earlier results for spill counts.

Have the numbers of smaller firms actually increased in response to the introduction of strict liability at the state level, following the pattern described by Ringleb and Wiggins (1990)? These authors find that after strict liability was instituted for long-term health effects on workers occupationally exposed to hazardous substances, many small firms were attracted into the industries with the highest potential liability. Could a similar effect be at play here, with a proliferation of smaller businesses in states that impose strict liability on responsible parties at hazardous waste sites?

We do not believe so. We reached this conclusion after we separated the data into the three subsamples representing 'early adopters', 'non-adopters' and 'recent adopters' of strict liability. We reasoned that if wealthier firms are truly divesting into smaller companies to escape liability, then the ratio of the smaller firms to larger firms should have increased in the presence of strict liability.

We found no evidence supporting this hypothesis. First, both small and large establishments are more numerous in states which impose strict liability on polluters. Second, the ratio of small plants to large plants varies across industries and, if anything, appears to be higher in the states that maintain negligence-based liability. The values of this ratio in states that recently adopted strict liability are generally intermediate between those of early adopters and non-adopters. There are, on average, 2.39 small manufacturing plants for each large plant in states that adopted strict liability before 1987, 2.89 in states that continue to rely on negligence-based liability, and 2.19 in states that passed strict liability provisions between 1987 and 1995.

When attention is restricted to establishments in the chemical and petroleum-refining industries (which traditionally handle large quantities of chemicals, create large amounts of hazardous wastes, and are held as responsible parties at many Superfund sites), these figures are 1.75, 2.31 and 1.89, respectively. In the instruments industry (reported in Ringleb and Wiggins 1990 to have the highest levels of workers' exposure to carcinogens), they are equal to 2.03, 2.98 and 1.88.

To sum up, our results suggest that small firms may engage in riskier activities, but provide no widespread evidence that corporate structures have evolved to exploit limitations in small-firms' exposures to strict environmental liability.

CONCLUSIONS

We have estimated models of chemical-spill frequencies to see if they are influenced by state environmental policies based on liability. We find that unintended pollution releases are – all else remaining the same – reduced by imposition of strict liability. It appears that states have adopted strict liability because of their tendency to experience numerous spill events, and have managed subsequently to reduce spill events over time thanks to strict liability.

We find evidence consistent with the hypothesis that firms have developed behavioural responses to avoid liability when they are strictly liable for releases of hazardous chemicals into the environment. In states with strict liability, greater spill severity and frequency are associated with smaller production units (our proxy for firms with fewer assets), whereas this association is not present in states following negligence-based liability.

Two possible explanations can be produced for this finding: (a) in a strict-liability regime, firms deliberately select their corporate structures and asset levels to avoid liability; or (b) small firms have tended to specialize in riskier processes, while keeping their investment in safety at a minimum.

The first explanation suggests that the number of small firms to each large firm might be expected to increase in states that impose strict liability of polluters. We did not find any evidence of such a tendency: if anything, the ratio of small to large establishments tended to be lower (often declining over time) in states upholding strict-liability provisions in their clean-up laws, even in the manufacturing sectors most heavily involved with the use of toxic chemicals, generation of hazardous waste, and nomination as responsible parties at contaminated sites. The small-firm phenomenon may therefore be due to explanation (b), with the caveat that whatever restructuring of production processes was spurred by the imposition of strict liability on polluters at the state level, it does not bear on the numbers of small plants.

NOTES

1. A well-known example is Allied Chemical's 1973 decision to subcontract its production of the pesticide Kepone to a small company, Life Sciences Products. The firm was owned and run by two former Allied Chemical employees, and was to purchase raw materials from and

sell Kepone to Allied Chemical. It was soon discovered that both Life Sciences and Allied Chemical were illegally discharging Kepone in the James River, and that Kepone dust covered the floor of the Life Sciences plant and contaminated its indoor air. Air emissions from the plant occasionally halted the traffic in the surrounding neighbourhood and irritated the skin and eyes of the employees of a nearby ice distribution plant. The EPA determined in 1975 that the Life Sciences plant should be dismantled and its site decontaminated, and assessed Life Sciences a fine of $3.8 million. The fine was never paid, since at the time of the assessment the firm was only worth $32 (Wentz 1989). Boyd (1996) cites another example of how the option of declaring bankruptcy is always available to firms. A 1989 fish kill in Virginia alerted state officials to widespread contamination originating from the Kim-Stan landfill. The facility was charged fines of $1.5 million, but filed for bankruptcy and ended up paying only $100,000.

2. See Alberini and Austin (1999b) for reporting requirements and criteria.
3. In a negative binomial λ_{it} is no longer a fixed parameter, but a draw from a gamma distribution with parameters (γ_{it}, δ), with $\gamma_{it} = \exp(x_{it}\beta)$, while δ is the same across sample units and over time, and the draws λ_{it} are independent over time. The negative binomial model allows for overdispersion, a problem frequently encountered in practice, and reduces to the Poisson as δ tends to infinity, or $(1/\delta)$ tends to zero.
4. In reality, the state legislature does not pick the liability structure alone, but in concert with other liability and programme attributes meant to influence firms' exposure to clean-up and damages claims. For example, the state may uphold joint-and-several liability, and impose punitive damages on recalcitrant firms. This suggests that k should really denote one of the many possible combinations of indicators and real-valued variables capturing liability and other attributes of the state's programme, and that the appropriate econometric model is a multinomial logit model explaining the choice of one combination of attributes over all other possible combinations. However, Alberini and Austin (1999a) show that a multinomial logit model explaining adoption of several liability attributes (strict v. negligence-based liability; proportional v. joint-and-several liability; presence or absence of provisions authorizing punitive damages against recalcitrant responsible parties) can be collapsed to a simple binary model describing just the presence or absence of strict liability.
5. Although establishments with fewer than 20 employees account for only about 2 per cent of the total value of shipments from manufacturing firms, they are very numerous, making up about two-thirds of the total number of establishments. We repeated our analyses for other breakdowns into small and large establishments (for example, establishments with fewer or more than 50 or 100 employees), and obtained qualitatively similar results.
6. In the early 1990s, Ohio briefly reverted to a policy based on negligence, reinstituting strict liability in its mini-Superfund programme by 1995. Illinois repealed strict liability in 1995.
7. The coefficient $(1/\delta)$ is estimated at 0.19, and the likelihood ratio statistic is equal to 67.88, falling in the 1 per cent rejection region of the chi square with one degree of freedom.
8. An F statistic equal to 12.67 rejects the pooled data model in favour of the fixed effects at the conventional significance levels.
9. Our probit model treats all observations as serially independent within a given state. Alberini and Austin (1999a) fit fixed-effects logit equations and obtain qualitatively similar results.
10. Replacing S_{it} with $\hat{\Phi}_{it}$ introduces heteroscedasticity in the equations for spill frequency, and requires appropriately correcting the standard errors of the estimates, following the general expressions in Murphy and Topel (1985). Unfortunately, neither the LIMDEP packaged routine nor our own GAUSS code were able to produce finite estimates of the corrected covariance matrix of the estimates for the Poisson model, and we were forced to use the 'all-purpose' heteroscedasticity-robust covariance matrix calculated as $V^{-1} \cdot I \cdot V^{-1}$, where V is the outer product of the first derivatives of the Poisson log likelihood function, and I is the information matrix (Fahrmeir and Tutz 1994).
11. Of the alternative features of state clean-up programmes, only the strict liability policy is retained in these specifications, due to the difficulty of modelling several policy dummies as endogenous, and to the little effect that the other policy dummies seemed to have on spill outcomes.
12. A formal test of the null hypothesis that the strict liability indicator is exogenous with respect to log CERCLA spills rejects the null at the 1 per cent significance level.

13. In equation (E) of Table 5.3 the difference between the fit of the Poisson and that of the negative binomial model becomes blurred, and a likelihood ratio tests finds the Poisson equation acceptable. In both the Poisson and linear regression models small and large mining establishments were found insignificant, and were hence dropped.

14. As before, care must be taken to derive the covariance matrix that corrects for the use of estimates in the second-stage Poisson regression. Formulae for the corrected covariance matrix of the Poisson coefficients, derived following Murphy and Topel (1985), are presented in Greene (1995). Once again, however, we encountered difficulties in applying these formulae, and were forced to use the heteroscedasticity-consistent covariance matrix $V^{-1} \cdot I \cdot V^{-1}$.

REFERENCES

Alberini, Anna and David Austin (1999a), 'Off and on the liability bandwagon: explaining state adoptions of strict liability in hazardous waste programs', *Journal of Regulatory Economics* 15(1): 41–63.

Alberini, Anna and David Austin (1999b), 'Strict liability as a deterrent in toxic waste management: empirical evidence from accident and spill data', *Journal of Environmental Economics and Management* 38: 20–48.

Beard, Randolph T. (1990), 'Bankruptcy and care choice', *RAND Journal of Economics* 21(4): 626–34.

Boyd, James (1996), 'Banking on "green money": are environmental financial responsibility rules fulfilling their promise?', Resources for the Future Discussion Paper 96–26, Washington, DC, July.

Environmental Law Institute (1993), 'An analysis of state Superfund programs: 50-state study. 1995 update', prepared for the US Environmental Protection Agency, Washington, DC, December.

Environmental Law Institute (1995), 'An analysis of state Superfund programs: 50-state study. 1993 update', prepared for the US Environmental Protection Agency, Washington, DC, December.

Fahrmeir, Ludwig and Gerhard Tutz (1994), *Multivariate Statistical Modelling Based on Generalized Linear Models*, New York: Springer-Verlag.

Gastel, Ruth (1998), 'Environmental Pollution: Insurance Issues', Washington, DC: Insurance Information Association.

Greene, William H. (1995), *LIMDEP 7.0 User's Manual*, Plainview, NY: Econometric Software.

Hall, Bob and Mary Lee Kerr (1992), *The 1991–92 Green Index*, Covelo, CA: Island Press.

Murphy, Kevin M. and Robert H. Topel (1985), 'Estimation and inference in two-step econometric models', *Journal of Business and Economics Statistics* 3(4): 370–79.

Pitchford, Rohan (1995), 'How liable should a lender be? The case of judgment-proof firms and environmental risk', *American Economic Review* 85: 1171–86.

Ringleb, Al H. and Steven N. Wiggins (1990), 'Liability and large-scale, long-term hazards', *Journal of Political Economy* 98(31): 574–95.

Shavell, S. (1984), 'A model of the optimal use of liability and safety regulation', *RAND Journal of Economics* 15: 271–80.

Tietenberg, Tom H. (1989), 'Indivisible toxic torts: the economics of joint and several liability', *Land Economics* 65(4): 305–19.

Tolley, George, Donald Kenkel and Robert Fabian (eds) (1994), *Valuing Health for Policy: An Economic Approach*, Chicago: University of Chicago Press.

US Environmental Protection Agency, Office of Emergency and Remedial Response (1989), *An Analysis of State Superfund Programs: 50-State Study*, Washington, DC: US EPA.

US Environmental Protection Agency, Office of Emergency and Remedial Response (1990), *An Analysis of State Superfund Programs: 50-State Study. 1990 Update*, Washington, DC: US EPA.

US Environmental Protection Agency, Office of Emergency and Remedial Response (1991), *An Analysis of State Superfund Programs: 50-State Study. 1991 Update*, Washington, DC: US EPA.

US General Accounting Office (1987), *Hazardous Waste: Issues Surrounding Insurance Availability*, Report to the Congress, PB88–123138, Washington, DC: US Government Printing Office.

Wagner, Travis P. (1999), *The Complete Guide to Hazardous Waste Regulations: RCRA, TSCA, HMTA, OSHA*, 3rd edn, New York: John Wiley.

Wentz, Charles A. (1989), *Hazardous Waste Management*, New York: McGraw-Hill.

6. The economics of clean-up and implications for legal design

Carl V. Phillips and Richard J. Zeckhauser[*]

INTRODUCTION

Most environmental regulation depends on the setting of standards. If environmental quality falls below the standard, the responsible party is deemed to be a violator. The penalties are usually civil, though in rare cases they are criminal. In this manner, the government's role in ensuring environmental quality is analogous to its role in ensuring civil rights: punishment is to be meted out – through fines or mandates for compliance – if particular lines are crossed. In both areas, private liability actions are often the first step in identifying violations.

The civil rights approach to environmental protection departs sharply from economics-based models for environmental regulation, which are sometimes called 'second generation' regulations. One aspect of the economics-based approach is the theory that potential polluters should be given appropriate incentives to reduce pollution, whatever its current level, and that efficient pollution levels are found when the benefits of reducing pollution just equal the costs of achieving the reduction.[1] Since both incremental benefits and costs may depend on local circumstances, particular standards of quality are not sacrosanct.

Though it violates many economists' norms, the standards system does put some economic incentives into action by encouraging privately instigated litigation and liability-based damages in many situations. A strength of the system is that the incentives to avoid injuring natural resources are in some sense proportional to the level of harm avoided. An important disadvantage of the environmental liability system is that its arbitrariness, uncertainty, high transactions costs, and misguided laws (for example, the Comprehensive Environmental Response, Compensation, and Liability Act – CERCLA) keep it from achieving an appropriate balance of benefits and costs (Arrow *et al.* 1996). For one of the many overviews of these well-known limitations, see Phillips and Zeckhauser (1995).

How can economics help us do better? We address this question by considering a resource that has been injured.[2] The standard economic model of the environment assumes that cost and benefit functions are 'well behaved': that is, with quality as the independent variable, marginal cost is assumed to be increasing throughout and marginal benefit falling. The global optimization simply identifies where the two curves cross and restores the resource up to that point. Restoration should occur immediately.

The well-behaved marginal cost and benefit curves are well justified for certain classes of environmental problems, including situations where a large resource is being contaminated from multiple sources. Two good examples are air pollution in a city or fertilizer effluent in a large body of water. In such cases, the large number of possible methods for reducing pollution, when taken in the efficient order, yield an approximately continuous, upward-sloping cost curve for quality improvement. Marginal costs of clean-up are clearly increasing. Moreover, across a large region, it is reasonable to assume that marginal benefits are downward sloping.

By contrast, we focus on the far different problem of remediating an injury at a single site, say a toxic waste dump or a tarred beach. For such situations, the core assumptions of the standard theory – continuity, diminishing marginal returns to effort and quality, increasing marginal costs of production – are typically inaccurate. Instead, many resources subject to injury experience significant economies of scale in remediation, since it costs nearly as much to remedy high levels of injury as it does low levels.

The physical reality of restoring an injured resource – anything from cleaning up a Superfund site to restoring a coastal area after an oil spill, to getting lead out of the soil in an urban neighbourhood – departs from the standard model's assumptions. Clean-up is often characterized by what we label *destination-driven costs*, where the cost of restoration depends primarily on the final level of restored quality and little, if at all, on how damaged the resource was. These physical properties imply that there is no function with the 'right' marginal properties that can be solved to find the optimal level of response. In other words, clean-up costs are not convex in the amount cleaned up or in the amount of injury remediated.

The principal economic argument of this chapter is that the standard well-behaved economic model fails to capture the essence of many real world environmental situations. As a consequence, extrapolations from that model prescribe restoration efforts and instantaneous quality levels that are not appropriate.

The chapter's principal policy argument is that regulation and liability rules that are based on the standard 'well-behaved' model will inevitably be inefficient, creating the wrong incentives for protection, disposal of pollutants and restoration. For example, pristine environments may be spoiled because they start above the environmental standard; and pollutants may be spread out among many sites, in situations where concentrating them would cause less total harm.

While our concern is with costs, not benefits, poor behaviour on the benefits side, and their sequelae, are well known in environmental problems. When a resource is severely injured, human activities that depend on it may stop (or move elsewhere). If so, the marginal benefits curve for environmental quality will be poorly behaved (non-convex), falling to zero below the shut-down point, whereas standard theory would have it positive and increasing with decreases in quality (see Starrett and Zeckhauser 1971). Such shut-down possibilities make it desirable to concentrate rather than to spread pollution, and argue against the use of standards.

On the cost side, we are concerned with the shape of the cost-of-restoration curve. The standard model assumes it is smooth and that marginal cost has a convenient upward slope. This formulation has a good basis in many situations, but is misleading here. To pin down the facts, we turned to the engineering literature to assess the cost structure for cleaning up a site. That literature takes as given that restoration costs are largely destination driven, treating this as a fact that hardly needs to be mentioned. The engineering literature reports costs of cleaning up land and groundwater pollution in terms of the treatment technology and such things as the number of offset wells to drill, tons of earth to dig or gallons of water to process. A remediation effort might consist of extracting water to evaporate volatile organic chemicals, digging up and washing the soil, introducing bacteria that break down pollutants, adding chemicals to chelate metals, or any of dozens of other well-known and widely employed techniques. In most cases, neither the cost nor the end result depends substantially on the initial quantities of the pollutants, but rather on the technology employed (Holden *et al.* 1989; Nunno 1990; Vidic and Phland 1995). Methods to estimate the cost of a project entail dozens of factors, but the concentration of contamination often plays little role (though it does have indirect effects, such as the amount of protective gear that is needed, and perhaps the size of the area polluted) (Stillman 1993).[3]

Engineering discussions that address real world restorations contrast sharply with the standard well-behaved economic model. Marginal cost functions that slope smoothly upward are not to be found.

The replacement of an injured resource, either on the injured site or with another site, is a second approach to site remediation. Replacement has similar cost curve implications. It might involve removing contaminated topsoil and permanently storing it, replacing oil-covered sand on a recreational beach, or simply capping and abandoning a site and substituting another. If a water source becomes unsafe to drink, an alternative supply can be purchased; similarly, if a wetland is hopelessly injured from a toxic spill, another potential wetland can be recovered from agricultural use for some fixed cost (Parks and Kramer 1995). Replacement will sometimes be more efficient than trying to salvage a particularly badly injured site, providing more net environmental gain for less cost

(Campbell 1994). For example, when the dioxin contamination of Times Beach, Missouri, was discovered in 1982, the immediate solution was for the Superfund to pay $33 million to relocate all residents and businesses to a safer location, a cost that was independent of the quantity of the pollutant (Tietenberg 1984: 386). In replacement efforts, the total cost will vary with some measures of the size of injury (such as total area polluted), but not with others (such as the amount of contaminant per cubic foot). The level of injury will not affect the final outcome, but may have a substantial effect on the cost.

Consider an analogy outside the politically charged realm of natural resource injury, the case of a building that is injured by a fire. Up to a certain level of injury, the building will be salvaged and restored (though the last bit of smoke damage may not be repaired). Such restoration may follow the standard incremental cost assumptions. But for injury past a certain level, the building will be torn down and replaced (possibly with a design that better meets modern needs). Replacement produces economies of scale, due to an element of indivisibility. A similar principle applies to automobiles: enough damage to a car will 'total' it, resulting in its replacement. (The quality of the replacement may be higher or lower than that of the old car.) In these cases, as with optimal environmental restoration, the cost of remediation may be unrelated to the level of injuries over a wide range. There is nothing terribly unusual about these situations. Similar non-convexities and economies of scale appear in many realms of decision-making. For example, a municipality might want to expand its airport to reduce limited overcrowding, but enough congestion will lead it to build a whole new facility.

The following analysis examines the nature of optimal restoration when costs are destination driven, and examines the implications for regulatory regimes and environmental quality. The next section looks at liability-based regulation and the benefits of environmental quality. The third section looks at the cost side, and explores the nature of restoration costs, and the fourth tells how and when restoration should be undertaken when at least some costs are destination driven. Next, the implication of these findings for regulatory and liability policy are presented, suggesting an extension of the standard economic principles of environmental liability. The proposal is argued to provide a conceptual solution to the troubling problems of brownfields. This is followed by a conclusion.

LIABILITY-BASED REGULATION AND THE BENEFITS OF ENVIRONMENTAL QUALITY

The use of the liability system to control environmental quality works best when there is a single party responsible for the injury. Given that, two assumptions make the liability system's cost structure tractable. Let $V(q)$ be the total discounted value of the stream of benefits a resource produces at quality level q.[4] The standard assumptions are that:

$$\frac{\partial V(q)}{\partial q} > 0, \ \frac{\partial^2 V(q)}{\partial q^2} < 0. \qquad (6.1), (6.2)$$

That is, by (6.1) the value of a resource increases with quality but by (6.2) marginal value is diminishing, so the loss resulting from an injury to a natural resource is convex in the level of injury. If (6.2) holds true, the liability approach is not well equipped to deal with multiple polluters. If it is not clear whom to blame for the last bit of injury (the final lowering of q) to a natural resource, we might be forced to charge each polluting party for the marginal harm, which is the largest harm per unit of injury. Total liability would be substantially greater than the total harm. This creates the problem of equitably dispersing funds: the damages collected will exceed the combined cost of restoring the resource and making the victims whole.[5] As is well known in the law and economics literature, it is impossible to use a single instrument (the liability damage award) to optimize both incentives and compensation. (Excessive funding for environmental protection and compensation is not as much of a problem as funding shortfalls.)

Assumption (6.2) is correct for many cases, such as minor discharges that represent a low-level threat to ecosystems, or certain environmental insults to health, those that have the property that the human body can cope with a certain level but will suffer harm at an increasing rate as the insult increases. But (6.2) is severely misleading for many important cases, such as recreational and aesthetic uses and severe injury to a resource.

Marginal harm (measured in human, plant or animal suffering) from an injury to a natural resource often does not increase with the magnitude of injury. For uninjured resources, the first unit of pollution may impose a much higher marginal cost than subsequent units. For example, a light coating of oil on a beach endangers the native fauna and flora and dramatically diminishes the recreational and aesthetic value; doubling the volume of oil would far less than double the impact. Similarly, 10 pieces of litter on a mountain trail diminish the wilderness experience substantially more than one-third as much as 30 pieces would (Schelling 1984: 131).

Non-convexities in damage also arise when losses are severe. For major injuries, there is likely to be a point beyond which the resource has very little human or ecological value left to lose (Helfand and Rubin 1994); this is a shut-down point. At that point, further quality reduction would entail little further loss, implying diminishing marginal costs. Moreover, people can avoid a resource with lowered quality (though other animals and of course whole ecosystems often do not have that option). Human activity will move on when quality drops below a certain point, even if some value remains (Starrett and Zeckhauser 1971). For example, once there is enough litter on a trail, people will choose another, and no one will swim at an oil-coated beach, even if the coating is light. For people who are no longer using a resource, additional injury causes no loss of benefit. In short, a one-size-fits-all economic model of restoration misses reality and cannot serve as the basis for efficient regulatory and liability structures. Designing economically efficient liability schemes or regulatory structures becomes much more complicated when (6.2) does not apply due to high initial costs of injury or low marginal costs for increases in large injuries.

If an entire injury can be attributed to a single activity of a single party, like an oil spill or a leaking storage tank, the complicated shape of the injury–harm curve causes fewer conceptual problems: the entire harm, whatever it turns out to be, should be borne by the responsible party. But when multiple activities contribute to the injury, and there are non-convexities in damages, how should liability be assigned? If it is clear that a party only added to the injury after the worst of the harm was done, then its liability or regulatory sanction should be low. If no one can be identified as either causing the initial injury or as the one that did the greatest harm, it is not clear who should pay the bulk of the damages. (After all, later polluters have done right by merely polluting an already low-quality site, rather than a clean one, and should not be asked to pay a share of the large harm inflicted by the initial polluter.) Trying to optimize incentives by sorting out who is responsible for which layer of injury is likely to be impossible.

These complexities, which impede the liability approach to environmental regulation, suggest that it may be too much to ask for economics-based incentives to function effectively on a decentralized basis in many areas of environmental regulation. In the face of a too-complex ideal, we are inclined to retreat to simpler methods, such as simply imposing standards and fining those who violate them. Though these methods are familiar, that does not mean they are optimal. In fact, an accurate perception of the economics of restoration, our next subject, suggests a major change in the way environmental quality should be controlled and liability should function.

THE NATURE OF RESTORATION COSTS

What does it cost to restore an injured resource to a reasonable level of quality? We start by understanding the standard economic theory, which presents the restoration decision as fundamentally incremental. Define s as the starting quality of the resource. Define t as some higher target quality level to which the resource could be raised (and assume for concreteness that the resource would be restored following some injury). Let $C(s,t)$ be the dollar cost of restoring the resource from quality s to quality t. It is usually assumed that:

$$\frac{\partial C(s,t)}{\partial t} > 0, \quad \frac{\partial^2 C(s,t)}{\partial t^2} > 0 \text{ for } s \text{ constant.} \qquad (6.3), (6.4)$$

The inequalities reflect the assumption that the marginal cost of restoration is positive and increasing in the target quality level (holding the pre-restoration level constant). These assumptions result in, for the given s, an upward-sloping marginal cost curve for restoration (that typically crosses the downward-sloping benefits curve that follows from (6.1) and (6.2)). When these conditions are explicitly assumed, it is generally implied that there is some function of quality, $c(q)$, such that:

$$C(s,t) = \int_s^t c(u)\,du, \qquad (6.5)$$

with $c(q)$ positive and increasing. That is, there is some marginal cost function that describes the cost of incremental restoration at any given quality level, is independent of s or t, and that meets conditions (6.3) and (6.4). Drawing a marginal cost curve and using it to discuss different possible levels for s and t implies that there is a $c(q)$ as defined by (6.5). Incremental restoration from any level of quality to any other level of quality is possible and practical under this formulation.

Economists tend to think of most decisions – in this case, restoration projects – as being incremental. Total cost is the sum of the costs of incremental steps, and the project can stop at any step. This view may result from an analogy to multiple-site or multiple-source environmental injuries, where substantial injury reduction does result from many small projects that are assumed to be undertaken in the order of diminishing efficiency. Under those circumstances, conditions (6.3)–(6.5) hold and all restoration projects follow the path traced by the universally applicable marginal cost curve. Local optimization efforts lead to the global optimum. We label the standard model, characterized by (6.5) as *invariant marginal costs* (IMC).

It follows from the existence of $c(q)$ as described in (6.5) that:

$$\frac{\partial C(s,t)}{\partial s} < 0 \text{ for } t \text{ constant.} \tag{6.6}$$

Both (6.3) and (6.6) can be interpreted as 'the bigger the restoration, the more it costs', but the two conditions are different. Condition (6.3) says that the higher the target level of restoration, the higher the cost (for the same starting level); condition (6.6) says the higher the starting level, the lower the cost (to get to the same target level).

Now let us turn to the case where costs are destination driven. We shall use the terminology *invariant total costs* (ITC) to refer to this case. With destination-driven costs, the distinction between (6.3) and (6.6) becomes important. When costs are destination driven, (6.6) is false (the derivative is *equal to* zero) as are (6.5) and (6.4), though (6.3) is generally true.[6] Condition (6.2), whose potential to mislead has already been addressed, is not crucial for the remainder of the analysis. However, it is worth noting that the loss due to an injury depends on how the injury will be remedied. This can make the shape of the function relating value of harm to magnitude of injury even more complicated. If restoration costs are destination driven and the restoration is assuredly going to take place soon, then further injury to a site would have no net impact.

Naturally, few projects have costs that are completely independent of *s*, and are thus purely ITC. For example, additional injury may create some additional cost of removing a greater volume of material or require greater safety precautions for workers during clean-up. The cost of stabilizing the injury (for example, to prevent geographic expansion) might increase as *s* falls even if the cost of the eventual restoration did not. Thus, most restoration projects' total costs will not be perfectly invariant to the starting point. This does not change the basic analysis, and these minor deviations (which still leave (6.5) inapplicable) will be ignored since the key point here is not to develop perfect optimization calculations, but to show that the ITC is frequently a reasonable approximation and the IMC formulation often extremely misleading.

OPTIMAL RESTORATION DECISIONS

To what level should a resource be restored? How should work proceed: in many small steps or all at a time? The optimality calculations for IMC restoration decisions when the incremental conditions (6.1)–(6.4) are true are exactly those of a standard optimal production problem. Specifically, we should produce (that is, restore) until the rising marginal cost curve crosses the falling marginal benefit curve or, if we are already at a higher level of *q* than that intersection, we should do nothing.[7] An implication of this is that there are two possible efficient final states following this decision: q_e, the point where the curves cross (more formally defined such that $\partial V(q_e)/\partial q_e = \partial C(s,q_e)/\partial q_e$), and the initial quality level, s (with no restoration undertaken).[8]

With ITC restoration, the optimization is more complex, since there are multiple discontinuous options for repairing or replacing an injured natural resource. For example, to restore a wetland that is polluted with toxins, we could remove the contaminated water and soil and try to recreate a working wetland; remove the contaminants but fail to rebuild the wetland; or just pave the mess over and build a new wetland elsewhere (with a range of possible expenditures at the new site). Fortunately, while there are many restoration options, one of them will be economically superior. Each project will have a constant cost and final quality level, t. Hence, we are picking the maximum net benefit, $V(t) - C(s,t)$, regardless of s or the inapplicable function in (6.5).[9]

Call the project that maximizes net benefits P, which has cost C(P) and resulting quality q_P. Then if we consider only destination-driven projects, our two candidates for the optimal post-restoration quality are s (which will result if no restoration is undertaken) and q_P.

If both incremental projects and destination-driven projects are possible – that is, we could clean up a little at a time up to some final level or carry out an optimal integrated project – then after an injury that lowers quality to s, there are three possible efficient post-restoration quality levels: s, q_e, and q_P. Figure 6.1 illustrates the optimization decision. The curve $B(s_1,q)$ (defined by $B(s,t)$ $\equiv V(t) - V(s)$), denotes the *total* benefits of a restoration project as a function the final quality, starting from initial quality $s = s_1$.[10] The $C_I(s_1 q)$ curve gives the cost of incremental restoration from s_1 to q. If IMC projects were the only option, then for any $s < q_e$ incremental restoration to q_e should be carried out. At target level q_e, the vertical distance between curve C and curve B is greatest (that is, net benefits from incremental restoration are maximized). This distance, the maximum net benefit from an incremental project, is labelled NB_I. The optimal destination-driven project yields quality of q_P and costs $c_D(q_P)$, which we denote as C(P). This project is labelled P, and yields net benefits $B(s_1,q_P)$ $= NB_D$. If both types of projects are available, their maximum net benefit levels must be compared. In the case illustrated in Figure 6.1, with initial level s_1, this comparison favours the destination-driven project since $NB_D > NB_I$.

Incremental projects are more attractive than doing nothing if and only if $s < q_e$. The optimal destination-driven project will be more attractive than doing nothing if and only if $B(s,q_P) > C(P)$. Since $\partial B(s,q_P)/\partial s < 0$ and $\partial^2 B(s,q_P)/\partial s^2 \leq 0$, there will be a threshold, q_{DN}, such that for $s < q_{DN}$ project P yields positive net benefit, implying that destination-driven restoration is superior to doing nothing. Specifically, q_{DN} is defined such that $B(q_{DN},q_P) = C(P)$, or equivalently, such that the point $(q_P,C(P))$ lies on the total benefit curve for restoration originating at q_{DN} (as illustrated in Figure 6.1).[11]

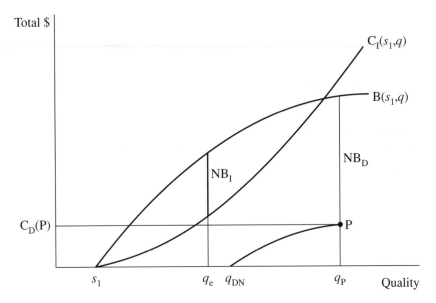

Figure 6.1   Comparison of IMC and ITC Projects

Project P is more attractive than incremental restoration if and only if:

$$[B(s,q_P) - C(P)] - [B(s,q_e) - C_I(s,q_e)] > 0, \qquad (6.7)$$

which is equivalent to:

$$C_I(s,q_e) > C(P) - B(q_e,q_P), \qquad (6.8)$$

since $B(s,q_P) - B(s,q_e) = B(q_e,q_P)$ by the definition of B given that $q_P \geq q_e$.

The right-hand side of (6.8) is constant over s (identically equal to the constant $B(q_{DN},q_e) = B(q_{DN},q_P) - B(q_e,q_P) = C(P) - B(q_e,q_P)$), and the left-hand side is decreasing in s. If the inequality is satisfied for any s, it will hold for all s less than some q_{DI}, the threshold for preferring the destination-driven project to the incremental project, defined such that $C_I(q_{DI},q_e) = C(P) - B(q_e,q_P)$, if such a q_{DI} exists. Theoretically, incremental costs could approach zero fast enough for low q that the destination-driven project may never be attractive, but this seems unlikely. If the physical reality offers either incremental or destination-driven projects, what are the possible orderings of q_e, q_{DN} and q_{DI}, and how can we interpret them? There are two possible cases, since the ordering of q_e and q_{DN} determines as well the ordering of q_{DI}. The first case is $q_{DN} < q_e$, illustrated in Figure 6.2. Given that $q_{DN} < q_e$, it must be that $q_{DI} < q_{DN}$, since for $s = q_{DN} - \varepsilon$, the benefit from P is infinitesimal while the benefit from incremental restoration to q_e is first order. For this case, we would want to do project P if and only if there were an injury to the resource sufficiently large to drive quality below q_{DI}. (No value for q_{DI} is shown on the diagram.) Otherwise, incremental restoration would be efficient, and q_{DI} would never be reached. The second possibility, illustrated in Figure 6.1, is $q_e < q_{DN}$ (in which case q_{DI}, as defined above, does not exist). In this case, project P is always more attractive than incremental restoration. The site should be restored to q_P if and only if $s < q_{DN}$; otherwise it should not be restored. Project P is a much better deal than any incremental project, and thus $q_{DN} > q_e$.[12]

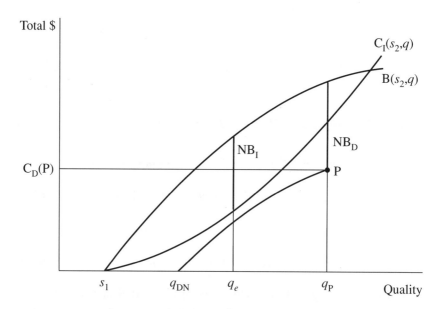

Figure 6.2   Comparison of projects with $q_{DN} < q_e$

The ordering presented in Figure 6.2, where an IMC restoration is the optimal choice over some range and project P does not become optimal unless the quality drops below q_{DI}, probably describes many large-scale or ongoing environmental concerns, such as a river polluted by agricultural runoff, and some trivial cases, like urban littering. For the cases emphasized in this chapter – individual sites suffering from specific industrial injuries – it does not seem to accord with the actual restoration activity, which is represented by Figure 6.1, where incremental restoration is never efficient.

OPTIMAL LIABILITY AND REGULATORY SYSTEMS

These results relating to destination-driven costs have three important sets of implications for regulation and liability policy. First, restoration standards should consider the optimal post-restoration quality level independent of the pre-injury quality level. Second, regulations that tend to spread out pollution are inefficient compared to ones that encourage greater concentrations of pollution in fewer places. Third, liability rules should pay careful attention to the quality of a resource prior to its injury or acquisition by the party who is ultimately liable for restoration costs.

Optimal Post-restoration Quality

When the costs of cleaning up pollution or restoring natural resources are primarily destination driven, the optimal level of restoration depends on the current state of a resource. The efficient final quality might be s, q_e, or q_P. That is, it may be optimal to do nothing, restore fully or restore partially, or to improve the resource's quality beyond its pre-injury level (q_P can be above or below the initial quality level). This implies that policies which set a single standard for a resource's restored quality level would be inefficient even if the standard were based on perfect knowledge of restoration costs and benefits.

When improvement beyond the resource's pre-injury state is optimal, then the injury and restoration produce a net improvement. For example, when a vacant city lot is sufficiently strewn with tyres, it may attract attention and be turned into neighbourhood gardens. A beach that has long suffered minor pollution from offshore bilge cleanings may become cleaner if a tanker spill leads to a major cleansing or replacement. Following a storage tank leak, an established industrial site with its accumulated toxins may be restored to a quality level it had not seen for a century. Regulatory requirements and civil liability rules should take into account that 'making whole' – requiring that everyone be made as well off as they were before the injury in question – might be a remarkable waste of an opportunity to increase social welfare at little cost.

Pollution Concentration

Current environmental rules frequently put the wrong resources at risk. With affluence, willingness to pay to enjoy very high-quality natural resources (via recreation, aesthetic use or existence value) increases substantially. At the same time, unspoiled sites, particularly pristine or long-undisturbed sites that are readily accessible, are becoming increasingly scarce. (Such resources are impossible to create at any price, but can be preserved.) Everything from a small unpolluted green space in an urban area, to a state park outside of town, to a virgin forest or coastline a few hours away is escalating in value. Yet various policies ignore low levels of contamination, make it easier to acquire and alter pristine sites than already injured ones, and otherwise undervalue the destruction of that which we hold most dear. These policies make it difficult to reuse sites efficiently that have already been injured by previous (usually industrial) activity.

A first-best solution would include a dynamic optimization that considered trends in preferences and resource availability, the inaccuracy of condition (6.2), and even of condition (6.1). We should recognize that our descendants will very likely prefer more unspoiled environmental amenities than the spinoffs from the material wealth we are generating by spoiling those resources. Even if we do not design policies that actively support our descendants' preference, we should at least steer clear of policies that encourage just the opposite, as do many current policies.[13] Such policies appear to be partially attributable to a failure to appreciate the implications of ITC restoration. (Some laws which were created with little regard for economics do emphasize pristine areas. The Clean Air Act includes 'Prevention of Significant Deterioration' rules which provide higher standards for high quality areas.)

The rhetoric surrounding pollution reduction, and the resulting policy, tends to focus on cases of extreme injury and treats them as if they were the bulk of our concern. Descriptions such as 'pollution levels are 100 times the safe level' or 'the ecosystem will take 200 years to recover' ignore the fact that the cost of restoration at the sites in question is about the same as it would be if those numbers were 10 and 20, and fail to ask where else the pollution would go. We would often be much better off if one site were polluted to the higher level and nine left pristine, rather than ten being injured at a lower level. In contrast, policies that freely allow pollution up to certain threshholds, or require the substantial degradation of an ecosystem before anyone objects, will leave us with few resources of extremely high quality and a need for some sort of restoration everywhere.

If a site is already due for a restoration effort, and particularly if it is unlikely to generate much value until it is restored, then the marginal cost of additional injury is low and may be zero. In such cases, it is desirable to shift risks or injuries from healthier sites to the already badly injured one. With IMC restoration, we get some gain from concentrating injury rather than spreading it across many sites due to the decreasing marginal cost of restoring the increased injury (which follows from (6.4) and (6.5)). But the benefits of concentrating pollution are dramatic under ITC, particularly when the environmental value of a site is already near zero. Consistent with popular intuition – but contrary to some of the implications of the standard economic theory – resource-injuring industries should be strongly encouraged to locate or otherwise function adjacent to each other and on the sites of previous dirty industries, all else being equal.[14]

The geographic concentration of waste disposal or of polluting industries in industrial parks is in the spirit of this type of regulatory response. Zoning or other regulations that concentrate industrial facilities reduce the cost of the externalities created by their pollution. Policies that encourage concentration are often driven by well-known failures of conditions (6.1) and (6.2). But they also take advantage of ITC. Instead of having to restore the soil quality so it meets current contamination standards every time it drops below q_e, only to pollute and clean it again, the pollution is directed to a site over a period of time and must be cleaned up only when (and if) it reaches a higher level of contamination. If the use of a site creates contamination and does not demand immediate clean-up (for example, dirty manufacturing or resource extraction might be located in areas already unsuited for recreation or wildlife), it may be efficient to clean it up only when the area is converted to some more sensitive use (for example, housing or a public park) (Breyer 1993).

Unfortunately, most current environmental laws give firms siting dirty industrial facilities or taking actions that risk discharges little incentive to adhere to these recommendations. Regulations based on ceilings for total load encourage firms to spread the injury across cleaner sites, since a firm will trigger a regulatory response demanding remedial action only if it pushes the pollution load at a site beyond the acceptable levels. Under the IMC formulation, this remediation would be relatively inexpensive if the injury were just short of the level that triggers the regulation (whether that level is q_e or not). But where ITC is the right model, as it often is, triggering a remediation brings on a large cost. While the net result might be a quality improvement in the resource, this is likely to be of little value to the firm, and thus the firm will take costly steps to avoid having to carry out the restoration. For example, it may leave a resource in its current use, rather than turning to a high-valued new use – possibly with a sale to another party – that would trigger restoration. The incentives are wrong: society's costs are continuous at the trigger point, while the firm's take a leap.[15]

Similarly, we would like to shift risks of catastrophe, such as an oil tanker spill, from high-quality sites (pristine coastlines, ecologically important areas) to lower-quality ones. But if the cost, C(P), and resulting quality level, q_p, from the restoration effort a firm would have to finance are the same whatever the initial quality of the site, as in our liability system, then there is no incentive to protect the higher-quality site.

Environmental economics has long observed that regulatory thresholds have disadvantages if either abatement costs or benefits vary across firms or sites. We have added a third argument against standards: destination-driven costs argue for concentrating, not spreading, pollution, even if all firms and benefit functions are identical, for two reasons: first, concentration reduces the costs of periodic clean-ups; second, even if there are strong arguments for a regulatory threshold – perhaps because concentrating pollution creates a disproportionate

health risk – the discontinuous cost of an ITC restoration will produce inefficient incentives for firms.

Regulations should be designed to reflect the real structure of restoration
costs, and destination-driven costs and diminishing marginal benefits often
characterize reality. Where standard economics, with its well-behaved cost
and benefit functions, may have led us astray, politics sometimes helps out. A
negotiated shrug regarding concentrated pollution or a higher fine when there
is public outcry about damaging a particularly valuable resource help get the
incentives right. We turn now to an economic model that allows for a richer
array of benefit and cost functions, and that would surely improve on these
ad hoc methods.

Liability to Take Account of Initial Quality

In the liability system, legally defensible property rights are often the primary
source of environmental regulation, especially for major injuries (Phillips 1995).
Such regulation takes the form of lawsuits brought by the holders of regulatory
property rights, or their agents, to protect the benefit they receive from the
resources.

By far the strongest disincentives for efficient pollution choices in the United
States, particularly efficient concentration of resource injuries, are the liability
rules. A firm or local government that acquires a highly polluted site is likely
to have to pay to restore its environmental quality, regardless of its lack of culpability in the pollution. Frequently the clean-up costs and benefits will result
from a pre-existing injury. Most often this is simply because the injury was not
previously identified or a liable party with money could not be found. Or, in
keeping with the present theory, this might be because an earlier restoration
would not have been efficient and it was only the current owner whose actions
pushed the quality below q_{DN}.

US environmental liability policy, particularly the Superfund laws and regulations, have been soundly and justifiably criticized for many reasons. One of
the most common criticisms is the assignment of 'responsible party' (RP) status,
and the responsibility for restoration costs, on a joint and several basis. As a
result, a current owner can be forced to finance the entire restoration effort.
This creates a huge disincentive to acquire polluted properties for any use,
resulting in the abandonment of injured sites and new pollution of much more
valuable, clean sites. So who is to pay for the efficient restoration of polluted
places? A simple solution can be found in the economics of liability, expanded
to recognize ITC.

The core result from the economics of environmental liability is that
efficiency is achieved if a polluter (a) pays to restore the injured natural resource
up to the point where the (increasing) cost of marginal restoration just equals

the (decreasing) benefit of increased quality, plus (b) pays damages equal to the net external harm remaining after restoration. That is:

$$\text{Efficient damage payment} = \text{Cost of efficient restoration} \\ + \text{Net harm after restoration.} \qquad (6.9)$$

For optimal incentives to avoid pollution, it is only necessary that the polluter pay the sum of these costs, regardless of who collects the payment or whether the restoration is actually carried out.

The standard economic model of natural resource injury, as described by conditions (6.1)–(6.6), includes continuous valued quantity options, increasing marginal costs and decreasing marginal benefits from the good. This, combined with the economic principle that getting anything 100 per cent perfect is too expensive, results in the unstated assumption that the residual harm is always positive.

But in fact the net residual change in quality might be positive. The damage award calculation should subtract the value of the net quality increase from the amount spent on remediation.[16] It is possible, in cases where the restoration was already justified by previous injuries, but not carried out, that this would make the net liability negative. One way to think of this is that the system would give the RP property rights over the net value it generated (as we would if it created a consumer product), and then create a market for selling back to society the portion of that value not flowing to the RP.

The equity rationale for this approach is that it ensures the fair treatment of an RP that is not actually responsible for most of the injury it is required to repair. The main economic rationale is that this approach is necessary to create incentives for efficient actions. When liability rules impose a threshold below which restoration is required, then a potential RP will take socially inefficient actions to avoid hitting the threshold, even though the net social cost is continuous at that point and the marginal cost of clean-up is zero below the threshold. The party owning or controlling a site would have less incentive to try to hide environmental injuries, and might even have the incentive to seek out efficient restoration options that could be undertaken.

Proper credit for net quality improvements would also ensure that restoration would take place where the combination of environmental/health benefits and economic benefits more than covered the cost of restoration. A patchwork of policies have been constructed at the local level to try to encourage reuse of injured sites, what are often referred to as brownfields, largely to encourage urban revitalization. But these are complicated, have shown limited success, and cannot pre-empt federal liability laws. Setting the right liability rules would eliminate the need for Rube Goldberg approaches to policy. A firm that acquires a site that is found to be in need of clean-up will not have to pay a net cost for the clean-up. The parties actually responsible for the pollution would still be liable if they could be identified and were not judgment-proof; otherwise, government would pay.[17]

Naturally, the net result of setting liability too high in some cases is a net reduction in environmental injury. However, it does so by raising the implicit value of low-quality sites. It would be more efficient to reduce environmental damage through a more general shift in the tradeoff between environmental protection and industrial activity: one shift that raises the implicit value of all natural resources, or of high-quality ones preferentially.

A disadvantage of giving firms and other entities credit for net environmental improvements is that it would create a budget imbalance. Restoration costs could exceed total net damages collected, creating the need for additional funding. This funding could come out of general revenues in the form of tax credits, though this would certainly create a political challenge. (It is easy to envisage the cries that we are paying polluting firms to clean up the mess they made, even though this should not actually occur.) One possible solution would be for the government to start collecting fees or liability awards for the net environmental harm that is done but not restored. Economic analysis of environmental policy constantly advises that such fees be collected, but it almost never actually happens. Collecting these funds would serve the dual purpose of discouraging harm and financing restorations that are not fully covered by net liability payments. If compensation for every harm were paid into a fund, it would necessarily exceed the cost of carrying out all efficient restorations. More realistically, if fees were collected for a large number of harms, it would fund a large number of efficient restorations.

Government funding of part of the restoration costs would also encourage it to write more realistic rules about how much clean-up is warranted. It is easy for the government to tell a firm that it must clean up a site so that it is clean enough for housing, when actually it is going to remain part of an oil refinery complex, or to tell a city that it can have a decommissioned military base if it assumes the liability for clean-up, even though it will be used as an airport. Regulators might reconsider such wasteful expenditures if part of the cost were put on budget.

CONCLUSION

Economic analysis and incentive-based environmental regulations help identify the optimal balance between the costs of injuries and the costs of avoiding or reversing them. Unfortunately, the traditionally posited shapes of marginal benefit and cost curves often bear little resemblance to the realities of restoring or replacing an injured site. In many important cases, remediation costs are destination driven. The implications of this contrast sharply with the constant quality and instantaneous clean-up prescriptions that emerge from the standard model.

The economic theory that influences regulatory and liability rules must attend to physical realities. In particular, the economic principle that responsible parties should pay the net cost of the harm they create must be extended so that they receive compensation for over-restoration, just as they would be charged for an unrestored injury. Only by understanding that cost functions for the remediation of injuries are often discontinuous can we craft rules that will foster efficient levels of environmental risk and appropriate polices for remediation.

NOTES

* Some of the material contained in this chapter (in particular parts of the third section) were previously published in the *Journal of Environmental Economics and Management* (Phillips and Zeckhauser 1998). The authors acknowledge the helpful comments of Rob Stavins.
1. The other main aspect of the economics-based approach involves the means of achieving targets and market-based mechanisms.
2. We use the term *injury* to refer to the physical loss in quality of a resource. *Harm* refers to the resulting loss of welfare.
3. Once remediation is underway, the same equipment must be used regardless of pollutant concentration, and the total cost and final outcome depend overwhelmingly on the choice of technology and its limitations rather than the starting quality level. Such factors as the types of contaminants, soil composition and moisture content affect the choice of technology. But the concentration of contaminants is only occasionally a major consideration in engineering discussions of technology choice, cost or target outcome (Holden *et al.* 1989; Nunno *et al.* 1990).
4. Utility can change depending upon how a situation is framed (Tversky and Kahneman 1986), and the change in the quality of a resource, rather than just the absolute level, might matter (Tversky and Kahneman 1991). Determining the shape of the curve (that is, measuring the value of natural resources) is also problematic (Phillips and Zeckhauser 1995). However, since the present analysis is normative in nature, it seems reasonable to assume the existence and measurability of V, despite the widely documented anomalies and measurement difficulties.
5. Complications of dividing compensation fairly arise if more than one party is injured. Compensation is beyond our scope, given that our focus is on optimal pollution control.
6. Strictly speaking, in the cases we are discussing, condition (6.3) may not hold, but a very similar stepwise inequality will. Also, the present discussion applies to cases where (6.6) is true but $c(q)$ approaches zero as s decreases. Details of these points are omitted for clarity of exposition.
7. For readers unfamiliar with the details, they can be found in Phillips and Zeckhauser (1998) or any environmental economics textbook.
8. Much of this analysis relies on the assumption that further injury to the resource is improbable. If there is a high enough probability of further injury, then it might be efficient to delay restoration under either IMC or ITC. With ITC, the optimal destination-driven project may result in quality higher than q_p, to compensate for expected future quality loss. See Keohane *et al.* (2000), for an analysis of this dynamic restoration case.
9. A more formal statement of this result, as well as mathematical conditions that are unimportant from a practical perspective, can be found as Proposition 1 in Phillips and Zeckhauser (1998).

10. The curves shown are for linear marginal costs and benefits (and thus quadratic total costs and benefits), as in a typical textbook model. The results apply to any cost and benefit curves that meet conditions (6.1)–(6.6).
11. The point can be identified in closed form as $V^{-1}[V(q_p) - C(P)]$, where V^{-1} is the inverse of the value function, $V(q)$, which must exist since $V(q)$ is strictly monotonic. Recall that since P has the greatest net benefit, whatever the value of s, of any ITC project, if doing nothing is superior to P then it is superior to every ITC project.
12. The discussion in this section is distilled into Proposition 2 in Phillips and Zeckhauser (1998).
13. Some such policies fail even in the traditional economic model. For example, policies that allow logging of old-growth forests often do not come close to passing muster in a cost–benefit analysis that considers all values that the forest creates. Similarly, regulations that treat pollution up to some threshold equivalent to no pollution at all (as opposed to charging for the social cost of the externality or offering rewards for not imposing that cost, even if it is small) encourage an initial pollution level that may have high marginal costs. To be fair, environmental health models, which are the basis of many such regulations, usually say that the first bit of pollution has less marginal impact than does further pollution. In many cases, however, there is little evidence that this is true.
14. This ignores other siting considerations. If a highly valuable resource is already suffering more injury than is optimal, we would not, of course, want to concentrate even more injury there. We do not want more industries that pollute the air to concentrate in densely populated areas, for example.
15. This also makes the firm excessively risk averse, accepting too much additional pollution to lower the variance of the pollution level.
16. This principle has implications for calculating values outside the realm of liability. For example, the city of Boston could respond to a hypothetical rise in sea level as a result of global warming by erecting a dike along its current coastline at some large expense. But in an informal assessment, Dutch engineers suggested that it would not be much more expensive to build the wall across the mouth of Boston Harbor, taking advantage of existing islands, and thereby claim hundreds of square miles of new land from the sea, relieving the congestion of the crowded urban area that cannot expand to the east. (This assessment was recounted by Thomas Schelling, personal communication.) Estimates of the net cost of global warming, then, should add in the cost of the long seawall, but it also should subtract the benefit of the newly reclaimed land.
17. There is a Coasean argument that as long as the property has value, making the new owner pay merely lowers the sale price, and effectively charges the prior owner.

REFERENCES

Arrow, K., M. Cropper, G. Eads, R. Hahn, L. Lave, R. Noll, P. Portney, M. Russell, R. Schmalensee, K. Smith and R. Stavins (1996), 'Is there a role for benefit–cost analysis in environmental, health, and safety regulation?', *Science*, 12 April.

Breyer, S. (1993), *Breaking the Vicious Circle: Toward Effective Risk Regulation*, Cambridge, MA: Harvard University Press.

Campbell, T.A. (1994), 'Managing ecological liability through use of restoration/acquisition alternatives', manuscript, Washington, DC: National Legal Center for the Public Interest.

Helfand, G.E. and J. Rubin (1994), 'Spreading versus concentrating damages: environmental policy in the presence of nonconvexities', *Journal of Environmental Economics and Management*, 27: 84–91.

Holden, T., J. Newton, P. Sylvestri and M. Diaz (1989), *How to Select Hazardous Waste Treatment Technologies for Soils and Sludges*, Park Ridge, NJ: Noyes Data Corporation.

Keohane, N., B. Van Roy and R.J. Zeckhauser (2000), 'Controlling stocks and flows to promote quality: the environment, with applications to physical and human capital', mimeo, John F. Kennedy School of Government, Harvard University.

Nunno, T. (1990), *International Technologies for Hazardous Waste Site Cleanup*, Park Ridge, NJ: Noyes Data Corporation.

Parks, P.J. and R.A. Kramer (1995), 'A policy simulation of the Wetlands Reserve Program', *Journal of Environmental Economics and Management* 28: 223–40.

Phillips, C.V. (1995), 'Assignment of property rights as a mode of regulation', doctoral dissertation, Harvard University.

Phillips, C.V. and R.J. Zeckhauser (1995), 'Confronting natural resource damages: the economist's perspective', in R.B. Stewart (ed.), *Natural Resource Damages: A Legal, Economic, and Policy Analysis*, Washington, DC: National Legal Center for the Public Interest.

Phillips, C.V. and R.J. Zeckhauser (1998), 'Restoring natural resources with destination-driven costs', *Journal of Environmental Economics and Management* 36: 225–42.

Schelling, T. (1984), *Choice and Consequence*, Cambridge, MA: Harvard University Press.

Soesilo, J. and S.R. Wilson (1997), *Site Remediation: Planning and Management*, Boca Raton, FLA: CRC Press.

Starrett, D. and R.J. Zeckhauser (1971), 'Treating external diseconomies: markets or taxes?', in J.W. Pratt (ed.), *Statistical and Mathematical Aspects of Pollution Problems*, New York: Marcel Dekker.

Stillman, R.G. (1993), 'Estimating the remediation of hazardous waste sites', in R.A. Selg (ed.), *Hazardous Waste Control*, New York: Marcel Dekker.

Tietenberg, T. (1984), *Environmental and Natural Resource Economics*, Glenview, IL: Scott, Foresman.

Tversky, A. and D. Kahneman (1986), 'Rational choice and the framing of decisions', in R.M. Hogarth and M.W. Reder (eds), *Rational Choice*, Chicago, IL: University of Chicago Press.

Tversky, A. and D. Kahneman (1991), 'Loss aversion in riskless choice: a reference-dependent model', *Quarterly Journal of Economics* 106: 1039–61.

Vidic, R.D. and F.G. Phland (eds) (1995), *Innovative Technologies for Site Remediation*, New York: American Society of Civil Engineers.

7. Environmental liability in practice: liability for clean-up of contaminated sites under Superfund

Hilary Sigman

In the late 1970s, residents of Love Canal (a suburb of Niagara Falls, New York) noticed discolouration of their lawns and basement walls. It turned out that their homes were built on land that had been used for disposal of chemical wastes in the 1940s and 1950s. In response to the public outcry from this incident, the US Congress hurriedly passed the Comprehensive Environmental Response, Compensation, and Liability Act (CERCLA) in December 1980. Under CERCLA, the Environmental Protection Agency (EPA) identifies abandoned sites with hazardous contamination, evaluates the dangers present, and ensures that either the government or private parties clean up the contamination. Because Congress established a large trust fund to pay for site clean-up, the programme became known as 'Superfund'.

Under the Superfund programme, EPA can conduct, or order private parties to conduct, small-scale emergency clean-ups and large-scale lengthy clean-ups, with the latter restricted to sites on the National Priorities List (NPL). The NPL included 1405 sites by September 1997; sites typically qualify for the NPL based on a rudimentary risk assessment.

Superfund relies heavily on legal liability rules to pay for clean-up at NPL sites. Private parties or government agencies associated with a site pay for most clean-up. Potentially Responsible Parties (PRPs) often undertake clean-up themselves under agreements with EPA. EPA estimates that it had reached agreements for clean-up cumulatively worth over $11.9 billion through September 1996. Alternatively, EPA can pay for clean-up using the Superfund Trust Fund and then sue the PRPs to recover its costs. Through September 1996, EPA had collected $1.4 billion in cost recoveries.[1]

There is widespread concern about the costs and consequences of Superfund liability. The US Congress has repeatedly considered restricting its application in future legislation. In developing its environmental liability regime, the European Union seeks more limited liability rules, in part because of the perceived failures of Superfund. This chapter discusses empirical research on the effects of Superfund liability, both on Superfund itself and, more briefly, on the rest of the economy. Although the empirical evidence is still far too incomplete to form a final judgement about the desirability of liability financing, this chapter outlines its advantages and disadvantages.

THE STRUCTURE OF SUPERFUND LIABILITY

Superfund imposes liability for clean-up on parties whose actions contributed to contamination at the site. Parties whom EPA may hold liable are called Potentially Responsible Parties (PRPs) and may include the past and present owners of the disposal site, waste generators, and parties who originally transported hazardous substances to a site.[2] Probst *et al.* (1995) estimate that the chemical industry will bear 25 per cent of the total cost for non-federal sites on the NPL, followed by the mining industry at 11 per cent.

Superfund liability is retroactive: PRPs may be held liable for activities that took place well before the advent of Superfund. Retroactive liability is a source of acrimony. Liable parties point out that they bear high costs for activities that were in full compliance with contemporaneous rules and for which there was no expectation of liability. However, retroactive liability is a large component of Superfund financing. If retroactive liability were eliminated at multiparty sites, Probst *et al.* estimate that the costs of Superfund to private parties would fall by 24 per cent. Because there is also retroactive liability at single-party sites, this value provides a lower bound on the total retroactive component of Superfund.

In addition to being retroactive, courts have interpreted Superfund liability to be 'joint and several': any defendant at a multiple defendant site may be required to pay the entire clean-up cost, regardless of its responsibility for contamination. PRPs who do pay all damages can then sue other PRPs for compensation. Joint and several liability affects the incidence of Superfund clean-up and transactions costs. For example, PRPs who remain in business must pay costs that should have been attributable to parties who are longer viable. In addition, PRPs who initially pay damages must bear the costs for later suits for contribution from other PRPs.

Joint and several liability may also affect incentives to settle and therefore the social costs of resolving Superfund disputes. Whether joint and several liability promotes or deters settlements is ambiguous theoretically. Kornhauser and Revesz (1994) present a formal model in which joint and several liability encourages settlements if trial outcomes are sufficiently correlated but discourages settlements if they are independent.

Chang and Sigman (2000) examine this relationship empirically by modelling the determinants of settlement rates and time-to-settle in Superfund litigation.

The results are consistent with a settlement-promoting effect from joint and several liability. An extension of the Kornhauser and Revesz model to the case of N defendants predicts that settlement rates should rise with the number of defendants if outcomes at trial are highly correlated; this relationship is observed in the estimated equations. In addition, the empirical results support the theoretical prediction that correlation in trial outcomes promotes settlement. Defendants appear to settle more frequently or more rapidly when this correlation is high. Thus, the empirical research supports the view that joint and several liability does not deter settlement.

LITIGATION COSTS

In evaluating the success of Superfund liability, the first factor to consider is the direct cost of liability. The programme has generated a large amount of litigation. Not only does EPA sue PRPs, but PRPs also sue one another over their shares of clean-up costs. PRPs also sue their insurance companies over whether general liability policies that the PRPs held before Superfund cover clean-up costs.

All of this litigation is likely to be costly. Researchers at RAND asked PRPs and their insurers to estimate the share of their Superfund costs that consist of legal and administrative costs. Because many of these transaction costs come early in the process before the actual clean-up begins, transaction costs may initially seem to be a higher share of costs than they will be by the end. The RAND researchers forecast the final transaction cost share to be 19–27 per cent of PRPs' total Superfund costs and 69 per cent of their insurers' Superfund costs (Dixon 1995). Putting these values together, they estimate that private parties' transaction costs will amount to 23–31 per cent of their Superfund expenditures. There are also legal costs to the federal government and the administrative costs of the courts, which should be added to this figure for the full social costs.

Comparing Superfund transaction costs to the transaction costs of other tort litigation in the US suggests that Superfund is not unusually costly. For example, Kakalik and Pace (1986) study tort litigation finished in 1985. They conclude that defendants' legal and administrative expenses amounted to 28–30 per cent of their total expenditures. These values suggest a transaction cost share similar to those predicted for Superfund by Dixon (1995). Thus, the high transaction cost may not indicate any special problems with Superfund liability, but rather the general cost of litigation-related activities in the US.

Before judging liability to be inordinately expensive, we should consider the costs of alternative funding sources, such as taxes. Until authorization expired in 1995, Superfund was partly financed by special environmental taxes, including taxes on corporate income and on feedstock chemicals. Fullerton (1996) calculates that the administrative cost of Superfund's corporate income tax may about equal the revenues collected, making the transaction costs associated with liability seem a bargain. Although this tax has exceptionally high compliance costs, other taxes, such as individual income taxes, can impose excess burdens comparable in magnitude to the transaction cost share of Superfund liability.[3] Thus, it is unclear that replacing Superfund liability with taxes would lower social costs.

EFFECTS OF SUPERFUND LIABILITY ON CLEAN-UP

In addition to these direct costs, Superfund liability may have had costs and benefits because it influences Superfund outcomes. Empirical research has focused on the influence of liable parties on two outcomes: the choice of remedies and the speed of clean-up.

Remedy Choices

Liability financing may influence the nature of remedies that EPA chooses for Superfund sites. EPA chooses remedies on a site-by-site basis and has considerable discretion. Options range from extensive clean-ups that may involve excavating and treating large volumes of waste to simple remedies, such as providing alternative drinking water sources to local communities.

Liability may increase or decrease the extent of clean-up. PRPs probably prefer less extensive remedies to save themselves money. To encourage less costly remedies, they may influence the decision process directly by participating in the studies that precede clean-up. They may also apply pressure more indirectly through the courts or Congress. On the other hand, PRP funding could also increase the chosen extent of clean-up. EPA may treat PRPs' expenditures as less important or more effective than its own, leading it to select more extensive clean-up when PRPs are expected to pay. For example, the regulations explicitly permit EPA to relax clean-up standards when it faces a tradeoff across sites for funds; it does not face these tradeoffs when it expects liable parties to pay. Given these offsetting effects, the direction in which liability funding alters the extent of clean-up is ambiguous *a priori*.

Several studies have examined the determinants of the remedies chosen at Superfund sites. Although these studies do not focus on the role of PRP, they include variables indicating whether PRPs undertake the studies and/or clean-up in estimated equations that model the determinants of remedy choice. Table 7.1 provides a summary of the results of these studies. These studies have mixed results about the relationship of PRP participation with remedy selection. When

Table 7.1 Summary of studies: effects of liable parties on remedy selection

Study	Dependent variable	Variable for liable party role	Results
Gupta (1993)	Anticipated remedy cost	PRPs conduct studies	Lower cost for wood preserving sites, but not PCB sites
Gupta et al. (1995)	Target risk level	PRPs conduct studies	Higher risk level in some specifications for wood preserving sites, but not PCB sites
Hird (1994)	Anticipated remedy cost and planned obligations	EPA designated in charge of site	Higher cost and obligations with EPA in charge
Sigman (1998)	Remedy type	Orphan status and depth of PRP pockets	Less extensive remedies with greater likelihood of PRP funding
Stratmann (1998)	Public spending	Orphan status and presence of litigation or ongoing negotiation	Higher spending at orphan sites and contentious sites
Viscusi and Hamilton (1999)	Target risk level	PRPs designated in charge of site	Higher level than sites without designation, not different from sites with EPA in charge

PRPs are involved, Hird (1994) and Gupta *et al.* (1995) find evidence of less costly and less permanent remedies, respectively. By contrast, Viscusi and Hamilton (1999) find higher target risk levels (indicating less stringent clean-ups) when the PRPs or government fund activities than when the funding source has not yet been determined. Although they do not report an explicit test, the coefficients on PRP funding and government funding are similar in magnitude, so they do not suggest a relationship between PRP funding and target risk levels.

These studies may not fully identify the effects of liability on decision-making for two reasons. First, PRPs may influence EPA's decision-making even at sites where they have yet to agree to fund study or clean-up. Thus, the estimated coefficients may not truly capture the effects of liability. Second, PRP partic-ipation may be endogenous to the remedies chosen by EPA: for example, PRPs may decline to participate when extensive remedies are chosen.

Sigman (1998) addresses these issues by examining the empirical relation-ship between remedy choice and the likelihood that PRPs will fund clean-up. A small percentage of sites are 'orphan' sites, where EPA has identified no viable PRPs. At these sites, EPA expects to finance the entire clean-up, providing a direct comparison of Superfund activities with and without liability.[4] For other sites, the depth of pockets of the PRPs measures the likelihood that PRPs will fund clean-up. Courts have interpreted Superfund to leave PRPs very little way out of liability, except by being judgment-proof. Thus, PRPs' depth of pocket is the best available measure of the likelihood that PRPs will fund clean-up. Depth of pocket is measured by whether the PRP is a large publicly traded corporation (many PRPs are individuals or small firms) and, if so, a measure of its bankruptcy probability.

The analysis focuses on a qualitative measure of the extensiveness of the remedy: whether it involves treatment of contaminants. It is difficult for PRPs or EPA to manipulate this measure for public relations purposes, unlike measures used in earlier studies, such as anticipated clean-up costs and target risk levels.

The empirical results suggest that EPA chooses less-extensive remedies when PRPs are expected to bear a large share of costs. Orphan sites are 54 per cent more likely to have treatment remedies than comparable sites. By contrast, EPA chooses less-extensive remedies for sites with PRPs with deeper pockets. These results are consistent with the hypothesis that PRP expenditures receive greater weight than public expenditures.

Thus, most empirical evidence supports the view that legal liability reduces the extent of Superfund clean-up. The welfare implications of this effect, however, are still subject to debate. A full evaluation requires an assessment of whether clean-ups would be more extensive than the efficient level in the absence of PRP pressure. Hamilton and Viscusi (1999) compare the costs of clean-up at a sample of Superfund sites with the number of cancer cases avoided. For 70 per cent of the sites they study, the cost per cancer case avoided exceeds $100 million (in 1993 dollars), indicating that remedies are too extensive.[5] If liability financing of these sites has resulted in less-extensive remedies, it has unequivocally improved efficiency. However, the average cost per cancer case avoided in their study is $3 million, so if liability financing pulls down the extent of clean-up at the small number of sites with very favourable spending per cancer cost avoided, it could also reduce welfare.

In addition to altering the remedies selected, liability financing may change the costs of undertaking a given remedy. Through 1995, PRPs had undertaken clean-up at 75 per cent of sites that had experienced some clean-up. Private parties may also have stronger incentives to control costs than government agencies and thus undertake study and clean-up more cost-effectively. A government analysis of clean-up at Department of Energy sites (cited by CBO 1994: 24) suggests that private parties have a 13 per cent cost advantage over the public sector. If government cannot write contracts that achieve private sector efficiencies, this cost saving should be considered an advantage of liability funding.

The Pace of Progress

PRPs' involvement may affect not only how clean-up is done but how rapidly it proceeds. Superfund's progress has been a major source of concern. By early 1997, 16 years after Congress enacted the legislation, only 11 per cent of NPL sites had been declared clean and deleted from the list. Some analysts have pointed to liability financing as a major source of delays.

PRPs may use their influence to speed or delay progress, depending on the circumstances. The time value of money gives PRPs incentives to use direct involvement and political influence to delay progress and thus postpone their costs. PRPs' expected costs also might change over time either because contamination diffuses making clean-up more costly or because contamination naturally attenuates making clean-up cheaper. With these conflicting factors, the direction of PRP influence, as well as its existence, is an empirical issue.

A survey of EPA's site managers suggests that PRPs may play an important role in the pace of progress (Beider 1994). The managers consider unusually cooperative PRPs to be among the most important characteristics of sites with rapid progress. They also report negotiation with PRPs as one of the most common sources of delay at sites with unusually slow progress.

Several studies have examined determinants of Superfund delays, including the role of PRPs. Hird (1994) examines the time it takes to list sites on the NPL. He finds some indication that sites where the government is in charge have slower times until listing, suggesting that PRPs actually speed listing. However, the result is statistically significant at the 10 per cent level only.

As with the studies of remedy selection, this study faces the difficulty that sites where PRP participation may be endogenous may not indicate all of the ways that PRPs wield influence. As before, this problem can be addressed by comparing orphan sites with other sites. Beider (1994) examines estimated time to completion, using actual times for the few sites that have completed clean-up and times forecast by site managers for the remainder. He finds orphan sites complete the process more rapidly. However, site managers' impressions that it is easy to work on sites without PRPs may influence his findings because the duration for most sites is based on managers' forecasts.

Sigman (forthcoming) also examines the effect of orphan status on clean-up time. In addition, the study considers the effects of the likelihood of PRP funding, as measured by depth of PRP pockets. These variables may affect the length of three stages of Superfund progress: the time from discovery of the site to listing on the NPL (prioritization phase), from listing to remedy selection (decision-making phase), and finally clean-up of the site. The duration of the three stages is analysed in a model of multiple sequential durations, with unobserved heterogeneity that may affect all three stages.

The results suggest that liable parties delay Superfund progress. Orphan sites experience decision-making that is 29 per cent faster than other sites. Sites with large publicly traded PRPs, who have the strongest incentives to delay progress, spend 15 per cent longer in the clean-up stage. However, sites with these large PRPs experience faster decision-making. Large PRPs are more likely to be active in the studies and public oversight process that precede remedy selection (Sigman 1998), so the result may be evidence that such PRP involvement in decision-making expedites it. The net effect of PRPs is still to slow decision-making, but these particular PRPs mitigate this delay somewhat.

The welfare implications of these delays depend on the net benefits of clean-up across sites. As discussed above, Hamilton and Viscusi (1999) find an average cost per cancer case avoided that might be consistent with positive net benefits of Superfund clean-up. Thus, delaying clean-up would have costs by delaying these benefits. With any PRPs present, clean-up is delayed by 1.8 years. Assuming that the net benefits of clean-up arise entirely at completion and using a 5 per cent social discount rate, this delay reduces the net benefits of clean-up by 8 per cent. When large PRPs are present, the net delay is 2.5 years, which would reduce net benefits by 12 per cent.

Although these results hold on average, delay could be welfare improving at many sites because the clean-up would not pass a cost–benefit test. However, the research on remedy selection discussed above suggests that EPA selects less-costly remedies under liable party influence, so net benefits when PRPs delay progress may tend to be more favourable than average. Thus, the costs of PRP-induced delay seem likely to outweigh its benefits.

OTHER EFFECTS OF SUPERFUND LIABILITY

In addition to its effects on the conduct of Superfund, liability may affect other economic activities. Three effects of Superfund liability have been studied in the literature: the incentives that liability provides for precaution in handling hazardous substances; the obstacles that it may create for land development; and the costs of the risks it imposes.

Incentives for Precaution

Superfund liability may alter contemporary handling of hazardous substances. If firms expect to bear clean-up costs for future contamination, they may generate less waste and use more permanent treatment and disposal than they would in the absence of liability. Even Superfund's retroactive liability (which concerns activities that it is too late to change) may create some incentives if it puts polluters on notice that current behaviour may later be judged by even stricter standards.

Of course, the desirability of such incentives depends upon the efficiency of the control they encourage. If Superfund clean-ups are too expensive for their benefits, then liability may actually encourage excessive precaution. In addition, firms are subject to environmental regulations, such as requirements for the management of hazardous waste under the Resource Conservation and Recovery Act (RCRA). Superfund liability may not encourage a degree of precaution beyond that required by such other environmental statutes. Empirical research related to such incentives for precaution is discussed elsewhere in the book.

Brownfields

Fears of Superfund liability may discourage the sale or redevelopment of land with actual or potential contamination (Boyd *et al.* 1996; Segerson 1993). Suspicious sites, often in old industrial areas, are referred to as 'brownfields'. To the extent that Superfund deters use of developed land, it may encourage development of pristine land as a substitute.

Expected clean-up costs should be capitalized into land values, so liability does not necessarily discourage sales. However, there is the potential for adverse selection in the land market, dampening transactions that might lead to development, as well as for courts to reallocate liability after the sale in a way that makes transactions unfavourable. More importantly, decisions to sell or develop land may trigger inspections that would alert authorities to contamination and perhaps instigate clean-up that might not be required if land is left dormant. In response to these concerns, EPA has begun a programme of agreements with prospective site purchasers, in which purchasers undertake some clean-up in return for assurances that EPA will not sue them. The extent to which Superfund liability has deterred land development and the success of the new prospective purchaser agreements remain to be studied empirically.

Cost of Capital

Garber and Hammitt (1998) argue that Superfund liability may permanently raise the cost of capital for affected firms because it creates undiversifiable risk for investors. They look for empirical evidence of higher returns to capital associated with measures of firms' Superfund exposure. They conclude that this exposure has a large and statistically significant effect on returns. This result is surprising because Superfund liability seems largely idiosyncratic relative to market risk. However, if true, it would add a social cost from the need to bear the risks that liability creates.

THE INCIDENCE OF SUPERFUND LIABILITY

Setting aside the efficiency concerns above, proponents of Superfund liability often argue that liability is desirable from a fairness perspective because it follows a 'polluter pays principle'. However, if the equity principle at stake is that the beneficiaries of pollution should bear the costs of cleaning it up, the liability system may not live up to this goal.

In thinking about the incidence of Superfund liability, we should distinguish retroactive liability from liability for harms that occurred after Superfund was anticipated. Once Superfund liability was anticipated, expected liability costs should have become a factor in prices and profits, passing these costs to the beneficiaries of pollution. Thus, the prospective component of Superfund liability appears to meet the fairness goal.

For retroactive liability, the comparison is more complicated. The beneficiaries of pollution are those who gained from lower production costs because of contamination. Based on concentration ratios for industries frequently involved in Superfund sites, Fullerton and Tsang (1996) argue that the industries are largely competitive. Therefore, they conclude that the avoided costs were largely passed through to consumers in the form of lower product prices. Because the affected industries, such as chemical manufacturing and mining, produce inputs that are widely used in the economy, benefits would likely have been distributed in a similar manner to consumption of goods during the time in question.

However, the distribution of costs is probably different. Retroactive liability does not affect the costs of current production and thus competitive firms cannot pass it forward to consumers. Instead, retroactive liability may be borne by owners of capital in affected firms and by their insurers. When Superfund liability became anticipated, the change probably decreased the value of corporate assets for firms expected to be held liable.

A few empirical studies have attempted to assess the impact of Superfund on asset values. They use event study methodologies, estimating abnormal returns associated with various Superfund-related information. Muoghalu and Rogers (1992) examine market reaction to Superfund lawsuits from 1980 to 1990. They find that firms experienced a 1.2 per cent abnormal return in the two days around the publication of the lawsuit, corresponding to an average loss to shareholders of $43 million. This loss is consistent with at least full capitalization of Superfund liability and perhaps more. Average costs for NPL activities are about $30 million per site, not including transaction costs (Probst *et al.* 1995: 36).[6] Multiple parties are typically named in a lawsuit and at a site, so liability per party should be only a share of these costs.

Some liability costs are already expected by the time that EPA files litigation against the firm. When Superfund began, the market should immediately have expected costs for firms in some industries, such as the chemical industry, with high exposure. As predicted, Dalton *et al.* (1996) find negative effects of events leading up to passage of Superfund on the chemical and petroleum industries. In addition, by the time a lawsuit is filed, the fact that the firm is a PRP at the site is already known. Harper and Adams (1996) find that notification of this PRP status was also associated with abnormal negative returns in the early years of the programme (but not in later years). These factors suggest the effect on asset values is even larger than the value cited above.

In addition to losses to liable parties, insurers too found themselves facing higher costs because Superfund gave rise to unanticipated claims under general liability policies. Although the applicability of these policies to Superfund liability has been under dispute, courts have sometimes concluded that the policies apply. Thus, some of the burden is likely to be a capital loss to insurers. It is possible that some bankruptcies result, spreading the burden more broadly to other insured parties. However, Probst *et al.* (1995) suggest that Superfund-induced bankruptcies are not that frequent. They compare Superfund losses to losses in a Florida hurricane, which caused few insurers to fail; the retroactive component of Superfund liability is comparable in magnitude to loss from the hurricane.

Thus, empirical evidence supports the view that retroactive Superfund liability is largely a capital levy. This incidence may be desirable in some ways, for example, falling by burdening the rich disproportionately and by limiting any distortions that might be created by the need to finance clean-up. On the other hand, it probably means that there is not a close correspondence between the beneficiaries of the pollution and the burden of clean-up costs, at least for the retroactive component of costs.

CONCLUSION

Given the controversy over Superfund's liability system, Congress has debated restricting its scope. For example, proposed changes would eliminate liability for contamination before the passage of Superfund or use taxes to pay for liability shares of PRPs who are no longer financially viable. Empirical economics research does not provide a definitive recommendation as to whether liability financing should be kept or scrapped, but it does suggest the tradeoffs that may be involved.

The consideration that has perhaps received the most attention in policy circles is the direct cost of using the legal system. Superfund liability does generate high transactions costs. However, these costs may not be excessive when compared to tax alternatives.

This chapter argues that other effects of Superfund create costs and benefits that should be balanced against these direct legal costs. Liability involves private parties in the conduct of clean-up. They may influence the remedies selected, exerting cost control that is likely to be desirable at most sites. They may also delay clean-up, which can be helpful at sites with negative net benefits, but could be costly on average if it causes delays at a few sites with high positive net benefits.

In addition to its influence on the Superfund programme, liability also creates other incentives. It may encourage precaution in managing hazardous wastes and discourage development of old industrial sites. However, there is limited empirical evidence on the extent of these responses or their consequences for economic efficiency. Thus, the missing information is too great for a judgement about whether costs or benefits dominate.

Advocates of liability often point to fairness principles, rather than to such efficiency concerns. For the retroactive component of Superfund liability, the evidence does not support a standard argument for the fairness of liability: that liability imposes the burden of pollution on its beneficiaries. However, liability related to activities since Superfund began may meet this fairness goal.

NOTES

1. These values are in nominal dollars. For comparison, EPA spent about $9 billion from taxes and general revenues on clean-up over the same period. In comparing government and PRP spending, one should note that the PRP settlements reflect future commitments rather than expenditures that have occurred to date.
2. In addition, banks that lend money to the owners of the site can be liable. EPA promulgated a rule to eliminate this liability under CERCLA in 1992, but a court overturned EPA's rule in 1994. In 1996, however, Congress amended Superfund substantially to protect lenders from liability.

3. Superfund liability may also impose efficiency losses if it changes polluters' behaviour in ways that do not give rise to net social benefits. Thus, there may be costly distortions comparable to the excess burden from liability as well.
4. Stratmann (1998) also compares orphan sites with other sites and finds higher public spending levels at orphan sites. However, it is unclear whether to interpret this result as an affirmative policy choice or the absence of other funding sources.
5. Some caveats are necessary in considering these values. They address only the cancer reduction and not other health and environmental benefits of clean-ups. Hamilton and Viscusi (1999) rely on official EPA estimates of risk levels, which could be manipulated for political purposes and include other biases, such as the use of upper bound estimates of risks. Finally, it may be inappropriate to compare these cost per cancer cost avoided values to conventional accident-based values of a statistical life because of the latency of cancer and the costs associated with cancer morbidity.
6. The comparison of losses to site costs is necessarily inexact because the estimated abnormal return appears to be in nominal dollars and because the lawsuits correspond to a selected sample of sites that may not be characteristic of the entire NPL.

REFERENCES

Beider, Perry (1994), 'Analyzing the duration of cleanup at sites on Superfund's national priorities list', Washington, DC: Congressional Budget Office Memorandum.
Boyd, James, Winston Harrington and Molly Macauley (1996), 'The effects of environmental liability on industrial real estate development', *Journal of Real Estate Finance and Economics* 12: 37–58.
Chang, Howard F. and Hilary Sigman (2000), 'Incentives to settle under joint and several liability: an empirical analysis of Superfund litigation', *Journal of Legal Studies* 29: 205–36.
Congressional Budget Office (1994), *The Total Costs of Cleaning Up Nonfederal Superfund Sites*, Washington, DC: Congressional Budget Office.
Dalton, Brett, David Riggs and Bruce Yandle (1996), 'The political production of Superfund: some financial market results', *Eastern Economic Journal* 22: 75–87.
Dixon, Lloyd S. (1995) 'The transactions costs generated by Superfund's liability approach', in Richard L. Revesz and Richard B. Stewart (eds), *Analyzing Superfund: Economics, Science, and Law*, Washington, DC: Resources for the Future, pp. 171–85.
Fullerton, Don (1996), 'Why have separate environmental taxes?', in James M. Poterba (ed.), *Tax Policy and the Economy*, vol. 10, Cambridge, MA: MIT Press, pp. 33–70.
Fullerton, Don and Seng-Su Tsang (1996), 'Should environmental costs be paid by the polluter or the beneficiary? The case of CERCLA and Superfund', *Public Economics Review* 1: 85–127.
Garber, Steven and James K. Hammitt (1998), 'Risk premiums for environmental liability: does Superfund increase the cost of capital?', *Journal of Environmental Economics and Management* 36: 267–94.
Gupta, Shreekant (1993), 'Do costs and benefits matter in environmental policy? An analysis of EPA decisions under Superfund', PhD Thesis, College Park MD: University of Maryland.
Gupta, Shreekant, George Van Houtven and Maureen L. Cropper (1995), 'Do benefits and costs matter in environmental regulations? An analysis of EPA decisions under Superfund', in Richard L. Revesz and Richard B. Stewart (eds), *Analyzing Superfund: Economics, Science, and Law*, Washington, DC: Resources for the Future, pp. 83–114.

Hamilton, James T. and W. Kip Viscusi (1999), 'How costly is "clean"? An analysis of the benefits and costs of Superfund site remediations', *Journal of Policy Analysis and Management* 18: 2–27.

Harper, Richard K. and Stephen C. Adams (1996), 'CERCLA and deep pockets: market response to the Superfund program', *Contemporary Economic Policy* 14: 107–15.

Hird, John A. (1994), *Superfund: The Political Economy of Environmental Risk*, Baltimore, MD: Johns Hopkins University Press.

Kakalik, James S. and Nicholas M. Pace (1986), *Costs and Compensation Paid in Tort Litigation*, Santa Monica, CA: RAND Corporation.

Kornhauser, Lewis A. and Richard L. Revesz (1994), 'Multidefendant settlements: the impact of joint and several liability', *Journal of Legal Studies* 23: 41–76.

Muoghalu, Michael and John E. Rogers (1992), 'The economic impact of Superfund's litigation on the value of the firm: an empirical analysis', *Journal of Economics and Finance* 16: 73–87.

Probst, Katherine N., Don Fullerton, Robert E. Litan and Paul R. Portney (1995), *Footing the Bill for Superfund Cleanups: Who Pays and How?*, Washington, DC: Resources for the Future.

Segerson, Kathleen (1993), 'Liability transfers: an economic analysis of buyer and lender liability', *Journal of Environmental Economics and Management* 25: S46–S63.

Sigman, Hilary (1998), 'Liability funding and Superfund clean-up remedies', *Journal of Environmental Economics and Management* 35: 205–24.

Sigman, Hilary (forthcoming), 'The pace of progress at Superfund sites: policy goals and interest group influence', *Journal of Law and Economics*.

Stratmann, Thomas (1998), 'The politics of Superfund', mimeo, Montana State University.

Viscusi, W. Kip and James T. Hamilton (1999), 'Are risk regulators rational? Evidence from hazardous waste decisions', *American Economic Review* 89: 1010–27.

8. Self-enforcement of environmental law

Robert Innes

When environmental laws are breached, violating firms can often engage in remediation activity that reduces the harm caused by their violation. Polluters can clean up contaminated sites and act quickly to end their discharges. A possible objective of law enforcement is what I shall call *self-policing* of behaviour, when violators voluntarily engage in these sorts of remediation activities. A further objective of law enforcement may be the *self-reporting* of environmental offences to government authorities, and firm investments in environmental *self-auditing* programmes that enable firms to discover their offences, report them and clean them up.

In this chapter, I consider how government enforcement programmes can prompt firms to engage in these self-enforcement activities, and the economic merits of doing so. At the crux of this inquiry is the premise that law enforcement is costly, so that prompting firms to exercise due care in preventing harmful environmental accidents – and cleaning them up when they occur – cannot be accomplished with the free imposition of sanctions for inefficient conduct. Instead, the government must monitor potential violators with cost, and optimal regimes of monitoring and sanctions must account for both the societal benefits of the harm that is prevented and the government enforcement costs that are borne.[1] As will be seen in what follows, such enforcement costs can provide a powerful economic motive for eliciting the self-initiated enforcement actions at issue in this chapter.

I begin this inquiry in the next section by focusing on the scope for *self-reporting* of behaviour to improve efficiency in law enforcement, studying five economic motives for this practice and describing the implications of these motives for optimal enforcment policy. I turn next to the implications of *self-auditing* programme investments – as the necessary antecedent to self-reporting – for the merits and design of enforcement regimes that prompt these investments. Finally, in the third section, I focus on whether and how optimal enforcement regimes can elicit voluntary violator remediation, or *self-policing*.[2] The fourth section concludes.

SELF-REPORTING

The Basic Model

A fixed number of identical, risk-neutral and profit-maximizing firms engage in activities that can cause accidents. Accidents damage the environment, which is costly to the general public. Each firm can exert non-negative accident-prevention effort (or care) that reduces the risk of an accident. With $x \in [0,\mathbf{x}]$ denoting a firm's investment in care, the probability that a firm will have an accident is $p(x)$, where $p'(x) < 0$ and $p''(x) > 0$ (care reduces accident risk at a decreasing rate), $p'(0)$ is arbitrarily large, and $p'(\mathbf{x})$ is arbitrarily small. When an accident occurs, the resulting harm is h.

Each firm has private information about its level of care x and, absent government monitoring, about whether or not an accident has occurred. However, if the government invests g dollars (per firm) in enforcement, it can detect an accident with probability $r(g,z)$, where $r \in [0,1]$, $r_g > 0$ (enforcement effort raises detection rates), and z is a parameter which will be defined in alternative ways below.

The government's regime of post-apprehension sanctions can have two components. If a firm self-reports its accident, it faces the monetary sanction s. If, instead, a firm does not self-report and is apprehended, it faces the fine f. Neither sanction can exceed an exogenous maximum (such as firm assets), $\mathbf{f}$. Moreover, for simplicity, I assume that sanctions cannot be negative – that is, a firm cannot be rewarded for accidents/violations.

Care

Let F denote the expected penalty that a firm faces if it has an accident. If a firm self-reports, for example, F simply equals s. If a firm does not self-report, F generally equals the probability that the government detects the accident, $r0$, times the penalty levied when detection occurs f. Given F, the firm will choose care to solve the following problem:

$$V(F) \equiv \min_{x} x + p(x)F \quad \text{s.t.} \quad x \in [0,\mathbf{x}]. \tag{8.1}$$

The firm minimizes the sum of its costs of care and the expected costs that it must bear from prospective accidents. By construction of $p(x)$, problem (8.1) has an interior solution for all positive and bounded F. This solution is also unique (by convexity of $p(x)$) and will be denoted by $x^*(F)$. Note that in a first-best world (without government costs of monitoring), the average accident sanction will simply be set equal to true societal harm, $F = h$, thus prompting care of $x = x^*(h)$.

Alternative Motives for Self-reporting

I shall now incorporate a variety of economic phenomena that provide efficiency motives for self-reporting enforcement regimes. For conceptual clarity (and simplicity), I model each of these motives one at a time.

Direct enforcement economies (Model 1)

Following Kaplow and Shavell (KS1994) and Malik (M1993), let us now suppose that accidents are detected in the course of government audits of firms, where m denotes the government's cost per audit. If there is no self-reporting of behaviour, the per-firm government enforcement expenditures required to support the apprehension probability r is:

$$g = mr. \tag{8.2a}$$

However, with self-reporting of offences, the government no longer needs to monitor violators – those firms which have accidents and thus self-report. Hence, in order to achieve a monitoring probability r for potential (non-reporting) violators, the government needs only expend (per firm):

$$g = mr(1 - p(x)), \tag{8.2b}$$

the cost per audit (m) times the probability that a non-reporting firm is audited (r) times the fraction of the population that does not self-report $(1 - p)$. Combining (8.2a) and (8.2b), we have:

$$r(g,z) = g/[m(1 - z)] \tag{8.3}$$

where $z = \phi p(x)$, with $\phi = 0$ with no self-reporting (NSR) and $\phi = 1$ with self-reporting (SR).

Clearly, self-reporting directly reduces the government's cost of apprehending potential violators with a given probability. Following KSM, we shall now see how the government can design its enforcement regime in order to reap these savings.

No self-reporting (NSR)   With no self-reporting, firms face the average accident sanction, $F = rf$. Firms thus exert care (per problem (8.1)), $x = x^*(rf)$. Given this care response, a benevolent (welfare-maximizing) government will choose its regime of sanctions and monitoring, (f,r), to minimize the sum of per-firm enforcement costs ($g = rm$), accident prevention costs (x), and accident harm ($p(x)h$), as follows:

$$J^{N*} \equiv \min_{(r,f)} J^N(r,f) = rm + x^*(rf) + p(x^*(rf))h \quad \text{s.t.} \quad r \in [0,1], f \in [0,\mathbf{f}]. \quad (8.4)$$

A solution to problem (8.4) is easily seen to have the following properties:

Proposition 1 (KSM) In an optimal NSR regime (Model 1), (a) there is positive government enforcement effort, $r > 0$;[3] (b) the post-apprehension sanction is set maximally, $f = \mathbf{f}$ (Becker 1968); and (c) relative to a first-best, accidents are underdeterred, $r\mathbf{f} < h$ and $x = x^*(r\mathbf{f}) < x^*(h)$.

By setting a maximal sanction, the government can achieve a given accident deterrent (rf) with the minimum possible monitoring rate r; enforcement expenditures can thus be reduced without compromising deterrence (the famous Becker 1968 logic). Because higher rates of deterrence require higher enforcement expenditures (that is, higher r), an optimal policy will trade off harm-reduction benefits of marginal deterrence against attendant enforcement costs; this tradeoff leads to an optimal level of deterrence that is somewhat less than first-best (where marginal deterrence benefits alone are set to zero).

Self-reporting (SR) In order to elicit self-reporting, the government must offer self-reporters a sanction that is no greater than the average sanction that would otherwise be faced:

(SR$_1$) $\qquad\qquad\qquad\qquad\qquad r \leq rf.$

In view of constraint (SR$_1$), consider how the government can improve upon the NSR optimum described above. Specifically, suppose that the government replicates the deterrence achieved under the NSR regime by (a) setting the same monitoring rate, r; (b) setting the same non-reporter sanction, $f = \mathbf{f}$; and (c) just barely eliciting self-reporting by setting $s = r\mathbf{f}$. Because firms anticipate the same accident sanction as before, they exert the same level of care (by construction), $x = x^*(s) = x^*(r\mathbf{f})$. The only change is that the enforcement economies described at the outset are realized: under the revised (self-reporting) regime, per-firm government enforcement expenditures decline from rm (under the NSR regime) to $rm(1 - p(x^*())) < rm$.

Proposition 2 (KSM) In Model 1, an optimal self-reporting enforcement regime will welfare-dominate any NSR enforcement regime.

With self-reporting, the government's choice problem becomes:

$$\min_{(r,s,f)} rm(1 - p(x^*(s))) + x^*(s) + p(x^*(s))h \quad \text{s.t.} \quad (\text{SR}_1), r \in [0,1], f \in [0,\mathbf{f}].$$

$$(8.5)$$

Several properties of this solution are easily derived:

Proposition 3 (KSM)   In an optimal SR regime (Model 1), (a) enforcement effort is positive, $r > 0$; (b) the non-reporter sanction is set maximally, $f = \mathbf{f}$ (Becker 1968); and (c) the SR sanction is set exactly equal to the average non-reporter sanction, $s = r\mathbf{f}$.

The idea here is to achieve a given accident deterrent (s) at minimum possible enforcement cost, subject to the self-reporting and feasibility constraints. If the self-reporting constraint were slack ($s < rf$), the government could lower its monitoring rate r – thus lowering its enforcement costs – without upsetting firms' incentive to self-report or, therefore, their choice of care. Hence, an optimal policy must involve a binding self-reporting constraint $s = rf$. With $F = s = rf$, the Becker (1968) logic again implies that enforcement effort is minimized with a maximal non-reporter sanction.

Violator remediation (Model 2)
I shall now suppose that direct enforcement economies of self-reporting are absent.[4] The probability of violator apprehension r thus depends only upon the per-firm government enforcement expenditures, $r = r(g) \in [0,1]$.[5] The innovation here (following Innes 1999a) is that damages from an accident can depend upon whether or not the firm engages in post-accident clean-up. I shall assume that clean-up either takes place, at net positive cost c, or does not take place.[6] If clean-up occurs, remaining damages are D_c. If clean-up does not occur, damages are h_n, where $h_n \geq D_c + c \equiv h_c$ (optimal clean-up cannot increase total damages). Because clean-up is efficient, the government mandates clean-up whenever a violator is apprehended or self-reports.

The no-self-reporting (NSR) optimum   With no self-reporting of behaviour, a violating firm faces the expected penalty, $F = r(g)f$, which prompts the care choice, $x^*(F) = x^*(r(g)f)$. When an accident is not detected, the firm will not choose to clean up (because clean-up is costly), leading to the societal accident damages h_n.[7] Expected accident damages thus equal the probability that an accident occurs, $p(x^*())$, times average harm, given that the accident has occurred, $r(g)h_c + (1 - r(g))h_n$. This logic yields the following government problem (minimizing costs of monitoring, care and accidents):

$$\min_{(g,f)} g + x^*(r(g)f) + p(x^*(r(g)f))[r(g)h_c + (1 - r(g))h_n] \quad \text{s.t.} \quad f \leq \mathbf{f} \Rightarrow (g^{\text{NSR}}, f^{\text{NSR}}).$$
$$(8.6)$$

With remediation benefits, the standard Becker (1968) logic for maximal sanctions no longer holds. The reason is that the government may no longer want to minimize the monitoring rate r needed to achieve a given accident deterrent, because lowering r has the direct cost of reducing the frequency with which socially beneficial clean-up occurs.[8] In particular, consider problem (8.6) without the constraint $f \leq \mathbf{f}$. So long as *ex post* benefits of clean-up are strictly positive, $h_n - h_c > 0$, and the marginal effectiveness of infinitesimal government monitoring investments, $r'(0)$, is sufficiently large (as assumed here), this problem has a solution, (f^*, g^*):

$$f^* = h(g^*)/r(g^*), \text{ where } h(g) = r(g)h_c + (1 - r(g))h_n \qquad (8.7a)$$

$$g^*: 1 - p(x^*(h(g)))\, r'(g)\, (h_n - h_c) = 0. \qquad (8.7b)$$

Clearly, if f^* is less than the maximal sanction $\mathbf{f}$, the constraint in problem (8.6) will not bind; equation (8.7) will describe the optimal enforcement policy without self-reporting; and the optimal fine will not be set maximally.

Proposition 4 In an optimal (Model 2) enforcement regime without self-reporting, the optimal fine for an accident, f^{NSR}, is set below the maximum possible level $\mathbf{f}$, provided the following condition holds: $\mathbf{f} > h(g^*)/r(g^*)$.

Self-reporting Self-reporting can now be elicited if $s \leq r(g)f$, which prompts the care response, $x = x^*(s)$. Moreover, self-reporters need not be 'detected' in order for clean-up to be mandated; hence, post-accident clean-up benefits are always obtained. The government's policy choice problem thus becomes:

$$\min_{(g,s,f)} g + x^*(s) + p(x^*(s))h_c \quad \text{s.t.} \quad s \leq r(g)f \text{ and } f \leq \mathbf{f}. \qquad (8.8)$$

Two sets of conclusions can be derived from the study of problem (8.8): (a) prospective benefits from enacting a self-reporting mechanism in place of a non-self-reporting mechanism, and (b) attributes of the optimal self-reporting regime.

On the first front, consider the following strategy: (a) set the self-reporting penalty, s, equal to the optimal expected penalty in the NSR regime, $s = r(g^{\text{NSR}})f^{\text{NSR}}$; (b) set the non-reporting penalty as high as possible, $f = \mathbf{f}$; and (c) set government monitoring expenditures to just preserve firms' incentives to self-report:

$$g = g_0: s = r(g^{NSR})f^{NSR} = r(g_0)\mathbf{f}. \qquad (8.9)$$

This strategy achieves the same incentives for accident prevention effort, x, as does the optimal NSR regime, while reducing societal costs in two ways: first, the self-reporting regime achieves *ex post* benefits of clean-up 100 per cent of the time, compared with $r(g^{NSR})$ per cent of the time under the NSR regime. And second, whenever the optimal NSR regime specifies a less-than-maximal accident penalty, $f^{NSR} < \mathbf{f}$, the self-reporting regime can provide the same level of accident deterrent incentive with a lower level of g by setting the non-reporting penalty maximally, at $f = \mathbf{f}$. That is, when f^{NSR} is less than $\mathbf{f}$, g_0 in equation (8.9) is less than g^{NSR}.[9]

> **Proposition 5** In Model 2, the optimal self-reporting regime is strictly superior to the optimal enforcement regime without self-reporting whenever there are positive *ex post* benefits of clean-up, $h_c < h_n$.

Minimizing enforcement costs of deterrence yield further properties of an optimum:

> **Proposition 6** In an optimal (Model 2) self-reporting enforcement regime, (a) the self-reporter sanction equals the average non-reporter sanction, $s = r(g)f$; (b) the non-reporter fine is maximal, $f = \mathbf{f}$; and (c) the self-reporting penalty, s, is less than the accident damages, h_c, prompting a care choice that is less than first-best, $x^*(s) < x^*(h_c)$.

Penalty assessment costs (Model 3)
Under a self-reporting regime, penalties are always assessed when an accident occurs. Without self-reporting, in contrast, penalties are only assessed with a probability less than one, namely, the probability of detection. When there is a fixed administrative cost of assessing a penalty, the self-reporting regime can therefore lead to higher administrative costs than an enforcement regime without self-reporting. This logic, as developed in KSM, suggests that the desirability of a self-reporting mechanism depends upon the relative weights of its enforcement-cost-reducing advantages and its administrative-cost-increasing disadvantage. Such a conclusion, however, hinges upon an implied restriction on the government's enforcement capabilities. If the government can randomly select a *fraction* of self-reporters to be penalized – and exempt the others from penalty – then a self-reporting regime can replicate an optimal NSR regime by penalizing the same proportion of self-reporters as would be detected in the NSR regime, and levying the same penalty on the penalized firms. This strategy yields an exact equivalence between optimal SR and NSR regimes in this

chapter's basic model: self-reporting cannot make things better, but needn't make matters worse. What is more, when penalty assessment costs depend upon the level of the penalty in a plausible way, they provide additional economic weight to the argument *for* self-reporting. I now turn to the modelling of these costs and their implications for optimal enforcement, abstracting from both the remediation and direct enforcement economies considered above.

Generalized penalty assessment costs　Scholars studying regulatory enforcement have noted that greater regulatory effort is generally needed to secure higher fines for violations of law (for example, see Garvie and Keeler 1994). For example, courts may require more compelling evidence if they are to sanction higher penalties on polluting firms. Moreover, as Garvie and Keeler (1994) point out, regulatory efforts to raise penalties are likely to exhibit diminishing returns as courts require increasingly compelling evidence to impose increased sanctions when the sanction for a given violation is already high. Defendants (firms) will also fight higher sanctions with increased vigour. Such logic implies that administrative costs of assessing penalties not only rise with the penalty level, but rise at an increasing rate. Formally, we have:

$$b(f) = \text{administrative cost of levying a fine of } f \text{ on a firm,} \qquad (8.10)$$

with $b'(f) > 0$ and $b''(f) > 0$ for $f > 0$, and $b(0) \geq 0$. Accident damages *without penalization* are now h (as before); *with penalization*, they are $h + b(f)$.

　　Let us first suppose that $b(0) = 0$, so that there are no fixed costs associated with levying fines. The penalty assessment costs are then as depicted in Figure 8.1. In an optimal NSR regime, each firm will face the expected accident penalty, $r(g^{NSR})f^{NSR}$, and average (post-accident) penalty assessment costs are $r(g^{NSR})b(f^{NSR})$, the probability that the penalty is imposed times the administrative cost incurred when it is.[10] In a self-reporting regime, the government can impose a penalty on all self-reporters that yields the same expected penalty as the NSR regime, $s = r(g^{NSR})f^{NSR}$. As illustrated in Figure 8.1, a convex $b(f)$ function implies that the latter penalty will yield strictly lower administrative costs – and higher economic welfare – than the NSR regime.

Proposition 7　In Model 3, with $b(0) = 0$, an optimal self-reporting regime: (a) yields higher economic welfare than can be achieved with any NSR regime; (b) sets a non-stochastic self-reporter penalty equal to the expected non-reporter penalty, $s = r(g)f$; (c) sets the non-reporter penalty maximally, $f = \mathbf{f}$; and (d) sets the self-reporter penalty below the level of actual accident damages, $s < h + b(s)$.

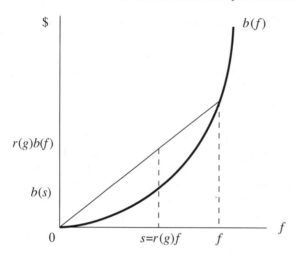

Figure 8.1   Penalty assessment costs when b(0) = 0

Now suppose instead that b(0) is positive, so that assessing any penalty is costly. Here, two cases need to be distinguished: case (1): when $b'(\mathbf{f}) > b(\mathbf{f})/\mathbf{f}$; and case (2): when $b'(\mathbf{f}) \leq b(\mathbf{f})/\mathbf{f}$. In case (1), as illustrated in Figure 8.2, there is a feasible fine, $f^* < \mathbf{f}$, that minimizes the penalty costs per-dollar-of-fine:

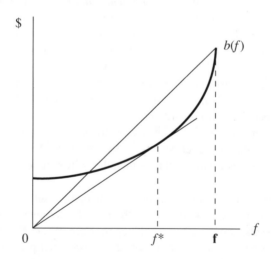

Figure 8.2   Penalty assessment costs when b(0) > 0 *and minimizing per-dollar costs is feasible*

$$f^* = \operatorname{argmin}\,(b(f)/f) < \mathbf{f}. \tag{8.11}$$

In an optimal enforcement regime without self-reporting (NSR), it can be shown that the government will set the fine, f^{NSR}, above f^*. By marginally raising f above f^* and lowering g in tandem to preserve the expected penalty, $r(g)f$, administrative costs stay approximately the same (by the definition of f^*) and, hence, total costs are reduced by the reduction in g.

Lemma 1 In case (1), $f^{NSR} > f^*$.

Lemma 1 is important because it implies that an optimal NSR regime does not minimize the administrative costs associated with achieving a given expected accident penalty. As a result, we shall see, a self-reporting regime can do better. In particular, consider a self-reporting regime in which the proportion α of self-reporters are assessed a penalty s and the proportion $(1 - \alpha)$ are not penalized. Furthermore, let (α, s) be selected so as (a) to achieve the same expected accident penalty as in the optimal NSR regime, $\alpha s = r(g^{NSR})f^{NSR}$; and (b) to minimize administrative costs of doing so by setting:

$$s = \max(f^*, r(g^{NSR})f^{NSR}) < f^{NSR}, \text{ and } \alpha = \min(r(g^{NSR})f^{NSR}/f^*, 1), \tag{8.12}$$

where the inequality follows from Lemma 1 and $r(g) < 1$. Finally, we set the non-reporter penalty maximally at $f = \mathbf{f}$ and the government monitoring expenditure exactly high enough to elicit self-reporting:

$$g^{SR}: r(g^{SR})\mathbf{f} = \alpha s = r(g^{NSR})f^{NSR}, \tag{8.13}$$

where $g^{SR} < g^{NSR}$ if $f^{NSR} < \mathbf{f}$ and $g^{SR} = g^{NSR}$ if $f^{NSR} = \mathbf{f}$.

 This enforcement programme achieves the same accident prevention effort as does the NSR regime, but with lower administrative costs and no higher government monitoring costs. For example, suppose that f^* is greater than $r(g^{NSR})f^{NSR}$, as depicted in Figure 8.3. Under the replicating self-reporting programme just described, the average administrative costs, A^{SR}, are lower than under the optimal NSR programme, A^{NSR}:

$$
\begin{aligned}
A^{SR} &= \alpha\, b(f^*) = r(g^{NSR})f^{NSR}\,(b(f^*)/f^*) \\
&< r(g^{NSR})f^{NSR}\,(b(f^{NSR})/f^{NSR}) = r(g^{NSR})b(f^{NSR}) = A^{NSR},
\end{aligned} \tag{8.14}
$$

where the inequality follows from the definition of f^* (which minimizes $b(f)/f$) and Lemma 1 ($f^{NSR} \neq f^*$). The same logic applies when $r(g^{NSR})f^{NSR}$ is above

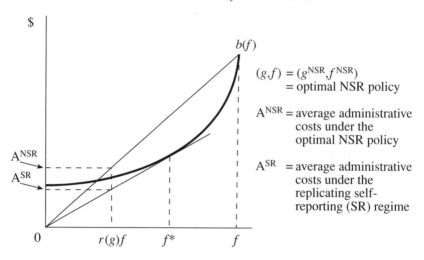

Figure 8.3   Average penalty assessment costs under the optimal NSR regime and a replicating SR programme

f^*. The difference in total (per-firm) costs under the NSR and SR programmes is thus:

$$(g^{NSR} - g^{SR}) + p(x^*(r(g^{NSR})f^{NSR})) [A^{NSR} - A^{SR}] > 0. \qquad (8.15)$$

When the accident penalty is high enough – as it is with the optimal NSR regime in case (1) – the average level of the net penalty assessment costs can be reduced by lowering the penalty level and preserving the average penalty by raising the proportion of the time that firms causing accidents are fined. Under a self-reporting regime, this can be done costlessly; in an NSR regime, this can only be done at the cost of a greater monitoring investment, g. As a result, self-reporting enjoys a cost-saving advantage over an enforcement regime without self-reporting.

Proposition 8   In Model 3, with $b(0) > 0$ and $b'(\mathbf{f}) > b(\mathbf{f})/\mathbf{f}$, an optimal self-reporting regime: (a) is superior to any NSR enforcement regime; (b) can be characterized by the policy (α, s, f, g), where α = proportion of self-reporters who are penalized, s = penalty imposed on those self-reporters who are penalized, f = penalty imposed on non-reporters = $\mathbf{f}$, and (α, s) is set to just elicit self-reporting, $\alpha s = r(g)\mathbf{f}$; (c) sets a self-reporting penalty no lower than f^*, $s \geq f^* = \operatorname{argmin}(b(f)/f)$; (d) penalizes self-reporters with probability one, $\alpha = 1$, if s is set higher than f^*, and sets $\alpha < 1$ only if s is set equal to f^*;

(e) sets the expected self-reporter penalty below the level of actual accident damages, $\alpha s = r(g)\mathbf{f} < h + \alpha b(s)$; and (f) sets $s = f^* < \mathbf{f}$ and exempts some proportion of self-reporters from penalty, $\alpha < 1$, if $f^* \geq h + b(f^*)$.

In case (2), in contrast, lowering the penalty below its maximum level, $\mathbf{f}$, raises per-dollar penalty costs. An optimal NSR regime then minimizes both administrative and monitoring costs of achieving a given level of accident deterrence by setting a maximal fine, $f = \mathbf{f}$. A self-reporting regime, at best, can only mimic this NSR optimum by setting maximal sanctions, $s = f = \mathbf{f}$, and penalizing self-reporters with the same probability as non-reporters, $\alpha = r(g)$.

We thus find that administrative costs do not disadvantage self-reporting enforcement regimes – and strictly advantage them whenever $b'(\mathbf{f}) > b(\mathbf{f})/\mathbf{f}$, a condition which is more likely to hold when: (a) $b(0)$ is smaller; (b) the maximal sanction, $\mathbf{f}$, is larger; and (c) the curvature in the net penalty assessment cost function, $d\ln b(f)/d\ln f$, is greater.

Heterogeneous probabilities of apprehension (Model 4)

Firms may have different – and privately known – probabilities of apprehension.[11] This source of asymmetric information may not only explain the presence of both self-reporters and non-reporters. Often, it will also motivate the use of self-reporting despite the absence of any other self-reporting benefits.

The setting Following Innes (2000a), let us consider the basic model on p. 151, with firms now distinguished by a privately known parameter δ that determines accident-detection rates:

$$\text{Probability of apprehension} = r(g)\delta,$$

where $r(g) \in [0,1]$ is as defined on p. 152. In the population of firms, δ is distributed with a continuous density (relative frequency) $q(\delta)$ and cumulative density $Q(\delta)$, on the interval between $\underline{\delta}$ and one, where $0 < \underline{\delta} < 1$.

Analysis Because higher δ-type firms have a greater incentive to self-report than do lower δ-types, we can think of the government as choosing a critical δ^* such that firms with $\delta \geq \delta^*$ self-report and firms with $\delta < \delta^*$ do not; the critical δ^* and the self-reporting fine s are related as follows (see Figure 8.4):

$$s = r(g)\delta^* f. \tag{8.16}$$

Now note that, for any $\delta^* \geq 1$, no firms self-report; without loss of generality, we can thus restrict δ^* to be no greater than one. Similarly, for any $\delta^* \leq \underline{\delta}$, all firms self-report. And for $\delta^* \in (\underline{\delta}, 1)$, some firms self-report and some do not.

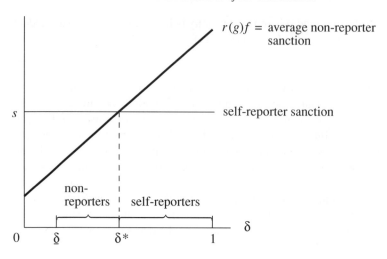

Figure 8.4   Derivation of the non-report/self-report intervals

The government's problem is to choose its policy, (g, f, δ^*), to minimize the (per-firm) average costs of accidents, accident prevention, and enforcement:

$$J(g, f, \delta^*) \equiv g + \int_{\underline{\delta}}^{\max(\delta, \delta^*)} \left\{ x^*\left(r(g)\delta f\right) + p\left(x^*\left(r(g)\delta f\right)\right)h \right\} q(\delta) d\delta$$

$$+ \left(1 - Q(\delta^*)\right)\left[x^*\left(r(g)\delta^* f\right) + p\left(x^*\left(r(g)\delta^* f\right)\right)h\right] \qquad (8.17)$$

subject to constraints that $\delta^* \leq 1$ and $f \leq \mathbf{f}$. The integral term in (8.17) gives the accident prevention costs and average accident damages for those low-δ firms that do not self-report and that thus exercise care in response to the average non-reporting sanction, $F = r(g)\delta f$. The last term gives the costs associated with the high-δ firms that self-report and that thus face the self-reporting sanction, $s = r(g)\delta^* f$ (from (8.16)).

Remark 1   In a Model 4 optimum, (a) non-reporters are maximally sanctioned, $f = \mathbf{f}$; (b) it is not the case that all firms are strictly advantaged by a self-reporting strategy: $\delta^* \geq \underline{\delta}$ or, equivalently, $s \geq r(g)\underline{\delta}f$; and (c) enforcement effort, g, is positive and bounded.[12]

Proposition 9   In the Model 4 optimum, some firms do not self-report, $\delta^* > \underline{\delta}$.

To understand Proposition 9, suppose that the self-reporting sanction is just low enough to prompt all firms to self-report, $s = r(g)\underline{\delta}\mathbf{f}$. Then marginally raising this sanction, by raising δ^* above $\underline{\delta}$ and thereby prompting some firms not to self-report, raises the accident penalty to *virtually all* firms. Marginal enforcement effort also has the benefit of marginally raising *all firms'* accident sanction, by permitting the s fine to rise without upsetting self-reporting incentives. With g chosen optimally, this marginal benefit exactly offsets the marginal direct cost of g. That is, there will be a strictly positive benefit of raising the accident penalty, which can be done costlessly with an increase in δ^* and only at positive cost with an increase in g. Hence, δ^* will be optimally raised above $\underline{\delta}$ in order to capture this benefit.

Turning now to the key issue – whether and when some self-reporting will be optimal – consider an enforcement regime without self-reporting. In such a regime, the government cannot tailor its accident penalties to the different firm types. Rather, it provides accident penalties that are higher for those firms with higher probabilities of being apprehended. An optimal enforcement strategy in this setting will often strive to achieve penalties that are closer, on average, to firms' respective accident damages – thereby eliciting more efficient choices of accident prevention effort – by underpenalizing some firms (the low δ-types) and overpenalizing others (the high δ-types). Adding a self-reporting component to the enforcement programme permits the government to screen the firms, with high δ-types self-reporting and low δ-types continuing to face the non-reporting sanctions. The self-reporting option lowers penalties to the high δ-types that can benefit from this option – and that are overpenalized in the NSR regime. The efficiency cost of enforcement is thereby lowered. Figure 8.5 illustrates this argument by graphing expected accident penalties under two regimes: (a) the optimal enforcement programme with no self-reporting (NSR), (g^{NSR}, $\mathbf{f}$, $\delta^* = 1$), and (b) an alternative regime in which δ^* is lowered from one to δ^*_1, without changing the government's enforcement effort, $g = g^{\mathrm{NSR}}$.

Proposition 10 In Model 4, suppose that the optimal NSR regime overpenalizes those firms with the highest probability of apprehension ($\delta = 1$), $r(g^{\mathrm{NSR}})\mathbf{f} > h$. Then it will be optimal to: (a) elicit self-reporting by firms with high probabilities of apprehension ($\delta \geq \delta^*$, with $\delta^* < 1$); (b) charge self-reporters for exactly the harm that they cause, $s = h$; and (c) underpenalize all firms that do not self-report, $r(g)\delta\mathbf{f} < h$ for $\delta < \delta^*$.

But will the most heavily penalized ($\delta = 1$) firms be overpenalized in the optimal NSR regime? Suppose instead that the highest δ-type firms are neither overpenalized nor underpenalized – and, hence, that average non-reporting sanctions are *less* than accident harm for all but the highest δ-types ($\delta = 1$). Then the penalty-raising effect of increasing government enforcement effort g

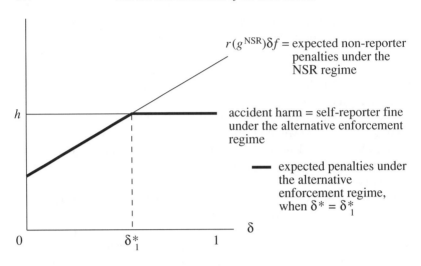

Figure 8.5   Expected accident penalties under two regimes

– due to the attendant reduction in the disparity between average sanctions and harm – is strictly welfare-enhancing for all firms (other than the $\delta = 1$ firms for which it is welfare-neutral). This welfare benefit is more likely to offset the direct cost of marginal enforcement effort when (a) the maximal sanction (or asset level) **f** is larger, and (b) the accident detection technology is more effective. Then lower levels of g – with correspondingly higher marginal detection benefits – are needed to achieve penalties that are close to accident damages. With a large **f**, increases in g also have large penalty-raising benefits, providing added motive for increased average sanctions.

Avoidance (Model 5)
Absent self-reporting, there are a wide variety of measures that violators can undertake to avoid apprehension. They can cover up incriminating evidence; they can flee the scene of an accident; they can lobby politicians to relax enforcement activity; they can dispose of contaminants in locations and in ways that are difficult to tie to their source; they can distance themselves from a violation using legal and other subterfuges. Such 'avoidance' opportunities impart an added eocnomic advantage to self-reporting enforcement regimes.

The model   Following Innes (1999b) (and building on Malik 1990), let us return to our basic model, with violator apprehension rates now depending upon both the government's monitoring effort (per firm) g and the violator's 'avoidance' effort a:[13]

probability of detection $= r(g,a) \in [0,1]$.

Enforcement with no self-reporting (NSR) Given g and f, a violator will select avoidance effort to minimize the sum of its direct cost and the resulting average sanction, $r(g,a)f$:

$$F(g,f) = \text{minimum average sanction} \equiv \min_{a \geq 0} (a + r(g,a)f). \qquad (8.18)$$

Remark 2 Violators exert positive avoidance effort whenever there is positive enforcement: $a(g,f) \in [0,a]$ when $g > 0$ and $f > 0$.

Given the average sanction $F(g,f)$ in (8.18), firms exert care, $x = x^*(F(g,f))$. The government's problem is to minimize the average net societal costs of these violations, the enforcement effort made to deter them, and the avoidance effort made by violators to reduce the likelihood of sanctions:

$$\min_{(g,f)} J(g,f) \equiv g + x^*(F(g,f)) + p(x^*(F(g,f)))(h + a(g,f)) \quad \text{s.t.} \quad f \leq \mathbf{f} \Rightarrow (g^{NSR}, f^{NSR}).$$
$$(8.19)$$

As shown by Malik (1990), the presence of avoidance activity can invalidate the standard logic that it is always optimal to set a maximal fine, $f = \mathbf{f}$. Here, higher fines have a direct cost: they give violators a greater incentive to avoid apprehension:[14]

$$\partial a(g,f)/\partial f = - r_a(g,a)/r_{aa}(g,a)f > 0. \qquad (8.20)$$

There is, therefore, a bounded fine which equates its marginal benefit in increased deterrence with its marginal cost in raising avoidance:

Remark 3 Problem (8.19), unconstrained by the limit on sanctions $\mathbf{f}$, has a positive and bounded solution, $(g^*,f^*) = \text{argmin } J(g,f)$.

Now note that if the maximal sanction is sufficiently high $-\mathbf{f} \geq f^* -$ then the unconstrained solution to problem (8.19) will also solve the government's constrained choice problem (8.19) subject to $f \leq \mathbf{f}$. However, if $f^* > \mathbf{f} -$ for example, because violator wealth is not sufficiently high – then the government cannot achieve the unconstrained solution to problem (8.19). In this case, the constraint on the fine must bind, $f = \mathbf{f}$, and the government will choose the monitoring effort, $g^{**} = \text{argmin } J(g,\mathbf{f}) \in [0,\mathbf{g}]$.

Corollary 1 An NSR regime elicits positive avoidance, $a(g^{NSR}, f^{NSR}) > 0$.[15]

Enforcement with self-reporting   Here, self-reporting requires:

$$(SR_5) \qquad\qquad s \leq F(g,f).$$

Now consider adding a self-reporting option to the optimal NSR regime, with a self-reporting sanction set to just satisfy (SR_5), $s = F(g^{NSR}, f^{NSR})$. Self-reporting is then elicited *before any avoidance effort is undertaken*. Moreover, the sanction for violations is the same as before, thus providing the same level of deterrence. Welfare costs will thus have been lowered by saving all avoidance costs.

Often, this logic understates the advantage of self-reporting. Recall that the optimal NSR regime often does not set a maximal non-reporter sanction because a higher sanction raises costs of avoidance. With self-reporting, however, no avoidance costs are actually borne. Hence, raising the non-reporter sanction yields the same benefits as identified by Becker (1968) without the additional avoidance costs identified by Malik (1990).

> **Proposition 11**   An optimal (Model 5) enforcement regime: (a) elicits self-reporting; (b) sets the non-reporter sanction maximally, $f = \mathbf{f}$; (c) sets the self-reporting sanction equal to the average non-reporting penalty, $s = F(g,\mathbf{f})$; and (d) underdeters violations by levying a penalty that is less than harm, $s < h$.

The government optimally sets a self-reporting sanction exactly equal to the average penalty that a violator otherwise faces, including the violator's cost of optimal avoidance. It thereby induces self-reporting without reducing deterrence. The added bonus is that self-reporting violators have no incentive to engage in any avoidance; avoidance costs are thereby saved and the enforcement economies of maximal sanctions can be freely reaped.

Implications

This section develops five distinct economic motives for environmental law enforcement regimes that prompt firms to self-report their violations. Self-reporting can directly reduce the government monitoring costs needed to achieve a given accident deterrent (KSM); increase the frequency of efficient remediation (Innes 1999a); sometimes reduce average penalty assessment costs; improve the targeting of sanctions to violators with heterogeneous risks of apprehension (Innes 2000a); and avoid costly violator efforts to avoid apprehension and punishment (Innes 1999b).

There are two potential counterpoints to these motives. First, if administrative costs of penalization are large and self-reporters cannot be randomly penalized (with a probability less than one), then self-reporting may be disadvantaged because it requires that administrative costs be borne on all violators (KSM). However, random penalization (if optimal) should not, I believe, be dismissed as 'unrealistic'. Intuitively, this practice may be thought of as letting some violators go with 'a slap on the wrist' and subjecting others to the full force of post-apprehension enforcement. Such behaviour is widely observed in practice, with government authorities and prosecutors often compelled, by budgetary limits, to pick and choose those violators against whom they proceed. Second, self-reporting may not be costless to violating firms, a topic to which I now turn.

SELF-AUDITING AND SELF-REPORTING

In the foregoing analysis of self-reporting, it is presumed that a firm freely observes its offences. In practice, however, the self-discovery of violations – the necessary antecedent to self-reporting – requires the costly acquisition of information. The purpose of this section is to study the implications of these information-acquisition (or self-auditing) costs for the optimality and optimal design of law enforcement regimes that elicit self-reporting of violations.[16]

The Self-auditing Model

Consider the accident regulation model developed above (p. 151). The twist now is that neither the government *nor a firm* can costlessly detect an accident when it occurs. By investing A dollars *ex ante*, a firm can detect its own violation (when it occurs) with probability $\rho \in [0,1]$; without investing, the firm cannot detect its accidents. As in Model 1 (pp. 152–4), I assume that the government monitors a firm at cost m; when it monitors, the government discovers whether or not an accident has occurred and also costlessly observes whether or not the firm has a self-auditing programme in place.[17] The government's enforcement regime now has four components: the monitoring rate, $r \in [0,1]$; the self-reporter sanction, $s \in [0,\mathbf{f}]$; and sanctions to non-reporting violators who have a self-auditing programme in place, $f_a \in [0,\mathbf{f}]$, and who do not, $f \in [0,\mathbf{f}]$.

Without self-auditing, law enforcement takes the no-self-reporting form described in (pp. 152–3) above, generating the minimum welfare costs J^{N*} of equation (8.4). The benefit of self-auditing is that it permits some self-reporting, which in turn permits the government to achieve a given apprehension probability r at a lower per-firm cost, $rm (1 - p(x) \rho)$ versus rm. The economic merits of eliciting self-auditing will turn on the relative weight of these enforcement cost savings and the self-auditing cost, A.

Optimal Enforcement with Self-auditing and Self-reporting

In choosing whether to self-audit or not, firms calculate the total average costs that they face under a self-auditing programme and compare these costs to those faced when they do not self-audit. When firms do not self-audit, they face an average accident sanction, $F = rf$, which yields the minimum cost $V(rf)$, where (per equation (8.1)):

$$V(F) = \min_{x \geq 0} x + p(x) F.$$

When self-auditing and self-reporting occur, the accident sanction (F) equals the average of the self-reporting sanction (s) and the self-auditor's non-reporting sanction (rf_a):

$$FS = \rho s + (1 - \rho)rf_a. \tag{8.21}$$

A firm's total cost of self-auditing is thus the auditing cost A plus the minimized accident and accident prevention costs, $V(F_S)$. In order for self-auditing to occur, the self-auditing strategy must yield (weakly) lower costs, as follows:

(SA) $A + V(F_S) \leq V(rf)$.

Now consider how the government can minimize welfare costs by choice of the average self-auditing sanction F_S, the monitoring rate r, and the no-auditing (NSA) sanction f, subject to eliciting self-auditing. With societal costs equal to the sum of the self-auditing investment (A), accident prevention effort (x), average accident damages ($p(x)h$), and enforcement expenditures ($mr(1 - p(x)\rho)$), this choice problem is as follows:

$$J^{S*}(A) = \min_{\{r, F_S, f\}} A + x^*(F_S) + p(x^*(F_S))h + mr(1 - p(x^*(F_S))\rho)$$

$$\text{s.t.} \quad (SA), F_S \geq 0, f \in [0, \mathbf{f}], r \in [0, 1]. \tag{8.22}$$

Remark 4   In any solution to problem (8.22), (a) the no-auditing sanction is set maximally, $f = \mathbf{f}$ (Becker 1968); (b) constraint (SA) holds with equality,

(SA′) $F_S = F(r, A) \equiv F: A + V(F) = V(r\mathbf{f});$

and (c) the average sanction F_S can be supported by a policy pair (s,f_a) that satisfies (i) equation (8.21) ($F_S = \rho s + (1 - \rho)rf_a$), (ii) the feasibility restrictions, $s \in [0,\mathbf{f}]$ and $f_a \in [0,\mathbf{f}]$, and (iii) the self-reporting constraint, $s \leq rf_a$.

Remark 4 establishes that the optimal average sanction (F_S) can always be supported by constituent self-reporting and non-reporting sanctions, s and f_a, that prompt self-reporting of self-detected violations, as implicitly assumed in (8.22). To understand this result, consider setting the sanction s so as to just elicit self-reporting, $s = rf_a$; now vary the non-reporting sanction f_a between its lower bound (zero) and its upper bound $(\mathbf{f})$. In this way, any F_S in the interval $[0,r\mathbf{f}]$ can be supported. Note finally that an optimal F_S must lie in this interval because (a) F_S is constrained to be non-negative (by (8.22)); and (b) F_S must be lower than $r\mathbf{f}$ in order to elicit self-auditing.

Given (SA′), the non-negativity restriction on F_S imposes an equivalent bound on the monitoring rate r:

$$F_S = F(r,A) \geq 0 \Leftrightarrow r \geq \underline{r}(A) \equiv r: V(r\mathbf{f}) = A, \qquad (8.23)$$

where $\underline{r}(0) = 0$, $\underline{r}'(A) > 0$, and $F(r,A)$ is as defined in (SA′). With $f = \mathbf{f}$, $F_S = F(r,A)$ (from (SA′)), and equation (8.23), the government's problem becomes:

$$J^{S*}(A) = \min_{r} A + x^*(F(r,A)) + p(x^*(F(r,A)))h + mr(1 - p(x^*(F(r,A)))\rho) \qquad (8.22')$$
$$\text{s.t. } r \in [\underline{r}(A),1].$$

I shall denote the solution to (8.22′) by $r^*(A)$.

Comparing the minimum welfare costs under self-auditing enforcement, J^{S*} in (8.22′), to its counterpart under enforcement with no self-auditing, J^{N*} in (8.4), we can now determine if and when self-auditing is optimal. Formally, define:

$$\Delta(A) \equiv J^{N*} - J^{S*}(A).$$

Enacting an optimal self-auditing programme will increase social welfare (by reducing welfare costs) if and only if $\Delta(A) > 0$.

Remark 5 (a) If $r^*(A) = \underline{r}(A)$, then $\Delta(A) < 0$. (b) When self-auditing costs are zero (A = 0), self-auditing is optimal: $\Delta(0) > 0$ (KS). (c) Define the maximum auditing cost that permits self-auditing to occur $\overline{A} \in [0,\mathbf{f}]$: $\underline{r}(\overline{A}) = 1$.[18] Self-auditing is not optimal if $A = \overline{A}$, $\Delta(\overline{A}) < 0$. (d) Societal benefits of self-auditing decline with the auditing cost A, $\Delta'(A) < 0$.

Proposition 12 There exists a positive critical self-auditing cost, $A_c \in [0, \bar{A}]$, such that (a) a self-auditing enforcement regime is strictly optimal whenever the true self-auditing cost A is lower than this critical level, and (b) self-auditing is not optimal whenever A is higher: $\Delta(A_c) = 0$, $\Delta(A) > 0$ for all $A < A_c$, and $\Delta(A) < 0$ for all $A > A_c$.

When there are no costs to self-auditing (as in KS), a self-auditing regime can achieve the same level of deterrence as an NSA regime without changing the government monitoring rate r; this strategy is advantageous because it reduces enforcement costs ($\Delta(0) > 0$). However, this strategy is not possible when there are positive costs of auditing ($A > 0$). In this case, eliciting self-auditing requires either raising the monitoring rate r or lowering the accident penalty F_S – or both – in order to raise the firm's penalty for refraining from auditing (with the higher no-auditor sanction, $r\mathbf{f}$) and/or reducing the sanction that self-auditors enjoy (F_S); self-auditors are thereby compensated for their investment A. In sum, eliciting self-auditing is costly, both directly and indirectly – and more costly as A rises ($\Delta'(A) < 0$). Hence, only when A is sufficiently small ($A \le A_c$) will self-auditing be optimal.

Proposition 13 Whenever self-auditing is optimal ($A \le A_c$), (a) the optimal government monitoring rate is positive and higher than its minimum level, $\underline{r}(A)$: $0 \le \underline{r}(A) < r^*(A)$; (b) the optimal average sanction is strictly positive: $F_S^* = F(r^*(A), A) > 0$; (c) optimal deterrence and care are less than first-best ($F_S^* < h$, $x^*(F_S^*) < x^*(h)$); (d) optimal deterrence falls when the self-auditing cost A rises: $dF(r^*(A), A)/dA < 0$; and (e) optimal deterrence is lower in the self-auditing enforcement regime than in the NSA enforcement regime ($F(r^*(A), A) \le r^N\mathbf{f}$), provided $A > 0$ and

$$\left| \, d\ln p'(x) \, / \, d\ln x \, \right| \le \left| \, d\ln p(x) \, / \, d\ln x \, \right| \text{ at } x = x^*(F_S^*). \qquad (8.25)$$

To understand Proposition 12, recall first that the purpose of enforcement is to provide deterrence. Hence, a self-auditing regime that provides no deterrence (by setting $r = \underline{r}(A)$ and $F_S = F(\underline{r}(A), A) = 0$) only wastes the self-auditing investment A; the government could do better with no monitoring and no self-auditing – providing zero deterrence at zero cost. For self-auditing to be optimal, positive deterrence must therefore be provided. However, because higher levels of deterrence require higher government expenditures on enforcement, optimal deterrence is less than first-best. When the self-auditing cost (A) rises, the enforcement effort required to achieve a given level of deterrence – and still elicit self-auditing – rises in tandem; with diminishing returns to enforcement effort, the marginal enforcement effort required to achieve marginal deterrence rises as well. As a result, optimal deterrence falls.

The relationship between optimal deterrence under self-auditing and NSA regimes (Proposition 13(e)) is determined by three offsetting forces. First, with self-auditing and self-reporting, there are smaller enforcement costs associated with any given monitoring rate r – because only non-reporters need to be monitored. This favours a *higher* level of monitoring and deterrence. Second, with self-reporting, higher levels of deterrence lead to fewer violators and, hence, a greater number of non-reporters who are subject to government monitoring. This implies an enforcement-cost-*raising* effect of higher deterrence that is absent when there is no self-reporting; a *lower* level of deterrence is thus favoured. Third, when the self-auditing cost A is positive, self-auditing requires higher monitoring rates in order to support given levels of deterrence – and greater increases in monitoring rates in order to raise deterrence marginally. Again, *less* deterrence is favoured.

Condition (8.25) ensures that the second (deterrence-reducing) effect of self-auditing dominates the first (deterrence-raising) effect. This condition is likely to hold in general; it simply requires that care does not have proportionately lower first derivative effects – *vis-à-vis* second derivative effects – on the probability of a violation.[19]

Because self-auditing can be either welfare-increasing or welfare-decreasing, it is of interest to evaluate how relevant economic parameters affect the critical value of A (A_c) that demarks these two cases. Recalling (8.24) and the definition of A_c $(\Delta(A_c) = 0)$, we can implicitly differentiate with respect to $z \in \{\mathbf{f},m,h,\rho\} \equiv Z$, as follows:

$$dA_c / dz = -\frac{\partial \Delta(A_c;Z)/\partial z}{\partial \Delta(A_c;Z)/\partial A} \overset{s}{=} \partial \Delta(A_c;Z)/\partial z,$$

$$= \left(\partial J^{N*}(\mathbf{f},m,h)/\partial z\right) - \left(\partial J^{S*}(A_c;\mathbf{f},m,h,\rho)/\partial z\right) \qquad (8.26)$$

where $J^{N*}()$ and $J^{S*}()$ are the minimum welfare costs defined in (8.4) and (8.22′); and the sign equality ($\underline{s}$) follows from Remark 5 $(\partial \Delta()/\partial A < 0)$. Evaluating the right-hand side of (8.26) gives:[20]

$$\partial \Delta(A_c;Z)/\partial \mathbf{f} \overset{\underline{s}}{=} \{m\, r^*(A_c;Z)\, (1 - p(x^*(F_S^*)\rho) - mr^N(Z)\} \overset{\underline{s}}{=} -\partial \Delta(A_c;Z)/\partial m \qquad (8.27a)$$

$$\partial \Delta(A_c;Z)/\partial h = p(x^*(r^N(Z)\mathbf{f})) - p(x^*(F_S^*)) \qquad (8.27b)$$

$$\partial \Delta(A_c;Z)/\partial r = m\, r^*(A_c;Z)\, p(x^*(F_S^*)) > 0, \qquad (8.27c)$$

where $F_S^* = F(r^*(A_c;Z);A_c,\mathbf{f})$ (from (SA')) and $r^N() = \text{argmin } J^N(r,\mathbf{f};Z)$ is the optimal NSA monitoring rate (from (8.4)). To interpret equation (8.27), note:

Remark 6 If self-auditing is weakly optimal $(A < A_c)$ and the optimal NSA regime yields a level of deterrence that is at least as high as does the optimal self-auditing regime, then average enforcement costs are strictly lower under the optimal self-auditing regime than they are under the optimal NSA regime, $m \, r^*(A_c;Z) \, (1 - q(x^*(F_S^*)\rho)) < mr^N(Z)$.

When self-auditing lowers (and thereby worsens) deterrence, then self-auditing must enjoy an enforcement cost advantage over the non-auditing (NSA) regime; otherwise, the self-auditing regime will not be optimal (Remark 6). Now recalling my earlier argument that self-auditing is very likely to lower deterrence (because condition (8.25) is likely to hold), we have the following results from equations (8.26)–(8.27):

Proposition 14 If condition (8.25) holds, then the critical auditing cost below which self-auditing is welfare-increasing (A_c) is higher when (a) the maximal firm sanction $(\mathbf{f})$ is lower, (b) the government auditing cost (m) is higher, and (c) the harm from a violation (h) is lower. A_c is also higher (whether (8.25) holds or not) when (d) the firm's auditing technology is more effective (with a higher level of ρ).

Underpinning Proposition 14 is the following logic. First, self-auditing is optimal in more cases (with a larger range of auditing costs A) when self-reporting produces greater enforcement savings, $rmp(x)\rho$. The latter economies are greater when the maximal sanction is lower and, as a result, achieving requisite deterrence in the NSA regime requires a large government monitoring rate r. These enforcement economies are also greater when the government's monitoring cost (m) is higher and its auditing technology is better (because ρ is higher). Second, under plausible conditions (equation (8.25)), a self-auditing regime is optimal only when it yields enforcement cost savings (net of the self-auditing cost A) that dominate its costs in depleting deterrence. Moreover, the welfare cost of worsened underdeterrence is greater when the harm from a violation is higher. As a result, self-auditing becomes optimal more often (for a wider range of A) when harm is lower.

Implications

Firms can and do invest in costly self-auditing programmes in order to determine whether and how they may be violating environmental or other laws. The societal benefit of these investments is that they permit firms to self-report their offences, which can improve social welfare for all of the reasons discussed in the first section, above. In the presence of positive self-auditing costs, an optimal enforcement regime balances these benefits of self-auditing against its costs, both direct and indirect. In studying how the government can make this optimization – when self-reporting enjoys the direct enforcement economies identified by KS and M – several qualitative implications are derived.

First, in order to elicit self-auditing programme investments – and attendant self-reporting – the sanction that is levied on self-reporting violators must be *strictly less than* the average sanction that is faced by non-reporting (and non-auditing) firms (per (SA′). In fact, the self-reporting sanction that supports an optimal self-auditing enforcement regime can be quite small in principle. This observation is of some practical interest. For example, extant theory suggests a test for an efficient self-reporting statute: are self-reporters levied a substantial sanction that leaves them almost indifferent between self-reporting and not? This test is failed by most state-level self-auditing statutes (Anderson 1996; Weaver *et al.* 1997). However, accounting for costs of self-auditing, this failure may not be cause for concern and, indeed, may be necessary for these statutes to efficiently prompt the self-auditing investments that are their goal.

Second, when an optimal enforcement regime elicits self-auditing, self-reporting need not (and likely will not) always occur. Because self-auditing is not a perfect process, self-auditors will not always detect their offences.

Third, only when self-auditing programme costs are sufficiently low will self-auditing enforcement regimes be optimal. Moreover, self-auditing is more likely to be advantageous (for a wider range of self-auditing costs) when maximal sanctions are smaller, violations are less harmful, government monitoring costs are greater, and the self-auditing technology is more effective. This logic suggests that smaller firms which can be subject to smaller maximal sanctions and which have less potentially harmful violations are particularly apt objects of self-auditing enforcement reforms.

VIOLATOR REMEDIATION AND SELF-POLICING

In the foregoing analysis of violator remediation (pp. 154–6), I implicitly assumed that the government cannot distinguish between pre- and post-apprehension remediation and, hence, can only prompt remediation by imposing post-apprehension clean-up mandates. Let us now consider the alternative, when the government *can* observe a firm's prior level of remediation when it discovers an accident. In this case, the government can elicit *self-policing* – voluntary pre-apprehension remediation – with the promise of reduced sanctions. This possibility raises two related issues: (a) What are the social costs and advantages of *eliciting* self-policing, rather than achieving remediation with government mandates? (b) How does the desire to achieve remediation affect the optimal design of law enforcement – the sanctions that are levied, the accident deterrence incentives that are afforded to potential violators, the government's investment in enforcement activity, and the extent and frequency of remediation activity?[21]

The Model

I again consider the standard accident regulation model described above (p. 151). The innovation here is that, once an accident has occurred, a firm can 'clean up'. Clean-up reduces the damages caused and can also reduce the risk to the firm that the government will detect the accident and levy a penalty. Clean-up can occur either before enforcement – that is, before the government detects accidents and penalizes firms that have caused them – or after enforcement.[22] I shall denote a firm's pre-apprehension clean-up level by $c \in [0,\mathbf{c}]$, and the sum of pre- and post-apprehension clean-up by $C \in [0,\mathbf{c}]$. C yields the accident damage $D(C)$, which is assumed to be decreasing and convex with $D'(\mathbf{c}) = 0$ and $\mid D'(0) \mid$ arbitrarily large. There is then the interior and unique first-best clean-up level:

$$c^* \equiv \text{argmin } h(C) \equiv (C + D(C)) \in [0,\mathbf{c}]. \qquad (8.28)$$

The probability with which the government detects a firm's accident depends upon its (per-firm) monitoring investment g and the firm's pre-apprehension clean-up c, $r(g,c)$.[23] In contrast to pp. 154–6, I now assume that the government can freely observe c whenever it detects an accident. I also suppose that the government can randomly penalize violators whom it has apprehended. In this environment, the government chooses its monitoring investment g and the probability with which a detected violator is penalized, ρ. For those firms that are penalized, the government levies a fine f and mandates a level of total clean-up, $C = c^M$. All of the penalization parameters can depend upon the observed level of c, $\rho = \rho(c) \in [0,1], f = f(c)$ and $c^M(c) \geq c$ for $c \in [0,\bar{c}]$. As before, fines are subject to upper and lower bounds, $0 \leq f(c) \leq \mathbf{f} - c$, with clean-up costs now separate and distinct from the fine. Moreover, when a positive fine is levied ($f > 0$) or a 'positive' clean-up mandate imposed ($c^M > c$), I assume that the government must bear a fixed administrative cost of $\beta > 0$, a cost which will be seen to motivate a policy of random penalization ($\rho < 1$).

The Clean-up Choice and Government Sanctions

Once an accident occurs, the firm's pre-apprehension clean-up choice problem is:

$$F = \min_{c \,\in\, [0,c]} c + r(g,c)\rho(c)(f(c) + c^M(c) - c). \qquad (8.29)$$

The minimand in (8.29) gives the firm's direct cost of pre-apprehension clean-up (c) plus the expected cost of accident penalties. The latter cost equals the joint probability of government detection and penalization, $r(g,c)\rho(c)$, times the sum of fines levied ($f(c)$) and post-apprehension clean-up that is mandated ($c^M(c) - c$) when the firm is penalized. The firm's total accident penalty, F, is the minimal average post-accident cost given in (8.29).

A constraint on the government's policy choices is that the pre-apprehension clean-up level 'targeted' by the government, let us call it c_T, solves problem (8.29). Now note: if an optimal enforcement regime elicits $c = c_T$, then this regime is economically equivalent to another that maximizes penalties to a firm that chooses any clean-up level other than c_T, and sets identical penalization parameters for a firm that chooses $c = c_T$. Under the alternative regime, the firm's incentive to choose c_T is at least as great as before; hence, c_T continues to satisfy the incentive constraint (8.29). Moreover, the actual penalties levied, clean-up mandates imposed and accident damages caused are the same as before; so too, therefore, is the firm's elicited level of 'care'. That is, all economic outcomes are the same. Therefore, without loss of generality, we can assume that the penalization regime takes the 'negligence' form,

$$\{\rho(c),f(c),c^M(c)\} = \{\rho,f,c^M\} \text{ for } c = c_T \qquad (8.30)$$
$$\{1, \mathbf{f} - c, c\} \text{ for all } c \neq c_T.$$

This penalization regime yields a simplified incentive constraint, where I now use an unsubscripted c to denote the 'target' clean-up level:

$$F = c + r(g,c)\rho(f + c^M - c) \leq \min_{c' \,\in\, [0,c]} [c' + r(g,c')(\mathbf{f} - c')] \equiv Q(G). \qquad (8.29')$$

Optimal Clean-up Mandates

If a firm (a) has had an accident, (b) has engaged in less than first-best clean-up, $c < c^*$, (c) has been detected, and (d) is being penalized, then it will be optimal for the government to mandate first-best clean-up, $c^M = c^*$, in order to minimize the *ex post* damage, $h(C) \equiv C + D(C)$. Thus, we have:

$$c^M = \max(c,c^*). \qquad (8.31)$$

With detection and penalization, total post-accident costs are $h(\max(c,c^*)) + \beta$. If either detection or penalization does not occur, then the firm only bears its pre-apprehension clean-up costs c, and damages are $h(c)$. Total expected accident damage is thus:

$$\text{Expected accident damage} = r(g,c)\rho[h(\max(c,c^*)) + \beta] + (1 - r(g,c)\rho)h(c). \tag{8.32}$$

Optimal Enforcement Policy

Given the average accident penalty described in (8.29′), the mandate policy in (8.31), and the average accident damages in (8.32), the government's societal cost minimization problem can be stated as follows, with $c^M = \max(c,c^*)$:

$$\min_{\{\rho,g,f,c\}} g + x^*(\text{F}) + p(x^*(\text{F}))\{r(g,c)\rho[h(c^M) + \beta] + (1 - r(h,c)\rho)h(c)\} \tag{8.33}$$

subject to (8.29′), $f + c^M \leq \mathbf{f}, f \geq 0, \rho \in [0,1], c \in [0,\mathbf{c}]$. Observe that if either $\rho = 0$ or $c \geq c^*$, then problem (8.33) (with $c^M = \max(c,c^*)$) reduces to a simpler problem (SP) (8.33) with $c^M = c$:

Lemma 2 Suppose that a solution to problem (SP) ((8.33) with $c^M = c$) sets $c > c^*$ whenever it sets $\rho > 0$. Then any solution to (SP) also solves (8.33) (with $c^M = \max(c,c^*)$).

In due course, we shall see that the premise of Lemma 2 is valid. For the moment, note that problem (SP) is indeed 'simpler' because it implies that there are no *ex post* societal benefits of penalization and attendant mandates that first-best clean-up be performed. Rather, average accident damages reduce to $h(c) + r(g,c)\rho\beta$, the sum of accident damages with only pre-apprehension clean-up, and average administrative costs of penalization. A solution to (SP) will therefore achieve a given level of accident deterrence, $\text{F} = c + r(g,c)\rho f$, with a minimum possible probability of penalization ρ, in order to minimize the average administrative costs $r()\rho\beta$. This objective is achieved by setting the fine as high as possible:

Lemma 3 A solution to (SP) will set f maximally, $f = \mathbf{f} - c$, whenever it sets $\rho > 0$. (When $\rho = 0$ in the optimum, f can also be set maximally without loss of generality.)

With $c^M = c$ (by the construction of (SP)) and $f = \mathbf{f} - c$ (Lemma 3), (8.29′) becomes:

$$\text{F} = c + r(g,c) \rho (\mathbf{f} - c) \leq \min_{c' \in [0,\mathbf{c}]} [c' + r(g,c')(ff - c')] = Q(g). \tag{8.29″}$$

Clearly, the revised constraint (8.29″) can be slack *only if* the penalization probability ρ is less than one. Therefore, (8.29″) must bind in a solution to (SP) because, if it were slack, ρ could be raised and the government monitoring investment *g* lowered in tandem so as to preserve the total probability of penalization, $r(g,c)\rho$; this strategy would preserve accident deterrence and damages, and directly lower enforcement costs.

Lemma 4   Constraint (8.29″) binds in any solution to (SP), and suffices to ensure that ρ is no greater than one.

Substituting for $f = \mathbf{f} - c$ (from Lemma 3) and for F and ρ (from (8.29″), given Lemma 4), problem (SP) now reduces to:

$$\min_{\{g,c\}} g + x^*(Q(g)) + p(x^*(Q(g)))\{r(g,c)\rho(g,c)\beta + h(c)\} \qquad (8.34a)$$

subject to:

$$\rho(g,c) \equiv [Q(g) - c]/[r(g,c)(\mathbf{f} - c)] \geq 0. \qquad (8.34b)$$

There are two possible cases: (a) When ρ > 0 in the solution (that is, (8.34b) does not bind); and (b) when ρ = 0 (that is, (8.34b) binds). In the first case, an optimal clean-up target minimizes average post-accident damages and costs by either being set maximally (at $c = \mathbf{c}$) or by solving the following optimality condition:

$$h'(c) = [\beta/(\mathbf{f} - c)][1 - \rho(g,c)r(g,c)] > 0, \qquad (8.35)$$

where the inequality follows from $\mathbf{f} > \mathbf{c} \geq c$, $\beta > 0$, $\rho(g,c) \leq 1$, and $r(g,c) < 1$. Because the inequality, $h'(c) > 0$, implies that c is greater than c^*, *the premise of Lemma 2 is validated*, and we have (from Lemmas 2–4):

Proposition 15   Whenever an optimal enforcement regime penalizes detected violators with a positive probability (ρ > 0), it (a) elicits a higher level of pre-apprehension clean-up than is first-best, $c > c^*$, and (b) under-deters accidents with an accident penalty F that is less than total *ex post* accident costs, $h(c) + r()\rho()\beta$.[24]

Optimal clean-up is above its first-best level because marginal clean-up enjoys an additional economic benefit, over and beyond lowering accident damages: a higher clean-up level directly raises the firm's cost of an accident, thus lowering the expected accident fine that is needed to provide a given level of accident deterrence. By doing so, it permits a given accident deterrent to be achieved with a lower probability of penalization ρ, and hence, a lower level of average administrative cost, $\beta\rho r(g,c)$.

This logic, of course, requires that the penalization probability *can* be lowered, a valid premise when ρ is positive but not when ρ is zero. In this second case (when (8.34b) strictly binds), problem (8.34) can be reformulated by substituting $\rho() = 0$:

$$\min_{g} g + x^*(Q(g)) + p(x^*(Q(g)))h(Q(g)) \qquad (8.36)$$

where $c = Q(g)$. There are now two offsetting forces that drive the relationship between an optimal cleanup target c and the first-best clean-up level c^*. First, an increase in c requires an attendant increase in the government monitoring investment g in order to raise the firm's penalty from failing to meet the higher clean-up standard and thereby provide the needed financial incentive for the firm to bear the additional clean-up cost. Second, a higher level of c improves accident deterrence by raising the accident penalty to violating firms. Because the 'monitoring cost of clean-up' favours a lower c, and the deterrence benefit favours a higher c, *an optimal clean-up target can be either higher or lower than first-best,* c^*.[25] Note, however, that *positive self-policing, c > 0, is always optimal*; in a zero penalization regime, the clean-up target is set equal to the maximum possible (and positive) accident deterrent $Q(g)$ in order to secure benefits of both deterrence and remediation.[26]

In sum, when allowing for continuous clean-up and random penalization, we find that an optimal enforcement regime not only elicits self-policing but elicits more clean-up than is first-best so long as firms are ever sanctioned for their violations. The extra clean-up substitutes for post-detection sanctions that are costly to impose, thus permitting a saving of enforcement resources. Voluntary (pre-apprehension) clean-up is optimally elicited using a 'negligence' rule that maximally and certainly penalizes any firm which fails to meet the requisite standard of remediation, and offering a reduced risk of penalty to those firms which do meet the clean-up standard. To elicit remediation without compromising deterrence, the reward to clean-up – the reduction in the expected sanction – is just sufficient to cover the clean-up costs that the firm must bear.

Implications: Self-reporting and Self-policing

In this section's optimal enforcement regime, voluntary violator remediation is elicited without self-reporting of behaviour. Hence, when sanctions *can* be conditioned upon prior remediation, self-reporting is no longer motivated, *per se*, by the desire to achieve early and certain clean-up (as on pp. 154–6). However, self-reporting may still enjoy the other benefits identified in the first section.

If so, the logic of this analysis favours *both* self-reporting and self-policing. To economize optimally on administrative costs of penalization, self-reporters are only penalized with a probability less than one; self-policing incentives – with explicit rewards for voluntary remediation – are thus needed to ensure that efficient remediation always occurs.

CONCLUSION: IMPLICATIONS FOR US ENVIRONMENTAL POLICY

This chapter presents a standard conceptualization of environmental law enforcement that yields a variety of economic motives for enforcement regimes which prompt firms, using appropriate incentives, to self-report their offences; to conduct environmental self-audits that permit them to uncover and report violations of environmental law; and to engage in self-initiated remediation when harmful accidents (such as pollutant releases) are discovered. How do these conclusions relate to observed practice in the US?

Many US environmental statutes stipulate explicit penalties for violators who do not self-report their offences, thereby providing some limited incentive for violators to self-report.[27] In addition, over twenty states have recently enacted laws that encourage firms voluntarily to audit their environmental performance and self-report violations of environmental statutes (Anderson 1996; Weaver *et al.* 1997); to provide these incentives, state laws promise a combination of liability protections and privilege for information contained in environmental self-reports and self-audits. Together, the US Environmental Protection Agency (EPA) and the US Department of Justice (DOJ) have also reformed their law enforcement and criminal prosecution policies in order to encourage environmental self-audits and self-disclosure. In 1995, the EPA enacted a policy stipulating that, for qualified self-reporters, the agency will seek reduced penalties, not recommend criminal prosecution, and 'not request or use an environmental audit report to initiate a civil or criminal investigation'.[28] The DOJ has directed its prosecutors to consider a violator's efforts to monitor its compliance with environmental laws and to promptly report and correct any violations, as mitigating factors in a decision on whether or not to prosecute.[29]

Despite these reforms, legal analysts and the regulated community have criticized federal enforcement policy for providing little incentive for regulated firms to self-audit. Beyond direct costs of environmental self-audits are a number of perils which face regulated firms that conduct these audits and report any detected violations. First, a self-reporter's eligibility for favourable regulatory treatment by the EPA can be costly and unclear due to a number of onerous requirements for this eligibility (Weaver *et al.* 1997). Moreover, experience with the EPA's self-disclosure policy indicates that self-reporting firms have none the less been subject to large monetary sanctions (McIntyre 1997). Second, current federal laws and regulations give no evidentiary privilege protections to environmental self-audit reports. The EPA's option of obtaining audit results can place a self-reporter at risk for other civil enforcement actions (Shearer 1996). The ability of the EPA to protect self-reported information from others is also unclear in view of the Freedom of Information Act's requirements (ibid.). As a result, self-reporters can risk the loss of trade secrets and proprietary business information that is important to their competitive advantage. In addition, self-reports might be used by private citizens in toxic tort actions against the firm and citizen suits that seek sanctions and injunctions not sought by government authorities (Weaver et al. 1997).[30] Third, under the responsible corporate officer doctrine, an environmental self-audit (by identifying acts that may violate environmental law) can lead to criminal liability for corporate employees – even if the employees have neither any knowledge that the company's acts constitute a violation nor any *intent* to violate the law (Frost 1991). This risk is particularly vexing in view of environmental regulations that are frequently changing and rather complex.

Given the risks that firms face when they self-report their environmental violations, it is perhaps not surprising that federal policies to encourage this practice have had only modest success (Weaver et al. 1997). This chapter suggests that there may be substantial economic dividends from stronger incentives for environmental self-reporting, self-auditing and self-initiated remediation – including saved avoidance costs, reduced enforcement costs and an increased frequency of appropriate remediation.

NOTES

1. This inquiry, of course, builds upon a law enforcement literature that is too vast to cite appropriately here. See, for example, the classic papers of Becker (1968) and Stigler (1970), and the more recent work of Shavell (1991), Mookherjee and Png (1992), and Polinsky and Shavell (1992). Important related work on environmental law enforcement includes Grieson and Singh (1990), Harrington (1988), Harford and Harrington (1991), Heyes and Rickman (1999), Russell et al. (1986), and Garvie and Keeler (1994). Most closely related is a rather recent literature on self-reporting, including the key works of Kaplow and Shavell (KS, 1994) and Malik (M, 1993); see also interesting papers by Harford (1987) and Swierzbinski (1994), who study self-reporting in environmental regulation but do not focus on the relative efficiency properties of self-reporting and non-reporting enforcement regimes that are at issue in this chapter.
2. Proofs of all results contained in this chapter are available from the author.
3. Positive enforcement effort follows from my simplifying premise that marginal care is extremely effective in reducing accident risk ($p'(0)$ arbitrarily large), which also implies that marginal enforcement effort enjoys arbitrarily large accident-risk-reduction benefits. However, KS consider a setting in which zero enforcement effort is possible and show that self-reporting is none the less welfare-enhancing.

4. This specification is also realistic when enforcement occurs by *monitoring*, which KS describe as 'the posting of enforcement agents to observe violations among any of a population, such as when police are stationed at the roadside'. In such cases, self-reports have no effect on the number of – or investment in – monitoring posts that is required to achieve a given likelihood of detecting a non-reporter's violation.

5. For g below a finite threshold $\mathbf{g}$, I shall assume that $r'(g) > 0$ and $r''(g) < 0$, $r(0)$ is arbitrarily small, $r'(0)$ is arbitrarily large, and $r'(g) = 0$ for $g > \mathbf{g}$ (ensuring that positive and bounded enforcement effort is undertaken).

6. For notational simplicity, I shall subsume the clean-up cost in the fines; hence, actual fines are less than the notional fines f and s by the amount c.

7. Implicit in this argument is the premise that the government cannot condition its sanctions on a firm's level of pre-apprehension clean-up. The third section below considers the reversal of this premise.

8. There is a rather extensive literature that identifies reasons for the failure of the Becker (1968) logic. See Bebchuk and Kaplow (1992) for a succinct and complete review of this literature.

9. Both of these cost-reducing effects of self-reporting occur only when there are positive *ex post* benefits of clean-up; without any clean-up benefits, f^{NSR} equals f and, hence, $g_o = g^{NSR}$.

10. It is presumed here – and easy to show – that the optimal NSR regime will have the property that the government imposes a common (non-stochastic) fine on all firms whose accidents have been detected. Otherwise, it could lower g and increase the proportion of 'caught culprits' that it penalizes, preserving both accident prevention incentives and *ex post* expected accident damages.

11. Firms may also be distinguished by other attributes about which they may have private information, but which are unlikely to alter the qualitative implications of interest in this chapter. For example, KS show how qualitative conclusions on self-reporting enforcement strategies can be extended to allow for heterogeneous accidents damages.

12. If either $f < \mathbf{f}$ or $s < r(g)\mathbf{\delta}f$, g could be lowered and all firms' accident deterrent preserved. Note, however, that when the probability of apprehension is not multiplicatively separable in g and δ, the Becker result may not always hold. Bebchuk and Kaplow (1993) develop this point in an enforcement model without self-reporting. Qualitative conclusions developed here – other than the Becker result – are robust to alternative specifications for the apprehension probability.

13. I assume $r_g > 0$ and $r_{gg} < 0$, $r_a < 0$ and $r_{aa} > 0$ (avoidance effort lowers detection risk at a diminishing rate), and $r_{ga} \leq 0$ (avoidance effort does not raise marginal benefits of enforcement effort), all on the compact set $[0,g]\times[0,a]$; for all a, $r(0,a) = 0$, $r_g(0,a)$ is arbitrarily large, and $r_g(g,a) = 0$ for $g \geq \mathbf{g}$; and for all $g > 0$, $|r_a(g,0)|$ is arbitrarily large, and $r_a(g,0) = 0$ for $a \geq a$. These premises ensure positive (and bounded) enforcement and avoidance effort.

14. Equation (8.20) is obtained by differentiating the first-order optimality condition from problem (8.18), $1 + r_a() s = 0$.

15. With $g^{NSR} > 0$ and $f^{NSR} > 0$, $a(g^{NSR}, f^{NSR}) > 0$ by Remark 2.

16. This inquiry (following Innes 2000b) implicitly builds upon classic works on the efficient acquisition of information (and legal advice), as well as the self-reporting literature. This prior literature, however, does not explore the linkages between the costs and design of government enforcement, on the one hand, and the acquisition of information, on the other (although Kaplow 1990 discussses this link briefly). See Innes (2000b) or Kaplow and Shavell (2000) for surveys of this prior work.

17. For simplicity (and because it is generally realistic), I shall assume that the maximal sanction $\mathbf{f}$ is greater than accident harm h and that the monitoring cost m is less than harm.

18. With $V(r\mathbf{f}) > 0$ and $V(r\mathbf{f}) < \mathbf{f}$ (by $p(x) < 1$ and $r \in [0,1]$), $\bar{A} \in [0,\mathbf{f}]$ exists by the Intermediate Value Theorem and the definition of $\underline{r}(A)$ in equation (8.23).

19. For example, when $p(x)$ takes the exponential form, $p(x) = (1 + e^x)^{-1}$, $|$ dln $p(x) /$ dln $x \mid - \mid$ dln $p'(x) /$ dln $x \mid = p(x)x > 0$, thus satisfying condition (8.25).

20. Recall from Proposition 12(a) that $r^*(A_c;Z) > \underline{r}(A_c;Z)$. Therefore,

$$\partial J^{S^*}(A_c;Z)/\partial z = [\partial J^S(r^*(A_c;Z);A_c,Z)/\partial r] [\partial r^*()/\partial z] + \partial J^S(r^*();A_c,Z)/\partial z = \partial J^S()/\partial z,$$

where the last equality is due to (a) $\partial J^S(r^*();.)/\partial r = 0$ if $r^*() < 1$, and (b) either $\partial J^S(r^*();.)/\partial r = 0$ or $\partial r^*()/\partial z = 0$ if $r^*() = 1$.

21. This section builds most closely upon Innes (1999c), where I study self-policing in a model which does not include administrative costs of penalty assessments and also does not consider the potential dependence of a firm's apprehension risk on its clean-up level. See also Polinsky and Shavell (1994) for a study of violator remediation without enforcement problems.

22. The two types of clean-up, pre- and post-apprehension, are implicitly assumed to be perfect substitutes in reducing damages. In practice, pre-apprehension clean-up is likely to have greater damage-reducing effects that swamp the discounting benefits of deferring clean-up costs until after enforcement occurs. I ignore both of these effects for the sake of simplicity and because I do not want to motivate self-policing by obvious timing advantages.

23. For generality here, I do not restrict the sign of $r_c(g,c)$. However, for environmental examples, it is likely that clean-up lowers detection risk, $r_c(g,c) \le 0$. To ensure that positive and bounded enforcement effort is undertaken, the following restrictions are also assumed to hold: $r_{gg}(g,c) < 0$, $r(0,c)$ is arbitrarily small, $r_g(0,c)$ is arbitrarily large, and $r_g(g,c) = 0$ for $g > \mathbf{g}$.

24. The second (underdeterrence) result of Proposition 15 is obtained from the necessary condition for an optimal level of g in problem (8.34a). Intuitively, monitoring and penalization costs of achieving accident deterrence motivate a lower level of deterrence than would otherwise be optimal.

25. Formally, differentiating (8.36) gives us the following marginal net societal cost of G (after substituting from the optimality condition from the firm's care choice problem (8.1)): $1 + Q'x^{*\prime} p'D(c) + Q'p h'$. For example, at a monitoring level that supports the first-best clean-up c^*, $g > 0$: $h'(Q(g)) = 0$, this derivative will be negative – and thus justify a higher-than-first-best clean-up target – if the deterrence benefit of additional penalization (the derivative's second term, which is negative) is larger than the requisite monitoring cost of one (the first term).

26. Combined with Lemma 2 and Proposition 15, the proof of Lemma 4 establishes that g is positive in any enforcement optimum. Therefore, when $\rho = 0$ in the optimum, we have that $c = Q(g) > 0$.

27. The Comprehensive Environmental Response, Compensation, and Liability Act (CERCLA, or Superfund), for example, explicitly provides for non-reporting penalties (42 U.S.C., sec. 9603(b)). Similar provisions are contained in the Clean Water Act and Clean Air Act (Russell *et al.* 1986).

28. EPA Final Policy Statement on Incentives for Self-policing: Discovery, Disclosure, Correction and Prevention of Violations, 60 Fed. Reg. 66,706, 66,710 (1995).

29. 'Factors in Decisions on Criminal Prosecutions for Environmental Violations in the Context of Significant Voluntary Compliance or Disclosure Efforts by the Violator' (1 July 1991), reprinted in 21 *Environmental Law Reporter* (Envtl L. Inst.) 325, 399 (July 1991).

30. Although some environmental statutes bar citizen suits when specific regulatory actions have been taken, Shearer (1996: 53) concludes that 'the majority of courts ... generally permit citizens to bring a legal action that the regulator has failed to take'.

REFERENCES

Anderson, M. (1996), 'The state voluntary cleanup program alternative', *Natural Resources and Environmental Law Newsletter* Winter: 22–6.

Bebchuk, L. and L. Kaplow (1992), 'Optimal sanctions when individuals are imperfectly informed about the probability of apprehension', *Journal of Legal Studies* 21: 365–70.

Bebchuk, L. and L. Kaplow (1993), 'Optimal sanctions and differences in individuals' likelihood of avoiding detection', *International Review of Law and Economics* 13: 217–24.

Becker, G. (1968), 'Crime and punishment: an economic approach', *Journal of Political Economy* 76: 169–217.

Frost, E. (1991), 'Voluntary environmental compliance audits: a DOJ policy failure', *Toxics Law Reports*: 499.

Garvie, D. and A. Keeler (1994), 'Incomplete enforcement with endogenous regulatory choice', *Journal of Public Economics* 55: 141–62.

Grieson, R. and N. Singh (1990), 'Regulating externalities through testing', *Journal of Public Economics* 41: 369–87.

Harford, J. (1987), 'Self-reporting of pollution and the firm's behavior under imperfectly enforceable regulations', *Journal of Environmental Economics and Management* 14: 293–303.

Harford, J. and W. Harrington (1991), 'A reconsideration of enforcement leverage when penalties are restricted', *Journal of Public Economics* 45: 391–5.

Harrington, W. (1998), 'Enforcement leverage when penalties are restricted', *Journal of Public Economics* 37: 29–53.

Heyes, A. and N. Rickman (1999), 'Regulatory dealing: revisiting the Harrington paradox', *Journal of Public Economics* 72: 361–78.

Innes, R. (1999a), 'Remediation and self-reporting in optimal law enforcement', *Journal of Public Economics* 72: 379–93.

Innes, R. (1999b), 'Self-reporting and avoiding avoidance in law enforcement', Working Paper, University of Arizona.

Innes, R. (1999c), 'Self-policing and optimal law enforcement when violator remediation is valuable', *Journal of Political Economy* 107: 1305–25.

Innes, R. (2000a), 'Self-reporting and optimal law enforcement when violators have heterogeneous probabilities of apprehension', *Journal of Legal Studies* 29: 287–300.

Innes, R. (2000b), 'Self-auditing and self-reporting in optimal law enforcement', Working Paper, University of Arizona.

Kaplow, L. (1990), 'Optimal deterrence, uninformed individuals, and acquiring information about whether acts are subject to sanctions', *Journal of Law, Economics and Organization* 6: 93–128.

Kaplow, L. and S. Shavell (1994), 'Optimal law enforcement with self-reporting of behavior', *Journal of Political Economy* 102: 583–606.

Kaplow, L. and S. Shavell (2000), 'Economic analysis of law', in A. Auerback and M. Feldstein (eds), *Handbook of Public Economics*, in press (forthcoming).

Malik, A. (1990), 'Avoidance, screening and optimum enforcement', *Rand Journal of Economics* 21: 341–53.

Malik, A. (1993), 'Self-reporting and the design of policies for regulating stochastic pollution', *Journal of Environmental Economics and Management* 24: 241–57.

McIntyre, K. (1997), 'Voluntary disclosure', *Natural Resources and Environment*, Spring: 52.

Mookherjee, D. and I. Png (1992), 'Monitoring *vis-à-vis* investigation in enforcement of law', *American Economic Review* 82: 556–65.

Polinsky, M. and S. Shavell (1992), 'Enforcement costs and the optimal magnitude and probability of fines', *Journal of Law and Economics* 35: 133–48.

Polinsky, M. and S. Shavell (1994), 'A note on optimal cleanup and liability after environmentally harmful discharges', *Research in Law and Economics* 16: 17–24.

Russell, C.S., W. Harrington and W.J. Vaughn (1986), *Enforcing Pollution Control Laws*, Baltimore, MD: Johns Hopkins University Press.

Shavell, S. (1991), 'Specific versus general enforcement of law', *Journal of Political Economy* 99: 1088–1108.
Shearer, R. (1996), 'Costs and benefits of audit disclosure', *Natural Resources and Environment* Summer: 48.
Stigler, G. (1970), 'The optimum enforcement of laws', *Journal of Political Economy* 78: 526–36.
Swierzbinski, J. (1994), 'Guilty until proven innocent: regulation with costly and limited enforcement', *Journal of Environmental Economics and Management* 27: 127–46.
Weaver, J., R. Martineau and M. Stagg (1997), 'State environmental audit laws advance goal of a cleaner environment', *Natural Resources and Environment* Spring: 6.

9. The theory of penalties: 'leverage' and 'dealing'

Winston Harrington and Anthony Heyes

INTRODUCTION

It risks banality to say that penalty – actual or threatened, real or perceived – is fundamental to the effective operation of any enforcement regime. This is true regardless of the policy instrument adopted, and whether enforcement occurs through the channels of administrative, criminal or civil law. The aim here is to outline the simplest economic theory linking penalty levels (and structures) to population compliance rates, and then to consider how that theory has been extended in recent years to take account of the fact that enforcement agencies and regulated firms will typically interact both repeatedly and in a variety of different contexts.

The basic economic theory linking penalty and compliance incentives predicts, simply, that a penalty will induce compliance (under standard assumptions) if the expected value of the penalty exceeds the cost of complying and hence avoiding that penalty. Consider, first, a firm facing a 'binary' – or 'yes/no' – compliance problem. Such problems may arise in some real situations, such as where a polluting firm is required to install a particular piece of safety equipment and either does or doesn't, though such specification can more generally be thought of as a modelling convenience (and one very commonly used). If violation is detected with probability p and the penalty for such violation is F then a firm will maximize profit by choosing to comply if and only if:

$$pF > c$$

where c is the firm's cost of compliance. If the cost of compliance (but not the enforcement parameters) varies across firms in the regulated population according to some distribution function g (with associated cumulative G), then the simple theory predicts that the rate of compliance across the population will be $G(pF)$. Notice that the pattern of compliance induced by any expected penalty pF will be cost-effective: no firm will ever be in compliance at the same time as a lower cost counterpart is in violation. Cost-efficiency cannot be assessed without knowing the value of damage proscribed by compliance.

This simplest version of the model can, then, provide a benchmark against which richer and more complex models can be compared. It can readily be extended to incorporate continuity in the compliance decision (as in, for example, Shavell 1992), risk aversion (Sandmo 1998), 'appealability' of penalties (Kambhu 1989; Jost 1997), the risk of type II monitoring errors (Segerson 1988), the inclusion of an element of self-reporting in compliance-assurance (Livernois and McKenna 1999), the potential inability of those penalized to pay the fine (Shavell 1986), the scope for firms to invest in making themselves difficult to inspect (Heyes 1994), non-profit-maximizing behaviour on the part of the firm (Haltiwanger and Waldman 1993), and in a wide variety of other ways.

The basic model provides some stylized predictions about how compliance in a population should relate to expected penalties for non-compliance. Assuming that g is not such that a lot of firms are bunched around $c = 0$, most apparent amongst these are: (a) if expected penalties are zero (or very small) then compliance rates will be zero (or very small); and (b) increasing expected penalties will increase population compliance rates. As complications are added, either singly or in combination, the predictions of the model – both positive and normative – become less clear-cut. In general, however, these basic predictions are sustained (for a summary of circumstances in which they may not be, see the survey provided by Heyes 2000) and they can reasonably be labelled 'conventional wisdom'.

Some interesting inconsistencies arise, however, in relating such conventional predictions to observed patterns of behaviour in a number of settings. In the context of environmental regulation Harrington (1988) notes that despite the fact that (a) when the EPA observes violations it rarely pursues the violator, and (b) the expected penalty faced by a violator who is pursued is small compared to the cost of compliance, it remains the case that (c) firms comply a significant portion of the time. Evidence of these and other stylized facts is provided by Harrington (in particular on pp. 29–32, and in table 1):

> When a violation is discovered by far the most common response is for the agency to send the firm a notice of violation (NOV) but take no further action. The reticence to use penalties is exhibited in Table 1 which reports the results of an RFF survey of state-level enforcement activity conducted in 1984. Most states levied penalties for less than 5% of NOVs issued. Also the size of the penalties is generally very small. (Harrington 1988: 30)

To take a typical example – that of Connecticut – of 800 known violations (that is, cases where NOVs were issued) in an average year penalties were assessed in only 21 cases and the average penalty collected in those cases was $221.

The expected penalty for violating the environmental rules covered under the survey during the survey period appears, then, to have been negligible (perhaps better measured in cents rather than dollars) and yet compliance, whilst less than full, was substantial.

Similar empirical regularities – with compliance seeming to be higher (often substantially higher) than justified given the frequency with which violations are penalized and the size of those penalties – have been noted in other countries (see, for example, Hawkins 1983) and in non-environmental settings (for example, Slemrod 1994 in the context of income tax compliance, Cowell 1994 for a survey).

A number of rationales can be given for such apparent overcompliance, and the appropriate explanation (or combination explanations) is likely to vary according to setting. In explaining the accuracy of individuals in completing income tax returns, for example, introspection suggests that it might be appropriate to invoke widespread overestimation of the probability that under-reporting will be detected, and inherent honesty (civic responsibility). Such explanations are less satisfactory when thinking about the compliance behaviour of firms – to whom the empirical literature on EPA enforcement cited here is freely available from any good library, and who are compelled (the standard story of market discipline predicts) to act to maximize expected profits.

Much of the answer for the apparent paradox (what Heyes and Rickman 1999 refer to as the 'Harrington Paradox') may lie in the failure of empirical analysts, particularly those early in the field, to account for the 'full' costs and benefits of compliance.

On the benefit side, the management guru Michael Porter and his disciples have promoted the idea that there may be secondary benefits to firms 'going green', in terms of improved customer or employee morale, incidental innovation or in other ways.

On the cost side there is growing interest in the role of so-called 'market penalties', falls in a quoted firm's stock market valuation in response to environmental infringement. Pioneering event studies were conducted in the context of prosecution for corporate fraud (Karpoff and Lott 1993) and airline safety (Borenstein and Zimmerman 1988), and a variety of applications are collected in a special issue of the *Journal of Law and Economics* edited by Lott (1999). Badrinath and Bolster (1996) examine the stock market reactions to US Environmental Protection Agency (EPA) judicial actions on a sample of publicly traded firms between 1972 and 1991. They show that a firm's valuation declines 0.43 per cent in the week of settlement, which for anything but the smallest firm translates into a dollar amount far in excess of the nominal penalty. This implies that the response of financial markets can substantially reinforce fiat penalties, and in so doing bolster the incentive that current shareholders have to ensure that their managers do not transgress. Other work on investor response to environmental infringements includes Laplante and Lanoie (1994) and Hamilton (1995). Interestingly, the response appears comparatively insensitive to the size of the violation, more pronounced for citations under the Clean Air Act than other statutes (the Clean Water Act, Toxic Substances Control Act and so on). The response is also found to be greater for more recent violations, suggesting an increasing role for this sort of 'private' discipline.

Of course, in so far as the apparently anomalous behaviour of firms is explained by the failure of those observing them to take full account of the private costs and benefits of compliance and violation, actual behaviour should remain consistent with the original model – once the measurement of p and c has been corrected – with population compliance at a rate $G(pF)$. The aim in this chapter, on the other hand, is to outline how relaxation of the (implicit) assumptions made in the basic model in ways that mean that one or both parts of the conventional wisdom stated break down.

The first of those assumptions is that the agency–firm relationship can be treated as a single-shot game. In reality the enforcement agency (such as the EPA in the US) and firm are likely to interact repeatedly through time, and the compliance incentives generated by a particular penalty strategy are unlikely to be comprehensible in a static formulation. Harrington (1988), building on the insights of Greenberg (1984) and Landsberger and Meilijson (1982), develops a theory of 'penalty leverage'. As the name suggests, by exploiting the scope for leverage the enforcement agency is able to get 'more than its money's worth' when the maximal penalty is restricted. In a similar spirit, Heyes and Rickman (1999) show that when the agency and firms interact in more than one 'domain' – which is likely, again, to be the norm – then a compliance-maximizing penalty regime will not, in general, involve maximal penalties. It will, rather, require that the agency exploit 'issue linkage', tying the way in which transgression is penalized in one domain with the firm's behaviour elsewhere.

PENALTY LEVERAGE

In Harrington's original model leverage is achieved by differentiating the treatment of polluters depending on their previous behaviour. A few years later, Livernois and McKenna (1999) identify another leverage mechanism, one that depends on the behaviour of the firm after a violation has occurred.

State-dependent Enforcement

In Harrington's model the enforcement process is modelled as an infinitely repeated game between the firm and the regulatory agency. At the beginning of the game the enforcement agency sets the probability of inspection and penalty in each state. Each period thereafter, the agency inspects according to these probabilities, and the firm decides whether it will comply with the regulation.

In each period the firm decides whether it will comply with a regulation that imposes a cost of c on the firm. The agency classifies the firm in one of two states, S_1 and S_2, with firms in S_2 facing more stringent enforcement than firms in S_1, and moves the firm from one state to the other depending on its performance in previous periods. Let p_i and F_i respectively denote the probability of inspection and the fine for a firm in state i and assume $p_1 < p_2$ and $F_1 < F_2$. Violations discovered for a firm in S_1 are further punished by exile into state 2, and compliance discovered in S_2 is rewarded by a chance of a return to S_1. Let u denote the probability that a firm found in compliance in S_2 is returned to S_1. The payoffs to the firm in any period depend on both the actions of the firm and the agency in the period and the firm's initial state, as shown in Table 9.1.

Table 9.1   Payoff matrices for the enforcement game

	State 1		State 2	
	Comply	Violate	Comply	Violate
No inspection	c	0	c	0
Inspection	c	F_1 $\rightarrow S_2$	c $P(\rightarrow S_1) = u$	F_2

For the firm, the movement from one state to another can be described as a Markov chain, but with the added property that the transition probabilities depend not only on the firm's current state, but also on the action the firm takes during the period, that is, whether to comply or not. The two transition matrices for complying and cheating are given in Table 9.2.

Table 9.2   Transition probabilities

	Comply			Cheat	
	S_1	S_2		S_1	S_2
S_1	1	0	S_1	$1 - p_1$	p_1
S_2	$p_2 u$	$1 - p_2 u$	S_2	0	1

Because the payoffs are time-independent, the firm's optimum policy is also, so that the action taken by the firm in any period depends only on the state of the firm during the period. Thus there are only four candidate optimum policies. We denote them by f_{00}, f_{01}, f_{10} and f_{11}, where, for example, f_{10} is the policy of cheating while in S_1 and complying while in S_2.[1] The optimum policy f_{opt} depends on the firm's compliance cost and the characteristics of the agency's enforcement policy. It turns out that f_{01} is never optimal, and for a fixed enforcement policy, the optimum policy depends on the cost of compliance c. When $c = 0$, the optimum policy is f_{00}, and as c increases the optimum policy changes, first from f_{00} to f_{10} and then from f_{10} to f_{11}:

$$
f_{opt} = \begin{cases} f_{00} & \text{if } c \leq L_0 \\ f_{10} & \text{if } L_0 \leq c \leq L_1 \\ f_{11} & \text{if } L_1 \leq c \end{cases}
$$

where the breakpoints L_0 and L_1 are given by:

$$
L_0 = p_1 F_1
$$

$$
L_1 = p_2 F_2 + \frac{p_2 \beta u (p_2 F_2 - p_1 F_1)}{1 - (1 - p_1)\beta}, \tag{9.1}
$$

In the denominator of (9.1) β is the discount factor $1/(1 + r)$. f_{opt} is a concave and piecewise linear function.

In other words, firms with low compliance costs (below L_0) always comply, and those with high compliance costs (above L_1) never comply. The most interesting firms here are those with compliance costs in the interval $[L_0, L_1]$, for in this case the firm cheats when it is in S_1 and complies when it is in S_2. The irony of this model is that the firms considered to be 'good guys' are the ones who can afford to cheat, while those with a 'bad guy' reputation comply until they are moved back into S_1.

Note that as long as there is some difference in the expected penalty for violations in the two states, $L_1 > p_2 F_2$. Some compliance can be achieved for firms with compliance cost that exceeds the expected penalty. From (9.1), the magnitude of this 'leverage' is a linear function of the difference in the expected penalties in the two states.[2] The average compliance rate is the firm's residence time in S_2:

$$
C_{10} = \frac{p_1}{p_1 + p_2 u}, \tag{9.2}
$$

and the agency's average inspection rate is:

$$I_{10} = \frac{p_1 p_2 (1+u)}{p_1 + p_2 u}. \qquad (9.3)$$

The policy of the enforcement agency is determined by five parameters: p_1, F_1, p_2, F_2 and u, the escape probability from S_2. In the original article the agency's problem was specified as a cost-minimization problem: minimize the cost of inducing a target level of compliance in a firm with compliance cost less than some specified maximum c^*. Harrington shows that the optimum penalties in the two states S_1 and S_2 are 0 and the maximum penalty F^*, respectively. With this penalty structure, penalties are only observed if the firm is an f_{11} firm, whose compliance cost exceeds c^*. f_{10} firms violate standards, but only in S_1 where no penalties are exacted. Thus the paradox is resolved.

This specification of the agency's objective function has turned out to be the most troublesome aspect of the original article. Is the agency setting policy for its dealings with a single firm or with many firms? How much information does the firm have about the firm's compliance costs? And what is the appropriate objective function for the agency? Implicitly, Harrington was only concerned with the relationship between the agency and a single firm. The agency assumed that it could determine the firm's abatement costs, or at least estimate an upper bound. Also, its objective function – minimizing the cost of achieving a compliance target – was a cost-effectiveness (CE) rather than a net-benefit (NB) criterion. Indeed, the model was so simple, with an either–or compliance decision and no consideration of environmental damages, that the CE and NB criteria were indistinguishable.

The importance of the optimization criterion was clarified in a subsequent article by Harford and Harrington (1990), which extended the original Harrington model to give firms an explicit abatement cost function with a variable pollution output. This allowed consideration of a model in which the NB criterion no longer collapsed into the CE criterion. In this model the Environmental Protection Agency sets the emission standard and the enforcement policy simultaneously. The optimum policy in this world is for the agency to make the emission standard less stringent, so much so that the firm's best policy is to comply with the standard all the time. This policy exposes an inherent inefficiency in the simple state-dependent enforcement strategy. State-dependent enforcement requires firms to install abatement equipment but then deliberately creates conditions under which they will fail to operate it properly.

It is not surprising that economic efficiency is served by the simultaneous determination of these two policy variables. And yet, this is not the way environmental policy is done in the real world. Almost without exception, the emission standard and the enforcement policy are determined sequentially, often by different governmental bodies.[3] If we require a sequential policy in the model, then the NB criterion also produces the central paradoxical result of the paper, namely that some compliance can be achieved without penalties being assessed.[4]

The second reconsideration of the model arose in reaction to the model's focus on only one firm. The emissions from that firm may or may not be known, but the agency knows the penalty structure that maximizes the range of compliance costs for which the target level of compliance can be achieved. Raymond (1999) pointed out that most enforcement agencies had to deal with many firms. In his model he assumed that the agency would not have firm-specific information on abatement costs, but it would know their distribution. He showed that it may no longer be cost effective for the agency to set the penalty in S_1 at 0. While doing so may maximize the abatement cost for which the target emission reductions may be achieved, it also sacrifices emission reductions from firms with low abatement costs. Setting $F_1 = 0$, in other words, can result in many firms being f_{10} firms that, with slightly higher penalties in F_1, might be f_{00} firms. There is a tradeoff, in other words, and the optimum policy depends on the distribution of abatement costs.

However, the agency is likely to have more information than this. Most enforcement programmes require sources to obtain construction and operating permits, often with emission certification tests, that contain valuable information about the firm's abatement technology. If this information could be used to estimate, albeit with error, each individual firm's abatement costs, or classify firms into classes with approximately equal abatement costs, it would be possible to tailor the enforcement parameters to each firm or group of firms, thus approximating the conditions of the original model.

Self-reporting and Voluntary Compliance

Livernois and McKenna (LM) (1999) use a model featuring self-reporting of pollution violations to provide another explanation for the paradox, and though their model relies on an entirely different mechanism from Harrington's, the results are strongly similar.

In the LM model, pollution violations are assumed to arise from stochastic machine failures. The firm can repair these failures immediately, notify the regulator of the violation, or keep silent. These three strategies are denoted respectively by S_{CT} (full compliance and truth-telling), S_{NT} (non-compliance and truth-telling), and S_{NF} (non-compliance and false reporting). All equipment failures, whether reported or not, are assumed to be repaired before the end of the next period. If the firm adopts S_{CT}, there is no penalty. Choosing S_{NT} carries a certain penalty of F_1 and S_{NF} a possible penalty of F_2, depending on whether the regulator makes a random inspection while the equipment is not working properly. The two penalties F_1 and F_2, together with the random inspection frequency π, comprise the regulator's enforcement policy. We must have $F_1 < \pi F_2$ if the firm is to have any incentive to self-report violations.

As in the Harrington model, for a given an enforcement policy the cost of each of the three strategies is an increasing linear function of the abatement cost. Also, the envelope of cost functions is concave and piecewise linear, consisting of one, two or three linear pieces depending on the enforcement parameters and the slopes of the individual functions. In the most interesting case, the firm's best strategy is SCT if compliance cost per period is less than a threshold value $\hat{c}$, SNT if compliance cost is between $\hat{c}$ and an upper threshold value $\tilde{c}$ and SNF if compliance cost exceeds $\tilde{c}$.

To produce the desired result, it must be that F_1, the penalty for the strategy of non-compliance and truth-telling, is 0, and this is shown to be the case for all but extremely high compliance-rate targets.

REGULATORY DEALING

The starting point for the model of regulatory dealing presented by Heyes and Rickman (1999) is similar to Harrington in so far as a population of firms, each with private information regarding costs of compliance, faces a binary ('yes/no') compliance decision, and the maximal penalty that the EPA is able to impose is bounded and at such a level as to make full compliance unenforceable. It differs however, in (a) returning to a static formulation, and (b) recognizing that the enforcement agent and regulated firm interact in more than one 'domain'. (This section draws upon the simplest version of the model presented in Heyes and Rickman 1999; the interested reader is directed there for extended analysis and motivation.)

The assumption that the EPA and firm interact in more than one enforcement context is a realistic one. It may be that the Agency enforces the same rule at more than one plant of a multi-plant firm, in more than one of the geographical regions in which the firm operates, or may enforce several different categories of regulation (clean water, noise and so on) at a single plant. In this case linking enforcement action in one setting to performance in another (exploiting 'issue linkage') can be expected to enhance the efficacy of the compliance programme.

Consider the following, highly stylized, formulation. A population of firms and an EPA interact in two *ex ante* identical domains, in each of which each firm is required to comply with a particular regulation. The cost to firm i of complying in domain j will be denoted c_{ij}, where c_{i1} and c_{i2} are independent draws from a distribution $g(c)$ which is commonly known and has an associated cumulative $G(c)$. If the EPA observes non-compliance (and we shall assume, to take the starkest case, that it is costlessly able to observe all non-compliance) it has the option of taking the firm to court ('pursuing' the firm), which results in the firm being subject to penalty F with certainty. The model could straightforwardly be extended to take account of less-than-full detection of non-compliance by the Agency, and/or 'slippage' at the penalty stage. Importantly we retain the assumption that penalties are restricted, that is, $G(F) < 1$.

For the purposes of comparison we can characterize the full-pursuit benchmark: the equilibrium when the strategy adopted by the EPA is to pursue and penalize all cases of non-compliance that it observes. Faced by an EPA behaving in such a way, it is apparent that firm i will comply in domain j if and only if $c_{ij} < F$, implying a population compliance rate equal to $G(F)$. Suppose, instead, that the EPA offers each firm a regulatory 'deal' by which the EPA agrees to tolerate violations by the firm in one domain in exchange for the firm complying in the other. In thinking about the impact that such dealing would have upon population compliance it is useful to distinguish between four types of firm:

1. 'α-types' – firms with $F < \text{Min}\{c_{i1}, c_{i2}\} < 2F$. Under full pursuit a firm of this type complies in neither domain. It accepts the regulatory deal (if offered) and elects to comply in that domain in which its compliance cost is lower. The environmental damage inflicted by the firm across the two domains decreases from $2d$ to d.
2. 'β-types' – firms with $\text{Max}\{c_{i1}, c_{i2}\} < F$. Under full pursuit a firm of this type would comply in both domains. It accepts the regulatory deal and then complies only in the domain where its compliance cost is lower. The global environmental damage done by the firm goes up from 0 to d.
3. 'γ-types' – firms with $\text{Min}\{c_{i1}, c_{i2}\} > 2F$. Under full pursuit a firm of this type complies in neither domain. It rejects the regulatory deal and continues to inflict global damage equal to $2d$.
4. 'σ-types' – firms with $c_{i1} > F > c_{i2}$. Under full pursuit a firm in this class complies only in domain 2. It accepts the regulatory deal but continues to comply only in that domain, such that the total damage it inflicts remains d.

(Note that the classification is exhaustive and mutually exclusive: any firm will be in one and only one class.) Will such dealing – which entails, note, reducing the rate at which known violators are pursued – enhance compliance? The answer depends, not surprisingly, upon the distribution of firms between the four classes. From the point of view of aggregate compliance (aggregate environmental damage) we can ignore γ- and σ-types, whose compliance behaviour is unaffected (though for different reasons) by the offer of a deal. Given the simple two-domain structure of the model it is apparent that dealing will enhance compliance if (and only if) the distribution $g(c)$ is such that the number of α-types, whose damage goes up by d, exceeds the number of β-types, whose damage goes down by the same amount. (The restriction this implies on the form of g is explored in more detail in Heyes and Rickman 1999.)

That dealing has the potential to enhance compliance can readily be understood from a simple example. Consider a firm for which $c_{i1} = 12$ and $c_{i2} = 15$ in a world in which $F = 10$ (an α-type firm). If the EPA pursues all violations then the firm faces two separable decision problems: whether or not to comply in domain 1, and whether or not to comply in domain 2. As the cost of compliance in each domain is less than the maximal fine, non-compliance in both domains is the dominant strategy, implying a total cost for the firm of 20. Now suppose that the EPA offers the firm a deal of the type outlined. The firm will accept the offer and in 'exchange' for compliance in domain 1 (which costs it 12) will avoid penalty not just in that domain, but will have a 'blind eye' turned to its continued non-compliance in domain 2 (the EPA's part of the bargain). The firm's total costs may have gone down from 20 to 12, but the total damage it does has also fallen from $2d$ to d. Provided the distribution of costs and configuration of parameters is such that there are enough firms of this type in the population, then dealing will be good for the environment.

CONCLUSIONS

The theories of both penalty leverage and regulatory dealing provide ways of understanding the often-noted empirical regularity that firms tend to comply with regulations more readily than would be predicted by comparison of the (static, single-context) costs and benefits of so doing. Both theories are consistent with population compliance rates being substantially above zero, though less than full, *even though penalties are never levied upon those caught violating*, and with population compliance rates being increasing in expected penalties (conditional on a particular structure of those penalties).

It is important to recognize that whilst the two models generate distinct testable hypotheses, they are not mutually exclusive – acceptance of one should not be taken to imply rejection of the other. In general we would suppose that an enforcement agency will interact with a firm both (a) repeatedly and (b) across more than one domain. In that case compliance-maximizing enforcement is likely to involve intertemporal as well as cross-domain trading, with the enforcement stance in domain j in period t conditioned not just on the firm's compliance history in j but also on current and historical performance elsewhere. The extent to which enforcement programmes come close to being 'optimized' in this way would require detailed analysis – probably based on case studies –

of the anatomy of the 'horse trading' that Hawkins (1983), Yaeger (1991) and others evidence routinely occur between regulators and firms.

In either model the observed tolerance of the enforcement agency to observed non-compliance is an integral part of a compliance-maximizing strategy, rather than evidence that the agency has 'gone soft' on pollution or is being subject to capture by the polluting industry. The models point to ways in which the link between realized penalties and compliance incentives are likely to be significantly more complicated than suggested by basic theory.

NOTES

1. That is, 0 means 'comply' and 1 means 'cheat,' and f_{ij} is the policy to take action i when in S_1 and action j when in S_2.
2. At a 1987 workshop on the economics of enforcement sponsored by the USEPA, Cheryl Wasserman of EPA's Office of Enforcement described EPA's enforcement policy as one of 'stroke 'em and poke 'em', in terms that are quite evocative of the two-group model being described here (Wasserman 1987).
3. In the US, for example, federal emission standards are determined by the EPA or (in some cases) by Congress without specifying how they are to enforced. The enforcement is in most cases delegated to the states. An exception to the simultaneous determination of emission standards and enforcement can be found in Title IV of the 1990 Clean Air Act, which established the SO_2 trading programme. Title IV mandated the installation of continuous emission monitors for all plants participating in the programme.
4. In a subsequent paper, Harford (1991) introduces emission measurement error and shows that the optimal (NB) policy employs state-dependent enforcement but does not generally result in zero penalties in either state.

BIBLIOGRAPHY

Badrinath, S. and P.J. Bolster (1996), 'The role of market forces in EPA enforcement activity', *Journal of Regulatory Economics* 10(2): 165–81.

Borenstein S. and M.B. Zimmerman (1988), 'Market incentives for safe commercial airline operation', *American Economic Review* 78(5): 913–35.

Cowell, F. (1994), *Cheating the Government*, Cambridge MA: MIT Press.

Greenberg, J. (1984), 'Avoiding tax avoidance: a (repeated) game theoretic approach', *Journal of Economic Theory* 32(1): 1–13.

Haltiwanger, J. and M. Waldman (1993), 'The role of altruism in economic interaction', *Journal of Economic Behavior and Organisation* 21: 1–15.

Hamilton, J. (1995), 'Pollution as news: media and stock market reactions to the toxic release data', *Journal of Environmental Economics and Management* 28(1): 31–43.

Harford, J.D. (1991), 'Measurement error and state-dependent pollution control enforcement', *Journal of Environmental Economics and Management* 21(1).

Harford, J.D. and W. Harrington (1991), 'A reconsideration of enforcement leverage when penalties are restricted', *Journal of Public Economics* 45: 391–5.

Harrington, W. (1988), 'Enforcement leverage when penalties are restricted', *Journal of Public Economics* 37: 29–53.

Hawkins, K. (1983), 'Bargain and bluff: compliance strategy and deterrence in the enforcement of regulation', *Law and Policy Quarterly* 5(1): 35–73.

Heyes, A.G. (1994), 'Environmental enforcement when "inspectability" is endogenous', *Environmental and Resource Economics* 4(5).

Heyes, A.G. (2000), 'Implementing environmental regulation: enforcement and compliance', *Journal of Regulatory Economics* 17(2): 107–29.

Heyes, A.G. and N. Rickman (1999), 'Regulatory dealing: revisiting the Harrington paradox', *Journal of Public Economics* 72: 361–78.

Jost, P.J. (1997), 'Monitoring, appeal and investigation: the enforcement of legal process', *Journal of Regulatory Economics* 12: 127–46.

Kambhu, J. (1989), 'Regulatory standards, compliance and enforcement', *Journal of Regulatory Economics* 1(2): 103–14.

Karpoff, J. and J.R. Lott (1993), 'The reputational penalty firms bear from committing corporate fraud', *Journal of Law and Economics* 36(2): 757–802.

Landsberger, M. and I. Meilijson (1982), 'Incentive-generating state dependent penalty systems', *Journal of Public Economics* 19(3): 335–52.

Laplante, B. and P. Lanoie (1994), 'Market responses to environmental incidents in Canada', *Southern Economic Journal* 60: 657–72.

Livernois, J. and C. McKenna (1999), 'Truth or consequences: enforcing pollution standards', *Journal of Public Economics*, 72.

Lott, J.R. (1999), 'Public and private penalties: introduction to special issue', *Journal of Law and Economics*, XLII(1): 239–45.

Raymond, M. (1999), 'Enforcement leverage when penalties are restricted: a reconsideration under asymmetric information', *Journal of Public Economics* 73(2): 289–95.

Sandmo, A. (1998), 'Efficient environmental policy with imperfect compliance', Discussion Paper 8/98, Norwegian School of Economics and Business.

Segerson, K. (1988), 'Uncertainty and incentives for nonpoint pollution control', *Journal of Environmental Economics and Management* 15: 87–98.

Shavell, S. (1986), 'The judgement proof problem', *International Review of Law and Economics* 6: 45–58.

Shavell, S. (1992), 'A note on marginal deterrence', *International Review of Law and Economics* 12: 133–49.

Slemrod, J. (1994), *Why People Pay Taxes: Tax Compliance and Enforcement*, Ann Arbor, MI: University of Michigan Press.

Wasserman, C.E. (1987), 'Environmental compliance and enforcement: theory, practice and the challenge to environmental economists', prepared for the Association of Environmental and Resource Economists Workshop on Environmental Enforcement and Monitoring, 13–14 August, University of Delaware.

Yaeger, P. (1991), *The Limits of the Law: The Public Regulation of Private Pollution*, Cambridge: Cambridge University Press.

10. Criminal law as an instrument of environmental policy: theory and empirics

Mark A. Cohen

INTRODUCTION

This chapter explores the role of the criminal law as an environmental policy tool. The criminal law is both a powerful and a clumsy policy instrument. Its sanctions can be severe, putting firms out of business or jailing executives. Yet, criminal enforcement is highly decentralized and lacks clear policy guidance, often resulting in wide variations in treatment of offenders – whether measured across offenders, jurisdictions, or time. To those not well versed in criminal law, it might be surprising to learn that not only can individuals be charged with a crime, but so can corporations. To understand how the criminal law might be effectively used for environmental policy purposes, I start with some background on the purpose of the criminal law and how it is applied to environmental cases in the US. Next, I consider the economic theory of criminal sanctions including questions such as: What is the purpose of the criminal law? How are sanctions to be determined from an optimal penalty framework? When should the firm versus the individual be held criminally liable for environmental harm? Finally, I examine what little empirical evidence exists on the use of the criminal sanction for environmental offences.

CRIMINAL LAW: THEORY AND PRACTICE

There is no one legal definition of a crime. Instead, statutes generally define specific behaviour deemed to be criminal. But those statutes can change and behaviour that is criminal today might not be next year. Nevertheless, there are several characteristics of crimes that distinguish them from torts or regulatory violations. Many legal scholars argue that the single distinguishing characteristic of crime is 'moral culpability', where someone is not only legally taken to task for harm they cause, but is also held morally responsible. Thus, an accident such as an oil spill might require payment for harm, but unless the person or firm is held 'morally responsible' through gross negligence or even purposeful action, the offence might not be raised to the level of a crime.

The question of moral culpability was at the heart of the debate over whether criminal charges should be levied in the *Exxon Valdez* spill. Although there was little question that Exxon was liable under tort law for property damage and lost income to nearby residents, the question of criminal liability was an entirely different matter. Indeed, the debate over whether to impose criminal liability focused on whether Exxon was morally culpable for the spill. The prosecuting attorneys argued that since the captain of the ship was not 'competent ... culpability went beyond simple negligence to a much higher degree'. Commenting on Exxon's plea to criminal charges, the prosecuting attorney claimed that it reflected the moral sensibilities of the community (Crovitz 1991).

Traditional versus Regulatory Crimes

Traditional legal theory defines crimes by the notion of *mens rea* or criminal intent. A harmful action that is caused through negligence or ignorance is not generally considered criminal even if the consequences are dire. This view of crime has largely been discarded in the case of modern regulatory crimes. Thus, in the case of environmental violations, no criminal intent is generally required. We shall discuss this issue in more detail shortly. Finally, an act does not necessarily have to be harmful for it to be criminal. Unlike torts where there must be an injured party, one can commit a crime that harms no one. Thus, attempted crimes and other illegal activities that never succeed are still criminal offences.

There are two main bodies of criminal law in the US that relate to environmental violations. First, many environmental offences involve general criminal statutes such as conspiracies, mail or wire fraud, or false statements to the government. A minor regulatory violation can easily become a crime if it is subsequently hidden from government enforcement personnel. Second, virtually every environmental law in the US includes criminal provisions (Cohen 1992: 1066–70). These criminal provisions generally fall into two distinct categories: (a) strict liability, and (b) those requiring some form of knowing, wilful or negligent behaviour. Strict liability offences, as their name implies, require no degree of criminal intent or knowledge. Even in the case of 'knowing' offences, however, courts have been very broad in their interpretation. For example, failure adequately to prevent an accidental discharge of oil can result in 'criminal negligence'. More surprising, perhaps, 'knowing' a waste is hazardous can be deemed adequate culpability to impose criminal charges even though an individual did not know a violation was occurring.

Under US law, virtually any illegal activity by agents or employees of a corporation that takes place within the scope of their work can subject that company to criminal liability. This is true even if an employee acts against the wishes or direct instructions of company officials. This doctrine is known as 'vicarious liability'. Similarly, in some cases, corporate officers may be held criminally liable for their employees' or agents' actions even if those actions were neither condoned nor known about in advance. Under strict liability laws, simply being the 'responsible corporate official' who delegated responsibility may result in criminal liability. Even in the case of laws that require some degree of knowledge or wilful behaviour, a corporate official who fails to prevent a crime or tacitly acquiesces may be held criminally liable (Riesel 1985: 10073).

Since virtually all environmental crimes can also be dealt with through civil or administrative actions, the decision about whether to use the civil or criminal law (or in some cases, both) is largely at the discretion of criminal prosecutors. Since regulators have discretion over which offences they refer to criminal prosecutors, regulatory agencies also have some discretion in this regard. According to internal EPA policy, two primary factors will be considered when deciding whether or not to refer an offence to criminal investigators: significance of environmental harm and culpable conduct (US EPA 1994). The latter is defined to include the history of repeated violations, whether the misconduct was deliberate, any attempts to conceal or falsify records, tamper with monitoring or control equipment, and whether or not the firm or individual had obtained the requisite permits or licences to pollute. Another policy statement by the criminal prosecutors themselves describes factors that will be used to determine whether to pursue criminal charges when a polluter is otherwise in significant compliance and/or there is disclosure of the violation to regulatory authorities: '(1) whether the disclosure was voluntary, (2) degree of coopera-tion, (3) extensiveness of the compliance program and efforts to prevent violations, (4) pervasiveness of non-compliance, (5) internal disciplinary action, and (6) subsequent compliance efforts' (US Department of Justice 1991).

Criminal laws have different legal procedures, standards of proof and enforce-ment personnel. In general, it is thought that imposing a criminal sanction is more costly to the government than imposing a similar sanction through the administrative process.[1]

Legal Theories of Punishment

In addition to moral culpability and *mens rea*, criminal law is often 'defined' by its particular sanctions – most notably, incarceration. Legal theorists generally distinguish between four goals of criminal sanctions: deterrence, inca-pacitation, rehabilitation and retribution. Yet most of these goals can be accomplished with traditional civil or regulatory remedies.

Deterrence is obtained by imposing sanctions severe enough to convince potential offenders that they are better off not committing an offence. Certainly, civil monetary fines or tort damage claims can have a deterrent effect without ever imposing a criminal sanction. However, in some cases the penalty required to obtain optimal deterrence may be beyond the wealth constraint of the offender. As we shall discuss later, that is one possible justification for criminalizing environmental offences: the inability of the offender to pay the optimal civil penalty.

Incapacitation might be accomplished in some cases through civil actions. For individual offenders, incapacitation is normally carried out through incarceration, precluding a repeat violation during their term in prison. For a firm, incapacitation might involve prohibitions against certain activities to ensure it does not violate the law. For example, a firm that has repeatedly violated hazardous waste transporting rules might have its permit revoked. Although normally a form of criminal incapacitation, in some cases (for example, as part of a settlement agreement), regulatory agencies can also impose these types of sanctions.

Rehabilitation of individuals generally requires some form of treatment or education programme designed to affect future behaviour. For corporations, this might take the form of 'corporate probation' or other court ordered requirements such as an employee training programme, hiring a compliance officer or conducting third-party audits. Although a criminal sentencing judge may order these remedies, administrative agencies might also fashion similar remedies in drafting voluntary consent decrees.

Finally, retribution may be obtained through penalties that are 'higher' than otherwise needed for optimal deterrence purposes. This might be a possible justification for very large punitive damage awards in tort cases. Again, the criminal law is not necessarily needed to exact such a high penalty. Thus, it is primarily incarceration itself that truly distinguishes the civil from the criminal law.

Some scholars have added a fifth goal to the traditional ones discussed above: to shape preferences and 'educate' potential offenders about the moral consequences of their actions (Dau-Schmidt 1990). This goal most directly links to the traditional view that 'crime' generally involves moral culpability. By labelling an activity a crime, society is placing it outside the social norms of the community.

Note that 'restitution' is missing from the list of goals of criminal sanctions. Traditionally, restitution was deemed a matter for civil courts. However, the growing victim rights movement in the US led to the enactment of statutory mandates that judges impose restitution to make victims whole. In the environmental context, this might include restoration or payment for the estimated monetary value of natural resource damages.

Traditionally, judges had complete discretion in sentencing criminals as long as they did not impose more than the statutory maximum sentence.[2] That changed dramatically in 1987 when the US Sentencing Commission imposed mandatory guidelines that forced judges to impose sanctions according to these new standards. Although these guidelines cover individuals convicted of environmental crimes and include non-monetary sanctions for corporate offenders, as of this date they do not cover monetary fines for environmental crimes committed by corporations. The latter are still at the discretion of the sentencing judge. In contrast, the US EPA has a civil penalty policy that systematically assesses penalties according to a formula that considers both the savings to the firm from non-compliance and the magnitude of any harm caused (US EPA 1984).

In the eyes of the law, the fact that both a firm and several of its employees are convicted of the same identical offence, for example, does not necessarily reduce the severity of the sanction imposed on any one party. The only exception to this might be in the case of restitution, where, for example, one would not double the size of the payment when there are two offenders.

ECONOMIC THEORY OF CRIMINAL LAW

Unlike legal theory, economic theory does not generally distinguish between criminal, civil or administrative law. A penalty is a penalty regardless of who imposes it. However, as noted by Becker (1968), prison is a socially costly sanction, involving both lost productivity of the offender and the diversion of productive resources into building and operating prisons. In contrast, monetary fines are thought of as wealth transfers that do not result in socially inefficient allocation of resources. Thus, the only reason to use prison would be if the optimal monetary fine exceeded the wealth constraint of the offender.

The basic insight of Becker's (1968) seminal article is that potential criminals respond to both the probability of detection and the severity of punishment if detected and convicted. Thus, deterrence may be enhanced either by raising the penalty, increasing monitoring activities to raise the likelihood that the offender will be caught, or changing legal rules to increase the probability of conviction. Becker's model ultimately leads to an 'efficient' level of crime, whereby the marginal cost of enforcement is equated to the marginal social benefit of crime reduced.

As Cohen (1987) notes, the Becker (1968) model can be written as a special case of a more general model that takes into account the random nature of pollution. Although Becker is primarily interested in *ex post* penalties, his model can easily be adapted to include *ex ante* penalties for not taking proper care to prevent a crime from occurring. In Becker's model, crime is unambiguously 'caused' by the criminal, whereas in stochastic pollution, the extent to which a polluter took adequate care in preventing the externality is often an important issue to be resolved. This has important consequences in the context of environmental crimes committed by corporations, since high penalties can lead to 'overdeterrence', where firms might take socially costly actions to prevent themselves from being charged with criminal wrongdoing.

Optimal Penalty Theory and Monetary Sanctions

Although this chapter does not fully explore the intricacies of optimal penalty theory (see Cohen 1999), a brief review is in order to highlight how it relates to the use of criminal sanctions. We begin with the firm's problem. The firm is assumed to produce pollution (x) as a byproduct of its production process, and to expend some effort (e) to reduce pollution. By its nature, pollution is stochastic, and can be written as a random variable with distribution function $F(x,e)$. Under a command and control regime, the government requires a minimum level of effort, which might include installing and properly maintaining certain pieces of equipment, properly training employees, and so on. With probability $P_I(m_1)$, the firm will be inspected for compliance, where m_1 is the level of government resources devoted to compliance monitoring. If inspected and found to be in non-compliance (that is, $e < e^*$), the government will impose a penalty $T_I(e)$. This is an *ex ante* penalty, based on the level of effort devoted by the firm to prevent pollution.

If pollution occurs, the government may devote resources, m_2, to detect and punish the firm that caused it. Then, the probability of detection is $P_D(x,m_2)$, increasing in both the level of government detection resources and the size of the externality (larger emissions are presumably easier to detect). If pollution is detected and attributed to its generator, the government imposes a penalty, $T_D(x,e)$. The government does not directly observe the level of effort by the firm. Thus, if the government wants to condition its penalty on the level of effort (a negligence standard), it must expend additional *ex post* monitoring resources, m_3, to determine the culpability of the stochastic polluter. Finally, the existence of a stochastic externality may involve a private loss to the polluter, $v(x)$, the value of lost resources.

The firm's expected profit from polluting can be written as:[3]

$$EU(e) = -P_I T_I(e) - \int_x [v(x) + P_D(x) T_D(x,e)] \ f(x,e) \ dx - e. \qquad (10.1)$$

The government is assumed to be a social welfare maximizer. As such, it wants to minimize the sum of clean-up or recovery costs, $C(rx)$, where r is the fraction of pollution that is cleaned up; environmental damages, $D[(1 - r)x]$; private resource loss, $v(x)$; prevention expenditures, e; and government enforcement expenditures m_1, m_2 and m_3.

$$\text{EW}(e, m_1, m_2, m_3, r) = \int_x \{D[(1 - r) x]$$
$$+ C(rx) + v(x)\} \, f(x,e) \, dx - e - m_1, m_2, m_3. \tag{10.2}$$

The government has control over the level of monitoring, m_1, m_2, m_3, and can either mandate some level of recovery/clean-up or clean up the damage directly itself. However, level of effort cannot be observed directly and can only be inferred or imperfectly observed *ex post*. Thus, the government imposes a penalty to induce the firm to take the optimal level of effort. That penalty is:

$$T_D(x) = \frac{D[(1 - r)x] + C(rx)}{P_D(x)}. \tag{10.3}$$

Substituting (10.3) into (10.1), the polluter's problem becomes one of social welfare maximization, (10.2), where m_1, m_2 and m_3 are set equal to zero with no need for government monitoring. This penalty is just Becker's optimal penalty equal to the harm divided by the probability of detection, which induces the socially optimal level of effort.

The optimal penalty (10.3) varies with the probability of detection, a key parameter in the enforcement agency's tool kit. Since increasing the probability of detection requires some expenditure on government monitoring, Becker's policy prescription is to set $P_D(x)$ arbitrarily low, thus raising the penalty. However, there may be limits on how high a penalty is feasible: for political reasons, wealth constraints of polluters, and for purposes of preserving marginal deterrence (Polinsky and Shavell 1979).

In addition to determining the probability of detection, the optimal penalty (10.3) requires that the government decide whether to require clean-up of any harm caused by illegal pollution. The optimal recovery/clean-up rule equates marginal damages to marginal clean-up costs, $D'[(1 - r) x] = C'(rx)$. The clean-up rule is independent of either the level of care taken by the firm or mandated by the government, and is independent of the optimal penalty (Cohen 1987). This is consistent with 'restitution' in the criminal law, where offenders – once deemed criminals – are required to pay for the harm caused irrespective of other factors such as culpability, level of care and so on.

Note that the optimal penalty (10.3) does not depend on the level of effort undertaken by the firm. Thus, it is a strict liability standard, whereby the polluter is held liable without regard to his state of mind or to the fact that the polluting incident might have been beyond his control. If penalties are not constrained and costless to impose, such a penalty is best because it economizes on government resources (m_3) that might otherwise be devoted to an *ex post* investigation and potential adjudication or litigation costs associated with determining what level of care the firm actually took (Cohen 1987). To some extent, this fact has been used to justify the use of strict and vicarious liability in criminal environmental law instead of the older *mens rea* criteria. Most environmental offences are not deliberate acts like violent crimes. Instead, there is likely to be considerable uncertainty about the cause, level of care and so on. If culpability had to be established, it would not only be costly but there would also be a low detection/conviction rate.

Gain- versus Harm-based Sanctions

The optimal penalty derived in equation (10.3) is based on the harm caused by the environmental violation. The fact that the offender gained by violating the law is not relevant. Nevertheless, offenders generally do benefit from violating the law – otherwise, they would not risk being penalized. However, the government took account of that gain as an increase in social welfare when determining the optimal penalty. Note that social welfare maximization (10.2) includes $v(x)$, the value of resources lost if there is an accident, and e, the cost of the firm's preventive measures. These terms drop out in the optimal penalty calculation because they are included in the firm's decision (10.1). Since firms already minimize these costs in their own private calculation, there is no need to include them in the penalty calculation.

There is an ongoing debate between economists and criminal justice policy-makers about whether the penalty should be based on the harm, the gain, or both. A penalty based on gain to the offender would replace the term $D[(1-r)x]$ in equation (10.3) with a term such as $(e^* - e)$, to account for the difference between the mandated pollution prevention effort and the amount of effort actually expended. However, if the penalty differs from (10.3), the polluter will exert too little or too much effort/compliance relative to the social optimum. If we want to deter every violation of the law, we could impose a penalty equal to gain divided by the probability of detection. Then it would never be in the firm's interest to violate the law. However, pollution is a byproduct of a socially beneficial activity. In the jargon of the law and economics literature, pollution is a 'conditionally deterred' offence – one that we only want to prohibit when its social costs exceed its social benefits. To reduce pollution beyond that level would create inefficiencies and result in 'overdeterrence'. Some offences – such as violent assaults and rapes – are 'unconditionally deterred' offences that society would never condone regardless of the private benefit to the offender. In those cases, we simply ignore the offender's benefits, and the optimal penalty would be based on private gain divided by the probability of detection.

In practice, many government penalties are based on either gain or some combination of gain and harm. The US EPA (1984), for example, calculates its civil penalty based on a combination of gain and harm. It first imposes a gain-based penalty designed to take away any benefit from non-compliance, and then adds a 'gravity' component based on harm. The gain-based component of the penalty calculates the amount of money the violator saved by not complying with the law. The harm-based component is not as precise. Recently enacted Sentencing Guidelines for organizations convicted of federal crimes computes the monetary penalty based on the *maximum* of gain or harm.[4] One reason that is often mentioned for using gain is that it is easier to estimate than harm – especially for non-monetary harms such as environmental hazards. However, that rationale may be less valid than it used to be, given the growing literature on contingent valuation methods used to value environmental harms. Moreover, unless the private benefit (for example, less resources devoted to compliance) is somehow greater than the social benefit, society is better off letting that violation occur.

The Role of Non-monetary Sanctions

For very harmful crimes, the optimal penalty may be so high that it bankrupts the environmental violator. If the polluter is able to declare bankruptcy in some of the worst-case scenarios (for example, an extremely large stochastic pollution incident or unexpected compliance inspection), it has an incentive to take too much risk and thus less than optimal level of care (Cohen 1987: 33–4). This limit on the size of the penalty might force the government to increase *ex ante* monitoring, m_1, or to impose an *ex post* negligence standard (instead of a strict liability standard). An alternative approach to dealing with insolvency – and one that will reduce the cost of government monitoring – is to impose non-monetary sanctions on the offender.

As noted earlier, imprisonment is viewed as a socially costly alternative relative to monetary fines that are generally considered transfer payments. Thus, imprisonment is seen as a last resort when it is particularly costly to monitor *ex ante* and the *ex post* optimal penalty is so high that it would bankrupt the offender. Shavell (1985: 1236–7) identifies five factors that have a bearing on whether or not imprisonment is needed:

1. size of assets of the offender;
2. probability of detection and conviction;
3. size of private benefits from illegal activity;
4. probability that an act will cause harm in the case of *ex ante* penalties;
5. size of the harm if it occurs.

Incarceration is not the only form of non-monetary sanction. Individuals convicted of a crime may be placed on probation, forbidden from engaging in certain lines of business or professions, or may have certain restrictions placed on their rights (for example, ownership of firearms or voting rights). These sanctions largely serve the role of incapacitation. Similarly, organizations might be placed on 'probation' whereby the court or regulatory agency monitors their future compliance or remediation activity. Often, these remedies are meant to 'rehabilitate' the firm by instituting new compliance programmes. They might also lose certain rights, such as the right to sell goods or services to the government. Although designed primarily to 'incapacitate' firms convicted of fraudulent overcharges against the government from repeating their crime, these forms of sanctions have also been used in the environmental arena. Although the prospect of such a punishment would certainly provide a deterrent effect to potential environmental offenders, in most cases (that is, where insolvency is not a problem), the same level of deterrence can be achieved by imposing a higher monetary fine. More importantly, unlike a monetary fine that is a pure transfer, the debarment from future government contracts is inefficient and imposes a cost on the government, which now faces a less-competitive supplier market. This is a classic case of 'overdeterrence'. Of course, it is possible that the illegal disposal of hazardous waste lowered the cost of production to the firm, allowing it to become the low-cost bidder. That would still not justify the use of debarment as a deterrent. Instead, *if* the government believed that the firm would continue to violate the law, debarment might be used to incapacitate the offender.

Criminal Law as a Government Cost-saving Mechanism

As noted earlier, absent externally imposed constraints on penalties, risk aversion or insolvency, the optimal penalty is arbitrarily high and the optimal expenditure on monitoring approaches zero. However, both our social values of fairness and the risk of insolvency by very bad actors often preclude the use of such draconian policies. Thus, we are left with a government enforcement policy that requires a significant amount of monitoring expenditures. Several innovations have been suggested to reduce the need for expensive government monitoring. One innovation is to require firms to self-report any violation of pollution standards. Voluntary reporting is rewarded with more lenient treatment (Arlen and Kraakman 1997). Prosecutors might agree not to bring criminal charges or to reduce the severity of any sanction they do impose when a violation is self-reported.[5] Thus, the most severe sanctions – including criminal penalties – are reserved for offenders who fail to report or submit false reports. Such a policy may overcome the public's sense of unfairness in unleashing a harsh criminal sanction on white-collar offenders, while also reducing the cost of government monitoring.

A similar innovation has been proposed by Harrington (1988) and others (see Harrington and Heyes, Chapter 9 in this volume), whereby the enforcement agency uses differential monitoring and/or penalty schemes based on the past history of the firm. Firms found to be in non-compliance in one period are placed in a separate category that increases their chance of subsequent monitoring and increases the penalty if found to be in violation. This also has the effect of reducing the cost of enforcement for a given level of compliance. Although this model does not require a criminal sanction for the worst category of violators, depending on the parameters of the model and the risk of insolvency for potential violators, the criminal sanction (especially incarceration) might be the only way to implement such a scheme.

Criminal Liability for Employees of the Firm

Since firms often can afford larger penalties than their employees, the optimal penalty can often be imposed on the firm without coming up against the individual's wealth constraint. Indeed, that has been one argument in favour of charging corporations instead of employees or managers. Thus, when environmental crimes are committed within a corporate structure, incarceration of employees might only be justified as a method for the government to overcome the firm's insolvency constraint. Yet, that is not the only reason to impose criminal liability on individuals. Once we look inside the 'black box' of the firm, it is evident that managers have their own enforcement problem trying to convince employees to act on the company's behalf. For example, suppose corporate policy strongly favours compliance with hazardous waste regulations. A local manager whose bonus depends on his or her unit's profitability might decide to dispose of some hazardous wastes illegally to boost that bonus. Thus, employee shirking is always a possible source of emissions that are not only against the law but may also be against firm policy.

From an efficiency perspective, corporate and individual penalties are perfect substitutes if the employee can bear the full cost of the optimal penalty (Segerson and Tietenberg 1992; Polinsky and Shavell 1993). In that case, it does not matter if the individual or the company is fined, as the company can always pass the cost back on to the individual through its wage contract. Employee and employer sanctions may also be substitutes if the employer can observe the level of effort of the employee and use that knowledge to set wages. The firm can induce the individual to take the optimal level of care in preventing emissions beyond the legally allowable amount. If employees and employers are perfect substitutes, the government can arbitrarily decide how to allocate the optimal penalty between the two parties. However, if employer and employee are not able to shift penalties between themselves, they are no longer perfect substitutes. If the employee cannot bear the full burden of the optimal penalty, the government might still be able to impose the optimal penalty on the company. Since the penalty cannot be shifted to the employee, however, an alternative mechanism must be found. Either the firm spends more on *ex ante* monitoring of the employee's behaviour, or the government will be needed to impose incarceration. Thus, the criminal penalty becomes a mechanism by which the government helps the firm enforce its internal company policy of compliance. Of course, this model does not apply to the manager/owner who violates the law.

EMPIRICAL EVIDENCE ON CRIMINAL ENFORCEMENT OF ENVIRONMENTAL POLICY

Ultimately, one would like to know the extent to which the use of the criminal law has deterred environmental violations – and whether the benefits of improved environmental quality outweigh any costs associated with criminal enforcement. That is a lofty goal that is far from being met. The few studies that have empirically evaluated the deterrent effect of government monitoring and enforcement programmes have focused on administrative and civil remedies – not the criminal law. Cohen (2000) reviews this empirical literature and concludes that studies generally find a deterrent effect from increased inspections and government enforcement actions. However, there is little evidence on the effect of increasing monetary sanctions and none on the role of criminal sanctions.

One reason for the lack of empirical evidence is that data on criminal enforcement of environmental laws are sparse. Although the US Justice Department releases aggregate figures on the number of indictments, convictions, fines and prison sentences, these are of limited value since they are not disaggregated. More recently, the US Sentencing Commission has begun to make disaggregated data available on individuals and corporations sentenced under federal statutes. However, the data exclude any identifying information and it is nearly impossible to link a corporation to any individuals within that company who might have been convicted.

We do know, however, that there has been a dramatic growth in the use of the criminal law over the past 20+ years. Reportedly, there were only 25 criminal environmental cases prosecuted at the federal level during the entire decade of the 1970s (Habicht 1987: 10479). The 1980s brought about significant changes as both the US EPA and the Justice Department established special offices focusing on criminal enforcement, and Congress reclassified some environmental crimes from misdemeanours to felonies (Starr and Kelly 1990: 10097). Accordingly, the number of prosecutions has skyrocketed, from the handful per year in the 1970s to 40 per year in the early 1980s. From 1986 to 1991, there were an average of 115 prosecutions per year. That figure increased again to about 180 per year from 1992 to 1994 (Hutchins 1995). No comparable figures are available for prosecutions under state law.

Is the Criminal Law Efficient?

The few empirical studies on environmental criminal law to date have focused on determining the structure of current prosecution and sentencing policies. Although these studies cannot tell us if the current legal institutions are efficient, they can examine whether or not they are consistent with an optimal penalty framework. Cohen (1996b) derived several testable implications from the optimal penalty literature and compared them to 961 corporate criminal sentences – about 10 per cent of which were environmental crimes. Here, I re-examine these implications in the context of environmental crimes.

Sanctions should be an increasing function of harm

Since the basic optimal penalty model does not distinguish between criminal and civil monetary sanctions, the theory only predicts that the 'total sanction' be increasing in harm.[6] Cohen (1992) examines total monetary sanctions imposed on 116 corporations that were convicted of violating US environmental laws and compares the penalty structure to what we would expect under an optimal penalty. One of the difficulties with this type of analysis is the lack of comprehensive data on harm. In the absence of such data, Cohen (1992) used monetary harm – any known restitution or payments for direct losses suffered by victims, plus clean-up costs. Both criminal fines and total monetary sanctions are found to increase with this measure of harm. Sanctions are also higher for hazardous waste violations, which are generally more harmful than other violations. Thus, there is evidence consistent with the first proposition.

Sanctions should be a multiple of harm, inversely related to the probability of detection

Cohen (1992: 1080–81) also found that the total monetary sanction imposed on corporations convicted of environmental crimes roughly equalled the monetary harm for those cases where harm could be estimated *and* where the company could afford to compensate for the harm. Interestingly, the criminal fine only represents about 20 per cent of the total monetary sanction (and hence, about 20 per cent of the harm). Clean-up costs far exceed any criminal penalty. If such a penalty structure were optimal, it would imply that the probability of detection is one for environmental crimes. Note, however, that because monetary estimates of harm were seldom available, these findings are based on only eight cases – far too few to draw any significant conclusions.

Even less is known about the probability of detection for environmental offences. However, it would appear that many of the largest environmental crimes are almost certainly detected with probability one. The question with incidents such as the *Exxon Valdez* is not whether it will be detected, but what punishment will be imposed. However, not all environmental crimes are as easily observable as the *Exxon Valdez*. For example, falsifying pollution monitoring tests or failing to notify authorities of an otherwise undetectable release are both difficult to detect. Perhaps that is part of the reason why the US Sentencing Commission Guidelines call for relatively severe punishments for deliberate record-keeping violations that result in no actual harm (US Sentencing Commission 1998: section 2Q1).

Criminal sanctions and other non-criminal penalties should be substitutes

Although Cohen (1992: 1087, 1097) provides anecdotal evidence that criminal sanctions are reduced when there are significant non-criminal penalties, there is no systematic empirical finding to that effect. For example, the judge who sentenced Ashland Oil for their oil spill in 1988 rejected the prosecutor's call for a $12 million fine and instead imposed a $2.5 million fine because the company had acted 'responsibly after the spill' by paying for clean-up and settling monetarily with local residents. More rigorous empirical evidence (Cohen 1996b: 406) shows that there is an explicit tradeoff between the criminal sanction and other monetary sanctions in a large sample of all corporate criminal sentences (about 10 per cent of which were environmental crimes). However, that study found that a 10 per cent increase in non-criminal sanctions reduces the criminal sanction by only about 1.8 per cent. Neither the anecdotal evidence of environmental crimes nor the statistical analysis of corporate crime in general supports a one-for-one tradeoff. This suggests that deterrence is not the only goal of sentencing.

Sanctions against the company and individuals should be substitutes

Instead, Cohen (1992: 1090, table 6) finds that corporate sanctions are higher when individuals are convicted along with their firms. These findings appear to be inconsistent with optimal penalty theory. Corporate sanctions were also found to be higher for larger firms. There is no economic reason to increase fines for larger firms – only for larger harms. However, since large firms are less likely to have individuals convicted for the same offence, the larger penalties might simply reflect the inability to trade off individual for corporate sanctions. That is, judges might be increasing the monetary penalty to companies when there is no individual to sanction. This is a plausible explanation, since in a restricted sample of small, privately held firms convicted of environmental crimes, monetary fines are found to be negatively related to the likelihood of an individual going to jail (Cohen 1992: 1095, table 8).

Individuals within a company are more likely to be prosecuted (and sent to prison) when their company cannot afford the optimal penalty

This is an extremely difficult proposition to test, since we do not know the optimal penalty, which depends on both the harm and probability of detection. Instead, in previous research, I have attempted to evaluate the firm's financial ability to compensate for the harm it caused – which would be an optimal penalty only in the case of certain detection. This is probably a reasonable approach, since it would include only the worst-off firms and the question is whether they are more likely than average to have an individual conviction. In Cohen (1992), I found no evidence that individuals were more likely to be prosecuted for environmental crimes when their company could not afford to compensate for the harm caused. However, given the small number of cases where harm could actually be estimated, this is not a very strong result. In the larger set of 961 corporate crimes (Cohen 1996b: 407–8), where monetary harm could be estimated for 285 firms, there was some evidence of this effect.

Individuals within a company are more likely to be prosecuted (and sent to prison) when firms themselves are unable to impose a large enough monetary penalty on employees or otherwise provide adequate incentives to deter crime

This is also a difficult proposition to test, since we have no data on individual income or wealth. We also have no idea what internal control measures the company has in place prior to the commission of the offence. However, is should be more difficult to impose an optimal penalty on individuals when the harm they cause is very large. Thus, individual prosecution and conviction rates should increase with harm. Once again, the sample of environmental cases was too small in Cohen (1992) to shed any light on this issue. On the other hand, in the sample of 285 corporate criminal convictions where harm was estimated, the magnitude of harm was a significant positive explanatory variable in a probit equation explaining the likelihood of an individual being convicted within the company (Cohen 1996b: 408, table 8). An interesting related result has been reported in an analysis of penalties to companies and employees in the Czech Republic. Earnhart (2000) finds that government authorities never fine employees in certain types of companies and industries (especially foreign firms and military operations), whereas it is common in other industries to fine both the employee and the company. He attributes this distinction to the ability of certain firms to better monitor and discipline employees, consistent with the Segerson–Tietenberg (1992) and Polinsky–Shavell (1993) results.

Criminal Law, Moral Culpability and Firm Reputation

Recall that one proposed goal of the criminal law is to shape preferences by labelling behaviour that is socially unacceptable. To the extent that this is true, being labelled a criminal should impose a cost on offenders. Indeed, there is evidence that individuals who are convicted of embezzlement and fraud suffer from long-term reputation losses as evidenced by lower lifetime earnings (Lott 1992). The extent to which this effect would carry over to environmental crimes is unclear. This might depend on the extent to which the crime involved a breach of trust, violation of company policy and so on.

Information that a firm has been labelled an environmental criminal may also be of interest to shareholders or lenders. To the extent that monetary sanctions reduce the expected value of the firm, this will affect the share price and/or bond rating of the firm. It may also give lenders pause before risking more capital on that particular firm. In addition to the direct monetary sanctions and clean-up costs associated with the enforcement action, the firm may incur additional costs in the future. For example, if being convicted of an environmental crime automatically causes a firm to be barred from doing business with the government, investors may take this additional information into account. Similarly, if the government enforcement agency follows the suggestion of Harrington (1988) and others, and implements a targeted enforcement strategy, the threat of future sanctions may now be higher. It is also possible that this environmental law violation will result in the loss of goodwill to employees or customers, thus reducing the long-run profitability of the firm. Some socially conscious investors might even shun the firm's stock, thereby depressing its value. Finally, it is possible that investors will update their assessment of the quality of management in the firm and take this environmental law violation as a signal that the firm is not as well managed as they had thought.

Various empirical studies have demonstrated that the stock value of publicly traded firms is reduced upon the announcement of a bad environmental outcome such as an oil spill or criminal prosecution. For example, one study of the *Exxon Valdez* incident estimated the total market value loss to be $10.1–11.3 billion (Jones *et al*. 1994). This is $1.2–2.4 billion more than the direct costs I estimate Exxon paid including clean-up costs, fines and civil settlements. If insurers paid a significant portion of those costs, the direct cost to Exxon might have been considerably less. Thus, it is possible that Exxon received an additional 'market' penalty from the bad publicity surrounding the *Valdez* incident. However, a recent study by Karpoff *et al*. (1998) of 77 such incidents found that the stock price effects are approximately equal to government-imposed penalties, clean-up costs and private settlements, suggesting there is no additional reputation loss. Perhaps more intriguing is that they found no additional penalty for being labelled a 'criminal' violation. In a regression analysis of the stock price effect, controlling for the type of pollution, monetary sanctions and so on, a dummy variable for a criminal label had no additional explanatory power. This calls into question part of the rationale for criminalizing environmental offences.

CONCLUSION

This chapter has explored the many ways in which criminal law can be used as an environmental policy instrument. Generally, economists view criminal sanctions to have civil counterparts with the same level of effectiveness. However, if we believe there is a moral stigma associated with being labelled a criminal, and that people somehow 'learn' social norms by observing what behaviour is criminal, it might have added value. Throughout, I have taken a pure economic efficiency approach in analysing the usefulness of using the criminal law. Thus, I have not considered the possibility that society values 'fairness' or 'retribution', for example.

Aside from this social norm explanation, the real value of the criminal law is the existence of non-monetary sanctions – including prison, debarment, probation and other mechanisms to restrict future behaviour of individuals or firms. Non-monetary sanctions, although costly and generally inferior to monetary sanctions, might be less costly than expensive *ex ante* monitoring or wealth constraints that limit monetary sanctions below the optimal penalty. However, non-monetary sanctions come with an additional potential cost: the risk of overdeterrence. For example, individual managers faced with the prospect of prison time for acts of their employees (admittedly a rare event) might take socially costly prevention measures such as adding several layers of monitoring or entirely closing up an operation.

Despite the fact that there is little empirical evidence on the efficacy of criminal environmental enforcement, the trend in the US has been to expand this tool dramatically over the past 20 years. What little evidence exists points to a system that is at least consistent with some of the implications of optimal penalty theory. However, there is no evidence of a stigma effect for publicly traded corporations convicted of environmental crimes.

NOTES

1. However, this may not always be true. In the US, for example, charging a corporation with a crime makes it easier for the government to obtain documents that might provide evidence against corporate officials who were involved in the criminal activity.
2. Minimum sentences are rare in the US system except for drug crimes and repeat violent criminals.
3. For our purposes, we assume that production costs depend only on output level and are separable from the pollution prevention decision. The results of these models generally hold even if production is explicitly included.
4. The fine provisions of the Sentencing Guidelines that became effective in 1991 do not apply to environmental violations. One reason cited by the Commission in postponing writing Guidelines for environmental offences was the fact that it is difficult to quantify harm.

5. Proposed Sentencing Guidelines for organizations convicted of environmental crimes in the US would provide such a reward for self-reporting (Bureau of National Affairs 1993). For a critique of that proposal, see Cohen (1996a).
6. The 'total sanction' should also include the pecuniary value of any non-monetary sanctions such as the reputation loss to the firm. However, as discussed below, there is little evidence of a reputation loss to firms convicted of environmental crimes.

REFERENCES

Arlen, Jennifer and Reinier Kraakman (1997), 'Controlling corporate misconduct: an analysis of corporate liability regimes', *New York University Law Review* 72: 687–779.
Becker, Gary S. (1968), 'Crime and punishment: an economic approach', *Journal of Political Economy* 76: 169–217.
Bureau of National Affairs (1993), 'Draft sentencing guideline issued for corporate environmental crimes', *Daily Report for Executives* 17 November.
Cohen, Mark A. (1987), 'Optimal enforcement strategy to prevent oil spills: an application of a principal–agent model with "moral hazard"', *Journal of Law and Economics* 30(1): 23–51.
Cohen, Mark A. (1992), 'Environmental crime and punishment: legal/economic theory and empirical evidence on enforcement of federal environmental statutes', *Journal of Criminal Law and Criminology* 82(4): 1054–1108.
Cohen, Mark A. (1996a), 'Environmental sentencing guidelines or environmental management guidelines: you can't have your cake and eat it too!', *Federal Sentencing Reporter* 8(4): 225–9.
Cohen, Mark A. (1996b), 'Theories of punishment and empirical trends in corporate criminal sanctions', *Managerial and Decision Economics* 17: 399–411.
Cohen, Mark A. (1999), 'Monitoring and enforcement of environmental policy', in Tom Tietenberg and Henk Folmer (eds), *International Yearbook of Environmental and Resource Economics*, vol. III, Cheltenham, UK and Northampton, MA: Edward Elgar, pp. 44–106.
Cohen, Mark A. (2000), 'Empirical research on the deterrent effect of environmental monitoring and enforcement', *Environmental Law Reporter* 30: 10245–52.
Crovitz, L. Gordon (1991), 'Justice for the birds: Exxon forgot to get a hunting license', *Wall Street Journal* 20 March: A23.
Dau-Schmidt, Kenneth G. (1990), 'An economic analysis of the criminal law as a preference-shaping policy', *Duke Law Journal* 1.
Earnhart, Dietrich (2000), 'Environmental crime and punishment in the Czech Republic: penalties against firms and employees', *Journal of Comparative Economics* 28 (2), 379–99.
Habicht, F. Henry II (1987), 'The federal perspective on environmental criminal enforcement: how to remain on the civil side', *Environmental Law Reporter* 20: 10478.
Harrington, Winston (1988), 'Enforcement leverage when penalties are restricted', *Journal of Public Economics* 37: 29–53.
Hutchins, Peggy (1995), 'Environmental criminal statistics FY83 through FY95', Memorandum, Environmental Crimes Section, US Department of Justice, 7 April (reprinted at Environmental Law Institute AD-1230).
Jones, J.D., C.L. Jones and F. Phillips-Patrick (1994), 'Estimating the costs of the *Exxon Valdez* oil spill', *Research in Law and Economics* 16: 109–50.

Karpoff, Jonathan M., John R. Lott, Jr and Graeme Rankine (1998), 'Environmental violations, legal penalties, and reputation costs', John M. Olin Law and Economics Working Paper No. 71 (2nd series), Law School, University of Chicago.

Lott, John R., Jr (1992), 'Do we punish high income criminals too heavily?', *Economic Inquiry* 30: 583–608.

Polinsky, A. Mitchell and Steven Shavell (1979), 'The optimal tradeoff between the probability and magnitude of fines', *American Economic Review* 69: 880–91.

Polinsky, A. Mitchell and Steven Shavell (1993), 'Should employees be subject to fines and imprisonment given the existence of corporate liability?', *International Review of Law and Economics* 13: 239–57.

Riesel, Daniel (1985), 'Criminal prosecution and defense of environmental wrongs', *Environmental Law Reporter* 15: 10065.

Segerson, Kathleen and Tom Tietenberg (1992), 'The structure of penalties in environmental enforcement: an economic analysis', *Journal of Environmental Economics and Management* 23: 179–201.

Shavell, Steven (1985), 'Criminal law and the optimal use of non-monetary sanctions as a deterrent', *Columbia Law Review* 85: 1232–62.

Starr, Judson W. and Thomas J. Kelly, Jr (1990), 'Environmental crimes and the sentencing guidelines: the time has come ... and it is hard time', *Environmental Law Reporter* 20: 10096.

US Department of Justice (1991), 'Factors in decisions on criminal prosecutions for environmental violations in the context of significant voluntary compliance or disclosure efforts by the violator', 1 July, Memorandum (now available at http://www.usdoj.gov/enrd/factors.htm).

US Environmental Protection Agency (1984), 'Policy on civil penalties', 16 February, reprinted in *Environmental Law Review* 17: 35083 (October 1987).

US Environmental Protection Agency (1994), 'Guidance on EPA's exercise of investigative discretion for environmental crimes', Memorandum from Earl E. Devaney, Director, Office of Criminal Enforcement, 12 January.

US Sentencing Commission (1998), *Guidelines Manual*.

11.   Citizen suits

Chad Settle, Terrance M. Hurley and Jason F. Shogren

Ultimately, the question we must ask ourselves is whether we are prepared to leave the public interest to hired hands.

Joseph L. Sax (1970)

INTRODUCTION

In January 2000, the United States Supreme Court upheld one of the most interesting legal tools for environmental protection: the ability of private citizens to use the courts to help enforce federal environmental policy. The Justices voted 7–2 in *Friends of Earth, Inc.* v. *Laidlaw Environmental Services (TOC), Inc.* (98–822), 149 F.3d 303, to preserve the rights of citizens to act as 'private attorney generals' for nature. Common folk can use the federal district courts to initiate suits if they can show they have an interest that is or might be adversely affected by violators who damage the natural environment. The end result of these citizen suits can be injunctive relief or civil penalties imposed on violators to give them incentive to comply with environmental regulations. The idea is to empower ordinary citizens to take control over their own environmental destiny. After all, many people believe as strongly as Justice Warren Burger did in 1966 that '[c]onsumers are generally among the best vindicators of the public interest' (quoted in Sax 1970: 244; also see Epstein 1998).

Now to be sure, private citizen involvement in the enforcement of federal laws is an old idea. Private citizens helping to enforce laws dates back over 600 years to a 1388 statute in England (Dickinson 1997). But at least in the United States until the 1970s, the ordinary citizen was shut out of the debate because most environmental decisions were left in the hands of government bureaucrats and technicians (Sax 1970). Interestingly, the case for citizen suits was not made so much to protect the private persons from *market failure* (for example, externalities and the like), but rather to protect them from *administrative failure* by the government agencies tasked to address issues with the market misallocation. Not that administrators were argued to be operating with malice towards the public, but rather that administrative complexities, red tape and politics kept the common citizen at arm's length from most environmental decisions. Re-emergence of interest in citizen suits for environmental protection began in earnest in the 1960s, as air and water pollution and threatened species became hotly contested issues. People and legislators began to realize that weak punishment mechanisms in environmental legislation were a problem.

This realization and the political climate led to the creation of citizen suit provisions in federal legislation in 1970, that is, section 304 of the Clean Air Act (Miller 1987). The goal was not to replace legislative process, but rather as 'a means of providing realistic access to legislatures so that the theoretical processes of democracy can be made to work more effectively in practice' (Sax 1970). This goal of more access, however, was not given much attention until after the Clean Water Act (CWA) was passed in 1972. After the CWA was passed, citizen suits became increasingly popular and now most of those suits brought are a direct result of the Act (Flora 1997). Throughout the 1970s and 1980s, as the power to enforce several federal laws was put into citizens' hands as well as those of the federal government, the number of citizen suits began to multiply and become a useful tool for those interested in environmental protection. Today, although the Supreme Court has raised the bar for the ordinary person to get into court over the past decade, the *Friends of the Earth* v. *Laidlaw Environmental Services* ruling suggests that citizen suits are likely to remain an important tool in the US (Glaberson 1999; Echeverria and Zeidler 1999). And interest in citizen suits probably will continue to spread globally, as suggested by test case suits in less-likely places such as China, where a Mr Zhang Jinhu sued his local government for compensation for losses suffered due to pollution (Rosenthal 2000).

The question of citizen suits becomes an issue to those interested in environmental economics if one wants to understand the efficiency consequences of how different legal rules either promote or inhibit the expenditure of effort to win a legal contest. Some rules decrease efficiency by increasing the effort expended in the conflict at no gain in environmental quality; other rules decrease efficiency when they bias the expected results away from those persons who value the outcome the most. Some rules can increase efficiency if they reduce the effort expended or make it more likely that those who value the environment the most, either for preservation or development, secure control over the resource.

Here we examine the recent economics literature on citizen suits within a class of environmental conflict models. We start with a brief overview of the recent history of citizen suits in environmental policy, focusing on the case of the United States as the motivating example. We then introduce a general environmental conflict model between a citizen group and a firm competing for a different environmental policy or level of enforcement. We consider how differences in ability, reimbursement of effort, valuation and information affect effort expended in the conflict. We consider how firms have fought back against citizen suits with the SLAPP – the *strategic lawsuit against public participation*. Finally, we extend the model to a repeated contest in which firms use the SLAPP to build a reputation in order to scare citizens from using their legal right to sue.

RECENT HISTORY OF THE CITIZEN SUIT IN ENVIRONMENTAL POLICY

Consider now a brief history of citizen suits in environmental policy in the United States. Three waves of public participation have become apparent over the last 30 years. The first wave was a time of expansion of citizen suits. The second wave saw the power of citizen suits threatened and their use restricted. Finally, in the past few years, the power of citizen suits has started to come back and their use broadened. As we discuss each wave, we find it helpful to characterize citizen suits as having either an *expansionist* or a *restrictive* approach (Dickinson 1997). The *expansionist* approach views citizen suits as helping the federal government in enforcing environmental regulations. The *restrictive* approach views citizen suits as both a nuisance that ties up our courts and as a mechanism that allows citizens to take over the power that should be delegated to federal agencies in enforcing these regulations (ibid.).

The first wave started in the 1970s and 1980s. In early 1970s, the US Congress enacted several major environmental regulations, including the Clean Air Act and the Clean Water Act (CWA) which included provisions for citizen participation. The CWA, for instance, allows the federal government and the states to allocate permits to limit the discharge of pollutants, and to establish monitoring and reporting actions. Under §505(a) of the CWA, any citizen has standing to initiate a suit to enforce any limit set by a permit; in this a *citizen* is 'a person or persons having an interest which is or may be adversely affected' (33 U.S.C. § 1365(a), (g)). But first the citizen must give 60 days' notice to the United States Environmental Protection Agency (EPA) of the alleged violation and alleged violator. The notice allows the alleged violator a chance to get into compliance, such that the citizen suit is unnecessary. The CWA authorizes district courts in citizen suits to enter injunctions and to assess civil penalties, payable to the United States Treasury. In addition, the court 'may award costs of litigation (including reasonable attorney and expert witness fees) to any prevailing or substantially prevailing party, whenever the court determines such award is appropriate' (§1365(d)).

Over this time, citizen suits were mostly seen as a help to federal agencies in enforcement. As a result of the positive climate for citizen suits in the 1970s and early 1980s, the number put into court increased each year (Miller 1987). The number of suits expanded so quickly that several suits were even brought against one polluter: the Tennessee Valley Authority (TVA) had five citizen suits and one state suit brought against it in June 1977 alone (TVA 1977). The fact that the TVA was a federal agency had led to leniency over many previous violations. It also led to leniency in these cases, but the large number of citizen suits were responsible for bringing violations to light and serving as a private punishment mechanism. These suits were large in number and each polluting firm had to worry whether they would be the next TVA. This meant firms violating federal pollution laws had to worry about enforcement from both the federal government and private citizens.

The spread of citizen suits was helped in part by lawyers themselves. An example of how clinics helped spread the number of citizen suits was one at Rutgers University, the Environmental Litigation Clinic. This helped citizens deal with potential cases (Carney 1985). The clinic was brought about in part due to the small number of cases filed in New Jersey despite the large number of violations in the state.

The *expansionist* approach is not limited to cases and issues from the 1970s and 1980s: there have been recent cases that help the power of citizen suits. A 1996 ruling mandated attorney's fees be paid for work that didn't directly lead to results in the case; the ruling stated that the work done 'was a catalyst for the settlement' and as a result the fees should be paid (Ruggles 1998). The *expansionist* approach was echoed in Heyes (1998), which cited citizen suits as a cheaper alternative to enforcement by direct regulatory agencies. Further research has been done to determine if states that had a more *expansionist* view, measured by whether the state was a right-to-sue or a right-to-know state, affected the level of emissions. The research concluded that these states did in fact have lower emissions than other states (Grant 1997). This research into the effect of citizen suits suggests that they and positive state views towards these suits have helped the environment.

These rulings prompting the *expansionist* approach are an exception. Over the past 15 years, as the number of suits has continued to grow, the first wave of expansion has come to an end and the second wave of restricting the power and use of citizen suits has started. Most rulings were now coming down in favour of the *restrictive* approach. Fear of the outcome of a widespread permission for citizen suits has a long history. As far back as 1980, fear of the potential damage they could cause was voiced. Many were being brought upon companies that had little or no insurance to pay for the resulting damages from the suits (Terry 1980). A portion of the public feared that firms would not be able to pay the large fees resulting from citizen suits, which could cause those firms to file for bankruptcy.

A key issue in restricting the domain of citizen suits is deciding who has *standing*: who is entitled to prosecute a particular legal claim in court. The Supreme Court has said that citizens must meet three constitutional requirements to have standing in court: (a) they must show that they have suffered an 'injury in fact'; (b) they must establish *causation*: the injury 'fairly can be traced to the challenged action'; and (c) they must show that the injury 'is likely to be redressed by a favorable decision' of the court. As we shall see, increasing restrictions on standing raise the bar for citizen suits high enough for some to worry that 'the evolution of standing doctrine over the last decade [1990s] has been a case of heads we lose, tails they win' (Echeverria and Zeidler 1999).

Court rulings in the early 1980s came down against the growing number of citizen suits. A 1981 ruling (*Middlesex County Sewer Authority* v. *Sea Clammers*) threw out a case in court for failing to give notice before filing suit; the citizen suit provisions mandate that a filer 'give 60 days' notice to the Environmental Protection Agency, their local states, and the alleged violators' (Court 1981). The 60-day rule was initially brought about to allow the Environmental Protection Agency or local states to bring a suit against a firm for violations – a last resort to allow the government to bring suit for violations (Miller 1987). The court's ruling on this case forced filers to comply with the 60-day notice or have their case thrown out of court.

The backlash against citizen suits became a hot issue when James Watt came into focus in the early 1980s as a part of the Reagan Administration. Directly after the Supreme Court ruled to limit the fees given to successful citizen suits, the Reagan Administration drafted new legislation that would limit the power of citizen suits (Yost 1983). The push towards reducing the power given in the Clean Water Act was finally brought before Congress and passed in a 1986 bill amending the original Act. The 1986 amendment limited the power of suits, claiming that no 'double penalties' could be awarded; citizen suits could not be brought for violations already addressed in other litigation or by federal agency investigations (Clauson 1997). The tables had been completely turned on citizen filers. The second wave of restricting the power of citizen suits had fully began. The move was back towards an *expansionist* approach.

Further rulings continued to come down from the court restricting both the power and frequency of citizen suits. An 8–0 decision from the Supreme Court in *Gwaltney of Smithfield Ltd.* v. *Chesapeake Bay Foundation* ruled that citizens could not file suit for 'wholly past violations'. A violator in a citizen suit had either to be continuously violating pollution laws or to have shown a threat of doing so in the future as a result of long and steady past violations. If a firm had violated the law in the past but had resolved the dispute in a timely manner, thus showing willingness to comply with the law, the citizen group would not be awarded victory (Johnston 1999; Leonard 1998; Taylor 1987; Young 1987). Even greater hits were taken when a bill that passed the Senate took away the power of citizens to bring suit against the government. A Bush–Senate deal took back the power of the citizens to bring suit against government agencies for failing to supply clean air to the US (Billings 1990). The federal government was no longer responsible for providing its citizens with clean air. This ruling held up under a different context, when a Florida case, *Seminole Tribe of Florida* v. *Florida*, ruled that citizens could not bring suit against their state in federal court for failing to comply with federal regulations (Reynolds 1996). It appeared that the future of citizen suits was under severe attack.

Even more scrutiny came against the citizen suit provisions when the Environmental Protection Agency developed its stormwater rule for small communities. The rule, for a certain class of suits, reversed the earlier decision and once again allowed citizen suits to be filed against small communities as it placed the responsibility back on the government with regard to the disposition of stormwater. No longer would the government be free of citizen suits. The first of the suits brought against local government was in 1993 when the Natural Resources Defense Council brought suit against the communities of Beverly Hills, El Segundo and Hermosa Beach for failure to provide toxic water clean-up and threatened to bring suit against Rancho Palos Verdes, Redondo Beach, Culver City and Westlake Village if they didn't clean up their cities' runoff (Fuetsch 1993). The expansion of citizen suits continued when the second phase of the stormwater rule was coming into effect (Jenkins 1997). Small communities feared that the phase two regulations would bring about more public scrutiny. This fear of citizen suits was not limited only to local communities. Some even compared the citizen suit power provided in environmental protection laws to that of 'vigilante justice' that needed to be stopped (Pendley 1994). All these fears seemed to enhance further the view that the power from citizen suit provisions needed to be stripped at least partially from citizen groups.

Two more cases reduced citizen suit power. The first case, brought by the Defenders of Wildlife, saw the Supreme Court uphold a George Bush Administration policy that limited the power of the Endangered Species Act to cases in the United States. A citizen suit to protect the ESA could not be brought against United States funded projects that were completed outside the United States (Hamburger 1992). Probably the biggest case in the 1990s was, ironically, what might have given citizen suits their respectability again in the view of society. The Supreme Court ruled, in *Bennett* v. *Spear*, that any citizen can bring suit over an environmental law. Land developers, farmers and ranchers could now use the citizen suit provisions to bring suit that these laws were too restrictive and overprotective of the environment (Savage 1997; Greenhouse 1996). If a person was being harmed by the action of the federal government and felt the actions taken were too severe, s/he could bring a citizen suit against the government for being too strict with respect to federal environmental law. The ability to have both sides of a protection issue come to court now gave citizen suits a new look. This case was first viewed as another victory against citizen suits brought against developers.

Ironically, while this last case seemed to be an overriding victory for developers and farmers who wanted less environmental protection, it gave respectability back to the citizen suit provisions. The last part of the 1990s saw a return to the *expansionist* approach as the third wave of broadening came about. Citizen suits had two notable victories in 1998. The first dealt with the issue of 'wholly past violations'. The Fourth Circuit court ruled on remand of *Chesapeake Bay Found* v. *Gwaltney of Smithfield, Ltd* that even if the violations were taken care of in the period between the filing and the time the case went to court, the plaintiff would still be due fees; this was upheld in other cases, *Atlantic States Legal Found* v. *Tyson Foods, Inc.*, *Natural Resources Defense Council* v. *Texaco Ref. & Mktg, Inc.* Now the term 'wholly past violations' meant only if the violations had been cleaned up prior to the filing of the case (Johnston 1999). The second victory came when the Supreme Court ruled in *Steel Co.* v. *Citizens for a Better Environment* that 'wholly past violations' only covered the Clean Water Act and the Emergency Planning and Community Right to Know Act, which allowed citizens to sue for past violations (Johnston 1999). Now, citizen suits could be brought under other Acts beyond the Clean Water Act for violations that occurred at any time. These two rulings were the first major victories for citizen suits rights in over 15 years. It appears that citizen suits are once again in favour.

Citizen suits found another foe in the 1990s. Lawsuits can be filed on behalf of firms that have citizen suits filed against them. These lawsuits, Strategic Lawsuits Against Public Participation (SLAPP), the phrase coined by George Pring and Penelope Canan, filed in the US are brought against citizens for speaking out against development or any action that brings a citizen to speak out against the firm. Firms can take citizen groups to court for complaining about development. This action is a pre-emptive strike against other citizen groups, acting to stop others from speaking out. Such suits are a legal trick, since speaking out publicly against development or other actions is protected by the first amendment for free speech in the US. To bring a SLAPP lawsuit, the firm must show that this speech is infringing their rights in some legal way, whether it be libel, business interference or conspiracy (Pring and Canan 1995). This movement from an issue of public speech to a legal type of infringement is necessary to bring a SLAPP lawsuit.

Although the phrase was recently coined, SLAPPs have a long history. A SLAPP is simply legal recourse against citizens who speak out against someone who has power. The first type of these suits was brought when the United States was young, in the late 1700s. Citizens were sued when they spoke out against the government for suspected corruption (Pring and Canan 1995). These early SLAPPs, just as citizen suits did, disappeared for centuries until recent years. These suits spread in the US in the 1960s and 1970s with the resurgence of citizen suits and became almost commonplace in the 1980s and 1990s. Thousands of SLAPP suits have been brought against citizens for speaking out against firms and their activities. These lawsuits have been responsible for scaring citizens into silence, as intended.

Pring and Canan develop what they call the transition from a citizen speaking out to the SLAPP suit to the end of the case. Their three stages are (a) the citizen or group speaking out against the firm for real or perceived harms; (b) the firm bringing suit that transforms the case from a free speech case to a legal issue (the SLAPP is born); (c) the actual SLAPP case itself (Pring and Canan 1995). The third stage is the actual conflict in court; however, we need to inspect the economic motivation behind this same process. Why do we care? What is the economic issue behind SLAPPs?

The first stage essentially is when damages are first brought about. The damages are first brought by the firm whose activity is harming the citizen or citizen group. The citizen wants someone to hear and understand the harm. Speaking out in any public forum or raising public awareness of the issue is the response. Then, by speaking out, the citizen or group is inflicting harm on the firm. The citizen group is either harming the image of the firm or is potentially stopping the activity of the firm. Either way, the citizen's action is affecting either the potential activity of the firm or the firm's image. The SLAPP is the turnabout on the citizen group – moving the harm back on the citizen. This fight is an environmental conflict, which has been modelled extensively and will be explained in detail in this chapter. As citizen suits have come back into favour, some people are asking whether the SLAPP lawsuits should be banned. Anti-SLAPP bills in several different states continue to be considered by both Republicans and Democrats (Pring and Canan 1995). These bills ask the important questions: whether SLAPPs cause more harm than good, and whether SLAPPs should be banned.

We now consider the class of models commonly used to address these efficiency questions that arise when considering citizen suits in environmental conflicts.

MODELLING CITIZEN SUITS AS AN ENVIRONMENTAL CONFLICT

Citizen suits in environmental conflicts serve as a mechanism to promote the private enforcement of federal environmental regulations. Congress in effect deputized private citizens to help enforce environmental protection. The economic question is how different institutional rules, given the different endowments of players, affect the economic efficiency of some environmental conflicts. The model commonly used to capture the efficiency of these conflicts extends Tullock's (1980) seminal rent seeking framework (see Nitzan 1994 for an overview). Contest models have exploded in popularity over the past decade, probably because of their ability to capture strategic behaviour with broad explanatory power in a relatively parsimonious model.

We begin by presenting a general model of environmental conflict of which each of the models and results that are discussed represent a special case. Consider two agents, denoted by f and h, contesting the right to use an environmental good. For example, f can be thought of as an agent representing a firm seeking to develop environmentally sensitive land and h can be thought of as an agent representing a homeowner or group of homeowners opposed to development. The value of the right to use the environmental good to the ith agent is denoted as V_i. While the ith agent knows this value, his opponent may not, such that the contest is a game of incomplete information. Following Harsanyi (1967–8), the incomplete information game is transformed into an imperfect information game by assuming that *nature* randomly chooses the ith player's value, v_i, from the distribution $F_i(v_i)$ where $v_i \in [a_i, b_i]$ for $i = f$ and h. $V_i = v_i$ is immediately revealed to player i by *nature*, but not necessarily to player j, for $i = f$ and h and $i \neq j$. $F_i(v_i)$ is common knowledge for $i = f$ and h.

The ith player exerts observable, irreversible and reimbursable effort x_i to influence the probability of securing the right to the environmental good. The probability that agent f secures the right to the environmental good is denoted by $P(x_f, x_h)$, while the probability that agent h secures the right is $P(x_h, x_f) = 1 - P(x_f, x_h)$. $P_i(x_i, x_j), P_{ii}(x_i, x_j), P_j(x_i, x_j)$ and $P_{jj}(x_i, x_j)$ represent the first and second partial derivative of this contest success function with respect to agent i and j's efforts where $P_i(x_i, x_j) > 0, P_{ii}(x_i, x_j) < 0, P_j(x_i, x_j) < 0$, and $P_{jj}(x_i, x_j) > 0$.

Let β_i be the proportion of the ith agent's effort reimbursed by agent j given i wins the contest. Let s_i represents the proportion of player i's effort that is exogenously subsidized. Assuming risk neutrality, the ith agent's expected payoff is:

$$E\pi_i = \int_{a_j}^{b_j} \left\{ P\left(x_i, x_j(v_j)\right) \left(V_i + \beta_i x_i + \beta_j x_j(V_j)\right) - \beta_j x_j - (1 - s_i)x_i \right\} dF_j(v_j).$$

(11.1)

A variety of important questions regarding the nature and effect of citizen suits and SLAPPs have been addressed using special cases of this general model.

These questions address the effect of reimbursable and subsidized effort, the role of information and timing, and asymmetries in values and the ability to contest the environmental good. However, before reviewing these various issues, it is useful to explore the nature of the concepts used to characterize behaviour and measure performance in these environmental conflicts.

Two concepts are typically used to solve for equilibrium behaviour in models of environmental conflict. In a Nash contest, the presumption is that both agents choose effort simultaneously, so the Nash or Bayesian Nash equilibrium concept solves the game. In a Stackelberg contest, the presumption is that one agent has the opportunity to commit and reveal effort before his opponent's choice of effort, so subgame perfection or the perfect Bayesian equilibrium concept solves the game. The Nash and subgame perfect solution are for solving games where agents know each other's value – games of complete information. The Bayesian Nash and perfect Bayesian equilibria are for solving games where one or more players do not know their opponent's value – games of incomplete information.

First, consider the characterization of the Nash or Bayesian Nash equilibrium. The first-order condition for the ith agent is:

$$\frac{\partial E\pi_i}{\partial x_i} = \int_{a_j}^{b_j} \left\{ P_i\left(x_i, x_j\left(v_j\right)\right) \left(V_i + \beta_i x_i + \beta_j x_j\left(V_j\right)\right) + \beta_i P\left(x_i, x_j\left(v_j\right)\right) - \left(1 - s_i\right) \right\} dF_j\left(v_j\right) = 0.$$

$$(11.2)$$

When second-order conditions are satisfied, solving equation (11.2) for $x_j(v_j)$ and $x_h(v_h)$ yields the Nash or Bayesian Nash equilibrium.

Now consider the Stackelberg equilibrium where agent i chooses effort first followed by j. To solve for the subgame perfect or perfect Bayesian equilibrium, we start by finding j's optimal effort given i's effort. Since uncertainty regarding i's value enters j's payoff only through its influence on effort, once i's effort is revealed V_i is irrelevant to j. Therefore, j's first-order conditions is:

$$\frac{\partial E\pi_i}{\partial x_i} = P_j\left(x_j, x_i\right)\left(V_j + \beta_j x_j + \beta_i x_i\right) + \beta_j P\left(x_j, x_i\right) - \left(1 - s_j\right) = 0. \quad (11.3)$$

Assuming the second-order condition is satisfied, equation (11.3) implicitly defines j's best response $x_j^R(V_j)$ given x_i. Agent i then maximizes his expected payoff given this best response function. The first-order condition is:

$$\frac{\partial E\pi_i}{\partial x_i} = \int_{a_j}^{b_j}\left\{\left[P_i\left(x_i,x_j^R(v_j)\right)+P_j\left(x_i,x_j^R(v_j)\right)\frac{\partial x_j^R(v_j)}{\partial x_i}\right]\left(V_i+\beta_ix_i+\beta_jx_j^R(V_j)\right)\right\}dF_j(v_j)$$

$$+\int_{a_j}^{b_j}\left\{P\left(x_i,x_j^R(v_j)\right)\left(\beta_i+\beta_j\frac{\partial x_j^R(v_j)}{\partial x_i}\right)-\beta_j\frac{\partial x_j^R(v_j)}{\partial x_i}-(1-s_i)\right\}dF_j(v_j).$$

(11.4)

Equation (11.4) implicitly defines i's optimal level of effort assuming the second-order condition is satisfied. Substituting this solution into equation (11.3) and solving for x_j yields j's equilibrium effort.

Various performance measures have been used to judge the wastefulness of environmental conflicts. The most common is rent dissipation, which is defined as total effort expended: $R = x_f + x_h$. While rent dissipation is a useful and more tractable measure of performance, it fails to capture other important benefits and costs when agents value the contest differently because it does not account for the value of the environmental good to the winner of the contest. Hurley (1998) proposes an alternative measure, contest efficiency, that incorporates the expected value of the environmental good. Contest efficiency is defined as the proportion of the maximum obtainable benefits captured by the contest. Similarly, Heyes (1997) defines a social loss function that represents deviations from the maximum obtainable benefit. A slightly less onerous measure of performance is the expected value of the environmental good less the rent dissipated attempting to secure the good:

$$\xi = \int_{a_i}^{b_i}\int_{a_j}^{b_j}\left\{v_j+P_i\left(x_i(v_i),x_j(v_j)\right)\left(v_i-v_j\right)-x_i(v_i)-x_j(v_j)\right\}dF_j(v_j)dF_i(v_i).$$

(11.5)

The measures of efficiency defined by Hurley and Heyes represent relative measures of efficiency, while equation (11.5) is an absolute measure.

For all but the most basic questions, the general model is analytically intractable. A number of simplifying assumptions is used to gain additional insight into the nature of citizen suits and environmental conflict. The most prominent simplifying assumption is the use of the more tractable stylized logit contest success function: $P(x_f, x_h) = A_f x_f / (A_f x_f + A_h x_h)$ where A_f is an absolute measure of agent f's ability and A_h is an absolute measure of h's ability. When $A_f > (<) A_h$, f's effort is more (less) effective at influencing the outcome of the contest than h's effort. However, even with the logit contest success function, a convenient closed-form solution is not always attained. Therefore, researchers have further restricted and embellished the model to focus on specific questions.

Tullock Benchmark

Tullock's (1980) seminal work focused on rent-seeking behaviour in a much simpler model. His fundamental results serve as a convenient benchmark from which to compare the results of later models. Tullock used the logit contest success function with equal ability ($A_f = A_h$), equal and known payoffs ($\Pr(V_f = V_h = V) = 1.0$), and no reimbursement ($\beta_f = \beta_h = 0$) or subsidization ($s_f = s_h = 0$). What he found is that in either the Nash or Stackelberg equilibrium each agent expended one-quarter of the value of the contest ($x_f = x_h = V/4$). This result implied that together agents would waste half of the value of the environmental good in an attempt to secure the right to use it ($R = \xi = x_f + x_h = V/2$). An important implication drawn from this result is that, together, agents will not expend more than the value of an environmental good to secure its use.

Reimbursable Effort

Many citizen suits are brought about over environmental conflicts. A common type of this environmental suit is for private enforcement of federal environmental regulations. Baik and Shogren (1994) examine a class of conflicts in which information is symmetric and there is no subsidization, but reimbursements, abilities and rewards can all be symmetric or asymmetric. The baseline case is developed as a starting point with symmetric reimbursements, abilities and rewards. Asymmetric reimbursements is then considered since private enforcement of United States environmental laws only allow citizens' legal costs to be reimbursed in the case of victory. A firm's legal costs are not reimbursed even if they are victorious in the battle. Asymmetric values and ability are then discussed along with issues of timing.

The interior Nash equilibrium efforts with symmetric information, reimbursements, abilities and rewards and no subsidization [$\Pr(V_f = V_h = V) = 1.0$, $\beta_f = \beta_h = \beta$, $A_f = A_h$, and $s_f = s_h = 0$] are $x_f^N = x_h^N = V/4(1 - \beta)$, while rent dissipation is $R^N = V/2(1 - \beta)$. First, note that any reimbursement of effort results in more effort being expended by both players and greater rent dissipation when compared to Tullock. Also, as the reimbursement (β) increases, equilibrium efforts increase as does rent dissipation. The total level of effort exceeds the value of the prize when more than half of the effort is reimbursed in victory ($\beta > 0.5$). In this case, even though expected returns are negative (more than the prize is expended in effort), neither firm has an incentive to reduce effort to zero in equilibrium because both players could win the prize with 100 per cent probability by increasing their effort to any positive amount. This is a particularly worrisome result that Tullock had temporarily dispelled. The fact that such a different and wasteful result was obtained for an initially attractive institutional structure is an important result.

Now suppose only one player, the homeowner, is reimbursed for effort in victory ($\beta_f = 0$ and $\beta_h = \beta$). This is the case for environmental citizen suits in the United States where only the citizens group is reimbursed in victory. The Nash equilibrium efforts become:

$$x_f^N = \frac{V\left(1 - \sqrt{1-\beta}\right)}{2\beta} \quad \text{and} \quad x_h^N = \frac{V\left(1 - \sqrt{1-\beta}\right)}{2\beta\sqrt{1-\beta}},$$

while rent dissipation is:

$$R^N = \frac{V}{2\sqrt{1-\beta}}.$$

With reimbursement only for the citizens group (homeowner), the total level of effort will be lower for all values of reimbursement (for all values of β between 0 and 1). However, the homeowner is now exerting a higher level of effort than the firm. As such, the homeowner now has a greater than 50 per cent chance of winning the contest in equilibrium and is the contest favourite (Dixit 1987). Alternatively, the firm has less than a 50 per cent chance of winning the contest and is the contest underdog. Tullock found that agents were equally likely to win. This result was robust when symmetric reimbursement was considered, but stands in contrast to the case of asymmetric reimbursement.

The resulting lower level of effort supports previous work suggesting asymmetry can reduce the total level of effort in a contest (Tullock 1980). But now, even with symmetric ability, only having asymmetric reimbursement will reduce total effort when compared to symmetric reimbursement. The inability to recuperate effort in victory lowers the expected return for the firm and as such lowers the optimal level of effort by the firm. Although this suggests that asymmetric reimbursement decreases the loss from rent seeking (effort is lower), rent dissipation is still greater than with no reimbursement.

Also similar to the case of symmetric reimbursement is the resulting exorbitant effort when levels of reimbursement are high. When reimbursement increases, the level of effort by both players increases. This result is intuitive, since the firm has a greater loss to protect and the homeowner has a greater gain to seek. However, since the firm is not reimbursed for its effort, the homeowner's effort increases at a faster rate than that of the firm. Thus, the gap between the effort of the homeowner and the effort of the firm widens. With this increasing gap, a higher level of reimbursement will lead to a higher probability that the homeowner will win the contest.

Tullock's result that the Nash and Stackelberg equilibria are identical is not affected by reimbursement provided $0.5 \geq \beta > 0.0$. If $1.0 \geq \beta > 0.5$ and reimbursement is asymmetric, however, the Stackelberg equilibrium efforts when the firm chooses effort first are $x_f^{Sf} = 0.0$ and $x_h^{Sf} = \varepsilon$, where ε is the least amount of effort the homeowner can invest. If the homeowner and the firm are given the opportunity to decide who moves first, both prefer the firm to move first when $1.0 \geq \beta > 0.5$. Therefore, if the firm must reimburse more than half of the homeowner's effort, the firm is willing to move first and invest no effort, the homeowner gladly allows the firm to move and then invest minimal effort in order to claim the environmental good.

If the firm and homeowner also have different abilities ($\alpha = A_f/A_h \neq 1.0$), the Nash equilibrium becomes:

$$x_f^N = \frac{V}{2\alpha\beta\sqrt{(\alpha+1)^2 - 4\alpha\beta}}\left[\sqrt{(\alpha+1)^2 - 4\alpha\beta} - (\alpha+1-2\alpha\beta)\right] \text{ and}$$

$$x_h^N = \frac{V}{2\beta\sqrt{(\alpha+1)^2 - 4\alpha\beta}}\left[(\alpha+1) - \sqrt{(\alpha+1)^2 - 4\alpha\beta}\right].$$

The inclusion of ability with asymmetric reimbursement substantially complicates equilibrium behaviour. Effort for the homeowner will fall as the size of the firm's ability advantage increases. However, the firm's effort will initially increase and then decrease. Overall, the effect will be an initial increase in rent dissipation followed by a decrease. The level of rent dissipation compared to symmetric ability and reimbursement depends on the size of the firm's advantage in ability.

In addition to rent dissipation, which player is the favourite can be affected by asymmetric ability. As the firm's ability increases, its effort increases and the effort of the homeowner decreases. Thus, as the firm's ability increases, the firm has a better chance of winning the contest. With asymmetric reimbursement, the homeowner is the favourite and the firm is the underdog. However, if the firm has more ability, it can overcome the disadvantage of reimbursing homeowner effort. With enough ability, the firm can once again be the favourite. This result indicates that asymmetric reimbursement may serve as a useful tool to 'level the playing field' when some agents are perceived to have an unfair advantage in their ability to influence the outcome of the conflict.

Introducing asymmetric rewards increases the total effort expended in the contest. The homeowner will always increase effort if the relative reward of the homeowner increases. The firm will increase effort if it is the favourite and will decrease effort if it is the underdog. The overall effect will be an increase in rent dissipation. Once again who is the favourite is blurred. The difference in reward will give a further advantage to who values winning the contest more.

Asymmetric reimbursement changes the expected payoffs to the homeowner and the firm. Implementing asymmetric reimbursement pushes the game in favour of the homeowner. The homeowner's odds of winning the contest increase as does his/her expected returns. In addition to swinging the game in favour of the homeowner, asymmetric reimbursement has another effect: it can decrease the amount of the prize that is wasted in the contest.

Asymmetric Information

Hurley and Shogren (1997) argue that a firm will not know for certain the value to a homeowner of winning an environmental dispute because the homeowner's preferences are private and there are few market signals available to inform the firm. Alternatively, a homeowner will know the value to the firm of winning the dispute, since the firm's profits are driven by readily observable and informative market signals. Heyes (1997) tells a different tale. The homeowner does not know what the firm stands to gain because he/she does not know the firm's abatement cost. Whether the firm knows the value of environmental damage to the homeowner is irrelevant since the model focuses on a Stackelberg equilibrium that allows the homeowner to move first, resolving any uncertainty that could face the firm. In either case, the informational asymmetry is effectively one-sided – one player knows more about his opponent than the other. A third alternative discussed in Hurley and Shogren (1998a) is that both agents are uncertain about their opponents' values such that the informational asymmetry is two-sided. We now review the effect of asymmetric information on conflict behaviour assuming there is no reimbursement of effort ($\beta_f = \beta_h = 0$). While we do not address the subsidization of effort directly, with the logit contest success function the subsidization of effort is readily transformed into the ability parameters.

A convenient closed-form solution for the Nash contest with a two-sided information asymmetry does not exist. Therefore, Hurley and Shogren (1998b) use numerical methods to explore equilibrium behaviour. With one-sided asymmetric information where player i knows player j's value [$\Pr(v_j = V_j) = 1.0$], but player j does not know player i's value. The equilibrium efforts for the Nash contest are:

$$x_j^N = V_j \theta^N \quad \text{and} \quad x_i^N = V_i \left(\rho_j \sqrt{\theta^N} - \rho_j^2 \theta^N \right)$$

where:

$$\rho_j \equiv \sqrt{\frac{A_j V_j}{A_i V_i}} \quad \text{and} \quad \theta^N = \left(\frac{E_i(\rho_j)}{1 + E_i(\rho_j)^2 + \text{Var}_i(\rho_j)} \right)^2$$

are the player j's relative resolve and willingness to waste (ibid.) and $E_i(\cdot)$ and $\text{Var}_i(\cdot)$ are the expectation and variance operators defined over the distribution $F_i(v_i)$. Relative resolve is a measure of a player's ability and desire relative to an opponent's ability and desire. A player's willingness to waste is the proportion of the value of the reward a player expends in an attempt to capture the reward.

The effect of asymmetric information on effort and rent dissipation in the Nash contest depends on the mean and variance of the uninformed player's (j) relative resolve. If both players have equal ability and player i's value equalled player j's *ex post*, then player i expends more effort and will have a greater probability of victory than player j – player i is able to take advantage of the information asymmetry. With equal values and abilities *ex post*, rent dissipation will never exceed the value of the reward. If player j's expected relative resolve is 1.0, which indicates equal strength and desire on average, then rent dissipation is lower than Tullock. Also, the more uncertain j is about i's value the lower his/her effort and rent dissipation. Player i's effort may increase or decrease depending on whether s/he is an underdog or favourite.

With two-sided asymmetric information, the perfect Bayesian equilibrium in the Stackelberg contest is $x_j^{Sj} = V_j \theta^{Sj}$ and $x_i^{Sj} = V_i(\rho_j \sqrt{\theta^{Sj}} - \rho_j^2 \theta^{Sj})$ where j chooses effort first and $\theta^{Sj} = (E_i(\rho_j)/2)^2$ is j's willingness to waste. With one-sided asymmetric information, the solution does not change when j does not know i's value. When j does know i's value, the only difference is that j's willingness to waste is known for certain, $\theta^{Sj} = (\rho_j/2)^2$. Therefore, in the Stackelberg contest, the strategic commitment of effort eliminates the influence of risk on behaviour.

In Tullock's model, the Stackelberg and Nash contest results were identical. With asymmetric reimbursement, efforts and rent dissipation in the Stackelberg contest is lower than Nash, but only if the level of reimbursement exceeds a half ($\beta > 0.5$) and the player who does not get reimbursed exerts effort first. With one-sided asymmetric information, the Stackelberg contest leads to the same result as the Nash contest only by coincidence. If players have equal ability and values *ex post* and the expected relative resolve of the uninformed player is 1.0, then rent dissipation in the asymmetric information Stackelberg contest is equal to Tullock (1980).

When only one player is reimbursed for his/her effort, that player gains a strategic advantage over the opponent. Similarly, if a player knows more about his/her opponent than the opponent knows about them, that player gains a strategic advantage. Unlike with asymmetric reimbursement, this informational disadvantage can be reduced by strategically committing effort because it eliminates risk for the uninformed player. With asymmetric reimbursement, a strategic commitment of effort has no effect on the contest outcome or provides a greater advantage to the player whose effort is reimbursed.

Another important implication of introducing asymmetric information is that players may no longer agree on who should move first. Baik and Shogren (1992) show that underdogs prefer to lead, while favourites prefer to follow. Given the choice, players agree on when each should invest effort. With asymmetric information, the value of information can prevent players from agreeing who should move when. Thus, a more complicated game results and institutional mechanisms that characterize how the conflict is resolved become even more important.

The SLAPP

For a SLAPP to occur, a homeowner must forgo the opportunity to exercise its right to sue and assume the role of a plaintiff, which Heyes (1997) argues allows it to commit effort first. Instead, the homeowner complains, which the firm uses as standing in order to file a SLAPP, assume the role of the plaintiff, and commit effort first. In the context of Baik and Shogren (1992), the citizen's complaint and the SLAPP that follows can be interpreted as just a device that allows a favourite homeowner and an underdog firm to resolve more efficiently a conflict where both parties know what the other has to gain. A problem with this interpretation is that several states are currently considering legislation to ban SLAPPs due to citizen group pressure, which should not happen if the SLAPP provides the best course of action for both the homeowner and firm to resolve the conflict. Hurley and Shogren (1997) pursue this interpretation further with the addition of one-sided asymmetric information, such that the firm does not know the homeowner's value. With one-sided asymmetric information, some homeowners could benefit from banning SLAPPs and would support such legislation. The potential value of legislation banning SLAPPs in favour of these homeowners is one of the primary focuses of Hurley and Shogren (1997).

To understand the structure of the SLAPP model it is useful to consider the simplified one-shot game shown in Figure 11.1. The game involves two players in a contest, the homeowner and the firm. Nature determines whether the firm or the homeowner is the favourite, with each having a probability of one-half. Only the homeowner knows his/her type. After the move by nature, the homeowner moves, choosing either to sue or complain. If the homeowner sues, s/he then reveals his/her type by leading in a Stackelberg contest. If she complains, the firm uses this decision to update its beliefs about whether it is the favourite. It then chooses either to lead in a Stackelberg contest by investing a lot of effort (SLAPP-hard), to lead in a Stackelberg contest by investing a little effort (SLAPP-soft), or to move simultaneously in a Nash contest (lobby).

The one-shot game has two equilibria. The only equilibrium that survives Cho and Kreps' (1987) intuitive refinement is the separating equilibrium in which an underdog homeowner sues and a favourite homeowner complains, followed by the firm choosing SLAPP-soft. This separating equilibrium is

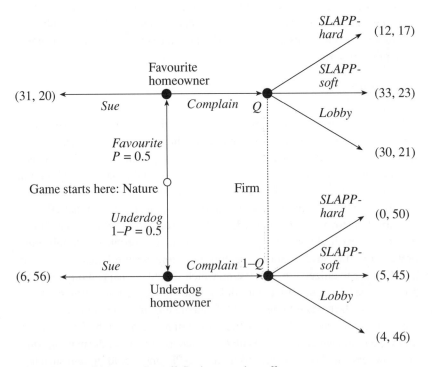

Note: Homeowner's expected payoff; firm's expected payoff.

Figure 11.1   The SLAPP game

efficient because it allows the underdog to move first, the favourite to follow, and both to expend less effort, thus wasting less of the reward in rent seeking. Banning the SLAPP in this game is equivalent to forcing the firm to choose lobby, which is inefficient because it does not allow the underdog firm to choose effort first. This leads to a higher level of rent seeking and more of the reward is wasted.

The formal SLAPP model allows for a continuous distribution of homeowner values and for players to explicitly choose their effort. If the homeowner starts the game by choosing sue, the firm and homeowner then play the Stackelberg contest where the homeowner leads. The solution to this contest is $x_h^{Sh} = V_h \theta^{Sh}$ and $x_f^{Sh} = V_f(\rho_h \sqrt{\theta^{Sh}} - \rho_h^2 \theta^{Sh})$ where $\theta^{Sh} = (\rho_h/2)^2$. If the homeowner chooses complain, the firm can choose to SLAPP or lobby. If it chooses SLAPP, the firm and homeowner play the Stackelberg contest where the firm leads resulting in $x_f^{Sf} = V_f \theta^{Sf}$ and $x_h^{Sf} = V_h(\rho_f \sqrt{\theta^{Sf}} - \rho_f^2 \theta^{Sf})$ where $\theta^{Sf} = (\mathrm{E}_i(\rho_f)/2)^2$. If it chooses lobby, the firm and homeowner play the Nash contest resulting in $x_f^N = V_f \theta^N$ and $x_h^N = V_h(\rho_f \sqrt{\theta^N} - \rho_f^2 \theta^N)$ where:

$$\theta^N = \left(\frac{\mathrm{E}_i(\rho_f)}{1 + \mathrm{E}_i(\rho_f)^2 + \mathrm{Var}_i(\rho_f)} \right)^2 .$$

As with the simplified game, two types of equilibria can arise: a pooling equilibrium and a partially separating equilibrium. In pooling equilibria, the homeowner always chooses sue regardless of how much he/she values the reward. In partially separating equilibria, the homeowner will either sue or complain depending on the value of their reward. If the homeowner chooses complain, the firm always chooses SLAPP.

Values of the reward that result in the homeowner choosing complain depend on the initial distribution nature uses to determine the homeowner's value, $G(v_h)$. By choosing complain, the homeowner may reveal valuable information to the firm. Therefore, after the firm updates its beliefs, $F_h(v_h)$ will in most cases differ from $G(v_h)$. In particular:

$$F_h(v_h) \equiv \begin{cases} 0, & \text{for } v_h < a_h \\ \dfrac{G(v_h) - G(a_h)}{G(b_h) - G(a_h)}, & \text{for } a_h \leq v_h \leq b_h \\ 1, & \text{for } b_h < v_h \end{cases}$$

where:

$$b_h = V_f \frac{A_f}{A_h}\left(1-\sqrt{1-2\sqrt{\theta^{Sf}}}\right)^2 \text{ and } a_h = V_f \frac{A_f}{A_h}\left(1+\sqrt{1-2\sqrt{\theta^{Sf}}}\right)^2.$$

The homeowner will choose complain when $b_h > V_h > a_h$.

Since the homeowner will not always choose to complain, choosing complain conveys important information to the firm that allows it to refine its beliefs about the homeowner's value. It is important to note that the homeowner may prefer the firm to lead in a Stackelberg contest, even if the homeowner knows he/she is an underdog. Alternatively, the homeowner may choose to lead in a Stackelberg contest when he/she is a favourite. These results are contrary to Baik and Shogren (1992).

Banning the SLAPP eliminates the firm's ability to lead in the Stackelberg contest. Therefore, if the homeowner refuse to take the lead by choosing complain, both the firm and homeowner must invest effort before knowing what their opponent did. Again, two types of equilibrium exist for the game. In pooling equilibria, the homeowner always chooses sue. In partially separating equilibria, whether the homeowner chooses sue or complain depends on the value of the reward. If the homeowner does choose complain, the firm updates its beliefs and a Nash contest ensues. The homeowner will choose complain when $b_h > V_h > a_h$ where:

$$b_h = V_f \frac{A_f}{A_h}\left(1-\sqrt{1-2\sqrt{\theta^N}}\right)^2, \quad a_h = V_f \frac{A_f}{A_h}\left(1+\sqrt{1-2\sqrt{\theta^N}}\right)^2 \quad \text{and}$$

$$F_h(v_h) \equiv \begin{cases} 0, & \text{for } v_h < a_h \\ \dfrac{G(v_h)-G(a_h)}{G(b_h)-G(a_h)}, & \text{for } a_h \leq v_h \leq b_h. \\ 1, & \text{for } b_h < v_h \end{cases}$$

If the firm knew the homeowner's value, the homeowner would always choose to lead in a Stackelberg contest as opposed to playing a Nash contest, which is not the case when information is incomplete. Information is valuable and by choosing to lead the homeowner gives up information. In some cases, the cost of giving up this information is not worth the benefit.

The results of a SLAPP ban are ambiguous due to two competing effects, the information and the timing effects. The information effect measures the difference between the homeowner's payoff under complete information and under incomplete information. How much does a change in information change the payoff to the homeowner? The timing effect measures how switching from sue to complain affects the homeowner's payoff. How much does a change in strategy change the payoff to the homeowner? These two effects work against each other and the question of which one dominates the other needs to be answered to determine whether a SLAPP ban will increase or decrease the efficiency of the equilibrium.

Since the effect of a SLAPP ban cannot be determined in general, Hurley and Shogren (1997) run simulations with a wide range of parameters to determine which parameter values lead to an increase or a decrease in the efficiency of the equilibrium after a SLAPP ban. Contest efficiency was used to measure efficiency. For some parameter values, the homeowner always chooses sue. In this region, a SLAPP ban has no effect on the efficiency of the equilibrium. All homeowners will sue regardless of whether or not the SLAPP is an option in the game. Over the rest of the range of parameters, the separating equilibrium is employed, where some homeowners sue and others complain. When this separating equilibrium is played, banning the SLAPP decreases the efficiency of the equilibrium.

If both the homeowner and the firm know each other's values, then the underdog will choose to lead in the contest and the favourite will be happy to follow. In this context banning the SLAPP will unambiguously reduce the efficiency of the conflict because it will take away the firm's ability to lead as an underdog. When the firm does not know the homeowner's value, an underdog homeowner may be unwilling to give up his/her information advantage by choosing to lead and revealing effort. But, by choosing not to sue, the underdog homeowner exploits this information advantage and introduces inefficiency into the contest. Banning the SLAPP does not force an underdog homeowner to reveal his/her value; therefore, it does not address the source of inefficiency in the conflict and is unlikely to improve it accept by coincidence.

REPUTATION-BUILDING IN ENVIRONMENTAL CONFLICTS

Firms use the SLAPP against citizens who complain about lax compliance with environmental rules and regulations. Many state lawmakers have reacted negatively to the SLAPP, proposing to ban its use in public debate since it removes a citizen's constitutional right to petition. And we have just seen that in one class of environmental conflict models suggest a SLAPP ban might be inefficient because it eliminates the efficient signalling equilibrium.

The original SLAPP conflict model was a one-shot contest with no exit strategy – the conflict is always played out, effort is always expended, and the game is played only once. These conflicts are efficient when a perfect Bayesian equilibrium exists in which the weaker player leads with his/her observable and irreversible effort, and the stronger player follows with his/hers (Baik and Shogren 1992). A SLAPP ban reduces efficiency because it prevents *all firms* from leading, including the weak ones which do move first to reduce the costs of rent dissipation, as society wants from an efficiency standpoint.

We now test the robustness of this result by extending the SLAPP conflict model to a repeated setting. We add reputation-building and an exit strategy, *back off*. Now firms use the SLAPP to build a reputation that *chills* homeowners into *backing off*, a potentially high opportunity cost outcome that makes a SLAPP ban look more attractive. A firm builds a reputation by choosing a suboptimal, off-the-equilibrium SLAPP strategy for several periods to induce some homeowner to exit the conflict. The firm can choose to take a short-run loss for its own long-run gain. From society's viewpoint, however, using the SLAPP to chill homeowners can be inefficient. The case for a SLAPP ban now makes more sense. The ban prevents the firm from *chilling* favourite homeowners, so they stay in the conflict, which can result in an efficient outcome: the weaker firm leads with its effort, and the stronger homeowners follow with theirs. But our results suggest that the inefficiency result remains relatively robust: a SLAPP ban only increases efficiency when firms do not use the SLAPP to build a reputation, which contradicts the spirit of why firms use it in the first place.

Figure 11.2 presents the extended SLAPP example, in which a homeowner and a firm are engaged in an environmental conflict. Without loss of generality, we use the example to construct the most favourable case for an efficiency-enhancing SLAPP ban. We extend the SLAPP conflict to a repeated game, in which (a) the firm can build a reputation to chill homeowners, and (b) the homeowners have an exit strategy, *back off* (the branches outside the dashed lines), to capture. Familiarity with the original example helps but is unnecessary as we explain the details below.

Consider the details of the game. A homeowner and firm can invest observable and irreversible effort to win an environmental conflict. Nature moves first and selects the homeowner's type: a contest underdog or favourite. An underdog is a player with a chance less than 50 per cent of victory at the Nash equilibrium; a favourite is the opposite (Dixit 1987). The homeowner knows his/her type, the firm does not: it has prior beliefs, P and $(1 - P) = 50$ per cent, that the homeowner is a favourite or underdog.[1]

After nature moves, the homeowner chooses between three actions: *sue*, *complain* and *backing off*. If the homeowner sues, s/he expends effort first and reveals his/her type, that is, s/he is the Stackelberg leader. If s/he complains, s/he

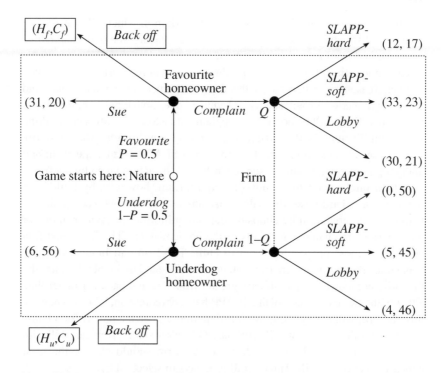

Note: Homeowner's expected payoff; firm's expected payoff.

Figure 11.2 Extended SLAPP game

signals his/her intent to fight but not his/her type. Given its updated beliefs, Q and $(1 - Q)$, about the homeowner's type, the firm responds to a complaint either with a *SLAPP-hard* – a high effort level; a *SLAPP-soft* – a low effort level; or *lobby*. Either a SLAPP-hard or SLAPP-soft response makes the firm the Stackelberg leader. Lobby implies the two parties play a simultaneous-move Nash game. If the homeowner backs off, the conflict ends without a fight. Figure 11.2 shows the numerical expected payoffs from these alternative actions; note we leave open-ended the payoffs from backing off (H_f, C_f) or (H_u, C_u).[2]

Recall that the basic one-shot SLAPP game (without backing off) has two perfect Bayesian equilibria, one of which survives the Cho and Kreps' (1987) intuitive refinement: the separating equilibrium in which an underdog homeowner sues, a favourite homeowner complains, and the firm responds with a SLAPP-soft. The separating equilibrium is efficient because it allows the underdog to move first and the favourite to follow, so both have incentive to invest less effort than any other strategy; that is, expected joint payoffs are maximized. Banning the SLAPP reduces efficiency by replacing the separating equilibrium with an inefficient pooling equilibrium in which all homeowner types sue. Efficiency drops because the weaker players, the underdog firms, are prevented from investing effort first.

The same efficient separating equilibrium exists at the start of our repeated conflict. Reasonable beliefs dictate that favourite homeowners will complain and underdog homeowners will sue with Q equal to one. Both types of homeowners believe that firms will respond to a complain with a SLAPP-soft. The resulting initial equilibrium is the efficient separating equilibrium: the favourite homeowner always complains followed by a SLAPP-soft by the firm; and underdog homeowners always sue regardless of the action taken by the firm.

A firm might want to change this equilibrium, however, by building a reputation as a hard nose who will punish any homeowner who complains. A firm builds a reputation by choosing out-of-equilibrium behaviour in one or more periods to change the beliefs of the homeowners.[3] The firm must first choose the most profitable action to chill. The firm can induce identical behaviour from homeowners from either a SLAPP-hard or a lobby because the favourite homeowner's payoffs are greater from sue and back off rather than either of the two chills: (complain, SLAPP-hard) or (complain, lobby). Knowing this, the firm will always chill by choosing lobby, since the payoff for a lobby (21) exceeds the payoff for a SLAPP-hard (17). Now since a firm can chill with either a lobby or a SLAPP-hard, a rational firm should choose the least expensive action to chill. Thus a chill is always to select lobby.

Three assumptions must hold for a firm to chill. First, *only* the firm knows there are n periods to the game. The assumption is based on only the firm having information about how long it will stay in business and be willing to fight citizens with SLAPPs. This assumption gives the firm and the homeowners different beliefs about when the game will end. Beliefs must differ so that backward induction does not ruin the threat of constant chills (Samuelson 1987).[4] Using these conditions, appealing to the Folk theorem allows these beliefs to be rational (Fudenberg and Tirole 1992). Since homeowners and firms have different beliefs about when the game will end, backward induction will not unravel perceptions that the firm will forgo profits in any one period to increase its profits in future periods. This is a necessary condition for a firm to chill.

Second, each risk-neutral, profit-maximizing firm faces each homeowner once, and each homeowner sees all past actions taken by the firm in conflicts with citizens. Finally, the homeowners must be Bayesians such that after k-consecutive chills of complaints, they update their beliefs to include chill as the expected response to a *complain*. And since the homeowner does not know the final period for the firm, s/he does not know when the last chill will appear, and thus the threat of a chill is never destroyed. This information is common to all players. The firm must also believe that future homeowners will observe a chill and update their beliefs accordingly. These assumptions make a chill a credible threat.

Does it pay to build a reputation? *No*, not if the firm plays against an underdog homeowner; but *maybe*, if the firm faces a favourite. The chill has no effect on the underdog's behaviour because s/he either leads or gets out of the way. The underdog homeowner's payoffs are the greatest when s/he moves first, and either sues or backs off, depending on which action pays more. She sues when $6 > H_u > 5 > 4 > 0$; otherwise she backs off $H_u > 6 > 5 > 4 > 0$.

A favourite homeowner's reaction to a chill is less clear-cut. If the favourite's payoff from back off exceeds the next best alternative, the separating equilibrium ($H_f \geq 33$), the favourite homeowner always backs off. Again the chill has no effect because the homeowner voluntarily exits the contest.

But if the favourite's payoff from back off is less than the separating equilibrium ($33 > H_f$), a chill does affect the favourite's behaviour. The question is whether the firm finds the chill strategy to be profitable. If the favourite's payoff from sue exceeds back off ($31 > H_f$), a chill is unprofitable to the firm. The firm chills and gets sued for its trouble, and thus earns less than if it had just played the separating equilibrium ($20 < 23$).

Potentially profitable chilling only exists when the favourite's payoffs from backing off fall between sue and complain, $31 < H_f < 33$. Now a firm that chills can induce the favourite to back off rather than sue. A firm that chills loses 2 units ($21 - 23 = -2$), and forces the homeowner who complains to lose 3 ($30 - 33 = -3$). Now complain looks bad. And with repeated chills, the favourite will eventually update his/her beliefs to believe a chill will come with every complaint. Since back off pays more than sue ($31 < H_f$), s/he exits the contest. Therefore, the firm's decision rule is: *Chill* if and only if (a) $31 < H_f < 33$, and (b) $C_f \geq + [(\gamma/\beta)*(23 - 21)]$; otherwise, do not *chill*.

A firm should chill if and only if the favourite has an incentive to complain but not to sue when chilled ($31 < H_f < 33$), and its marginal gains from a chill (C_f) exceed the lost profits from not playing the separating equilibrium (23) plus the reimbursement-weighted per unit cost of the chill [$(\gamma/\beta)*(23 - 21)$]. The reimbursement ratio (γ/β) represents how much of a chill the firm must make back in each reimbursement period. The number of periods it takes before the chill pays back depends on how the game is played. The firm may face all underdogs and never get the reward; or the firm may face all favourites and get the reward quickly, or some combination.

To illustrate, consider an example. Assume the game has two periods and that seeing one chill will force all favourite homeowners to update their beliefs, that is, $n = 2$, and $k = 1$, and $(\gamma/\beta) = (2/1)$.[5] This means that for every two chills, the firm gets one reimbursement period. Homeowners expect the firm to follow all complaints with a chill, and back off in the future. Four scenarios can unfold in this example. The firm confronts either:

1. two underdogs – one in each round;
2. an underdog homeowner in period 1 and a favourite in period 2;
3. a favourite homeowner in period 1 and an underdog in period 2; or
4. two favourites – one in each round.

In scenario (1), the firm never gets an opportunity to chill because s/he never faces a complain, underdog homeowners never take this action. In scenario (2), the firm does not chill the favourite homeowner in period 2 because the firm knows that this is the last period and a chill is simply forgone profits. In scenario (3), the firm chills, which forces homeowners to update their beliefs, but the firm never faces a second favourite homeowner to reap the rewards from the first chill. In scenario (4), the firm chills, and faces a second favourite homeowner who has already updated his/her beliefs and thus backs off.

For the firm to chill, it must make up all forgone profit from all potential chills. The firm will not chill in scenarios (1) and (2), but it will in (3) and (4). The firm chills in two of four scenarios but only reaps the reward in scenario (4). Since each of the four outcomes is equally likely, the firm must at least gain a profit of 4 under scenario (4) to make up for the lost profit of –4 (= –2 + –2) under scenarios (3) and (4). Therefore, due to the reimbursement ratio $(\gamma/\beta) = (2/1)$, they must reap twice as large a benefit from getting the homeowner to back off, since they have to chill in two different scenarios and reap only one reward (one back off). Since the firm can get a profit of 23 from SLAPP-soft, it must get a profit of 23 plus the forgone profit from chilling in scenarios (3) and (4) which equals a total of 27. A chill only occurs in this case if $C_f >$ $27 = 23 + (2/1)(23 - 21)$. If, for example, the game was of three rounds with only one chill needed to change beliefs ($n = 3$ and $k = 1$), then $(\gamma/\beta) = (6/5)$.[6]

We can now summarize two useful results. First, a firm never gains by chilling the underdog homeowner because s/he has no incentive to complain. A firm can profit from chilling a favourite homeowner if and only if the favourite's first intention is to complain but not to sue when chilled ($31 < H_f <$ 33), and its marginal gains from a chill exceed the lost profits from not playing the separating equilibrium plus the reimbursement-weighted per unit costs of the chill ($C_f \geq + [(\gamma/\beta)*(23 - 21)]$). Chilling occurs when the firm builds a reputation and increases the odds that the homeowner chooses actions that are less costly to the firm.[7]

Second, the reimbursement ratio (γ/β) depends on how many rounds are played in the game (n), and how many chills a firm must employ to induce a homeowner to back off (k). The reimbursement ratio increases when it takes fewer chills to change favourite homeowner behaviour and when there are more periods to collect the benefits of the chill (that is, less k, more n). Holding k constant, more rounds, n, leads to more periods in which a successful chill leads to the reward – a back off by the homeowner. And for low values of k, chills will become successful faster and will lead to the reward in more periods.

Having established the case for a profitable SLAPP, we now consider whether a SLAPP ban is still inefficient. A SLAPP ban prohibits the SLAPP-hard and SLAPP-soft actions in the separating equilibrium.[8] To determine the efficiency impacts, we compare expected payoffs in equilibrium with and without the SLAPP.

First consider the efficiency of the equilibrium behaviour for the underdog and favourite homeowner. A SLAPP ban has no effect on the underdog behaviour because they already ignore chills. Underdog homeowners never complain, as such they never evoke a SLAPP from the firm, and efficiency is identical with or without the SLAPP.

A SLAPP ban affects the favourite homeowner based on his/her relative payoffs. If the payoff from back off exceeds that in the separating equilibrium ($H_f \geq 33$), s/he always backs off, and a SLAPP ban has no effect. If back off is less than 33, two additional cases must be considered. If the favourite's payoff from sue exceeds back off ($31 > H_f$), a SLAPP ban reduces efficiency. This is because s/he chooses sue over backing off. The firm, realizing the homeowner will never back off, never chills. Restricting the SLAPP in this case would change the equilibrium from (complain, SLAPP-soft) to sue, which has smaller joint payoffs, that is, is less efficient.

But if the favourite's first intention is to complain but not to sue when chilled, $31 < H_f < 33$, s/he would complain until noticing k chills, and would then back off. If the firm profits from its reputation-building, the equilibrium outcome is for the homeowner to back off. If the SLAPP is banned, the equilibrium behaviour will still be for the homeowner to back off (since $H_f > 31$). Restricting the SLAPP does nothing to change the equilibrium and, therefore, does nothing to change efficiency.

But if it does not pay for the firm to build a reputation, the impact on efficiency is ambiguous. The change in efficiency is measured as the difference between the sum of expected payoffs in the SLAPP equilibrium (complain, SLAPP-soft), which is 59 [$= 0.5(6 + 56) + 0.5(33 + 23)$], and the expected payoffs from the SLAPP-ban equilibrium (back off), which is $\psi = 0.5(6 + 56) + 0.5(H_f + C_f)$. If $H_f + C_f > 56$, a SLAPP ban increases the efficiency of the equilibrium, $\psi - 59 > 0$; otherwise, the ban decreases efficiency, $\psi - 59 < 0$.

Banning SLAPPS to prevent undue exit from the conflict can increase efficiency. But this only holds when the favourite is like the Cowardly Lion in *The Wizard of Oz*: s/he wants to complain, but if chilled backs off ($31 < H_f < 33$). For all other payoff ranges, efficiency of the equilibrium decreases or remains the same with a ban. We can now summarize the equilibrium result: the only case in which a SLAPP ban increases the efficiency of the equilibrium in the repeated game is if and only if three actions hold:

1. the favourite homeowner's first intention is to complain, but
2. if chilled will back off $(31 < H_f < 33)$,
3. when the firm does not find it profitable to build a reputation by chilling the homeowner.

This result says that a SLAPP ban only improves efficiency when a firm chooses not to use the SLAPP to build a reputation, which contradicts the spirit of why it uses the SLAPP.

But a SLAPP ban might make economic sense if we focus our attention on the interim period between the start of the game and the ultimate equilibrium. A firm who chills k times to build a reputation both suffers and inflicts losses that reduce efficiency in the time it is building a reputation by chilling. These losses accumulate over the k chills until the homeowner finally updates his/her beliefs and decides to back off – the eventual equilibrium for favourite homeowners within the relevant reward range. In contrast, a SLAPP ban moves the game to this back-off equilibrium immediately. No interim losses are realized because no chills take place. Therefore a SLAPP ban eliminates the losses incurred during the chill period. Whether these interim losses justify a SLAPP ban depends on the magnitude of the losses per chill, the number of chills (k), and the frequency with which the favourite homeowner is within and outside the relevant reward range. Large loss per chill, many chills and a large fraction of homeowners within the reward range makes it more likely that a SLAPP ban would make economic sense. Otherwise, the case for the ban based on interim losses is weaker.

We now go over this secondary result. If a favourite homeowner's first intention is to complain but if chilled will back off $(31 < H_f < 33)$, a SLAPP ban can eliminate interim efficiency losses that occur when the firm chills the homeowners (that is, those between the start of the game and the equilibrium), and push players to the new equilibrium faster relative to the SLAPP game. If this is not a favourite homeowner's first intention, a SLAPP ban has no impact on interim efficiency losses since the equilibrium is the same because reputation has no effect.

CONCLUDING REMARK

Citizen suits have a role in the enforcement of environmental policy. These suits give voice to ordinary citizens who might otherwise be left out of contributing to public policy restricted by the 'mind-forged manacles' of administrative failure in the very agencies created to protect them. A question of interest to economists is whether the legal rules and institutional structures that define citizen suits increase or decrease the likely efficiency of the environmental conflicts. For the class of models we explore here, we see that the eventful impacts of an environmental conflict occur when some asymmetry exists, either in ability, valuation, reimbursement or information. Asymmetric reimbursement rules can decrease efficiency if they induce players to fight harder than they otherwise would, and that with asymmetric information banning the SLAPP does not increase efficiency and may actually decrease efficiency of the conflict by eliminating the most efficient outcome. The open question that deserves attention now is whether these theoretical distinctions matter from an empirical standpoint. The literature has yet to produce a measure of the efficiency losses that might exist. Producing such an estimate would help us understand better how cost-effective citizen suits have been in protecting our natural environment.

NOTES

1. One-sided asymmetric information has been shown to be sufficient in capturing the behavioural underpinnings of contest behaviour under uncertainty (Hurley and Shogren 1998a).
2. See Hurley and Shogren (1997) for how these expected payoffs were calculated.
3. A rational player believes that (a) underdog homeowners will *sue* if $H_u \leq 6$ and will *back off* if $H_u > 6$; (b) firms will respond to a *complaint* with *SLAPP-soft*; and (c) favourite homeowners will choose *complain*. If these beliefs hold over the entire game, no reputations are built and no homeowners will choose away from these strategy sets. But if the firm chooses to build a reputation, play out-of-equilibrium behaviour in one round, the homeowner may change his/her beliefs and start expecting the firm to chill all complaints.
4. Samuelson (1987) shows that when at least one party in a two-party contest is uncertain about the length of the contest, backward induction does not destroy the threat of punishment.
5. Note that, in general, $(\gamma/\beta) \neq (n/k)$. Rather the reimbursement ratio should be read as the number of rounds it takes to reap the rewards of a chill over the number of chills it takes to change beliefs.
6. Consider ordinal payoffs to see the generality of the result. Let the payoff to the firm for a *complain, SLAPP-soft* now be e rather than 23; and for a *complain, lobby* to be f rather than 21. The threshold value is the difference between the ordinal payoffs. The firm still must make back 6/5 of a chill for each reimbursement, however each chill now costs the firm $e - f$. Now each reimbursement must equal at least a payment of $((e - f) * 6) / 5$. The firm chills as long as $C_f \geq + ((e - f) * (6/5))$. This last example shows that when the number of chills necessary for a belief update stays constant (k), and n increases, the critical value at which the firm will chill (C_f) decreases. Conversely, if n stays constant and k increases, the critical value of C_f will increase.
7. To illustrate the generality of this result, we briefly consider ordinal payoffs. Assign each payoff a letter representing the payoff instead of a specific number. The payoff a favourite homeowner receives from: (a) *backing off* is still equal to H_f; (2) *suing* is now a instead of 31; (3) *complaining* followed by the firm choosing to *SLAPP-hard* is b instead of 12; (4) *complaining* followed by the firm choosing to *SLAPP-soft* is c instead of 33; (5) *complaining* followed by the firm choosing to *lobby* is d instead of 30. Each payoff holds the same ordinal ranking as before, $c > a > d > b$. With these ordinal payoffs, we can rewrite the cardinal results as follows: the relevant range of payoffs from *backing off* is the range $a < H_f < c$. The result from the cardinal analysis still holds: a firm builds a reputation when the payoff from *backing off* falls between the payoff between *suing* and *SLAPP-soft*.

8. We are banning only the SLAPP actions, but by doing so we only leave *lobby* as a possible outcome from a *complain*. Now the homeowner will either act in the same manner as before the SLAPP ban, back off (if they always do), or sue; or will back off. When they always back off or always sue regardless of chills and the SLAPP, they will still back off. There is no change in equilibrium. When they would complain and expect a SLAPP-soft in response, the firm has an incentive to chill and induce a back off. In the case of a chill, banning the SLAPP can move the game to the new outcome faster. It bans the potentially good outcome for the homeowner (complain, SLAPP-soft).

REFERENCES

Baik, K.H. and J.F. Shogren (1992), 'Strategic behavior in contests: comment', *American Economic Review* 82: 359–62.

Baik, K.H. and J.F. Shogren (1994), 'Environmental conflicts with reimbursement for citizen suits', *Journal of Environmental Economics and Management* 27: 1–20.

Billings, L.G. (1990), 'Grading the Clean Air Act: Bush–Senate compromise weakens law', *San Diego Union-Tribune*, 11 March, Opinion, Ed. 1, 2: C-1.

Brown, M. (1992), 'Appeals panel says coal suits can't be filed in Washington', *Courier-Journal* (Louisville, KY), 23 May, Late Kentucky Edition, News: 9A.

Carney, L.H. (1985), 'The environment', *New York Times*, 25 August, Late City Final Edition, section 11JN: 22, col. 1.

Cho, I.K. and D.M. Kreps (1987), 'Signaling games and stable equilibria', *Quarterly Journal of Economics* 102: 179–221.

Clauson, H. L. (1997), 'How far should the bar on citizen suits extend under section 309 of the Clean Water Act? (1996 Ninth Circuit Environmental Review)', *Environmental Law* 27(3): 967–90.

'Court limits citizen suits based on 2 pollution laws' (1981), *New York Times*, 26 June, Late City Final Edition, section B: 3, col. 5.

Dickinson, D. (1997), 'Is "diligent prosecution of an action in a court" required to preempt citizen suits under the major federal environmental statutes?', *William and Mary Law Review* 38(4): 1545–82.

Dixit, A. (1987), 'Strategic behavior in contests', *American Economic Review* 77: 891–8.

Echeverria, J. and J. Zeidler (1999), *Barely Standing: The Erosion of Citizen 'Standing' to Sue and Enforce Environmental Law*, Georgetown Environmental Policy Project, http://www.envpoly.org/papers/barely.htm.

Epstein, R. (1998), *Principles for a Free Society: Reconciling Individual Liberty with the Common Good*, Reading, MA: Perseus Books.

Flora, C.E. (1997), 'An inapt fiction: the use of the *ex parte* Young doctrine for environmental citizen suits against states after Seminole Tribe' (1996 Ninth Circuit Environmental Review), *Environmental Law* 27(3): 935–65.

Foster, A. (1998), 'Lawsuits force EPA to enforce the Clean Water Act; more than 30 lawsuits have been filed in 35 different states; Missouri facing impending suit over the polluted Mississippi River', *Chemical Week* 160(38): 74.

Fudenberg, D. and J. Tirole (1992), *Game Theory*, Cambridge, MA: MIT Press.

Fuetsch, M. (1993), '3 cities sued for cleanup of polluted runoff; environment: El Segundo, Hermosa Beach and Beverly Hills are accused of failing to enforce federal storm drain requirements', *Los Angeles Times*, 5 December, Home Edition, Westside, Part J: 5, col. 1.

Glaberson, W. (1999), '"Citizen suits" losing power as weapon against polluters', *Plain Dealer*, 6 June, section National: 18A.

Grant, D.S. II (1997), 'Allowing citizen participation in environmental regulation: an empirical analysis of the effects of right-to-sue and right-to-know provisions of industry's toxic emissions', *Social Science Quarterly* 78(4): 859–73.

Greenhouse, L. (1996), 'Justices weigh suits over going too far to protect environment', *New York Times*, 14 November, Late Edition-Final, section A: 19, col. 1.

Hamburger, T. (1992), 'Court limits citizen suits challenging policies on environment', *Star Tribune* (Minneapolis, MN), 13 June, Metro Edition, News: 1A.

Harsanyi, J. (1967–8), 'Games with incomplete information played by Bayesian players', *Management Science* 14: 159–82, 320–34, 486–502.

Heyes, A.G. (1997), 'Environmental regulation by private contest', *Journal of Public Economics* 63: 407–28.

Heyes, A.G. (1998), 'Making things stick: enforcement and compliance', *Oxford Review of Economic Policy* 14(4): 50(1).

Hurley, T.M. (1998), 'Rent dissipation and efficiency in a contest with asymmetric valuations', *Public Choice* 94: 289–98.

Hurley, T.M. and J.F. Shogren (1997), 'Environmental conflicts and the SLAPP', *Journal of Environmental Economics and Management* 33: 253–73.

Hurley, T.M. and J.F. Shogren (1998a), 'Effort levels in a Cournot Nash contest with asymmetric information', *Journal of Public Economics* 69: 195–210.

Hurley, T.M. and J.F. Shogren (1998b), 'Asymmetric information contests', *European Journal of Political Economy* 14: 645–65.

Jenkins, S. (1997), 'Being heard above the storm: small cities voice concern over Phase II regs', *American City and County* 112(8): 36(6).

Johnston, C.N. (1999), '1998 – the year in review', *Environmental Law* 29(1): 69.

Leonard, A.R. (1998), 'When should an administrative enforcement action preclude a citizen suit under the Clean Water Act?', *Natural Resources Journal* 35: 555–624.

Meier, B. (1987), '"Citizen suits" become a popular weapon in the fight against industrial polluters', *Wall Street Journal* 17 April, section 1: 17, col. 4.

Miller, J.G (1987), *Citizen Suits: Private Enforcement of Federal Pollution Control Laws*, New York: Wiley Law Publications.

Naysnerski, W. and T. Tietenberg (1992), 'Private enforcement of federal environmental law', *Land Economics* 68: 28–48.

Nitzan, S. (1994), 'Modelling rent-seeking contests', *European Journal of Political Economy* 10(1): 41–60.

Pendley, W.P. (1994), 'Strangled by citizen suits: environmental laws put power in which it doesn't belong', *Denver Rocky Mountain News* 24 April, Ed. F: 86A.

Pring, G.W. and P. Canan (1995), *SLAPPs: Getting Sued for Speaking Out*, Philadelphia, PA: Temple University Press.

Reynolds, J. (1996), 'Court ruling could affect environmental laws', *American City and County* 1(8): 65(1).

Rosenthal, E. (2000), 'China pollution victims starting to fight back', *New York Times* 16 May.

Ruggles, R. (1988), 'Asarco to pay lower fees after appeal', *Omaha World-Herald*, 11 March, Metro edition, News: 18.

Samuelson, L. (1987), 'A note on uncertainty and cooperation in finitely repeated prisoner's dilemma', *International Journal of Game Theory* 16: 187–95.

Savage, D.G. (1997), 'Supreme Court lets species act foes file suit', *Los Angeles Times* 20 March, Home Edition, Part A: 1.

Sax, J.L. (1990), *Defending the Environment: A Strategy for Citizen Action*, New York: Alfred A. Knopf.

Shogren, J., K.-H. Baik and T. Crocker (1992), 'Environmental conflicts and strategic commitment', in R. Pethig (ed.), *Conflicts and Cooperation in Managing Environmental Resources*, Berlin: Springer-Verlag, pp. 85–107.

Taylor, S. Jr (1987), 'Supreme court roundup; citizens' suits in pollution cases are limited', *New York Times*, 2 December, section A: 24, col. 4.

Tennessee Valley Authority (TVA) (1977), 'Failures and opportunities', *Washington Post*, 22 July, Final edition, first section, Editorial: A26.

Terry, S. (1980), 'Citizen suits against polluters increase – but can guilty pay?', *Christian Science Monitor*, 26 December, Midwestern edition: 11.

Tullock, Gordon (1980), 'Efficient rent seeking', in James M. Buchanan, Robert D. Tollison and Gordon Tullock (eds), *Toward a Theory of the Rent-seeking Society*, College Station, TX: Texas A&M University Press, pp. 97–112.

Yost, N. (1983), 'Don't further weaken citizens' lawsuits', *New York Times*, 12 November, Late City Final Edition, section 1: 23, col. 1, Editorial Desk.

Young, L.R. (1987), 'Environmentalists lose clean water suit', *Journal of Commerce* 2 December, Chem: 9B.

12. Law versus regulation: a political economy model of instrument choice in environmental policy

Marcel Boyer and Donatella Porrini[*]

INTRODUCTION

From a law and economics point of view, the regulation of environmentally risky activities is an alternative to a system of liability assignment. 'Regulation and tort law are alternative methods (though often used in combination) for preventing accidents. The former requires a potential injurer to take measures to prevent the accident from occurring. The latter seeks to deter the accident by making the potential injurer liable for the costs of accident should it occur' (Landes and Posner 1984: 417). In this chapter we shall review and characterize, in an incomplete information political economy framework, the conditions under which an environmental regulation approach is superior to an environmental liability one.

We develop here a formal analysis of the comparison between different policy instruments to implement a given set of environmental protection objectives,[1] including a political economy explanation of the choice of instruments.[2] The first instrument we consider is the assignment of a CERCLA type liability,[3] that is, a strict, retroactive, joint and several liability on the owners and operators of the firm responsible for a catastrophic environmental disaster. More precisely, we model an extended lender liability rule whereby private banks financing the responsible firm are considered as liable operators if the latter is unable to cover the damages and compensation from its own assets. The second instrument in our comparison consists in a regulation framework. After the environmental legislation of the 1970s in the United States, the federal government played an extensive role in regulating air pollution, water pollution, hazardous and solid waste disposal, as well as pesticide use, among other environmental risks. More precisely we consider here an incentive regulation system based on a menu of contracts and subject to capture by the regulated firms.

Boyer and Laffont (1999) argue that two types of meaningful comparisons of instruments are possible. In the first type, exogenous constraints on instruments are considered and then various constrained instruments can be compared. In the second type, instruments, equivalent in the complete contracting framework, can be meaningfully compared given some imperfections in the economy outside the control of the social or constitutional planner.[4] The origin of this imperfect control of the social planner must be carefully justified. Otherwise, the results could be simply a direct and uninteresting consequence of artificial constraints on the social planner.

The Extended Lender Liability Option

The common law tort system, administered by the courts and governed principally by state law in the United States, provides a mechanism for creating incentives for care and for compensating victims, property losses and health injuries by a strict liability system.[5] Alongside the tort system, there exists a system of private and public insurance both for the liability of firms and for the consequences on individuals. In the 1980s, the United States Congress enacted CERCLA and created a Superfund for the quick and effective clean-up of dangerous waste sites.[6] It gave the Environmental Protection Agency (EPA) the power to bring damage actions to recover clean-up costs against the owners and operators of the facility directly responsible for releases.

We wish to concentrate here on an important aspect of a liability system that makes all owners and operators retroactively, strictly, jointly and severally liable, namely the extension of liability to the lenders. In spite of a secured interest exemption clause protecting financial institutions holding indicia of ownership on the firm's assets,[7] the United States courts have repeatedly considered secured lenders as owners or operators under CERCLA, in so far as their involvement in the operations of the firm exceeded the level warranted to secure their interest.[8]

A lenders' liability system was defined by the courts' decisions, for instance in the following landmark cases involving the bankruptcy of the primary responsible firm: *USA* v. *Mirabile*,[9] *USA* v. *Maryland Bank and Trust*,[10] *USA* v. *Fleet factors*,[11] and *Bergsoe Metal* v. *East Asiatic*.[12] But these cases appeared to articulate potentially conflicting rules of liability regarding the type and degree of involvement making the lenders jointly liable with the responsible firms.[13] To clarify this confused situation, the EPA issued in 1992 the so-called *Final Rule*[14] under which a lender would be liable for clean-up costs if it participated in the management of the borrower's operations by exercising management control over either the day-to-day operations of the facility or its environmental compliance efforts. In the years following the EPA's final rule, some court decisions were based on this statement.[15] But in the 1994 case *Kelley* v. *EPA*,[16] the DC Circuit Court of Appeal held that Congress in enacting CERCLA did not give the EPA authority to effect the imposition of liability and therefore invalidated the EPA's final rule.[17]

In 1996, the Asset Conservation, Lender Liability, and Deposit Insurance Protection Act[18] clarified the limits of liability for secured creditors by validating the EPA's lender liability rule. According to this Act, lenders and secured creditors must 'participate in the management of the facility' to be held liable as an 'owner or operator' of a contaminated site and a secured creditor's simple financing transactions should not imply a joint, several, retroactive and strict liability for environmental contamination. But, while the Act provides welcomed relief for secured creditors, it does not completely insulate lenders and fiduciaries from environmental liability, and the question remains regarding the precise steps that must be taken to ensure a limitation of liability for lenders.[19]

In addition to the lender liability rule developed through the jurisprudence, the CERCLA liability system raises other issues. First, suing all the potentially responsible parties or targeting some 'deep pocket' ones to recover response, clean-up costs and damages, as well as coordinating numerous parties with conflicting interests and finding an agreement on a cost allocation plan may generate very high transaction costs. Second, the involvement of many potentially responsible parties implies that the distribution among polluting parties of the needed compensation costs can create incentive problems such as the allocation of resources to legal strategies rather than to accident prevention.[20]

As well as this transaction cost problem, the CERCLA liability system was not supported by a significant development in the insurance market.[21] The main problems are the following. The standard insurance policies do not fit the CERCLA retroactive liability system because they do not cover claims made before or after the validity period of the insurance contract. Moreover, because both the premium and the deductible in the policies are extremely high, only a few insurance companies in the United States issue them and many lending institutions opt for self-insurance.[22]

In Europe, a unified regime of liability for environmental damages is still in the making.[23] The problem of harmonizing different national legal regimes from the standpoint of both market integration and environmental protection that cuts across traditional administrative and legal boundaries raises difficult issues.[24] In this context, the White Paper on Environmental Liability of February 2000 issued by the European Commission aims at determining who should pay for the clean-up and restoration costs of the environmental damage resulting from human acts. The question whether the costs should be paid by society at large through the tax system or by the polluter when it can be identified was answered by the imposition of liability on the party responsible for causing the damage. The European Commission opted essentially for a strict (no fault) liability system that is effective only for future damage where polluters can be identified, damage is quantifiable and a causal connection can be shown. Given the general rule that the polluter must always be the first actor a claim is addressed to, the White Paper nevertheless recommends a form of extended liability rule. It states that the persons who exercise control (the 'operators') of an activity by which the damage is caused should be the liable party and it specifies that lenders not exercising operational control should not be liable. Furthermore, in the final part of the White Paper that deals with the overall economic impact of environmental liability in the European Community, it is stated that the liability system generally protects economic operators in the financial sectors, unless they have operational responsibilities.

The White Paper liability system, while similar to the United States system, differs from it on many important aspects. First, both of them are based on a strict liability regime in the sense that liability comes from the causal link between the actor and the damage and whether the actor's behaviour was proper or negligent is irrelevant. Second, while the CERCLA system is applied retroactively, the EC White Paper provides a non-retroactive application.[25] Third, only a mitigated joint and several liability regime is provided in the European case in the sense that a party is allowed to provide convincing arguments that it is only partially liable. Fourth, instead of covering every damage including the damage to natural resources, the European system covers only traditional damages, such as personal injury and damage to property, and the decontamination of sites. Fifth, the objective of the United States system of recovering the environmental damage from liable parties is supported also by the creation of a Superfund while no such fund is established by the White Paper. Sixth, the set of actors who can be held liable is the same, namely the 'operators' of the firm, and both systems specify that lenders not exercising operational control should not be held liable, the so-called secured interest exemption rule.[26]

The Regulation Option

An alternative instrument to implement the environmental policy is a regulatory system where an authority or an agency can use a number of ways to control environmental damages and reduce the probability of environmental accidents. The traditional approach is the command and control procedure of setting and implementing pollution standards. A more recent approach rests on incentive market-based instruments, such as emission taxation, marketable permits and offset trading.[27]

In the command and control approach based on a mandatory technology or abatement standard, the regulator, such the United States Environmental Protection Agency, can order the firms to limit their emissions, to emit no more than a specified amount of a pollutant and/or to install a particular abatement technology. The regulator monitors over the time the compliance of firms with the standards and emission limits through the conduct of inspections, actions in federal courts and negotiated settlements with polluters.[28]

The incentive market-based instruments are alternative tools that are typically based on the menu of contracts framework or on a system of marketable permits. The latter essentially works in the following way: the regulator grants a plant or public utility a number of permits to emit a given amount of a pollutant; if the facility is able to reduce its emissions, preferably through the use of newer technologies, it can sell its remaining emission permits to another facility that is unable to meet its quota.

Looking at the United States experience, air pollution control under the Federal Clean Air Act (1970–90) followed in its early stages a command and control approach but with the increasing knowledge of and experimentation with market-based solutions switched to markets of pollution 'rights'. Given that the main goal of the Clean Air Act was the attainment of national ambient air quality standards, the Congress asked the EPA to establish the National Ambient Air Quality Standards (NAAQSs) for pervasive air pollutants. Later, effluent taxes and marketable emission rights were taken into consideration in order to overcome the shortcomings of the command and control instruments in terms of monitoring, enforcement capabilities and their high level of administrative costs.

In the EC, the European Environmental Agency (EEA) has a limited regulatory role for two reasons. First, the EEA exercises mainly the role of providing objective, comparable and reliable information that member states or the Community at large may use to develop measures to protect the environment, to evaluate the results of the said measures, and to educate the public about the state of the environment. Second, the EEA has very limited resources: the Agency has a staff of approximately 60 persons and its limited financial resources curtail its capacity of addressing directly and credibly the environmental problems of the Community. Therefore in every single member state, the regulation follows the national legislation and the choice of instruments is specific to each state.

Liability versus Regulation

To compare the two policy instruments we can follow a law and economics approach analysing their impacts in terms of social welfare.[29] This kind of analysis balances the benefits from the risky activities with the costs of precautionary care, the expected level of damages (probability and severity), the administrative expenses associated with these policies, and the net social cost of the informational rents.

A strict liability system is typically applied to risks created by abnormally hazardous activities and against defendants for all injuries caused by their conduct. The victim files an action claiming a causal link between the defendant's conduct and the plaintiff's injury or disease and the system relies on a case-by-case adjudication. A strict liability regime has the advantage of internalizing environmental risks both from the incentive and the compensation points of view. But it has some practical disadvantages: in many cases the victims are widely dispersed and none of them is sufficiently motivated to initiate a legal action, harm may appear only after a long delay, specifically responsible polluters may be difficult to identify, determining the causal link may be difficult, inconsistent verdicts may emerge, delays in court proceedings may be very long and the system may be more profitable for lawyers and experts than for the victims.

On the other hand, a regulation system is typically characterized by a centralized structure. Its advantages are based on the fact that it is well suited to set policies regarding the definition and implementation of standards. The centralized search facilities, the continual oversight of problems and a broad array of regulatory tools can make the regulation system capable of systematically assessing environmental risks and of implementing a comprehensive set of policies. But regulatory agencies may be not very flexible in adapting to changing conditions and a centralized command structure relying on expert advice may be subject to political pressure as well as to collusion and capture by the regulated firms.[30]

We can compare the two policy instruments on the basis of the following features: the level of administrative costs; the magnitude of the damages in case of an environmental accident; the private knowledge of the parties regarding the causal factors of accident probability; and the risk of capture or collusion.

The cost of a liability system includes the administrative expenses incurred by the private and the public parties, namely the cost of optimally controlling the probability of accidents, the legal expenses and the public expenses for maintaining legal institutions. The cost of the regulatory system includes the public expenses for maintaining the regulatory agencies and the private costs of compliance. One advantage of the liability system is that a significant part of the administrative costs is incurred only if a suit occurs. On the other hand, the administrative costs of a regulation system are incurred whether or not the harm occurs because the process of regulation is itself costly and the regulator needs to collect information about the parties, their activities and the risks.

A second element of the comparison refers to the party who bears the cost of environmental damage. In a regulation system, the costs are usually directly or indirectly covered by the public parties when due care was exercised by the firms according to the standards defined by the regulatory agency. In a liability regime, these costs are imposed on the responsible private parties, if and when a suit occurs, given their capacity to pay and their limited liability. Both systems may require some form of compulsory insurance for the losses in excess of the assets of the firm but the liability system can also rely on an extended liability assignment according to which most or all deep-pocket stakeholders (suppliers, partners and financiers) of the firm may be made strictly, jointly and severally responsible for the damages.

A third important element of the comparison is the distribution of knowledge among parties regarding the benefits of activities, the cost of reducing risks and the probability and the severity of accidents. Sometimes the nature of the activities carried out by the firms is such that the private parties have better knowledge of the benefits and costs of reducing risks. In such a case a liability system has the advantage of making the private parties residual claimants of the control of risks while a regulation system suffers from the lack of information leading to overestimation or underestimation of the costs and benefits of the risks (probability and/or severity). But it may also happen that the regulator has better knowledge of those risks because of the possibility of centralizing information and decisions, in particular when a better knowledge of the risk factors requires a special expertise to be shared through different cases and situations.[31]

A fourth relevant feature in the comparison is the possibility of capture and collusion between the enforcers and the parties. The enforcers may be influenced by external pressure in both systems, but one may reasonably argue that the courts are less likely to be captured than the regulating agencies.

On the basis of these differences between the two policy instruments, we shall present in the next section a model based on the stylized features of an extended lender liability system and of an incentive regulation system where the asymmetric information between parties (moral hazard) and the possibility of capture are explicitly present.

THE MODEL

We consider a two-period context where a firm can, in each period, invest an amount F to generate a low profit level of π_L with probability θ or a high profit level of π_H with probability $(1 - \theta)$, with expected profit $\bar{\pi} = \theta\pi_L + (1 - \theta)\pi_H$.[32] The stochastic revenues are i.i.d. and the discount rate is zero. The firm can choose self-protection activities e that reduce the probability $p(e)$ of a major environmental accident generating damages of $d > \pi_H$. Therefore if a major environmental disaster occurs in period 2, it sends the responsible firm into bankruptcy. We shall assume that the self-protection activities are exerted in period 1 and that an accident can happen in period 2 only, if it does occur. The self-protection activities can be at the high level e_h or at the low level e_ℓ; we shall assume for simplicity that the cost of the low level e_ℓ is zero and that the (differential) cost of the high level is $\Delta\psi$. Let $p(e_h) = p_h$ and $p(e_\ell) = p_\ell$. We shall assume that $\Delta\psi < (p_\ell - p_h)d$ and therefore it is socially optimal in a first-best sense that the firm chooses the high level of self-protection activities.

We shall assume for simplicity that the firm has no equity and must borrow in each period the full amount F in order to remain in business. We consider two regimes. In the first regime, the firm interacts with a private banker who is the residual liable party for environmental damages caused by the firm, that is for damages above the assets of the firm. The firm is assumed to be risk neutral but with limited liability. The bank is assumed to be a deep-pocket private bank whose limited liability is irrelevant. In the second regime, the firm interacts with a regulator who is directly responsible for implementing environmental protection policies to maximize welfare but who is subject to capture by the regulated firm. Under the extended lender liability regime, the firm borrows from the private bank. Under the regulatory regime, we assume for simplicity that the firm borrows from the regulator. Clearly, a real regulator does not finance the firm but in his/her complex relationship with the firm, s/he would worry about the financial viability of the firm and also the impact of financial contracts on incentives for self-protection activities. Creating a direct financial link between the regulator and the firm is a reduced-form representation of the structural relationship between the regulator, the firm and the financial markets.

We wish to concentrate here on the prevention of environmental accidents and so the information structure we consider is as follows: although the realized profit level is observable by everyone, the level of self-protection activities is a private information of the firm and is therefore observable neither by the regulator nor by the bank. The timing of the interplay between the principal (either the public regulator or the private bank) and the firm is as follows in both regimes considered. The principal offers a financial contract to the firm making explicit the payments to be made in each period if the firm is financed. If the contract is accepted, the firm invests F and chooses the care level e. The profit level of the first period is then observed and a payment is made to the principal according to the financial contract. In period 2, the firm is refinanced or not, and if refinanced it invests F again, the profit level is observed and a catastrophic accident occurs or not. A payment is made to the principal according to the financial contract and, if an accident occurs, clean-up costs are distributed according to the liability system in force.

We shall characterize and compare three solutions. The benchmark solution will correspond to the case where a *benevolent* regulator, not subject to capture, chooses the financial contract offered to the firm in order to maximize a utilitarian social welfare function. The second solution will be obtained when a private bank, under an extended lender liability system, chooses and offers a financial contract that maximizes its own expected profit function in which the informational rent of the firm is not present. The third solution will be obtained when the *captured* regulator chooses the financial contract offered to the firm. In so doing, s/he maximizes a distorted social welfare function in which the informational rent of the firm will be overvalued. In a sense, there are three possible principals in this context: the benevolent regulator, the captured regulator and the private bank.

MORAL HAZARD IN ENVIRONMENTAL PROTECTION

Clearly, the asymmetric information structure and the limited liability of the firm make the internalization of externalities a difficult problem. If a major environmental disaster occurs, the firm will be 'judgment-proof' for damages above its value: that is, here, its profit level. Under limited liability, moral hazard variables cannot be costlessly controlled by imposing appropriate penalties on the risk-neutral firm and the latter will in general be able to capture an informational rent. Accident-preventing activities by the firm must then be induced by higher rewards rather than stiff penalties since the limited liability constraint imposes a limit on those penalties.

Given that the profit level is observed by all parties, the principal is able to offer a financial contract where the repayment level is a function of the profit level. But because the level of self-protection activities is not observed, the repayment level must be independent of those activities. So we shall assume that the financial contract stipulates that in period t the principal will lend the amount F and ask for repayment levels of R_L^t if realized profit is π_L and R_H^t if realized profit is π_H. A financial contract is therefore a 4-tuple of repayments for loans of F in each period: $(R_L^1, R_H^1, R_L^2, R_H^2)$. The objective function of the principal will depend on the setting, that is, on whether the principal is a benevolent regulator, a captured regulator or a private bank, and whether the principal has priority or not over the firm's profit in case of bankruptcy. We shall assume here that if an accident occurs the firm must pay for the damages at least up to the maximal amount made possible by its limited liability. Since $d < \pi_H$, it means that all its profit will be taken away if an accident occurs and no payment is then made to the principal.

Under our assumptions, the full-information first-best allocation entails clearly a high level of self-protection activities e_h and a loan/investment F in both periods iff:

$$2\bar{\pi} - 2F - p_h d - \Delta\psi \geq 0, \tag{12.1}$$

a condition which is satisfied if we have a benevolent regulator or a captured regulator. The two regulators differ by their treatment of the firm's informational rent but since the rent is zero under full information, this differential treatment has no impact. In the absence of extended lender liability, the private bank lends in each period iff:

$$\max\{2\overline{\pi} - 2F - p_\ell\overline{\pi}, 2\overline{\pi} - 2F - p_h\overline{\pi} - \Delta\psi\} \geq 0, \tag{12.2}$$

leading to overinvestment because of the partial, rather than full, internalization of the externality. With the extended liability of the deep-pocket private bank, the full-information first-best allocation is also achieved at the Nash equilibrium of the game played by the firm and the bank. The bank's liability induces it to fully internalize the externality and, being risk neutral, it prefers the optimal level of effort e_h. Hence, one may suggest that a possible solution to the full internalization of the externality created by environmental accidents is to make the private bank responsible for damages if the judgment-proof firm it finances causes a catastrophic environmental accident.[33]

But when the principal, whether it is the benevolent regulator, the captured regulator or the private bank, suffers from agency problems in its relationship with the firm, the possibility of achieving the first-best must be qualified. As mentioned before, we consider in this chapter that the firm's profit is observable by the regulators and the private bank but that they all face a moral hazard problem regarding the level of the firm's accident-preventing activities. We shall characterize first the social optimum to be used as a benchmark. This benchmark corresponds to the case of the benevolent regulator who maximizes the proper social welfare function but in so doing must take into account the private information of the firm regarding its self-protection activities. Next, we shall characterize the Nash equilibrium obtained for the game involving the firm and the private bank under the extended lender liability regime. Then, we shall characterize the solution obtained when the regulator is captured. Finally, we shall compare the three solutions and derive some propositions on the relative social efficiency of the regime of incentive regulation implemented by a captured regulator and the regime of extended lender liability.

The Social Optimum Under Moral Hazard

Because of asymmetric information, the full-information first-best allocation is not achievable any more. The proper benchmark for our analysis is the social optimum under moral hazard because even the benevolent regulator whose objective is to maximize social welfare must take into account the agency costs. We shall assume that the social welfare function (SWF) is utilitarian and that there is a social cost of public funds $(1 + \lambda)$ coming from distortions due to taxation: it costs $(1 + \lambda)T$ to raise T through general taxation.[34] The financial payments made by the firm to the benevolent regulator acting here as a financier together with the cost F invested by the benevolent regulator will enter the social welfare function with a weight of $(1 + \lambda)$, in the first case because they allow a reduction in taxation and in the second case because the investment F must be financed through taxation, directly or indirectly. We shall assume also that the expected damage of an accident enters the social welfare function with a weight of $(1 + \lambda)$ because the government will have to cover that cost in one way or another and finance it through taxation. Given that the firm's net utility (rent) is not observable by the benevolent regulator, and therefore not taxable, this net utility enters the social welfare function with a weight of 1. It will therefore be efficient for the benevolent regulator to recuperate any observable profit of the firm.[35] The firm will be left with its unobservable informational rent which will then have a weight of 1 in the social welfare function. The socially optimal programme of the benevolent regulator will therefore minimize the rent left to the firm because of its smaller weight in the social welfare function. The existence of a social cost of public funds is an important and realistic feature of regulatory frameworks. It makes income distribution relevant, although in an unusual sense, for environmental protection. Were that cost equal to zero, the regulator would not care whether the firm made monopoly profits or captured significant informational rents as long as the efficient production level were realized. The existence of a positive λ together with the assumption of a regulator acting as financier will allow us to develop a tractable yet realistic model of instrument choice in environmental protection policy.

The social optimum under moral hazard maximizes the expected social welfare under the incentive compatibility, limited liability and individual rationality constraints of the privately informed firm. The firm will choose a high level of self-protection activities iff it finds it profitable to incur the differential cost $\Delta \psi$, that is, iff its expected net utility is larger with $e = e_h$ than with $e = e_\ell$, that is iff:

$$(1 - p_h)[\bar{\pi} - (\theta R_L^2 + (1 - \theta)R_H^2)] - \Delta \psi \geq (1 - p_\ell)[\bar{\pi} - (\theta R_L^2 + (1 - \theta)R_H^2)]$$

which can be rewritten as:

$$\bar{\pi} - \theta R_L^2 - (1 - \theta)R_H^2 \geq \frac{\Delta \psi}{p_\ell - p_h}, \tag{12.3}$$

which is the incentive compatibility constraint to be satisfied if the principal wants to induce the firm to select e_h. The limited liability constraints of the firm simply require that the repayment levels do not exceed the corresponding profit levels. Finally, the firm's individual rationality constraint is that its net utility be non-negative (assuming an exogenous utility normalized at zero). The firm's expected net utility is 0 under $e = e_\ell$ and given by its informational rent under $e = e_h$: $\bar{\pi} - \theta R_L^1 - (1 - \theta)R_H^1 - \Delta\psi + (1 - p_h)\, (\bar{\pi} - \theta R_L^2 - (1 - \theta)R_H^2)$. Distortions created by the presence of moral hazard will occur only when the combination of the limited liability constraints and the incentive compatibility constraint (12.3) require giving up a (costly) rent to the firm. The existence of a social cost of public funds requires that $R_L^1 = \pi_L$, $R_H^1 = \pi_H$ and that (12.3) be satisfied with a strict equality: because $\lambda > 0$, it is socially better to use the profit of the firm to reduce the general distortionary taxes. Therefore, the net utility level or informational rent of the firm is:

$$\mathfrak{R} \equiv -\Delta\psi + (1 - p_h)\frac{\Delta\psi}{p_\ell - p_h} > 0. \tag{12.4}$$

Under the socially optimal financial contract, the benevolent regulator collects an expected amount of:

$$\bar{\pi} + (1 - p_h)(\theta R_L^2 + (1 - \theta)R^2_{\,H}) - p_h[\theta(d - R_L^2) + (1 - \theta)(d - R_H^2)] - 2F. \tag{12.5}$$

Proposition 1   If:

$$\frac{\lambda}{1 + \lambda}\mathfrak{R} + \Delta\psi \leq (p_\ell - p_h)d, \tag{12.6}$$

the social optimum (the benevolent regulator solution) is characterized by a high level of accident-preventing activities and an investment F in both periods iff:

$$2\bar{\pi} - 2F - p_h d - \Delta\psi - \frac{\lambda}{1 + \lambda}\mathfrak{R} \geq 0. \tag{12.7}$$

If (12.6) is not satisfied, the social optimum is characterized by a low level of accident-preventing activities and an investment in both periods iff:

$$2\bar{\pi} - 2F - p_\ell d \geq 0. \, \| \tag{12.8}$$

Proof: Let us first derive the social welfare when e_h is induced. We must solve the following programme:

$$\text{Max } \{(1+\lambda)[\theta R_L^1 + (1-\theta)R_H^1 + (1-p_h)(\theta R_L^2 + (1-\theta)R_H^2) - 2F]$$
$$- (1+\lambda)p_h(d-\bar{\pi}) + [(\bar{\pi} - \theta R_L^1 - (1-\theta)R_H^1 - \Delta\psi)$$
$$+ (1-p_h)(\bar{\pi} - \theta R_L^2 - (1-\theta)R_H^2)]\} \tag{12.9}$$

subject to the incentive compatibility condition (12.3) and the individual rationality condition:

$$\bar{\pi} - \theta R_L^1 - (1-\theta)R_H^1 - \Delta\psi + (1-p_h)(\bar{\pi} - \theta R_L^2 - (1-\theta)R_H^2) \geq 0. \tag{12.10}$$

The solution entails $\theta R_L^1 + (1-\theta)R_H^1 = \bar{\pi}$ and (12.3) satisfied with a strict equality because of the different weights in the SWF. Accordingly, the social welfare (12.9) can be written as:

$$(1+\lambda)\left[\bar{\pi} - 2F + (1-p_h)\left(\bar{\pi} - \frac{\Delta\psi}{p_\ell - p_h}\right) - p_h(d-\bar{\pi})\right] + \left[(1-p_h)\frac{\Delta\psi}{p_\ell - p_h} - \Delta\psi\right],$$

hence as:

$$(1+\lambda)[2\bar{\pi} - 2F - p_h d - \Delta\psi] - \lambda\left[(1-p_h)\frac{\Delta\psi}{p_\ell - p_h} - \Delta\psi\right],$$

that is:

$$(1+\lambda)[2\bar{\pi} - 2F - p_h d - \Delta\psi] - \lambda\mathfrak{R}. \tag{12.11}$$

Therefore, investment should take place if (12.7) is satisfied. If $e = e_\ell$, no rent is left to the firm, the social welfare becomes:

$$(1+\lambda)(2\bar{\pi} - 2F - p_\ell d) \tag{12.12}$$

and investment must take place in both periods if (12.12) is positive. Comparing the social welfare levels (12.11) and (12.12), we obtain that $e = e_h$ must be induced if:

$$\frac{\lambda}{1+\lambda}\mathfrak{R} + \Delta\psi \leq (p_\ell - p_h)d, \tag{12.13}$$

where the right-hand side is the incremental value and the left-hand side is the incremental cost, including the social cost of the informational rent, of the high level of accident-preventing activities. This completes the proof. ∎

Proposition 1 differs from the first-best full-information rule because of the presence of $\mathfrak{R}$, the rent to be given up to the firm when the benevolent regulator wants to induce a high level of accident-prevention activities. The benevolent regulator cannot avoid giving up that rent to induce a high level of accident-preventing activities and will therefore take into account the net social cost of that rent, namely $\lambda\mathfrak{R}$. If that cost is large, the benevolent regulator may prefer, in maximizing the SWF, to induce a low level of care e_ℓ generating a high probability p_ℓ of environmental accidents. It may even turn out that the firm will not be financed by the benevolent regulator even if it were to be in a full-information context. Both when making the investment decision and deciding on the optimal level of care activities, the social cost of this rent must be accounted for. As λ decreases, the net social cost of the firm's informational rent decreases and condition (12.13) converges to the condition for $e = e_h$ under full information. As λ increases, the net social cost of giving up a rent to the firm goes up and condition (12.13) converges to the condition, to be derived below, for $e = e_h$ under extended lender liability since $\lambda/(1 + \lambda)$ converges to 1 as $\lambda \to \infty$.

The Nash Equilibrium When the Firm Faces a Private Bank

We now consider the case where the firm faces a private banker who is liable for environmental damages caused by the firm when the latter is unable to cover those damages from its assets, here its profits. Clearly, as in the above case of a benevolent regulator acting as financier, the private bank can offer a care-inducing contract to the firm but in so doing will concede a rent to the firm as expressed by (12.3). Otherwise, the bank can capture the whole profit. The bank's expected profit under a contract inducing a high level of care activities e_h is, using (12.3):

$$\bar{\pi} + \left(1 - p_h\right)\left(\bar{\pi} - \frac{\Delta\psi}{p_\ell - p_h}\right) - p_h(d - \bar{\pi}) - 2F$$

that is:

$$2\bar{\pi} - 2F - p_h d - \left(1 - p_h\right)\frac{\Delta\psi}{p_\ell - p_h}, \qquad (12.14)$$

while under the alternative contract inducing the low level of care e_ℓ, its profit is:

$$2\bar{\pi} - 2F - p_\ell d. \tag{12.15}$$

Proposition 2 Under extended lender liability, the private bank induces a high level of accident-preventing activities less often than the benevolent regulator does. When the bank decides to induce $e = e_h$ conceding a rent $\mathfrak{R}$ to the firm, it lends less often than the benevolent regulator does. When, in spite of lender liability, the bank opts to induce the low level of care activities e_ℓ leaving no rent to the firm, it lends as often as the benevolent regulator does in that case. ‖

Proof: Comparing (12.14) and (12.15), the private bank opts for inducing $e = e_h$ iff:

$$\mathfrak{R} + \Delta\psi < (p_\ell - p_h)d \tag{12.16}$$

while the benevolent regulator induces such a level of care when (12.13) is satisfied. Comparing the two conditions shows that the private bank opts for the low level of care activities more often because:

$$\frac{\lambda}{1+\lambda}\mathfrak{R} + \Delta\psi < \mathfrak{R} + \Delta\psi.$$

Considering (12.14) and using (12.4), the private bank will lend with e_h iff:

$$2\bar{\pi} - 2F - p_h d - \Delta\psi - \mathfrak{R} \geq 0. \tag{12.17}$$

Comparing (12.17) and (12.7), obtained in the case of the benevolent regulator, shows that the private bank lends less often than the benevolent regulator does. Similarly, since (12.15) and (12.8) are the same then the private bank lends as often as the benevolent regulator does in that case since no rent is left to the firm and the bank internalizes completely the cost of an accident. ∎

The intuition behind Proposition 2 is that under the extended lender liability, the cost of an accident for the bank is the same as for the benevolent regulator and so the comparison between the two solutions rests on their different evaluation of the firm's rent when $e = e_h$ is induced. For the bank, the cost of the rent is equal to the value of the rent itself $\mathfrak{R}$ while for the benevolent regulator the net cost is smaller, namely $(\lambda/\lambda + 1)\mathfrak{R}$, because s/he considers the social value of that rent in the SWF. This makes the bank less willing than the benevolent regulator not only to lend but also to induce a high level of accident-preventing activities. Hence this unavoidable informational rent leads to insufficient financing and too few care activities induced by the bank. If the bank chooses to induce $e = e_\ell$, there is no rent and therefore the bank lends as often as the benevolent regulator.

The Biased Optimum When the Regulator is Captured

If the regulator is captured, s/he will in a sense benefit from the firm's rent one way or another, that is, through bribes, collusive interests, perks, future employment opportunities and so on. It will be as if s/he puts too much weight (overvaluation) on the firm's informational rent in the objective function, that is, as if s/he undervalues the social cost of that rent in comparison with the benchmark case of the benevolent regulator. This will make the captured regulator less keen to reduce this rent to its minimum.

We shall assume that the rent $\mathfrak{R}$ of the firm, when $e = e_h$ is induced, enters the captured regulator's objective function with a weight of K, where $1 < K < (1 + \lambda)$. The captured regulator's objective function is a biased version of the social welfare function, namely when e_h is induced:

$$(1+\lambda)\left[\overline{\pi} - 2F + (1 - p_h)\left(\overline{\pi} - \frac{\Delta\psi}{p_\ell - p_h}\right) - p_h(d - \overline{\pi})\right] + K\mathfrak{R},$$

that is, using (12.3):

$$(1 + \lambda)[2\overline{\pi} - 2F - p_h d - \Delta\psi] - (1 + \lambda - K)\mathfrak{R} \qquad (12.18)$$

and, when e_ℓ is induced:

$$(1 + \lambda)[2\overline{\pi} - 2F - p_\ell d]. \qquad (12.19)$$

We have:

Proposition 3 The captured regulator induces a high level of accident-preventing activities more often than the benevolent regulator does. When s/he induces $e = e_h$ conceding a rent to the firm, s/he lends more often than called for, conditionally on $e = e_h$, by the second-best optimal investment rule. When the captured regulator induces a low level of accident-preventing activities e_ℓ leaving no rent to the firm, s/he lends as often as called for, conditionally on $e = e_\ell$, by the second-best optimal investment rule. ||

Proof: Comparing (12.18) and (12.19), we obtain that the captured regulator induces $e = e_h$ iff:

$$\frac{1+\lambda-K}{1+\lambda}\mathfrak{R} + \Delta\psi < (p_\ell - p_h)d$$

which compared with (12.6) shows that the captured regulator induces e_h too often since:

$$\frac{1+\lambda-K}{1+\lambda}\mathfrak{R} + \Delta\psi < \frac{\lambda}{1+\lambda}\mathfrak{R} + \Delta\psi.$$

When e_h is induced, the captured regulator's objective function (12.18) is positive iff:

$$2\bar{\pi} - 2F - p_h d - \Delta\psi - \frac{1+\lambda-K}{1+\lambda}\mathfrak{R} \geq 0.$$

Since $(1 + \lambda - K)/(1 + \lambda) < \lambda/(1 + \lambda)$, the social cost of the rent is undervalued and therefore, the capture of the regulator leads to overinvestment, conditionally on $e = e_h$, in the environmentally risky activities. When e_ℓ is induced, we observe from (12.12) and (12.19) that the investment rules of the captured regulator and of the benevolent regulator are the same. ■

THE CHOICE OF INSTRUMENTS

Let SWF^{CR} be the value of the SWF (12.9) with the solution, level of care activities and investment rule, implemented by the captured regulator, as defined in Proposition 3. Let SWF^{PB} be the value of the SWF with the solution, level of care activities and investment rule, implemented by the private bank under extended lender liability, as defined in Proposition 2. Let us define the correspondences Ω, Φ, Γ as follows:

$$\text{SWF}^{CR} > \text{SWF}^{PB} \text{ iff } \Delta\psi \in \Omega\,(\lambda)$$
$$\text{SWF}^{CR} = \text{SWF}^{PB} \text{ iff } \Delta\psi \in \Phi\,(\lambda)$$
$$\text{SWF}^{CR} < \text{SWF}^{PB} \text{ iff } \Delta\psi \in \Gamma\,(\lambda).$$

We now turn to the characterization and illustration of those correspondences.[36] But first, let us recall the main result of our analysis so far.

When $e = e_\ell$ is induced, the investment rules are the same in the three cases considered, namely the benevolent regulator, the private bank and the captured regulator.

When the benevolent regulator is the principal, we obtain that the probability that $e = e_h$ will be induced is the probability that $\lambda/(1 + \lambda)\,\Re + \Delta\psi$ is less than $(p_\ell - p_h)d$ and the probability that an investment $2F$ will be made in the firm is the probability that $\lambda/(1 + \lambda)\,\Re + \Delta\psi$ is smaller than $2\bar{\pi} - 2F - p_h d$. This is the benchmark case corresponding to the second-best solution, that is, the social optimum under moral hazard.

When the private bank is the principal, the probability that $e = e_h$ will be induced is now the probability that $\Re + \Delta\psi$ is less than $(p_\ell - p_h)\,d$ and the probability that an investment $2F$ will be made in the firm is now the probability that $\Re + \Delta\psi$ is smaller than $2\bar{\pi} - 2F - p_h d$. Compared with the benchmark case, this solution represents a loss of social welfare because of *not enough* incentive for care, hence too many accidents, and *not enough* investment in the environmentally risky operations of the firm. The loss in welfare is due to the bank's *overvaluation* of the net social cost of the informational rent captured by the firm, that is to the bank's failure to consider the social value of the rent.

When the captured regulator is the principal, we then obtain that the probability that $e = e_h$ will be induced is the probability that $(1 + \lambda - K)/(1 + \lambda)\,\Re + \Delta\psi$ is less than $(p\ell - p_h)d$ and the probability that an investment $2F$ will be made in the firm is then the probability that $(1 + \lambda - K)/(1 + \lambda)\,\Re + \Delta\psi$ is smaller than $2\bar{\pi} - 2F - p_h d$. Again, compared with the benchmark case, this solution represents a loss of social welfare because of *too much* incentive for care, hence too few accidents (conditional on the level of financing), and *too much* investment in the environmentally risky operations of the firm. The loss in welfare is due to the captured regulator's *undervaluation* of the net social cost of the informational rent captured by the firm, that is the captured regulator's overweighing of the social value of the rent.

The investment rules in the three contexts are the same if $e = e_\ell$ is induced. But they differ if $e = e_h$ is induced. Moreover the conditions under which e_h is induced differ between the three contexts.

In the benevolent regulator (BR) solution:

$e = e_h$ iff:

$$\frac{\lambda}{1+\lambda}\,\Re + \Delta\psi \le \left(p_\ell - p_h\right)d,$$

that is, using (12.4) iff:

$$\Delta\psi \le \frac{(1+\lambda)(p_\ell - p_h)d}{1 + \lambda\frac{1-p_h}{p_\ell - p_h}}. \tag{12.20}$$

Investment $2F$ take will place iff:

$$2\bar{\pi} - 2F - p_h d - \Delta\psi - \frac{\lambda}{1+\lambda}\Re \ge 0,$$

that is, iff:

$$\Delta\psi \le \frac{(1+\lambda)(2\bar{\pi} - 2F - p_h d)}{1 + \lambda\frac{1-p_h}{p_\ell - p_h}}. \tag{12.21}$$

In the private bank (PB) solution:

$e = e_h$ iff:

$$\Re + \Delta\psi \le (p_\ell - p_h)d,$$

that is, iff:

$$\Delta\psi \le \frac{(p_\ell - p_h)^2 d}{1 - p_h}. \tag{12.22}$$

Investment $2F$ take will place iff:

$$2\bar{\pi} - 2F - p_h d - \Delta\psi - \Re \ge 0,$$

that is, iff:

$$\Delta\psi \le \frac{(p_\ell - p_h)(2\bar{\pi} - 2F - p_h d)}{1 - p_h}. \tag{2.23}$$

In the captured regulator (CR) solution:

$e = e_h$ iff:

$$\frac{1+\lambda-K}{1+\lambda}\,\mathfrak{R} + \Delta\psi \le (p_\ell - p_h)d,$$

that is, iff:

$$\Delta\psi \le \frac{(1+\lambda)(p_\ell - p_h)d}{K + \dfrac{(1-p_h)(1+\lambda-K)}{p_\ell - p_h}}. \qquad (12.24)$$

Investment $2F$ take will place iff:

$$2\bar{\pi} - 2F - p_h d - \Delta\psi - \frac{1+\lambda-K}{1+\lambda}\,\mathfrak{R} \ge 0,$$

that is, iff:

$$\Delta\psi \le \frac{(1+\lambda)(2\bar{\pi} - 2F - p_h d)}{K + \dfrac{(1-p_h)(1+\lambda-K)}{p_\ell - p_h}}. \qquad (2.25)$$

Suppose that $\lambda = 0$. In that case, the BR implements the first-best solution since, although the firm can capture an informational rent, that rent has no social cost. So the BR induces e_h since by assumption $\Delta\psi < (p_\ell - p_h)d$ and finances the firm iff $2\bar{\pi} - 2F - p_h d - \Delta y \ge 0$. The PB solution is independent of the value of λ. Using (12.4), we obtain that the PB induces e_h, leaving a rent $\mathfrak{R}$ to the firm, iff:

$$\Delta\psi \le \frac{p_\ell - p_h}{1 - p_h}(p_\ell - p_h)d.$$

Otherwise, the PB induces e_ℓ, leaving no rent to the firm. Conditionally on $e = e_\ell$, the private bank lends as often as called for by the first-best rule since there is no rent. The social loss in welfare in this case is the welfare loss due to inducing e_ℓ rather than e_h. Moreover, even when the PB prefers to induce e_h, it does not follow that it finances the firm. In fact, if:

$$\Delta\psi > \left(2\bar{\pi} - 2F - p_h d\right)\frac{p_\ell - p_h}{1 - p_h},$$

the PB will not finance the firm with $e = e_h$, contrary to the first-best rule. It may still finance the firm with $e = e_\ell$. But $(2\bar{\pi} - 2F - p_h d)\,(p_\ell - p_h)/(1 - p_h) > (p_\ell - p_h)/(1 - p_h)(p_\ell - p_h)d$, as below, iff $2\bar{\pi} - 2F - p_\ell d > 0$:

$$(\lambda = 0 \text{ and } 2\bar{\pi} - 2F - p_\ell d > 0)$$

	A		B		C		D	

$\longrightarrow \Delta\psi$

$0 \qquad \dfrac{p_\ell - p_h}{1 - p_h}(p_\ell - p_h)d \quad \left(2\bar{\pi} - 2F - p_h d\right)\dfrac{p_\ell - p_h}{1 - p_h} \quad (p_\ell - p_h)d$

Otherwise we have as shown next below.

- In A, we have $e^{PB} = e_h$ and $e^{BR} = e_h$, and financing occurs in both the BR and PB solutions: no welfare loss in the PB solution.
- In B and C, we have $e^{PB} = e_\ell$ and $e^{BR} = e_h$, and financing occurs in both the BR and PB solutions: the welfare loss in the PB solution corresponds to the higher than efficient level of accidents.
- In D, we have $e^{PB} = e_\ell$ and $e^{BR} = e_\ell$, and financing occurs in both the BR and PB solutions, since $2\bar{\pi} - 2F - p_\ell d \geq 0$, independently of $\Delta\psi$ which is not paid since $e = e_\ell$: there is no welfare loss in the PB solution.[37]

If $2\bar{\pi} - 2F - p_\ell d < 0$, then we have the following:

$$(\lambda = 0 \text{ and } 2\bar{\pi} - 2F - p_\ell d < 0)$$

	A′		B′		C′		D′	

$\longrightarrow \Delta\psi$

$0 \qquad \left(2\bar{\pi} - 2F - p_h d\right)\dfrac{p_\ell - p_h}{1 - p_h} \quad \dfrac{p_\ell - p_h}{1 - p_h}(p_\ell - p_h)d \quad (p_\ell - p_h)d$

- In A′, we have $e^{PB} = e_h$ and $e^{BR} = e_h$, and financing occurs in both the BR and PB solutions: no welfare loss in the PB solution.
- In B′, we have $e^{PB} = e_h$ and $e^{BR} = e_h$, but financing occurs only in the BR solution: the welfare loss in the PB solution corresponds to not realizing the investment.
- In C′, we have $e^{PB} = e_\ell$ and $e^{BR} = e_h$, but financing occurs only in the BR solution: again the welfare loss in the PB solution corresponds to not realizing the investment.

- In D′, we have $e^{PB} = e_\ell$ and $e^{BR} = e_\ell$, and financing occurs in neither the BR nor the PB solutions: no welfare loss in the PB solution.

Similarly, comparing the solutions under BR and CR for the case $2\bar\pi - 2F - p_\ell d > 0$, we obtain:

$$(\lambda = 0 \text{ and } 2\bar\pi - 2F - p_\ell d > 0)$$

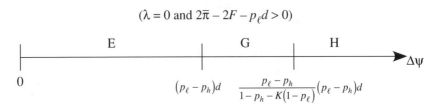

- In E, we have $e^{CR} = e_h$ and $e^{BR} = e_h$, and financing occurs in both the BR and CR solutions: no welfare loss in the CR solution.
- In G, we have $e^{CR} = e_h$, leaving a rent to the firm, and $e^{BR} = e_\ell$, leaving no rent to the firm, and financing occurs in both the CR and the BR solutions. The welfare loss in the CR solution corresponds to a level of accidents that is too low (from the level of care e_h generating a rent for the firm).
- In H, we have $e^{CR} = e_\ell$ and $e^{BR} = e_\ell$ and financing in both the CR and the BR solutions: no welfare loss in the CR solution.

Rather than proceed with a general analysis of the cases with $\lambda > 0$, let us consider the following illustrative numerical example:

$$\pi_L = 5, \pi_H = 10, \theta = 0.5, F = 5, p_\ell = 0.1, p_h = 0.05, d = 20, K = 1.2$$

for which $\bar\pi = 7.5$ and $(p_\ell - p_h)d = 1$. For this case, we can graph the frontiers (20) to (25) as on Figure 12.1, for $(\Delta\psi, \lambda) \in \{(0,0), (1,1)\}$.

Conditions (12.20), (12.22) and (12.24) relate to the decision about the level of care activities, namely $e^{BR} = e_h$ iff $\Delta\psi$ is to the left of (12.20) for a given λ, that is, iff λ is below (12.20) for a given $\Delta\psi$, $e^{PB} = e_h$ iff $\Delta\psi$ is to the left of (12.22), irrespective of the value of λ, and $e^{CR} = e_h$ iff $\Delta\psi$ is to the left of (12.24) for a given λ, that is, iff λ is below (12.24) for a given $\Delta\psi$. Conditions (12.21), (12.23) and (12.25) relate to the decision about the investment in the firm, namely BR invests with e_h iff $\Delta\psi$ is to the left of (12.21), PB invests with e_h iff $\Delta\psi$ is to the left of (12.23) and CR invests with e_h iff $\Delta\psi$ is to the left of (12.25). Therefore, for the example considered, all three principals invest if indeed they decide to induce e_h from the firm. When they induce e_ℓ, they all follow the same rule since there is then no rent left to the firm, namely they all

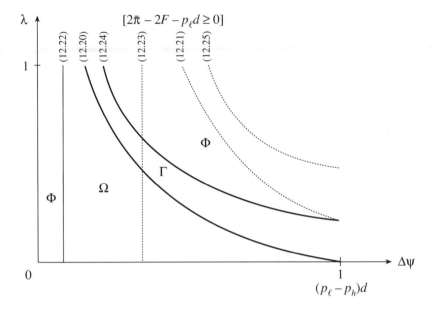

Figure 12.1   Comparison of regimes

invest iff $2\bar{\pi} - 2F - p_\ell d \geq 0$. If we assume that this last condition is satisfied, then there will always be investment in the firm. The difference between the three solutions comes from the different decisions regarding the inducement of care activities. Consider Figure 12.1. For a situation $(\Delta\psi,\lambda)$ to the left of (12.22), all three principals induce e_h and invest in the firm: the three solutions are the same. For a situation $(\Delta\psi,\lambda)$ between (12.22) and (12.20), $e^{BR} = e^{CR} = e_h$ but $e^{PB} = e_\ell$, while they all invest in the firm: in this region, the captured regulator solution is preferred to the private bank solution. For a situation $(\Delta\psi,\lambda)$ between (12.20) and (12.24), $e^{BR} = e^{PB} = e_\ell$ but $e^{CR} = e_h$, while they all invest in the firm: in this region, the private bank solution is preferred to the captured regulator solution, even if there will be more accidents in the former solution. The larger number, more precisely the higher probability, of accidents is more than compensated by the fact that there is no (costly) rent left to the firm. Finally for a situation $(\Delta\psi,\lambda)$ above (12.24), all three principals induce e_ℓ and invest in the firm: the three solutions are the same. Therefore:

Proposition 4   If $2\bar{\pi} - 2F - p_\ell d \geq 0$, that is, if the firm is socially profitable with a low level of care, then the 'extended lender liability' regime and the 'regulator subject to capture' regime are equivalent instruments for implementing the environmental policy if the differential cost between high and low levels of accident prevention activities is relatively small or relatively large (as a function of the social cost of public funds λ), that is, if:

$$\Delta\psi \in \Phi(\lambda) \equiv \left[0, \frac{(p_\ell - p_h)^2 d}{1 - p_h}\right] \cup \left[\frac{(1+\lambda)(p_\ell - p_h)d}{K + \frac{(1-p_h)(1+\lambda-K)}{p_\ell - p_h}}, \infty\right) \cup \left\{\frac{(1+\lambda)(p_\ell - p_h)d}{1+\lambda\frac{1-p_h}{p_\ell - p_h}}\right.$$

The 'regulator subject to capture' regime is a better instrument if the differential cost between high and low levels of accident prevention activities is in the lower intermediate range, that is, if:

$$\Delta\psi \in \Omega(\lambda) \equiv \left(\frac{(p_\ell - p_h)^2 d}{1 - p_h}, \frac{(1+\lambda)(p_\ell - p_h)d}{1+\lambda\frac{1-p_h}{p_\ell - p_h}}\right).$$

The 'extended lender liability' regime is a better instrument if the differential cost between high and low levels of accident prevention activities is in the higher intermediate range, that is, if:

$$\Delta\psi \in \Gamma(\lambda) \equiv \left(\frac{(1+\lambda)(p_\ell - p_h)d}{1+\lambda\frac{1-p_h}{p_\ell - p_h}}, \frac{(1+\lambda)(p_\ell - p_h)d}{K + \frac{(1-p_h)(1+\lambda-K)}{p_\ell - p_h}}\right). \quad \parallel$$

If investing in the firm is not socially desirable or profitable unless $e = e_h$ is induced, that is, if $2\bar{\pi} - 2F - p_\ell d < 0$, we obtain a configuration represented in Figure 12.2, where $p_\ell = 0.3$, for $(\Delta\psi,\lambda) \in \{(0,0), (5,1)\}$.

We observe the following. For a situation $(\Delta\psi,\lambda)$ to the left of (12.23), all three principals prefer to induce e_h and invest in the firm: the three solutions are the same. To the right of (12.23), the private bank does not invest any more because $\Delta\psi$ is too high. For a situation $(\Delta\psi,\lambda)$ between (12.23) and (12.21), $e^{BR} = e^{CR} = e_h$ and both invest in the firm: in this region, the captured regulator solution is preferred to the private bank solution. To the right of (12.21), the benevolent regulator does not invest any more. Although s/he would prefer to induce e_h (for $(\Delta\psi,\lambda)$ between (12.21) and (12.20)), $\Delta\psi$ is too high and therefore the rent to be left to the firm is too costly. Note that, as expected, the no-

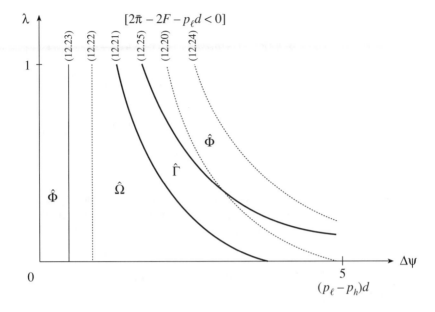

Figure 12.2   Comparison of regimes when investment in firm is socially desirable only if effort prevention is high

investment trigger value is decreasing in λ: the higher the social cost of public funds, the faster the benevolent regulator stops investing as the differential cost $\Delta\psi$ increases. For a situation $(\Delta\psi,\lambda)$ between (12.21) and (12.25), $e^{CR} = e_h$ and the captured regulator is the only principal still interested in investing in the firm: in this region, the private bank solution is preferred to the captured regulator solution. Even if the captured regulator induces the high level of care activities, his/her decision to invest in the firm is due to his/her undervaluation of the social cost of the rent left to the firm. In this region of parameter space, it is socially better not to finance the firm. Finally, for a situation $(\Delta\psi,\lambda)$ above (12.25), none of the three principals invests in the firm: the three solutions are the same. We obtain a comparison similar to the case of Proposition 4 but with different boundaries. We have:

Proposition 5   If $2\bar{\pi} - 2F - p_\ell d \leq 0$, that is, if the firm is socially profitable only with a high level of care, then the 'extended lender liability' regime and the 'regulator subject to capture' regime are equivalent instruments for implementing the environmental policy if the differential cost between high and low levels of accident prevention activities is relatively small or relatively large, that is, if:

$$\Delta\psi \in \hat{\Phi}(\lambda) \equiv \left[0, \ \frac{(p_\ell - p_h)(2\bar{\pi} - 2F - p_h d)}{1 - p_h} \right] \cup \left[\frac{(1+\lambda)(2\bar{\pi} - 2F - p_h d)}{K + \dfrac{(1 - p_h)(1 + \lambda - K)}{p_\ell - p_h}}, \infty \right]$$

$$\cup \left\{ \frac{(1+\lambda)(2\bar{\pi} - 2F - p_h d)}{1 + \lambda \dfrac{1 - p_h}{p_\ell - p_h}} \right\}.$$

The 'regulator subject to capture' regime is a better instrument if the differential cost between high and low levels of accident prevention activities is in the lower intermediate range, that is, if:

$$\Delta\psi \in \hat{\Omega}(\lambda) \equiv \left(\frac{(p_\ell - p_h)(2\bar{\pi} - 2F - p_h d)}{1 - p_h}, \ \frac{(1+\lambda)(2\bar{\pi} - 2F - p_h d)}{1 + \lambda \dfrac{1 - p_h}{p_\ell - p_h}} \right).$$

The 'extended lender liability' regime is a better instrument if the differential cost between high and low levels of accident prevention activities is in the higher intermediate range, that is, if:

$$\Delta\psi \in \hat{\Gamma}(\lambda) \equiv \left(\frac{(1+\lambda)(2\bar{\pi} - 2F - p_h d)}{1 + \lambda \dfrac{1 - p_h}{p_\ell - p_h}}, \ \frac{(1+\lambda)(2\bar{\pi} - 2F - p_h d)}{K + \dfrac{(1 - p_h)(1 + \lambda - K)}{p_\ell - p_h}} \right). \ \|$$

Proposition 6 The region in $(\Delta\psi, \lambda)$-space over which the captured regulator solution is better than the extended lender liability solution is independent of K while the region in $(\Delta\psi, \lambda)$-space over which the captured regulator solution is worse than the extended lender liability solution is expanding with K. $\|$

CONCLUSION AND POLICY IMPLICATIONS

We have analysed in this chapter a simple model which allows a comparison between different instruments for implementing an efficient environmental protection policy. More precisely, we considered a moral hazard context in which firms can take preventing actions to reduce the probability of environmental disasters. Those actions being a private information of the firm concerned will give rise to informational rents whose net social cost is positive because of the existence of a social cost of public funds. We first characterized the optimal rules a benevolent welfare-maximizing regulator would choose regarding the level of care activities a given firm should be exercising and the condition for financing the firm. Those rules differ from the first-best rules because the maximization of social welfare requires that the regulator minimizes the informational rent of the firm. We then compared the benevolent regulator solution rules to those rules a private bank would apply under the extended lender liability of the CERCLA type and to those rules a captured regulator, overestimating the contribution of the informational rent of the firm to social welfare, would choose.

The comparison of the three sets of rules led us to identify the region in the $(\Delta\psi,\lambda)$-space where the captured regulator rules and the CERCLA-liable private bank rules are equivalent to the benevolent regulator rules, the region where the captured regulator rules are better in terms of social welfare attained to the CERCLA-liable private bank rules, and finally the region where the CERCLA-liable private bank rules are better.

Our main results are summarized in Proposition 4 for the case where the firm is socially profitable when the level of care is high or low and in Proposition 5 for the case where the firm is socially profitable only if the level of care is high. In general, the captured regulator solution is better if the deterministic characteristic location of the economy in the $(\Delta\psi,\lambda)$-space falls in the lower intermediate range, that is if $\Delta\psi \in \Omega\ (\lambda)$ (or $\Delta\psi \in \hat{\Omega}\ (\lambda)$) and the CERCLA-liable private bank solution is better if the deterministic characteristic location of the economy falls in the higher intermediate range, that is if $\Delta\psi \in \Gamma\ (\lambda)$ (or $\Delta\psi \in \hat{\Gamma}(\lambda)$). It is interesting to note that the former region is independent of the capture parameter K while the latter region is expanding with increases in K: if the captured regulator's overestimation of the contribution of the informational rent to social welfare increases, within its reasonable interval, then the upper boundary of the region in $(\Delta\psi,\lambda)$-space where the CERCLA-liable private bank solution rules are better than the captured regulator's rules (condition (12.24) in Proposition 4 and condition (12.25) in Proposition 5) moves up.

The main conclusion of this chapter is therefore that choosing between a regulation framework and a legal framework to implement an environmental protection policy is not an easy matter. But our analysis provides some preliminary steps in determining a way to analyse such a choice. So the answer to the question regarding which instruments should be employed by the policy makers is that a case-by-case examination is required. But some of the important determinants of the relative efficiency with which different policy instruments maximize social welfare function have been characterized.

NOTES

*   We wish to thank Claire Domenget, Patrick Gonzalez, Yolande Hiriart, Ejen Mackaay and Stephen Shavell for their comments and assistance. Donatella Porrini acknowledges financial support from MURST project 'Regulation and Self-Regulation' (Universita LIUC – Castellanza, Italy). We retain sole responsibility for the content of this chapter.

1.   See Cropper and Oates (1992), Segerson (1996) and Lewis (1996).

2.   See Buchanan and Tullock (1975), Yohe (1976), Boyer (1979), Noll (1983), Hahn (1990), Laffont (1995) and Boyer and Laffont (1999).

3.   CERCLA: Comprehensive Environmental Response, Compensation, and Liability Act 1980, 1985, 1996.

4.   This is the case in Buchanan's (1969) example of a polluting monopolist when the subsidies required to correct the monopolistic behaviour are not available: Pigouvian taxes are then dominated by a quota which implements the second-best tax.

5.   See Calabresi (1970), Landes and Posner (1984, 1987), Shavell (1987), Menell (1991) and Boyer *et al.* (2000).

6.   The Superfund enabled the government to begin the clean-up of priority sites placed on the National Priority List (NPL) with money generated principally by taxes on crude oil, corporate income, petrochemical feed stocks, and motor fuels.

7.   'The term "owner or operator"' does not include a person, who, without participating in the management of a vessel or facility, holds indicia of ownership primarily to protect his security interest in the vessel or facility' (42 USAC., par. 9601, (21), 1988).

8.   See Strasser and Rodosevitch (1993), Pitchford (1995), Heyes (1996), Boyer and Laffont (1996, 1997), Boyd and Ingberman (1997), Dionne and Spaeter (1998), Gobert and Poitevin (1998) and Gobert (1999).

9.   15, *Environmental Law Reports* 20,994 (E.D. Pa 1985).

10. 632 F. Supp. 573 (d. Md. 1986).

11. 901 F. 2d 1550 (11th Circuit 1990) cert. denied, 498 USA 1046 (1991).

12. 910 F. 2d 668 (9th Circuit 1990).

13. See Chadd *et al.* (1991).

14. *National Oil and Hazardous Substances Pollution Contingency Plan; Lender Liability under CERCLA Final Rule*, 57 Fed. Reg. 18, 344 (1992), codified at 40 C.F.R. § 300.1100 to 1105 (1992).

15. *Publicker Indus., Inc.* v. *USA (In re* Cuyahoga Equip. Corp.*)*, 980 F. 2d 110, 118–119 (2d Cir. 1992); *Kelley ex rel. Mich. Natural Resources Comm'n* v. *Tisconia*, 810 F. Supp. 901, 907 (W.D. Mich. 1993); *Ashaland Oil, Inc.* v. *Sonford Prods. Corp.*, 810, F. Supp. 1057, 1060 (d. Minn. 1993), and others.

16. *Kelley* v. *USEPA*, 15 F. 3d 1100 (DC circuit 1994), cert. denied; *American Bankers Assoc. and Others* v. *Kelley*, 115 S. Ct. 900 (1995).

17. See Simons (1994).

18. H11766 Subtitle E, §§ 2501 to 2505 – Asset Conservation, Lender Liability, and Deposit Insurance Protection Act of 1996 (HR 3610).

19. See Henderson (1997).

20. See Kornhauser and Revesz (1994).

21. See Staton (1993).

22. For more on this issue, see *A. Johnson & Co.* v. *Aetna Casualty & Sur. Co.*, 933 F.2d 66 (1st Cir. 1991); *USA Fidelity & Guar. Co.* v. *George W. Whitesides Co.*, 932 F..2d 1169 (6th Cir. 1991).

23. In 1993, the European Commission published the *Green Paper on Remedying Environmental Damage* (COM (93) 47 final, Brussels, 14 May 1993, OJ 1993 C 149/12). It presented the broad concepts on which a liability system could be built and contained a description of the issues relevant to designing a Community-wide liability system. It led to discussions on the future EC liability regime through a debate aimed at collecting the opinions of the interested sectors and parties. It focused on the liability criteria, the definition of environmental damage, the right of non-governmental organizations to bring legal actions (the legal standing doctrine),

the insurability of environmental damage, the limitations of liability, the problem of rein-statement of the environment, the possibility of compensation funds financed by industries. In the same year, the Commission explored the possibility of joining the 1993 Council of Europe Lugano Convention, but a decision did not follow because of the intention to issue a specific White Paper and a Directive proposal. In November 1997, the *Working Paper on Environmental Liability* outlined the key elements of a proposed Directive on environmental liability and, in October 1998, a commitment to adopt a White Paper on Environmental Liability was stated (Commission Decision 2176/98 (24/9/98), *Towards Sustainability*, OJ 1998 L 2 75/12). The Commission published a detailed environmental liability model for the EC in March 1999.

24. See Bianchi (1994) and Poli (1999).
25. The European Commission justifies in the White Paper the choice of such a system as follows: first, the 'polluter pays principle' is more efficiently applied if the polluter must pay for the damages regardless of fault; second, the operator of a hazardous activity should bear the risk inherent in it; third, it can be difficult for the victims to prove the fault of the operator because of a lack of knowledge; fourth, a non-retroactive system allows a quicker consensus by restricting attention on care for future accident prevention only.
26. See Boyer and Porrini (2000).
27. Boyer and Laffont (1999) develop a theoretical model where the emergence of incentive market-based instruments is obtained endogenously rather than simply assumed.
28. See Cole and Grossman (1999).
29. See Cooter and Ulen (1999), Posner (1998), Chiancone and Porrini (1998).
30. See Laffont and Martimort (1999) and Boyer and Laffont (1999).
31. Considering the three elements, Shavell (1984) affirms that administrative costs and differences in knowledge favour liability, while incapacity to pay (or limited liability) and the probability of escaping suit favour regulation. In general, a liability system is more efficient when private parties possess better information and when accident has a low probability of occurrence. Regulation is better when harm is usually large, spread over many victims or takes a long time to show up, when accidents are not very rare events, and when standards or requirements are easy to find and control.
32. This framework is similar to the one proposed by Boyer and Laffont (1997). Although there is no direct role played in our current chapter by the two-period feature of the model, we elected to remain close to the Boyer–Laffont framework in order to reach a more integrated compared analysis with their paper and also with our forthcoming paper on the choice of instruments under adverse selection, where the multi-period feature is essential.
33. This corresponds to the basic reasoning of the judge in the *Fleet Factors* case.
34. The value of λ is non-negligible and considered to be of the order of 0.3 in developed countries and higher in developing ones.
35. Clearly the benevolent regulator as financier, as will be the case for the other principals, has market power in such a context but, increasing the firm's exogenous reservation utility would be equivalent to increasing the competitiveness of the lending market. No important result depends on this simplifying assumption of a zero reservation utility. Hence the approach taken here is more general than it may appear at first sight.
36. Although we concentrate here on $\Delta\psi$ and λ as variables and consider all other variables as parameters $(p_\ell, p_h, d, \pi_L, \pi_H, \theta, F, K)$, we could of course consider changes in any other parameters of the model.
37. *Stricto sensu* this case is ruled out if we stick to our assumption that $\Delta\psi < (p_\ell - p_h)d$.

REFERENCES

Bianchi, A. (1994), 'The harmonization of laws on liability for environmental damage in Europe: an Italian perspective', *Journal of Environmental Law* 6: 21–42.
Boyd, J. and D. Ingberman (1997), 'The search of deep pocket: is "extended liability" expensive liability?', *Journal of Law, Economics, and Organization* 13: 233–58.

Boyer, M. (1979), 'Les effets de la réglementation', *Canadian Public Policy/Analyze de Politiques* 4: 469–74.

Boyer, M. and J.J. Laffont (1996), 'Environmental protection, producer insolvency and lender liability', in A. Xepapadeas (ed.), *Economic Policy for the Environment and Natural Resources*, Cheltenham, UK and Northampton, MA: Edward Elgar, pp. 1–29.

Boyer, M. and J.J. Laffont (1997), 'Environmental risk and bank liability', *European Economic Review* 41: 1427–59.

Boyer, M. and J.J. Laffont (1999), 'Toward a political theory of the emergence of environmental incentive regulation', *Rand Journal of Economics* 41: 137–57.

Boyer, M., T.R. Lewis and W.L. Liu (2000), 'Setting standards for credible compliance and law enforcement', *Canadian Journal of Economics* (forthcoming).

Boyer, M. and D. Porrini (2000), 'The political economy of law versus regulation in environmental policy', mimeo, Université de Montréal and Università di Milano.

Buchanan, J.M. (1969), 'External economies, corrective taxes and market structure', *American Economic Review* 59: 174–7.

Buchanan, J.M. and G. Tullock (1975), 'Polluters' profits and political response', *American Economic Review* 65: 976–8.

Calabresi, G. (1970), *The Cost of Accident*, New Haven, CT: Yale University Press.

Chadd, C.M., T. Satinoven, L. Bergeson, R.W. Neuman and C.R. Briant (1991), 'Avoiding liability for hazardous waste: RCRA, CERCLA, and related corporate law issues', Corporate Practice Series 57, Washington, DC: Bureau of National Affairs.

Chiancone, A.and D. Porrini (1998), *Lezioni di Analisi Economica del Diritto*, 3rd edn, Rome: Giappichelli.

Cole, D.H. and P.Z. Grossman (1999), 'When is command-and-control efficient? Institutions, technology, and the competitive efficiency of alternative regulatory regimes for environmental protection', *Wisconsin Law Review* 45: 887–938.

Cooter, R. and T. Ulen (1999), *Law and Economics*, 3rd edn, New York: Addison-Wesley.

Cropper, M.L. and W.E. Oates (1992), 'Environmental economics: a survey', *Journal of Economic Literature* xxx, 1675–740.

Dionne, G. and S. Spaeter (1998), 'Environmental risks and extended liability: the case of green technologies', mimeo, École des HEC (Montréal).

Gobert, K. and M. Poitevin (1998), 'Environmental risks: should banks be liable?', mimeo, CIRANO, Université de Montréal.

Gobert, K. (1999), 'Responsabilité des créanciers en matière environnementale', mimeo, CIRANO, Université de Montréal.

Hahn, R.W. (1990), 'The political economy of environmental regulation: towards a unifying approach', *Public Choice* 65: 21–47.

Henderson, D.A. (1997), 'Congressional reform of lender and fiduciary liability under CERCLA and RCRA: is Fleet Factors finally dead?', *Banking Law Journal* 210–18.

Heyes, A. (1996), 'Lender penalty for environmental damage and the equilibrium cost of capital', *Economica* 63: 311–23.

Kornhauser, L.A. and R.L. Revesz (1994), 'Multidefendants settlements under joint and several liability: the problem of insolvency', *Journal of Legal Studies* 23: 517–42.

Laffont, J.J. (1995), 'Regulation, moral hazard and insurance for environmental risk', *Journal of Public Economics* 58: 319–36.

Laffont, J.J. and D. Martimort (1999), 'Separation of regulators against collusive behavior', *Rand Journal of Economics* 30: 232–62.

Landes, W. and R. Posner (1984), 'Tort law as a regulatory regime for catastrophic personal injuries', *Journal of Legal Studies* 13, 417–34.

Landes, W. and R. Posner (1987), *The Economic Structure of Tort Law*, Cambridge, MA: Harvard University Press.

Lewis, T.R. (1996), 'Protecting the environment when costs and benefits are privately known', *Rand Journal of Economics* 27: 819–47.

Menell, P.S. (1991), 'The limitations of legal institutions for addressing environmental risks', *Journal of Economic Perspectives* 5: 93–113.

Noll, R. (1983), 'The political foundations of regulatory policy', *Journal of Institutional and Theoretical Economics* 139: 377–404.

Pitchford, R. (1995), 'How liable should a lender be?', *American Economic Review* 85: 1171–86.

Poli, S. (1999), 'Shaping the EC regime on liability for environmental damage: progress or disillusionment?', *European Environmental Law Review* 11: 299–309.

Posner, R. (1998), *Economic Analysis of Law*, 5th edn, New York: Little, Brown.

Segerson, K. (1996), 'Issues in the Choice of environmental instruments', in J.B. Braden, H. Folmer and T.S. Ulen (eds), *Environmental Policy with Political and Economic Integration*, Cheltenham, UK and Brookfield: Edward Elgar.

Shavell, S. (1984), 'Liability for harms versus regulation of safety', *Journal of Legal Studies* 13: 357–74.

Shavell, S. (1987), *Economic Analysis of Accident Law*, Cambridge, MA: Harvard University Press.

Simons, R.P. (1994), 'The consequences of the overturning of the EPA lender liability rule', *Journal of Commercial Lending* 4: 43–7.

Staton, D.S. (1993), 'EPA's final rule on lender liability: lenders beware', *Business Lawyer* 49: 163–85.

Strasser, K.A. and D. Rodosevich (1993), 'Seeing the forest for the trees in CERCLA liability', *Yale Journal on Regulation* 10, 493–560.

Yohe, G.W. (1976), 'Polluter's profits and political response: direct control versus taxes: comment', *American Economic Review* 66: 981–2.

13. International harmonization of environmental law: theory with application to the European Union

Henry van Egteren and R. Todd Smith[1]

INTRODUCTION

The European Union has attempted, in recent years, to find the most effective manner in which to accommodate varying environmental traditions regarding liability for environmental damages. The two main traditions are negligence and strict liability.[2] Strict liability implies that an injurer is liable for the damages associated with an accident, regardless of the level of care taken by the injurer. Under simple negligence, the determination of liability for damages is a function of the injurer's level of care: if the injurer meets or exceeds the legal standard of care, as defined by the court, then the injurer's liability for damages is zero.

There are powerful distributional consequences associated with one type of tradition versus another. While negligence and strict liability both may be capable of inducing socially optimal levels of care, potential injurers would normally prefer negligence-based regulations since they can escape liability when they perform at a level of care at or above that which society deems 'optimal'.[3] Under strict liability, potential injurers are liable even when they accomplish what society deems optimal. In other words, a potential injurer is liable under more circumstances when strict liability is imposed than when negligence is imposed.

While the European Union would like to respect the environmental traditions of its member states, its most important objectives are to secure the environmental future of the region as well as to maintain or enhance the economic fortunes of its members. More often than not, these are conflicting goals. Therefore, in choosing a liability concept that will underpin important environmental statutes, policy-makers need to be aware of the differential impacts on environmental damage and economic activity one liability concept will have compared with another. In addition, implementation of this liability concept will be influenced by the distributional aspects identified above.

In this chapter we shall examine some of the theoretical (incentive) issues that arise in the harmonization of environmental statutes based on simple negligence or strict liability. Three types of harmonization are examined and compared to the socially optimal outcome. We begin by assuming that states all adopt negligence-based statutes but maintain the right to set legal standards of care (negligence with competing regulators). We then assume that states harmonize by agreeing to adopt environmental statutes based on strict liability. The final comparison involves negligence-based environmental statutes but this time we assume that individual states delegate standard-setting authority to a central planner (negligence with cooperating regulators).[4]

We find that strict liability and negligence with cooperative regulators can both implement the socially optimal outcome. Therefore, a group of states that compete for environmentally sensitive firms can achieve the socially optimal location pattern and levels of care for these firms by harmonizing their environmental statutes based on either strict liability or a negligence-based regime. The ability of cooperation to achieve the socially optimal outcome in a negligence-based regime is dependent upon one crucial assumption in the model referred to as unlimited scope of liability.[5]

The importance of the scope of liability was noted by, amongst others, Kahan (1989; see also Marks 1994). He argued that well-established economic models of torts (for example, Brown 1973: 323 or Shavell 1987) proceeded on the assumption that the scope of liability was unlimited. This meant that, if an injurer chose a level of care slightly lower than the legal standard of care, the injurer would be responsible for any accident that occurred, even if that accident would also have occurred had the injurer taken the legal standard of care. Alternatively, if an injurer chose a level of care equal to the legal standard of care, he would not be liable for damages if an accident occurred. Kahan argued that, in actual tort law, the scope of liability is limited, so that, when the injurer takes a level of care slightly below the legal standard of care, the injurer is liable only for accidents that occur because the level of care is lower, not for accidents that would have occurred anyway. He gave the following example, which is illuminating:

> Suppose the proper height of the fence is 10 feet, so that it is negligent to build a fence of less than 10 feet. Under the standard economic models of negligence, a cricket field owner who builds a fence 9 feet 11 inches rather than 10 feet is negligent and assumed to be liable for all injuries caused by balls that fly over the fence. In particular, he is assumed to be liable whether balls fly over at a height of 9 feet 11.5 inches, 11 feet, or even 100 feet.
>
> But, as a matter of common law, an injurer is only liable for accidents caused by his negligence. Therefore, the owner would not be liable for injuries from balls flying over the fence at heights exceeding 10 feet. Accidents caused by balls flying over at greater heights are not caused by his negligence since they would have occurred just

the same if the fence had been 10 feet high. Thus, if his fence is only 9 feet 11 inches rather than 10 feet, he is liable only for accidents caused by balls flying over the fence at a height between 9 feet 11 inches and 10 feet.[6]

In designing environmental statutes, however, legislators are not constrained by common law traditions. The scope of liability can be a choice variable rather than imposed by common law traditions. By choosing unlimited scope, so that the injurer is liable in a wider class of circumstances, our results show that a negligence-based regime can achieve the socially optimal outcome. Therefore, delegating responsibility for standard setting to a central authority, as might be feasible in the European Union, can implement the socially optimal outcome as long as potential injurers are responsible for any accident that occurs when they have less care than the legal standard specifies. By doing this, we maintain the distributional aspects of negligence-based regimes but do not sacrifice efficiency.

Several other studies have examined harmonization issues, for example, Carraro and Siniscalco (1992: 183); Hoel (1997: 241); Markusen *et al.* (1995: 55); Ulph (1996: 265); van Long and Siebert (1991: 296); Wellisch (1995: 290). None of these, however, has compared liability schemes – though they do use game theoretic techniques similar to ours. With special focus on the European Union, Rauscher (1991: 313) examines how the competition for firms by states within the Union impacts on economic welfare when there are transboundary externalities associated with the firms' activities. No mention, however, is made of alternative liability concepts (strict versus negligence-based). Our chapter does not allow for transboundary effects and focuses on alternative liability schemes. Oates (1998: 1) examines the claim that environmental standards need to be centralized. He summarizes the debate surrounding interjurisdictional competition but does not discuss the role of alternative liability schemes.

The legal literature also contains several studies that examine the issues surrounding harmonization within the European Union (for example, Bär and Kraemer 1998: 315 and Bianchi 1994: 21). None of these papers presents a formal model to analyse liability schemes and their impact on economic welfare.

In the next section, we present the model, originally introduced in van Egteren and Smith (2000). The third section introduces the benchmark case of the socially optimal locations and levels of care. We then discuss the first type of harmonization based on negligence with competing regulators. In the following two sections, we examine harmonization with strict liability and then harmonization with negligence and cooperating regulators. Conclusions are given in the final section. A technical appendix containing additional details of the derivations (and fully worked proofs of the propositions) is available from the authors or volume editor upon request.

THE MODEL

Assume there are two countries, $v \in \{j,k\}$, each interested in designing an environmental policy capable of balancing environmental concerns with economic concerns. The regulator wants to attract firms to its jurisdiction but at the same time, everything else equal, it wishes to minimize the environmental impact of attracting those firms. The set of relevant firms, $I = \{I, ..., n\}$, with typical element $i \in I$, includes only those firms capable of generating an environmental accident.

Countries first set environmental standards. Given these standards, firms then decide where to locate. Once located, firms choose a level of care. And finally, firms initiate production and nature determines which firms have environmental accidents.

Once the location decision is made, each firm combines local resources to produce output in that country. The only difference between firms is the inherent riskiness of production technologies. Since we assume unilateral precaution in accident prevention, riskiness is a function only of the firm's level of care $x \in X$, where X is a set of feasible care levels, as well as the firm's inherent risk type, $i \in I$. Thus, riskiness of production technologies is represented by the probability of having an accident, $P(x,i) \in [0,1]$, with the probability of an accident decreasing at a decreasing rate in the level of care, $P_x < 0$, and $P_{xx} > 0$; and, increasing at an increasing, constant or decreasing rate in the firm's risk type. The marginal productivity of care in reducing the probability of an accident can be increasing, constant or decreasing in the firm's risk type. We also assume that each firm is unique and that accident outcomes are independent across firms.

The firm's constrained expected profit function is:[7]

$$Y - C(x) - L \bullet AP(x,i), \qquad (13.1)$$

where Y is the fixed revenue of the firm, $C(x)$ is the constrained cost of care function and $L \bullet AP(x,i)$ is the expected liability of an environmental accident. This last component of firms' costs will depend on two things: the expected damages of an accident, and the proportion of these damages a firm is required to pay. This latter proportion is dependent on the liability scheme a particular jurisdiction has in place: simple negligence or strict liability.

If firm i locates in country v, and an accident occurs during the production process, then damages are measured by A_v, with $A_j > A_k$. Expected damages in jurisdiction v for a firm of type i are $P(x_{iv},i)A_v$, where x_{iv} is the level of care taken by a type i firm in country v. The proportion of these damages which the firm is required to pay is L. The value of L, which we discuss in detail below, is determined by the liability scheme in place. For now, we assume simply that $L \in [0,1]$.

For the constrained cost of care function, we assume $C(x) > 0$ for $x > 0$, and $C(0) = 0$. In addition, we assume costs of care are increasing at an increasing rate in the level of care so that $C'(x) > 0$, and $C''(x) > 0*$ for all $x \in X$.

We shall make no *a priori* judgement about how revenue varies across countries or across firms. Note that the set $\{Y_j, Y_k\}$ could depend on firm type i; though to lighten the notational burden we shall drop this index in the analysis that follows.

THE SOCIALLY OPTIMAL LOCATIONS AND LEVELS OF CARE

If the regulators can choose levels of care and locations directly, then they would be interested in maximizing aggregate net benefits defined as:

$$\sum_{v=j,k}\left[Y_v - C(x_{iv}) - P(x_{iv},i)A_v\right]. \tag{13.2}$$

Since revenues are fixed, finding the optimal location pattern and levels of care is equivalent to solving $\min_{x_{iv}} C(x_{iv}) + P(x_{iv},i)A_v$ for each jurisdiction.

While corner solutions are relevant (case iii below), it is useful to determine an interior solution by specifying the first-order condition for each $i \in I$ and $v \in \{j,k\}$ as:

$$C'(x^*_{iv}) + P_x(x^*_{iv},i)A_v = 0, \tag{13.3}$$

where $x_{iv} = x^*_{iv}$ is the standard that satisfies the first-order condition. This occurs when the marginal costs of care are just equal to the avoided marginal expected damages. Given this calculation, maximum net benefit possible in jurisdiction v is:

$$N_{Bv}(x^*_{iv}) \equiv Y_v - C(x^*_{iv},i) - P(x^*_{iv},i)A_v. \tag{13.4}$$

Regulators can now achieve their objective by forcing firms to locate in jurisdictions that produce the highest net benefits.

Optimal Location of Firms

Regulators must be concerned about three possible cases that can arise: (a) a firm could potentially generate positive net benefits in either jurisdiction (depending on the specified level of care); (b) a firm could generate positive net benefits in only one jurisdiction (regardless of the required level of care); and (c) a firm could generate only negative net benefits in either jurisdiction (for any level of care). The manner in which to interpret these changing assumptions regarding net benefits is to suppose that each of (cases i–iii) is associated with a different group of risk types. With that interpretation, as one considers increasingly risky firms, one moves from positive net benefits in both jurisdictions (case i) to positive net benefits in only one jurisdiction (case ii), and finally to the case where firm risk is so high that neither country can generate positive net benefits (case iii).

Consider case i and assume that maximum net benefits are higher in jurisdiction j, so society wishes the firm to locate in j. The socially optimal level of care is to have firm i operate at x^*_{ij}.

Alternatively, if maximum net benefits are highest in jurisdiction k, then the firm should locate in jurisdiction k and operate at x^*_{ik}.

In case ii, one jurisdiction can sustain only negative net benefits so society wants to ensure that the firm does not locate in jurisdiction k. It should locate in j at a care of x^*_{ij}.

The third case assumes that the firm cannot generate positive net benefits in either jurisdiction and as a result, the socially optimal outcome is to ensure that the firm shuts down. The levels of care that would ensure this are any $x_{ij} > x^s_{ij}$ and any $x_{ik} > x^s_{ik}$, where:

$$Y_j - C(x^s_{ij}) = Y_k - C(x^s_{ik}) = 0. \tag{13.5}$$

As the risk types for the firms vary, we can expect firms to locate in different jurisdictions depending on things like revenues, costs and expected liability in each jurisdiction. In general, one would expect a mix of risk types across countries. None the less, the following presents a special case in which it is socially optimal to have all firms locate in one jurisdiction.

Proposition 1   If $Y_k \geq Y_j$, then the socially optimal outcome is to have all firms locate in jurisdiction k regardless of their type.

This result is not surprising. If jurisdiction k has lower damages, $A_k < A_j$, and higher revenues, $Y_k \geq Y_j$, then at the socially optimal outcome all firms would locate in k. While this possibility is of some interest, we shall henceforth rule this out by assuming that $Y_j > Y_k$.

HARMONIZATION BASED ON NEGLIGENCE WITH COMPETING REGULATORS

If jurisdictional standard setting remains in the domain of individual states, then harmonizing negligence-based environmental regulations promotes competition for firms as regulators set standards strategically. Intuition – and popular conception – suggests that the incentive to undercut the standards of a rival jurisdiction leads to a race-for-the-bottom in standards. While this intuition is essentially correct, it is incomplete. In order to gain added insight into this problem, we analyse a strategic game involving two players, jurisdictions j and k. The strategies for each player are the regulatory standards that specify the levels of care for the firm which determine when the firm is liable for damages once an accident occurs.

The location decision of the firm, which we refer to as $\Lambda \in \{0,1\}$, is a function of the regulatory standards in each jurisdiction. Thus, $\Lambda_j(s_{ij},s_{ik})$ represents firm i's location decision. If this is equal to one, then the firm has decided to locate in jurisdiction j. If it is zero, then the firm has decided to locate in jurisdiction k.

Prospective firm profits across jurisdictions determine the location decision, and firm profits are influenced by whether or not the firm will choose to adhere to the standard. Firms attempt to maximize profits, but because revenues are fixed a firm will choose a level of care, and a location, based on the standards offered by the regulator. Given the standards in each jurisdiction, a type-i firm attempts to:

$$\min_{x_{iv}} C(x_{iv}) + L(x_{iv},s_{iv})P(x_{iv},i)A_v \qquad (13.6)$$

where $L(x_{iv},s_{iv})$ is the firm's liability under negligence. Specifically, liability is determined according to:

$$L(\cdot) = \begin{cases} 0 & \text{if } x_{iv} \geq s_{iv} \\ 1 & \text{if } x_{iv} < s_{iv}. \end{cases} \qquad (13.7)$$

When the scope of liability is unlimited, it is well known that $x_{iv} = s_{iv}$ solves (13.6) for all $s_{iv} \in [0,\bar{x}_{iv}]$, where $\bar{x}_{iv}$ is defined implicitly by:[8]

$$C(\bar{x}_{iv}) = \min_{x_{iv}} C(x_{iv}) + P(x_{iv},i)A_v. \qquad (13.8)$$

For standards above $\bar{x}_{iv}$ the firm can lower its costs by ignoring the standard even though it will now be liable for damages. If standards offered by the regulators are to be feasible, then they must be less than or equal to $\bar{x}_{iv}$. For all standards that are feasible, the firm finds it optimal to set its care level equal to the standard.

Under simple negligence, expected profits for firm i when it locates in jurisdiction $v \in \{j,k\}$ are:

$$\pi\left(x_{iv}, s_{iv}; Y_v, A_v\right) = \begin{cases} Y_v - C\left(x_{iv}\right) & \text{if } x_{iv} \geq s_{iv} \\ Y_v - C\left(x_{iv}\right) - P\left(x_{iv}, i\right)A_v & \text{if } x_{iv} < s_{iv}. \end{cases} \quad (13.9)$$

The expected net benefits to a particular jurisdiction will depend upon the location decision of the firm, the profits once the firm has made a positive location decision, and the expected accident costs. Therefore, the expected net benefits to jurisdiction j are:

$$EB_j(s_{ij}, s_{ik}) = \Lambda_j(s_{ij}, s_{ik})[Y_j - C(x_{ij}) - P(x_{ij}, i)A_j]. \quad (13.10)$$

Definition 1 Let $B_j(s_{ik}) = \{s_{ij} - EB_j(s_{ij}, s_{ik}) \geq EB_j(s_{ij}, s_{ik}) - s_{ij} \in X\}$ be jurisdiction $j = s$ best-reply mapping for a type i firm given $s_{ik} \in X$.

The best-reply mapping for jurisdiction k, $B_k(s_{ij})$, is defined in a similar manner.

Definition 2 A Nash equilibrium is a pair of strategies, (s_{ij}^n, s_{ik}^n), such that $s_{ij}^n \in B_j(s_{ik}^n)$ and $s_{ik}^n \in B_k(s_{ij}^n)$.

In what follows, we define each jurisdiction's best-reply mapping and then determine where these best-reply mappings intersect. These intersections will constitute the set of Nash equilibria.

To characterize the Nash equilibria, we first need to define some threshold values for the standards of care.

Definition 3 Let s^1, s^2, s^3, s^4 and s^5 be defined implicitly by the following conditions (these also apply if j is switched with k):

(a) s^1: $Y_j - C(s_{ij}^1) - P(s_{ij}^1, i)A_j = 0$ for any $i \in I$;

(b) s^2: $Y_j - C(s_{ij}^1) = Y_k - C(s_{ij}^2)$ with $i \in I$;

(c) s^3: $Y_j - C(s_{ij}^3) = Y_k - (s_{ik}^*)$ with $i \in I$, s_{ik}^* defined in (13.3);

(d) s^4: $Y_k = Y_j - C(s_{ij}^4)$ with $i \in I$; and

(e) s^5: defined in (13.8), as $s^5 = \bar{x}$.

The definitions are made more transparent after examining Figures 13.1 and 13.2. The standard s^1 identifies the level of care at which the regulator receives zero net benefit. The standard s^2 specifies a standard that makes the firm indifferent between jurisdictions given that the regulator is receiving zero net benefits. In Figure 13.1, indifference between jurisdictions is captured by the equality of the distances *ab* and *cd*.

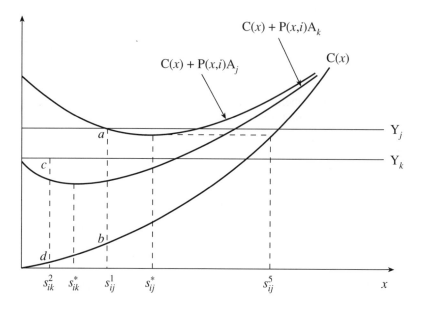

Note: $ab = cd$.

Figure 13.1   Definition 3

The standard s^3 ensures that the firm is indifferent between locations when the standard offered in the opposing jurisdiction is the standard that maximizes net benefits in that jurisdiction, s^*, $ab = cd$ in Figure 13.2.

The standard s^4 is found by specifying a standard that makes the firm indifferent between jurisdictions when the opposing standard is zero. This is $ef = gh$ in Figure 13.2. And finally, s^5 is defined in (13.8) and depicted graphically in Figure 13.1.

The Best-reply Mappings

The best-reply mappings, and any Nash equilibria, depend upon the potential net benefits available to the regulators. These are affected by the riskiness of the firm. As discussed above, there are three risk categories of relevance. The first category (case i) involves firms that have the potential to produce positive net benefits for any jurisdiction. This is not to imply that net benefits need always be positive, but rather, they are positive for at least one level of care.

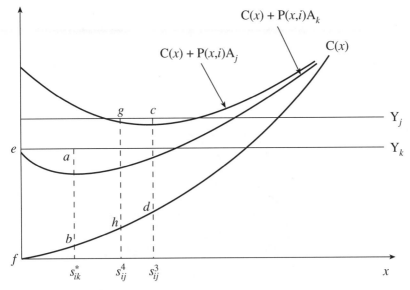

Note: $ab = cd$ and $ef = gh$.

Figure 13.2 Definition 3

The second and third risk categories follow logically from the first. As riskiness increases, the firm is capable of generating positive net benefits in only one and then in neither jurisdiction (cases ii and iii, respectively). To determine the equilibrium standards and location of firms as one moves across risk types, one simply uses the appropriate best-reply mappings as described in the three possible cases. The technical appendix available from the author contains a formal characterization of best-reply mappings for the three cases.

Case i: The firm can generate positive net benefits in either jurisdiction
Figure 13.3 depicts jurisdiction j's best-reply mapping.[9] Using jurisdiction j was an arbitrary choice and the symmetry of the two jurisdictions means that k's best-reply mapping could be represented simply by interchanging k with j in what follows.

Segment a The standard s_{ik}^2 defines a level of care that makes the firm indifferent between jurisdictions when j is offering a standard that allows it to receive zero net benefits. For all standards below s_{ik}^2, the firm would prefer to locate in k. Thus, in order to compete, the regulator in j would have to lower its standard resulting in negative net benefits for j (see Figure 13.1 for an aid in the

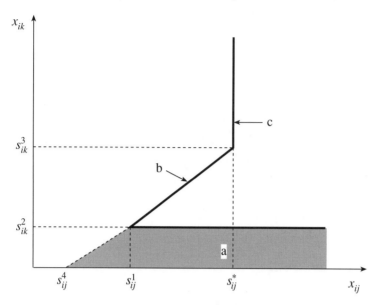

Notes: Since $s^4_{ij} > 0 \Rightarrow s^3_{ik} < 0$, by lemma (see technical appendix available from the author).

Figure 13.3   *Jurisdiction j's best-reply mapping for case i*

analysis). Thus, for standards below s^2_{ik}, the regulator is better off ensuring that the firm locates in k. Thus, for any of these low standards, the regulator in j finds a standard that would make the firm indifferent between locations and then offers anything higher. Formally, we have:

$$\text{for all } s_{ik} \in [0, s^2_{ik}], \; \{s_{ij} \mid s_{ij} > s^6_{ij}\} \in B_j(s_{ik}),$$

where s^6_{ij} satisfies $Y_k - C(s_{ik}) = Y_j - C(s^6_{ij})$.

Segment b   As the standard in k rises beyond s^2_{ik}, jurisdiction j is now capable of competing for the firm. Consequently, for any standard in k that is an element of $[s^2_{ik}, s^3_{ik}]$ the regulator finds the standard in j that makes the firm indifferent between locations and then undercuts this, thereby attracting the firm to j. Formally, we have:

$$\text{for all } s_{ik} \in [s^2_{ik}, s^3_{ik}], \; s_{ij} = s^6_{ij} - \xi \in B_j(s_{ik}),$$

where $\xi > 0$ and s^6_{ij} satisfies $Y_k - C(s_{ik}) = Y_j - C(s^6_{ij})$.

Segment c   When s_{ik} rises above s_{ik}^2, the regulator in j can attract the firm by offering s_{ik}^3, the standard that maximizes net benefits in j. Thus, for all standards above s_{ik}^3, the regulator does not wish to raise the standard in j as this would lower net benefits. Thus, we have:

$$\text{for } \{s_{ik} - s_{ik} > s_{ik}^3\},\ s_{ij} = s_{ij}^* \in B_j(s_{ik}).$$

Case ii: The firm can generate positive net benefits in only one jurisdiction

In this second scenario, one jurisdiction continues to have an interest in attracting the firm (net benefits are potentially positive), while the other jurisdiction will not be able to obtain positive net benefits regardless of what standard it offers. Not surprisingly, the best-reply mapping for the jurisdiction that may be able to generate positive net benefits is identical to the best-reply mapping described in case i. The best-reply mapping for the other jurisdiction is different from case i because this jurisdiction wishes to discourage the firm from locating in it under all circumstances. Specifically, assuming for illustration purposes that jurisdiction k is the jurisdiction that receives negative net benefits for any standard if the firm locates in k, $B_k(s_{ij})$ has three segments, as depicted in Figure 13.4.

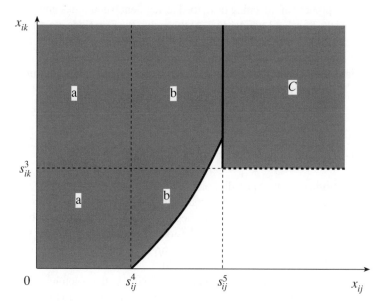

Notes: Since $s_{ij}^4 > 0 \Rightarrow s_{ik}^4 < 0$, by lemma (see technical appendix available from the author).

Figure 13.4   Jurisdiction k's *best-reply mapping for case ii*

Segment a   The standard s_{ij}^4 specifies a level of care in jurisdiction j that makes the firm indifferent between jurisdictions when it is assumed that the firm faces a zero standard in jurisdiction k. Thus, for all standards below s_{ij}^4 the regulator in k can keep the firm from locating domestically by offering any non-negative standard. This yields:

$$\text{for all } s_{ij} \in [0, s_{ij}^4], \{s_{ik} \mid s_{ik} \geq 0\} \in B_k(s_{ij}).$$

Segment b   Along this interval of standards for j, the regulator in k must be careful since some standards offered in k are now capable of attracting the firm, something the regulator in k does not want. Therefore, for any standard offered in j, the regulator in k finds a standard that makes the firm indifferent as to location and then offers any standard greater than this amount. Formally, we have:

$$\text{for all } s_{ij} \in [s_{ij}^4, s_{ij}^5], \{s_{ik} \mid s_{ik} > s_{ik}^6\} \in B_k(s_{ij}),$$

where s_{ik}^6 satisfies $Y_j - C(s_{ij}) = Y_k - C(s_{ik}^6)$.

Segment c   The process of matching described in segment b continues until the standard in j hits the threshold standard s_{ij}^5. At this point, the firm finds it optimal to ignore the standard set by the regulator and instead choose s_{ij}^* and face the liability. The regulator in k understands this and determines the standard s_{ik}^3 which will make the firm indifferent between locations. It then offers anything higher than s_{ik}^3. Formally, we have:

$$\text{for } \{s_{ij} - s_{ij} > s_{ij}^5\}, \{s_{ik} \mid s_{ik} > s_{ik}^3\} \in B_k(s_{ij}).$$

Case iii: The firm cannot generate positive net benefits in either jurisdiction

In this third possibility, neither jurisdiction is capable of achieving positive net benefits, even if standards are zero. One could imagine that such a scenario is plausible for higher-risk firms. Since only negative net benefits are possible, competition is re-established but now jurisdictions are competing to force the firm to locate in the opposing jurisdiction. This might be interpreted as a form of the 'not in my backyard', or NIMBY, scenario.

The intuition behind these best-reply mappings is simply that each jurisdiction chooses a sufficiently high standard that the firm either wishes to locate in the other jurisdiction or to shut down. The threshold standards s_{ij}^s and s_{ik}^s identify standards of sufficient stringency as to cause the firm to shut down or locate somewhere else. When the standard in the opposing jurisdiction exceeds the threshold, the best reply is to similarly impose a standard above the threshold in order to ensure the firm does not locate in your jurisdiction. In comparison, if the standard in the opposing jurisdiction is less than the threshold, then the required standard to ensure the firm locates elsewhere is correspondingly lower.

Figure 13.5 illustrates the best-reply mapping for jurisdiction j. This best-reply mapping is defined formally as follows:

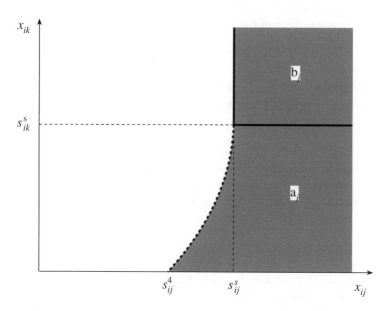

Notes: Since $s_{ij}^4 > 0 \Rightarrow s_{ik}^4 < 0$, by lemma (see technical appendix available from the author).

Figure 13.5   Jurisdiction j's *best-reply mapping for case iii*

Segment a

$$\text{for all } s_{ij} \in [0, s_{ik}^s], \{s_{ij} \mid s_{ij} > s_{ij}^6\} \in \mathrm{B}_j(s_{ik}),$$

where s_{ij}^6 satisfies $\mathrm{Y}_k - \mathrm{C}(s_{ik}) = \mathrm{Y}_j - \mathrm{C}(s_{ij}^6)$.

Segment b

$$\text{for } \{s_{ij} - s_{ik} \geq s_{ik}^s\}, \{s_{ij} \mid s_{ij} \geq s_{ij}^s\} \in \mathrm{B}_j(s_{ik}).$$

Nash Equilibrium

Nash equilibria are defined by the intersection of the two best-reply mappings we have outlined for the three cases. While we may have multiple equilibria in this model, depending upon parameters, we are only interested in standards of care and the location characteristics of any Nash equilibrium. As a result, refinements of the Nash equilibrium concept will not give us any new information on the characteristics about which we are interested.

Proposition 2   The set of Nash equilibria for case i can only involve intersections of the best-reply mapping for jurisdiction j and jurisdiction k, respectively, of the following segment types

$$(a_j, b_k), (a_j, c_k), (b_j, a_k), \text{ and } (c_j, a_k).$$

Since any equilibrium in case i involves segment a, one jurisdiction is earning zero net benefits . For all equilibria in which one jurisdiction is earning positive net benefits, the location pattern is determined by that country. Suppose the Nash equilibrium is (a_j, c_k) (the case (c_j, a_k) results in opposite location patterns). In this event, the firm will locate in jurisdiction k and face the standard, s^*_{ik}. This is optimal for jurisdiction j because the standard in jurisdiction k is low enough that it induces a negative net benefit in jurisdiction j if the regulator in j lowers its standard to attract the firm. Indeed, in order to avoid this j outcome, the regulator in j may actually raise its standard to ensure the firm locates elsewhere.

The equilibria in the proposition tell us that competition for firms need not erode environmental standards completely. It is possible to have equilibria involving the socially optimal standard. Moreover, regardless of whether standards in any equilibria are efficient or not, the location pattern need not be socially optimal. To see this, suppose maximum net benefits are higher in jurisdiction j and the type of Nash equilibrium that results from competition is characterized by jurisdiction j receiving zero net benefits and the firm locating in k (that is, an equilibrium of type (a_j, c_k)). If this were true, then competition for firms under simple negligence cannot replicate the cooperative location pattern, since the socially optimal outcome would have the firm locating in j, the jurisdiction capable of generating the highest net benefit. In order for this situation to arise, assuming (a_j, c_k) as the type of Nash equilibrium we are examining, we require net benefits to be higher in jurisdiction j and firm profits to be higher in jurisdiction k: $Y_j - C(s^*_{ij}) - P(s^*_{ij},i)A_j > Y_k - C(s^*_{ik}) - P(s^*_{ik},i)A_k$ and $Y_k - C(s^*_{ik}) > Y_j - C(s^l_{ij})$. These inequalities imply $C(s^*_{ij}) + P(s^*_{ij},i)A_j < C(s^l_{ij}) + P(s^*_{ik},i)A_k$, or $C(s^*_{ij}) - C(s^l_{ij}) < P(s^*_{ik},i)A_k - P(s^*_{ij},i)A_j$. Thus, the issue is whether or not the last inequality can be true given the assumptions of the model.

Figure 13.6 illustrates expected damages and demonstrates that this may or may not be true depending upon the value of the standards, the curvature of the probability function and the difference in damages. In this figure, there are two values for s^*_{ij}. The first value ensures that $P(s^*_{ik},i)A_k - P(s^*_{ij},i)A_j$ is positive. Thus, it is possible for our claim to be correct. The difference need only be larger than the difference in costs: $C(s^*_{ij}) - C(s^I_{ij})$. The second, higher value ensures that $(Ps^*_{ik},i)A_k - P(s^*_{ij},i)A_j$ is negative. In that case, our claim would not be true, since $s^*_{ij} > s^I_{ij}$ and $C' > 0$.

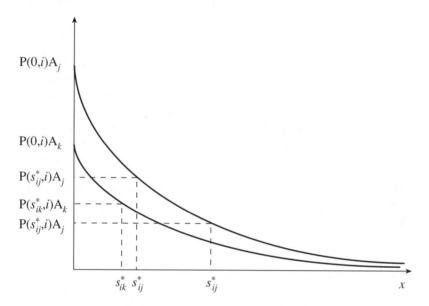

Figure 13.6 Expected damages

When there is potential to generate positive net benefits in either country, competition need not yield the socially optimal location pattern nor the socially optimal standards. It is possible then that firms locate in the wrong country and at standards that are too lax.

Proposition 3 The set of Nash equilibria in case ii can only involve inter-sections of the best-reply mapping for jurisdiction j and jurisdiction k, respectively, of the following segment types:

$$(b_j,a_k),(b_j,b_k), \text{ and } (c_j,b_k).$$

Case ii may be interpreted as a situation involving medium-risk firms that are capable of generating positive net benefits in only certain jurisdictions. As a result, there is no obvious competition for the firm. It should not be surprising then that negligence-based harmonization of statutes in which regulators compete in standards is now capable of achieving the socially optimal location pattern. In the case discussed here, location always occurs in jurisdiction j, the jurisdiction assumed to be capable of sustaining positive net benefits.

A surprising implication of the proposition is that the socially optimal standard is not guaranteed, even though there is no natural competition for the firm. It may arise as in the case of (c_j, b_k) intersection, but may also be below the socially optimal level as in intersections (b_j, a_k) and (b_j, b_k) This seems odd because both jurisdictions want the firm to locate in jurisdiction j, so why cannot we implement the cooperative outcome as a Nash equilibrium? This occurs because of the divergence between the firm's objective function and the regulator's objective function under negligence. Thus, it is not competition *per se* that generates the distortion in this case. Rather, it is the possibility that, at the socially optimal outcome, with net benefits higher in jurisdiction j, it is still possible that firm profits are higher in k. Because of this possibility, jurisdiction j and jurisdiction k are, in essence, working together, or towards the same objective when they distort standards away from their socially optimal levels.

Proposition 4   The set of Nash equilibria in case iii implement the socially optimal outcome and involve intersections of the best-reply mapping for jurisdiction j and jurisdiction k, respectively, of the following segment types:

$$(b_j, b_k).$$

This result implies that all Nash equilibria are characterized by the firm shutting down. Equilibrium standards are equal to or greater than the levels of care at which the firm would wish to shut down. As a result, negligence-based harmonization with competition in standards achieves the socially optimal outcome when the firm cannot generate positive net benefits in either jurisdiction.

In this case, one's intuition about a race for the top with respect to the environmentally risky firm is re-established. But again, the intuition of this argument is incomplete. Competition does lead to rising standards, but since net benefits in either jurisdiction are always negative, zero net benefits is a more desirable outcome. Therefore, competition is in some sense costless. If the outcome from competition is to shut the firm down, which ultimately will be the case, then both jurisdictions are strictly better off. In this scenario, both jurisdictions have an inexhaustible supply of higher standards with which to compete. In the end, it is the firm that runs out of feasible alternatives.

HARMONIZATION BASED ON STRICT LIABILITY

In this section, states agree to harmonize environmental statutes based on strict liability. This situation has been proposed recently by the European Union.

Under these circumstances, states agree that the firm will be automatically and strictly liable for all damages, regardless of the level of care it may have been using.

Proposition 5 Strict liability achieves the socially optimal outcome.

To see this, note that strict liability transforms the firm's objective into

$$\max\nolimits_{x_{ij}} Y_j - C(x_{ij}) - P(x_{ij},i)A_j. \tag{13.11}$$

The firm solves this problem for each jurisdiction and then compares the value of its profits in each country. These objective functions mirror those of individual countries in the socially optimal solution and thus the solutions will be $x^*_{ij} = s^*_{ij}$ and $x^*_{ik} = s^*_{ik}$. These standards effectively implement the socially optimal outcome because the firm is now comparing profits in the two countries where profits are exactly net benefits to the regulator. Thus, the firm will locate in the jurisdiction with the highest net benefits at a level of care which maximizes net benefits. But this means that, at these standards, the countries are achieving the same net benefits they would have received had a social planner chosen directly location and the firm's level of care.

In theory, then, the recent proposal by the European Union to adopt strict liability as the basis for adjudicating environmental accidents appears to make sense in that the socially optimal outcome can be achieved. However, this brings with it certain distributional consequences that may be controversial. Therefore, it is also of interest to explore negligence-based regimes that are capable of achieving the socially optimal solution.[10]

HARMONIZATION BASED ON NEGLIGENCE WITH COOPERATING REGULATORS

Suppose that harmonization involves regulations that are negligence-based so each jurisdiction has agreed to adjudicate environmental accidents using a legal standard of care that defines the circumstances under which a firm will be liable. The difference now, as compared to the case of 'negligence with competing regulators', is that the states have agreed to let a central authority specify these legal standards of care for each state.

Under full cooperation between regulators, the central planner will choose a pair of care levels for a specific firm type, one for each jurisdiction, so as to maximize aggregate net benefits. The planner, however, cannot choose directly the levels of care, x_{iv}, for the firm; it can only specify standards of care that induce appropriate levels of care and appropriate locations for firms. Consequently, the planner first solves the firm's problem in order to determine how the firm will respond to any given set of standards. Using this information, it can then choose standards so as to induce efficient care levels and location decisions so that (13.2) is maximized.

Optimal Standards and Location of Firms Under Cooperative Regulation

In light of the above discussion, the standards a planner would offer depend on the location that is capable of producing the highest net benefits for a firm of a given risk type. The three risk categories identified earlier are again relevant.

Suppose jurisdiction j is the socially preferred location in case i. Cooperative standards need to ensure that location occurs in j and that the firm's actual level of care maximizes net benefits, x^*_{ij}. If the regulator offers $s^*_{ij} = x^*_{ij}$, then the firm would choose to meet the standard if it located in j. The firm will locate in j only if its profits are higher in j than in k. Note that net benefits can be largest in j while profits are higher in k, depending upon what standards are offered. In order to determine the standard to be offered in k alongside s^*_{ij}, the regulators find the standard in k that makes the firm indifferent between locations. Specifically, the regulators calculate s^3_{ik}, where s^3_{ik} is defined implicitly by:

$$Y_j - C(s^*_{ij}) = Y_k - C(s^3_{ij}).$$ (13.12)

Upon finding this value, the regulators would offer s^*_{ij} and any $s_{ij} > s^3_{ik}$ as the cooperative standards. This will ensure the firm locates in j and operates at a level of care that maximizes net benefits.

In a similar fashion, when the socially optimal location is in k, the cooperative standards would be s^*_{ik} and any $s_{ij} > s^3_{ij}$.

If the firm is capable of generating positive net benefits in only one jurisdiction (case ii), with jurisdiction j being the socially preferred location, then cooperative standards are determined in the same manner as case i.

When the firm is very high risk (case iii), the socially optimal outcome is to ensure the firm shuts down. Thus, cooperative standards are any $s_{ij} > x^s_{ij}$ and $s_{ik} > x^s_{ik}$, where:

$$Y_j - C(x^s_{ij}) = Y_k - C(x^s_{ik}) = 0.$$ (13.13)

Summarizing the three cases yields:

Proposition 6   When the scope of liability is unlimited, negligence-based cooperative standards regulation achieves the socially optimal outcome.

While it may not be surprising that cooperation generates a socially optimal outcome, the result is important because it was shown in van Egteren and Smith (2000) that, when the scope of liability is limited, negligence-based cooperative standards regulation does not guarantee the socially optimal outcome. Our result indicates that if a group of states, such as the European Union, decides to delegate jurisdictional standard setting to a central authority, then negligence-based regulations that embody unlimited scope of liability are capable of achieving the socially optimal outcome. Unlimited scope would imply that, if an accident occurred and a firm had chosen a level of care different from that specified by the central authority as the legal standard of care, the firm would be liable automatically for damages. Alternatively, because regulations are negligence based, firms would not be penalized for pursuing the socially optimal level of care when an accident occurs.

CONCLUSIONS

The liability concepts inherent in many environmental regulations play an integral role in determining how firms choose levels of care and where they locate. These liability concepts influence the size and the frequency of environmentally hazardous accidents.

A key finding of the chapter is that harmonization can achieve the socially optimal location pattern and levels of care for the firm. If harmonization is negligence based, then states must be willing to delegate standard-setting authority to a central planner and adopt unlimited scope of liability. If states are unwilling to give up the autonomy required to achieve the social optimum under negligence-based harmonization, they can harmonize using strict liability as the basis for statutes. This brings with it a different distribution of benefits and costs as firms are liable for damages even if they achieve levels of care that would be deemed socially optimal. Alternatively, states may pursue negligence-based harmonization and maintain autonomy over standard setting. This will achieve the socially optimal outcome when firms are particularly risky, but will only achieve the socially optimal location pattern if firms are of medium risk. The major problem associated with adopting this type of harmonization is that it fails to generate the socially optimal location pattern and level of care when firms are low risk and most desirable in that they can produce positive net benefits in either jurisdiction.

The above results notwithstanding, there are several important considerations that need to be addressed in future research. Given what is already known about the impact of limited liability or inability to pay on the desirability of strict liability in other contexts, our assumption that firms have sufficient assets to cover environmental liabilities is particularly important. Indeed, the recent

White Paper issued by the European Union points to the fact that insurance is not required for firms that are environmentally risky. Thus, this area of research seems particularly important.

We have assumed that there are no transboundary effects associated with an environmental accident. Given the close proximity of states within the European Union, expanding this aspect of the analysis seems appropriate. Third, we have assumed that any profits earned by the firm remain within the jurisdiction in which they are located. While this may be true in many situations, it is certainly not true for all cases.

NOTES

1. Smith thanks SSHRC of Canada for financial assistance.
2. While these are common law concepts, civil jurisdictions within the European Union have similar concepts. See Faure and Van den Bergh (1987: 95–114) for an analysis of strict liability and negligence under Belgium's code civil.
3. See Cooter and Ulen (1996) for a demonstration of this result.
4. We do not examine negligence-based harmonization in which there are uniform standards across jurisdictions. The economics literature has dealt with this possibility and there appears to be a consensus that this type of response is rarely optimal when states are heterogeneous. Such is the case in this model, and it is fairly straightforward to demonstrate that uniform standards are not optimal.
5. If the scope of liability is limited, then giving up standard-setting autonomy to a central planner is not sufficient to ensure the socially optimal outcome as shown in van Egteren and Smith (2000).
6. Kahan (1989: 429).
7. A formal derivation of this function is in the technical appendix available from the author.
8. See for example, Cooter and Ulen (1996). See Figure 13.1 for a graphical interpretation.
9. Not all these segments need exist for every parameterization of the model. However, this is the most general representation.
10. Other aspects of strict liability and negligence-based regimes are discussed in the conclusions.

REFERENCES

Bär, S. and R.A. Kraemer (1998), 'European environmental policy after Amsterdam', *Journal of Environmental Law* 10(2): 315–30.

Bianchi, A. (1994), 'The harmonization of laws on liability for environmental damage in Europe: an Italian perspective', *Journal of Environmental Law* 6(1): 21–42.

Brander, J. and B. Spencer (1985), 'Export subsidies and market share rivalry', *Journal of International Economics* 18: 83–100.

Brown, J. (1973), 'Toward an economic theory of liability', *Journal of Legal Studies* 13: 323–49.

Carraro, C. and D. Siniscalco (1992), 'Environmental innovation policy and international competition', *Environmental and Resource Economics* 2(2): 183–200.

Cooter, R. and T. Ulen (1996), *Law and Economics*, 2nd edn, New York: HarperCollins.

Faure, M. and R. Van den Bergh (1987), 'Negligence, strict liability and regulation of safety under Belgian law: an introductory economic analysis', *Geneva Papers on Risk and Insurance* 12(43): 95–114.

Hoel, M. (1997), 'Environmental policy with endogenous plant locations', *Scandinavian Journal of Economics* 99(2): 241–59.

Kahan, M. (1989), 'Causation and the incentives to take care under the negligence rule', *Journal of Legal Studies* 18: 427–47.

Marks, S. (1994), 'Discontinuities, causation, and Grady's uncertainty theorem', *Journal of Legal Studies* 23: 287–301.

Markusen, J., E. Morey and N. Olewiler (1995), 'Competition in regional environmental policies when plant locations are endogenous', *Journal of Public Economics* 56: 55–77.

Oates, W. (1998), 'Environmental policy in the European Community: harmonization or national standards?', *Empirica* 25: 1–13.

Rauscher, M. (1991), 'National environmental policies and the effects of economic integration', *European Journal of Political Economy* 7: 313–29.

Shavell, S. (1987), *Economic Analysis of Accidents*, Cambridge, MA: Harvard University Press.

Ulph, A. (1996), 'Environmental policy and international trade when governments and producers act strategically', *Journal of Environmental Economics and Management* 30: 265–81.

van Egteren, H. and R.T. Smith (2000), 'Environmental regulations under simple negligence or strict liability', unpublished manuscript.

van Long, N. and H. Siebert (1991), 'Institutional competition versus *ex ante* harmonization: the case of environmental policy', *Journal of Institutional and Theoretical Economics* 147: 296–311.

Wellisch, D. (1995), 'Locational choice of firms and decentralized environmental policy with various instruments', *Journal of Urban Economics* 37: 290–310.

14. Insurability, environmental risks and the law

**Howard C. Kunreuther and
Paul K. Freeman***

INTRODUCTION

This chapter makes the case for utilizing insurance rather than the liability system to provide protection against some chronic or sudden environmental risks. A chronic risk has a long lead time between the actual exposure to a particular toxic substance and the occurrence of a disease. A classic example is the long delay (often 20 years or more) between exposure to asbestos and the contraction of mesothelioma (a cancer affecting the membrane lining of the chest cavity). A sudden risk is exemplified by releases of chemicals that can cause death or sickness at the time of the accident, such as the Union Carbide disaster in Bhopal, India in 1984.

There seems to be a growing consensus among researchers and practitioners that the current liability system in the United States is not working well in dealing with environmental risks. Rather than continuing to rely on the courts for addressing many environmental risks, we propose that a set of enforceable insurance contracts be developed that can be used in combination with other policy tools such as third-party inspections and/or well-specified performance standards. Insurance should protect a firm's assets from perceived random claims while providing compensation to a victim without the high transaction costs associated with the liability system.

The next section discusses the current liability system. The third section then considers when insurance may be a more promising policy tool for dealing with environmental risks by examining the conditions of insurability. We provide four illustrative examples as to how insurance coupled with other policy tools, such as inspections and well-specified standards, can be utilized for dealing with chronic risks. The concluding section compares an insurance-based system with the current liability system and suggests directions for future research.

LIMITATIONS OF CURRENT LIABILITY SYSTEM

Tort law is the body of common law that deals with wrongs committed between parties outside of contractual obligations. The two functions of tort law are: (a) to provide the basis for an injured party to recover damage, and (b) to deter others from engaging in similar activities. Over the past 40 years, an emerging development in tort law has been the concept of enterprise liability. Enterprise liability has emerged as the tort theory applicable to product liability claims (Priest 1985). By extension, it also has been adapted to environmental claims (Mielenhausen 1991).

Enterprise liability imposes strict liability on a defendant for injuries from environmental claims and toxic chemicals. One reason for this development was the argument by legal scholars, subsequently adopted by the courts, that manufacturers could police their products through quality control much more easily than consumers could detect defects (Shavell 1987). It was anticipated that enterprise liability would increase social welfare by forcing manufacturers to invest in loss-prevention activities until the point where the marginal benefits of reducing the loss equals the marginal costs of investing in the mitigation measures.

Enterprise liability is intended to play a risk-spreading function. By making manufacturers strictly liable for losses caused by their products or operations, the cost of this liability could be included in the higher selling prices they would charge. Funds accumulated would be available for any claimant establishing that a product damaged him or her regardless of the negligence of the manufacturer. In other words, the tort system, through strict liability, played one traditional insurance role: spreading risk across a population of similar risks (Landes and Posner 1987).

To examine how enterprise liability is supposed to work, consider the following simple example. A firm is involved in producing a product that could lead to the death of an individual with annual probability p. Should a fatality occur, the firm would be liable for L dollars. The firm knows that if it invests C dollars today in a protective measure, the probability of a fatality will be reduced to p^*. Suppose there are N individuals subject to possible fatalities from the product and the length of time that the firm is in operation is T years. Given an annual discount rate (r) the firm knows that if it invests in the protective measure then the expected benefit [E(B)] from the measure is the reduction in its discounted liability costs over the T years:

$$\text{E(B)} = \sum_{t=1}^{T} (p - p^*)NL / (1 + r)^t. \qquad (14.1)$$

Suppose $p = 1/1000$ and $p^* = 1/2000$, $L = \$2$ million, $N = 100$, $r = 0.10$ and $T = 10$ years. Then equation (14.1) yields an E(B) of approximately $\$620\,000$. Whenever $C < $ E(B) then it is cost-effective to invest in the protective measure; otherwise it is not.

In theory, enterprise liability is designed to play two roles that insurance has historically played. It encourages loss-prevention measures while providing compensation for losses. Several challenges emerge for enterprise liability in performing these two functions.

First, the enterprise liability system causes problems for both the plaintiff who may suffer harm from a toxic chemical or product, and the defendant charged with responsibility for the harm. The biggest problem for both sides is establishing a causal link between exposure to hazardous materials and the alleged injury or disease (Rabin 1987)). Many environmental risks involve substances that do not have a clearcut linkage with specific diseases, such as cancer. The fields of toxicology and epidemiology are limited in their ability to deduce human cancer risks from animal bioassays due to different sensitivities between humans and animals. Furthermore, the procedure of extrapolating findings from animal studies to human beings is fraught with uncertainty.

The inability of science to provide causal connections for most environmental risks has been discussed at length in the scientific literature. Toxicologists are reluctant to label more than just a few chemicals as carcinogenic and will rarely conclude that humans face a known risk because animals in a controlled experiment contracted a disease (Kraus et al.1992). Furthermore, there is little concrete evidence to suggest that more scientific studies and risk assessments will clarify the situation (Graham *et al.* 1988). Hence it is difficult to estimate the probability of a loss before investing in protective measures (p) as well as after such a measure is adopted (p^*). In addition it is difficult to know in advance what the courts will determine the value of L to be should there be a lawsuit. In other words, firms have a difficult time determining the E(B) of a protective measure and whether it is worth the cost (C).

Even for diseases such as asbestosis or mesothelioma, where there is normally greater understanding of causality, it is often difficult for the courts to assign liability.[1] There are thus likely to be enormous transaction costs and legal expenses incurred by companies in arguing who (if anyone) is responsible for specific losses when an individual claims injury. For example, the RAND study on asbestos litigation costs revealed that plaintiffs only receive an estimated 37 per cent of the total dollars spent by defendants and their insurers. The remainder is consumed in transaction costs, including legal fees (Kakalik *et al.* 1983).

It appears, then, that neither the deterrence function nor recovery function of tort law is served by the application of enterprise liability imposition since the plaintiff cannot adequately collect for damages and defendants are not convinced that liability is being justly imposed.

INSURABILITY AND MARKETABILITY OF ENVIRONMENTAL RISKS

Insurance has proven to be an effective tool for providing victims with compensation and in modifying behaviour for a series of environmental risks. It has done so at considerably lower transaction costs than experienced through the tort system. This section explores the requirements necessary for insurance to play its historical role as an effective risk-spreading and behaviour-modifying tool for environmental risk.

Conditions for Insurability

Two conditions must be met before insurance providers are willing to provide coverage against an uncertain event. *Condition 1* is the ability to identify and, possibly, quantify the risk. The insurer must know that it is possible to estimate what losses it is likely to incur when providing different levels of coverage. *Condition 2* is the ability to set premiums for each potential customer or class of customers. This requires some knowledge of the customer's risk in relation to others in the population so that problems of adverse selection and moral hazard do not occur.[2] If Conditions 1 and 2 are both satisfied, a risk is considered to be insurable. But it still may not be profitable. In other words, it may not be possible to specify a rate where there is sufficient demand to yield a positive profit from offering coverage. In such cases there will be no market for insurance.

Using the notation from the previous section, one needs to be able to estimate the probability of an event occurring (p) and the reduced probability (p^*) of incurring losses (L) after investing (C) in preventive measures. Insurance pays claims based on contractual terms. Hence it is possible to craft insurance policies to relax the requirements of causality as a precondition of claims payment. As shown with some of the examples in the next section, a claim can be triggered solely based on an event without regard to whether the event actually causes physical damage.

Even when outcomes are used as a basis for setting insurance premiums, fundamental problems arise when one tests the proposed product against the basic criteria of insurability indicated by Conditions 1 and 2. First, the courts have required insurers to pay damages for losses insurers never intended to cover. This is a direct result of policy coverage interpretation problems, which have intensified due to changing definitions of liability. Insurance is dependent on enforcement of specified language, since the language sets the terms of the risk for which the policy was priced. It is thus essential that the courts respect the terms of coverage specified in the policy.

A second fundamental problem is that many environmental problems lack the historical information necessary for traditional actuarial modelling. Without a measurable baseline standard of behaviour that is accepted by all potential insureds, it is impossible for the insurer to generate enough uniformity for the formulation of appropriate insurance coverage and underwriting of insureds. The uniform standard can arise from government regulation, from industry, from financial institutions or from other areas of influence. Insurance companies have historically proven to be ineffective in imposing new standards of behaviour for a market.

As a complement or substitute for historical data, environmental insurance providers have used scientific models to define the maximum possible loss, average loss and the frequency of loss. Rates are then based on these scientific models. These rates will normally reflect the degree of uncertainty associated with the risk. For example, suppose a group of experts agree that the best estimate of a person contracting cancer from being exposed to a particular substance is $p = 0.001$, but that there is a great deal of uncertainty surrounding this probability figure. A risk-averse insurer will want to specify a higher premium to cover this risk than if it had the same probability (that is, $p = 0.001$) but were more certain (for example, the chances of an automobile accident) if the events are not perfectly correlated (Hogarth and Kunreuther 1992).

To avoid moral hazard problems, the insured population must be closely monitored to ensure that their behaviour conforms to the original scientific model and the prescribed standard. Finally, as new scientific data and statistical information become available, they should be used to refine and adjust the scientific model.

Profitability of Insurance

Even if an insurer determines that a particular risk meets the above two insurability conditions, it will not invest the time and money to develop a product unless it is convinced that there is sufficient demand to cover the upfront costs for product development as well as the expenses associated with marketing and distribution.[3] The larger these costs, the higher the premium will have to be for a fixed number of customers. The final premium will be a function of these administrative costs and the elasticity of demand with respect to price.

Suppose that the insurer has specified an underwriting premium (P*) which represents its best estimate of the expected loss from a given risk without any consideration of the costs (F) of developing and/or marketing coverage. It must then determine its breakeven premium (P^*_i) as a function of the quantity of insurance (Q_i) it can sell over the lifetime of the product. The breakeven premium will then be defined as $P^*_i = P^* + F/Q_i$. Obviously the larger Q_i is, the lower the premium will be. The insurer needs to determine how large the demand for insurance is likely to be as a function of the premium it charges.

Let Q^*_i be the amount of insurance that the firm feels it can sell over the lifetime of the product at a premium P^*_i. The insurer knows that if $Q^*_i > Q_i$ it will be able to make a profit by charging a premium P^*_i. If there are several values of P^*_i where $Q^*_i > Q_i$, then the insurer will either choose the one which yields it the highest profit (if it has monopoly power) or it will be forced by competition to set the lowest premium which still yields zero profits.

FOUR ILLUSTRATIVE EXAMPLES

This section presents four examples where insurance appears to be an attractive alternative to enterprise liability in providing protection against specific environmental risks and encouraging firms to operate in a safer manner than they otherwise might. Each example involves the use of insurance in conjunction with other policy tools, such as property audits or inspections, well-defined performance standards and/or economic incentives. For each example we shall focus on the conditions that make the risk insurable and profitable to market and those factors that discourage insurers from providing protection against these risks.

Example 1: Asbestos Abatement Liability Coverage[4]

Characterizing the problem
Asbestos is the common name for a group of natural minerals that occur as masses of compact or relatively long, silky fibres. In the 1960s, the mineral was identified as a carcinogen – a product known to cause cancer in human beings. Medical evidence established that airborne asbestos fibres that are inhaled or swallowed are linked to a number of diseases, including asbestosis, lung cancer and mesothelioma. In the early 1970s, the US government began banning the use of asbestos.

Beginning in the early 1980s, significant pressure developed in American society to remove asbestos from existing structures. This pressure was fuelled by public concern over the health effects of asbestos exposure, as well as by government requirements that schools be surveyed to determine the extent of asbestos contained in their structures. In the early to mid-1980s, both the Environmental Protection Agency (EPA) and the Occupational Safety and Health Administration (OSHA) issued regulations for asbestos removal work.

The governmental regulations for asbestos removal contain clear specifications for job site monitoring, worker protection procedures, transportation and disposal of asbestos fibres and proper removal techniques. The job site monitoring requirement is to be carried out by independent industrial hygiene firms. Insurance has been an effective means of enforcing federal and state regulations related to asbestos as well as providing an efficient means of paying for damages related to asbestos removal activity.

Feasibility of insurance

Relying on this regulatory framework, insurance firms began offering insurance coverage for contractors involved in asbestos removal work. These policies assumed the liabilities of contractors for property damage and bodily injury created as a result of a release of asbestos fibres in excess of the permissible exposure levels at a job site location.

There are two key factors that relate to the environmental risk associated with an asbestos abatement liability policy: (a) the probability (p) that third parties are exposed to asbestos and will contract asbestosis or mesothelioma, and (b) the insurer payout (L) if an individual either contracts a disease or is vulnerable to experiencing it in the future having been exposed to the asbestos fibres.

With respect to the first factor, the scientific literature on the effects of exposure to asbestos clearly identified the key factors leading to disease manifestation: fibre concentration and duration of exposure multiplied by yield dosage. A careful examination of asbestos abatement methods and practices revealed that engineering protocols were available to limit asbestos fibre exposure, especially for third parties outside the work area. The ability to monitor the abatement contractor's adherence to these protocols was also present, with the possibility of cancelling an insurance policy if the contractor released an undue amount of asbestos fibres into the air.

Regarding the insurer payout (L), the policy was crafted to provide coverage for the insured's legally liable damages to third parties for bodily injury or property damage that occurs during the course of asbestos abatement activities. Customized policies were drafted which details definitions of occurrence, damages, coverage triggers, exclusions and exceptions to exclusions.

Since the policy required constant monitoring of contractors engaged in asbestos removal, a record exists of all asbestos exposure to third parties from the activities of the insured. For bodily injury claims, the issue of whether the insured was responsible for exposure is therefore resolved. The remaining issue is whether the claimant actually is damaged by the exposure. For property damage claims, the mere release of asbestos fibres outside containment barriers is sufficient to generate a legitimate claim for compensatory property damage claim. Because of ongoing monitoring required by the insurance coverage, the issues of causation are significantly simplified.

Loss model/pricing

An extensive review of the medical literature was undertaken with particular emphasis on dose response models articulated by OSHA. In promulgating standards regulating occupational exposure to asbestos for industry, OSHA developed quantitative risk assessment models to project excess mortality and morbidity as a function of dose. For each of four different disease classes (that is, lung cancer, mesothelioma, asbestosis and gastrointestinal cancer), mortality and morbidity were shown to vary with the concentration of airborne asbestos fibres and the duration of exposure.

In accordance with the OSHA models, it was possible to estimate the relative frequency of disease manifestation associated with specific exposure levels to asbestos fibre and to construct proprietary mortality/morbidity tables for each disease class for exposures anticipated from typical abatement activities. Abatement activities have lower exposure than levels associated with occupational hazards.

The expected loss frequency associated with abatement contractors required data on the number of third-party persons in close proximity to abatement activities, the asbestos fibre concentrations outside the work area and the duration of exposure during abatement needed to be calculated. These fibre data, along with project duration distributions accumulated from a sample of actual abatement projects, permitted estimates of the dosage of asbestos experienced by third parties outside the work area. Synthesizing these data with the mortality/morbidity tables described above, it was now possible to project disease manifestation frequencies in terms of contractor revenues.

Loss severity, or the cost associated with claims from asbestos abatement activities, was estimated from the comprehensive cost studies prepared by the RAND Institute of Civil Justice (Dixon 1993; Kakalik *et al.* 1983). These studies presented size of loss distributions from asbestos lawsuits prior to the 1982 Manville bankruptcy, providing breakdowns of victim compensation, defence litigation costs and unallocated loss expense. Conservative trend factors and disease latencies were selected to estimate ultimate loss distributions and expenses associated with adjusting losses.

Marketability of the product

Assessing the marketability of asbestos liability coverage did not require extensive analysis because obtaining liability coverage for abatement contractors was a precondition of their obtaining work. Building owners who have work performed by contractors generally require some type of indemnification against liabilities associated with the work to assure themselves that the company is financially viable. The standard forms of the American Institute of Architects for contract work contain the requirement that contractors purchase insurance against their liabilities prior to the commencement of their work. Once insurance became available for contractors performing asbestos removal work, the construction industry created instant demand for the coverage. In fact, such insurance became a virtual licence to do business. In other words, insurance was a type of 'good housekeeping seal'.

Example 2: Property Transfer Liability Coverage[5]

Characterizing the problem

The Comprehensive Environmental Response, Compensation, and Liability Act (CERCLA), commonly known as Superfund, governs hazardous waste produced and abandoned in the past. It mandates a strong liability scheme that dictates that those responsible for environmental contamination will, to the extent possible, pay the costs of clean-up. The courts have interpreted CERCLA as imposing a system of broad liability of three types:

1. *Joint and several liability*   Imposes liability without respect to proportioning liability among parties. If a business is liable for any portion of a contamination, it may have liability imposed for the full cost of the contamination clean-up.
2. *Retroactive liability*   Imposes liability on current owners of a property for all environmental clean-ups now required, even for activities undertaken by prior owners which may have been perfectly legal at the time the activity was carried out.
3. *Strict liability*   Imposes liability without requiring a showing of criminal intent or contribution. A business can be liable for a current environmental clean-up solely because contamination now exists at unacceptable levels, even if the current owner had always complied with prior standards of behaviour.

In order to protect themselves from the possibility of having to pay for clean-up costs, purchasers of property and their lenders perform pre-acquisition site assessments to identify potential contamination. Site assessments have significant limitations in detecting all contamination, leaving the new owner and the lender exposed to potentially significant liability. For this reason a large number of contaminated properties lie vacant at the heart of many large industrial cities in the United States. This so-called brownfield problem can be reduced with insurance that covers the unanticipated clean-up costs for contamination discovered after the land is purchased and redevelopment begun.

Feasibility of insurance

Property transfer insurance has been designed to protect commercial real estate purchasers and their lenders from liability for contamination that is present, but as yet undetected on the property. To obtain this coverage, a customer must obtain pre-acquisition site assessments from an independent engineering consulting firm that has been pre-qualified by the insurance company to conduct assessments.

Any contamination discovered during the site assessment will be excluded from coverage. The magnitude of the unknown risk (contamination that is not uncovered by assessment) is reflected in the insurance premium. In essence, this insurance becomes a tool both to discover and to quantify the costs associated with existing environmental contamination, making it a powerful instrument of environmental policy.

On a composite basis, 0.86 per cent of insured properties are expected to have an insurance-covered contamination. In other words, the probability of a claim is $p = 0.0086$. This calculation is based on an average contamination rate of 12.37 per cent for all properties. This percentage was calculated based on an assessment of 9000 commercial properties. In a review of environmental audits, it was found that 6.95 per cent of the environmental audits failed to detect existing environmental contamination. This provides a combined ratio of 0.86 per cent (12.37 per cent × 6.95 per cent = 0.86 per cent).

The other element necessary to determine an insurance premium is the magnitude of the claim (L) associated with contamination. To estimate the potential losses associated with contamination that was not detected by a pre-acquisition assessment, an examination of the costs of federal and state mandated clean-ups at more than 3000 sites was undertaken. Available data indicate that the average cost of remedial action (CORA) (1991 dollars) ranges from $135 000 for underground storage tanks (USTs) to just over $33 million for Federal National Priority List (NPL) sites.

Marketability of the product
Property transfer liability insurance was not marketable until potential customers were comfortable with the purchase of a pre-acquisition environmental assessment prior to purchasing property. Around 1992 these assessments were an accepted form of business practice and the majority of the nation's banks began to require assessments as preconditions for most bank-financed real estate transactions.

The product has not been widely used on all standard property acquisitions. Rather, it is purchased primarily when a third party (usually the financing institution) requires the insurance as an added layer of protection. In contrast to the asbestos coverage discussed above, there is no compelling industry-driven motivation to buy this insurance voluntarily.

Example 3: Underground Storage Tank Insurance[6]

Characterizing the problem
Leaking underground petroleum storage tanks represent one of the most serious environmental problems in the United States. The social costs of tank leaks, which can range up to millions of dollars, can easily dwarf a typical gas station

or distributor's ability to internalize them. Actuarial estimates place the *average* expected clean-up cost for an underground storage tank from $60 000 to $400 000, depending on the degree of soil and groundwater impacts and whether there is offsite migration. Costs can be much higher with offsite migration. Comparing this figure to the annual revenues from retail gas outlets, which can be as low as $25 000, makes clear the magnitude of the distributional impact on firms in the industry.

The clean-up of UST leaks is the only type of environmental remediation in the United States that has been consistently publicly financed since the mid-1980s. Regulations governing the use of USTs are a central component of the Resource Conservation and Recovery Act (RCRA). Since 1984, when the first UST amendments to RCRA were enacted, state and federal approaches to the environmental risks posed by USTs have undergone a significant evolution.

Two of the more important aspects of the existing programme are the requirement that UST owner/operators demonstrate financial responsibility and the development of state guarantee funds (SGFs) to help them meet this need. SGFs serve a dual role: they provide public financing for remediating existing leaks and serve as a source of compensation for prospective risks. Hence SGFs do little to deter future environmental problems while effectively eliminating the opportunity to use private insurance markets to promote risk reduction. Because the costs of SGF coverage are typically much lower than the premiums that private insurers would have to charge, there is little incentive for tank owners to purchase coverage.

Feasibility of insurance

The two key elements associated with setting premiums for UST insurance is the probability that a tank will leak (p) and the costs associated with cleaning up the contamination (L). Using past data on UST leaks compiled from various studies it is possible to determine the percentage of tanks of various ages likely to leak. By insisting on tank inspections prior to providing coverage, insurers should be able to discriminate between good and bad risks, thus refining the value of p through this additional information.

With respect to estimating L, the University of Tennessee conducted a study of total costs to clean up leaking USTs in the United States by surveying over 75 000 sites and estimated that the average cost to clean up USTs is $175 000 (University of Tennessee 1991). USTs appear to be an insurable risk if there were sufficient demand for coverage by tank owners. There is little ambiguity on the probability of a leak if one has good information on the characteristics of the tank. By requiring monitoring devices on tanks, insurers can detect leaks early and avoid large clean-up expenses. Each tank is independent and leakage from one tank will have no impact on others. The only issue regarding correlation of risks relates to changes in the liability laws regarding the degree to which clean-up needs to occur. New rulings on 'how clean is clean' would impact on the amount that insurers would have to pay on all tanks in their portfolio of policies.

Marketability of the product

The original financial responsibility requirements provided an opportunity for private insurance and loss-prevention techniques to be employed, but the SGFs effectively eliminated these opportunities. There is a joint role that SGFs could play in concert with private insurance, as pointed out by Boyd and Kunreuther (1997). They show that SGFs should be used to pay for past liabilities so that firms have incentives to take deterrent action combined with private financial responsibility to guarantee the internalization of future liabilities. In this sense private insurance can play an important role in providing prospective coverage against future leaks.

There is now an incentive for private insurers to enter the market since all SGFs are experiencing financial difficulty. UST owners have been advised to seek other sources of coverage in order to comply with RCRA's financial responsibility requirements. One of these options is private insurance.

Example 4: Providing Insurance Against Sudden Accidents

The passage of section 112(r) of the Clean Air Act Amendments (CAAA) of 1990 offers an opportunity to utilize a set of market-based mechanisms with insurance as an important component for dealing with these issues. As part of section 112(r) firms are required to develop risk management plans (RMPs) for preventing and mitigating major chemical accidental releases. There is an opportunity for utilizing insurance coupled with third-party inspections for encouraging firms to undertake preventive actions to reduce the chances of these accidents.

More specifically, a chemical plant has an opportunity to reduce future direct and indirect losses from accidents by implementing a risk management plan (RMP) which will reduce the probability of an accident from p to p^* at a cost of C. The value of C reflects the expenditures in both time and money in implementing a strategy for reducing the risks of future accidents. An RMP is a type of loss-prevention measure and its expected benefits [E(B)] is given by equation (14.1). To determine whether implementing an RMP is an attractive option, the E(B) can be compared with C.

As pointed out in Kunreuther *et al.* (2000) there are a number of reasons why chemical plants do not voluntarily undertake an RMP and incur the costs C to reduce the risk. These include misperceptions of the risk, short time horizons and capital constraints, particularly for small firms which would prefer to take the chances of an accident occurring rather than invest in protective measures.

The social consequences of this behaviour can be significant if there are externalities associated with chemical releases. For example, a chemical accident will have impacts on the residents in the area surrounding the plant but the industrial plant will not be liable for these costs. Hence they will not include them in their evaluation of an RMP. For example, if there are decreases in property values to homes in the surrounding area or there are disruptions in community life because of the accident, the chemical firm will *not* be held liable for these adverse impacts. By underestimating the benefits from an RMP, chemical plants may decide not to take action when it would be in the public's and society's interest for them to do this. Ashford (1993) has reported that for every $1 of direct cost associated with an accident there is $4–10 individual social costs not borne by the firm.

For these reasons it may be necessary for a government agency, such as the US Environmental Protection Agency (EPA), to require well-specified RMPs by firms that are covered by section 112(r) of the CAAA. The key question is how they can ensure that the RMPs are actually being developed and implemented. Third-party inspections coupled with insurance offer considerable promise in achieving this objective.

Under such a programme a qualified inspector determines whether a firm has implemented an RMP and provides this information to an insurance firm, which then sets a premium for coverage based on the results of the RMP. Those firms which choose not to develop an RMP face the risk of being audited by the EPA and having a fine levied on them. With a sufficiently large fine and a high enough probability of being audited by the EPA, there will be a sufficient financial incentive for the chemical plant to want to implement an RMP.[7]

A pilot experiment in Delaware is now under way which will provide data on the success of third-party inspections coupled with insurance. This activity, under the auspices of the Wharton Risk Management and Decision Processes Center, is being undertaken by a task force, consisting of the EPA's Chemical Emergency Preparedness and Prevention Office (CEPPO), EPA Region III, and the State of Delaware's Department of Natural Resources and Environmental Control (DNREC). To the extent that firms subject to section 112(r) are receptive to having audits and insurance premiums reflect the risk of these facilities, then an important step will have been taken to move in the direction of implementing market mechanisms in place of command and control procedures.

Lessons Learned

The above examples suggest a set of lessons regarding the role of insurance in reducing losses from environmental risks and providing financial protection relative to tort law. First, if it is based on performance standards or RMPs, environmental insurance can provide an effective means of institutionalizing regulations.

By monitoring insureds' activities as part of ongoing underwriting procedures, insurance companies provide economic incentives for their clients to comply with the standards. This is especially true when the insurance is either required or viewed as highly desirable. Two common situations are where insurance is needed to permit the insured to perform its core business activity (contractors must have insurance) or where it has an impact on the insured's ability to proceed with a new business transaction (acquisition of new property for example). This monitoring function also deters undesirable behaviour by increasing the consequences of non-compliance.

One of the two key functions of common law is to provide a means of recovery or compensation. As a contract, insurance can both broaden or narrow the conditions upon which payment will be made. Those conditions often rely on existing tort doctrines as preconditions for payments to be made. In areas such as perceived environmental risks, it may be easier and less costly to all parties to adopt contractual conditions of payment. For example, property transfer liability insurance responds to releases of hazards above permissible exposure levels without regard to actual harm caused.

CHALLENGES FOR THE FUTURE

This chapter has attempted to make the case for substituting performance standards, third-party inspections and insurance in some circumstances for the current legal liability system. To justify such a system, it is useful to examine how well it is likely to fare using the criteria of compensation and deterrence that are instrumental in promoting the enterprise liability system.

Comparing Environmental Insurance with Enterprise Liability

For the current liability system to be an effective deterrent with respect to environmental risks, there has to be some relationship between the actual regulation and the hazard itself. In the area of environmental risk, this relationship is distinctly absent even for substances, such as asbestos, where there is a causal link between exposure and the disease. In the case of asbestos, the long latency period, in addition to other factors that may cause cancer, prevent us from directly linking exposure to a fibre and the onset of disease.

Unless firms are able to determine what impact their actions will have on reducing the risks of disease, the liability system will not optimally satisfy its function of encouraging firms to allocate funds for loss-prevention activities.

Rather than encouraging firms to make inappropriate benefit–cost tradeoffs, we favour a system where the regulatory agency sets clear performance standards in consultation with other interested parties. This is likely to satisfy the deterrent objective far better than the current programme.

By coupling this performance standard with insurance, there will be incentives for firms and their insurers to undertake inspections. Insurers will want to engage in monitoring and control efforts and impose appropriate penalties and premium increases for insureds who fail to meet existing standards. Furthermore, industrial firms will be encouraged to pursue innovations that reduce future risks, something they would be more reluctant to do under enterprise liability.

Some type of insurance system in place of the current liability system can also allocate costs more efficiently to victims of diseases. Under this type of arrangement, the claims payments will flow either directly from the firm to the victim (social insurance) or from the firm to the insurer to the victim (private insurer). The costs of these transactions costs will be lower than under the current system.

Another advantage of insurance over enterprise liability relates to possible deterrence benefits. Assuming that the insurance needs are defined as 'mandatory', either because of government requirements or market conditions, the insurance company's annual renewal of the insurance policy provides at least a paper review of all operations. Often the insurance company monitors ongoing operations of the insured on a more frequent basis. In the asbestos example, monitoring data on each job must be maintained by the contractor and is subject to insurance company review.

In fact, there is an economic incentive for the insurer to assure compliance with standards since its loss experience is directly related to this activity. Under an enterprise liability system, where causality is difficult to prove, there is little incentive for the firm to engage in preventive activities if they believe that they will only be partially liable (if at all) for the losses.

Currently, most environmental risks do not satisfy the basic conditions of insurability or marketability, and hence insurers are reluctant to provide coverage against them. The private market place has attempted to develop coverage for underground storage tanks, lead-based paint exposures, landfills (both hazardous and non-hazardous), and other clearly identifiable exposures but has not been very successful in doing so for a variety of reasons. An understanding of the issues identified in this chapter may assist policy-makers in the design of regulations and creation of market conditions to permit the insurance industry to play a role in environmental policy. In large measure, the government can both create and destroy the conditions that would permit insurance to be developed and sold.

Future Research Issues

The development of enterprise liability arose because of perceived failures of the existing market for insurance to respond adequately to emerging liability concerns. Instead of creating alternative mechanisms to spread liability, policy-makers may be better advised to understand the tools required to permit the private market to respond to liability concerns.

Future research should be focused on the most efficient tradeoffs between government mandatory allocation of liability with high transaction costs, and the role the public sector can play in supporting market alternatives such as insurance to address liability concerns. This is especially critical for govern-mental-created environmental liabilities such as the clean-up costs associated with the Superfund programme. By focusing on insurance as an alternative to the liability system it may be possible to encourage cost-effective loss-prevention measures while still providing compensation to victims in a much more efficient manner.

NOTES

* Support from the Wharton Risk Management and Decision Processes Center is gratefully acknowledged. Special thanks to Dr Alan Potter, Chief Actuary for Eric Agency Inc. in Denver, CO for his helpful comments on earlier drafts.
1. For example, did the actor Steve McQueen contract mesothelioma by being exposed to asbestos while working in a shipyard during World War II or was it primarily due to the asbestos in his autoracing suit (Viscusi 1991)?
2. For more details on the concepts of insurability in relation to environmental risks see Freeman and Kunreuther (1997: ch. 4).
3. We are assuming that the marketing and distribution costs are fixed rather than a function of the number of policies sold.
4. See Freeman and Kunreuther (1997: chs 5–6) for more details on insuring asbestos risk.
5. Insurance for environmentally contaminated property is discussed in more detail in Freeman and Kunreuther (1997: ch. 7).
6. This section draws heavily from Boyd and Kunreuther (1997).
7. See Kunreuther *et al.* (2000) for more details on the features of this type of programme.

REFERENCES

Ashford, Nicholas (1993), 'The encouragement of technological change for preventing accidents: moving firms from secondary prevention and mitigation to primary prevention', Center for Technology and Industrial Development, Massachusetts Institute of Technology, April.

Boyd, James and Howard Kunreuther (1997), 'Retroactive liability or the public purse?', *Journal of Regulatory Economics* 11: 79–90

Dixon, Lloyd S. (1993), *Private Sector Cleanup Expenditures and Transaction Costs at 18 Superfund Sites*, Santa Monica, CA: RAND Institute for Civil Justice.

Freeman, Paul and Howard Kunreuther (1997), *Managing Environmental Risk Through Insurance*, New York: Kluwer Academic Publishers.

Graham, John, Laura Green and Marc Roberts (1988), *In Search of Safety*, Cambridge, MA: Harvard University Press.

Hogarth, Robin and Howard Kunreuther (1992), 'Pricing insurance and warranties: ambiguity and correlated risks', *Geneva Papers on Risk and Insurance Theory* 17: 35–60.

Kakalik, James S., Patricia A. Ebener, William L.F. Felstiner and Michael G. Shanley (1983), *Costs of Asbestos Litigation*, Santa Monica, CA: RAND Institute for Civil Justice.

Kraus, Nancy, T. Malmfors and Paul Slovic (1992), 'Intuitive toxicology: expert and lay judgements of chemical risks', *Risk Analysis* 12: 215–32.

Kunreuther, Howard, Jacqueline Meszaros and Robin Hogarth (1995), 'Ambiguity and underwriter decision processes', *Journal of Economic Behavior and Organization* 26: 337–52.

Kunreuther, Howard, Patrick McNulty and Yong Kang (2000), 'Third party inspection as an alternative to command and control regulation', in Kurt Deketelaere and Eric W. Orts (eds), *Environmental Contracts: Comparative Approaches to Regulatory Innovation in the United States and Europe*, New York: Kluwer Law International.

Landes, William and Richard Posner (1987), *The Economic Structure of Tort Law*, Cambridge, MA: Harvard University Press.

Landy, Mark K., Marc J. Roberts and Stephen R. Thomas (1990), *The Environmental Protection Agency: Asking the Wrong Questions*, New York: Oxford University Press.

Mielenhausen, Thomas C. (1991), 'Insurance coverage for environmental and toxic tort claims', 17 *Wm Mitchell Law Review* 945.

Rabin, Robert L. (1987), 'Environmental liability and the tort system', 24 *Houston Law Review* 27.

Priest, George L. (1985), 'The invention of enterprise liability: a critical history of the intellectual foundations of modern tort law', *Journal of Legal Studies* 14: 461–528.

Shavell, Steven (1987), *The Economics of Accident Law*, Cambridge, MA: Harvard University Press.

University of Tennessee (1991), *Underground Storage Tanks: Resource Requirements for Corrective Action*, Knoxville, TN: University of Tennessee Hazardous Waste Remediation Project. Waste Management Research and Education Institute (December).

Viscusi, W. Kip (1991), *Reforming Products Liability*, Cambridge, MA: Harvard University Press.

15. Environmental damages in court: the *American Trader* case

David J. Chapman and W. Michael Hanemann[1]

INTRODUCTION

On 7 February 1990 the steam tanker *American Trader* spilled 416 598 gallons of crude oil approximately one and one-half miles off the coast of Huntington Beach, California. Almost eight years later, a ten-week trial in an Orange County state court came to an end on 8 December 1997 with a verdict for the plaintiffs in the amount of $18 million – the first jury verdict for natural resource damages ever delivered in the United States.[2] Economics, and economists, played a central role in the trial, occupying four weeks of the trial testimony. This chapter describes the economic issues that were raised in the case and explains how they were treated, viewed from the plaintiffs' perspective. Because the *American Trader* case went to trial, unlike almost every other suit for natural resource damages including the one following the *Exxon Valdez* oil spill, the arguments of both sides and the analyses of their expert witnesses have been fully aired in public, making it possible to discuss this case in some detail.[3,4]

The 'polluter pays' principle is meaningful only if one can establish satisfactorily *how much* that should be. That was the main focus of the *American Trader* trial.[5] This case illustrates some of the issues that can arise in the course of implementing the liability approach to pollution control. More generally, it illustrates the issues that can arise when one applies economic analysis in litigation. There was no disagreement in this case regarding the appropriate economic methodology; all of the argument was about the empirical implementation of economic methodology. Consequently, issues relating to data collection, analysis and interpretation were at the heart of trial. This is a perspective which is sometimes lacking in the theoretical literature on the liability approach to pollution control.

The *American Trader* was carrying approximately 23 100 000 gallons of oil on the afternoon of 7 February 1990 when it approached the offshore sea berth of the Golden West refinery in Huntington Beach. The oil came from Alaska, had been shipped to Los Angeles where it was transferred to a smaller tanker, and was being taken for final delivery to the Golden West refinery. The captain was relatively unfamiliar with the refinery, there was a low tide, and as the ship attempted the difficult manoeuvre into the offshore mooring, which involves using its anchors as pivot points, it hit and punctured the hull and the front right storage tank with its own anchor.[6] The crew members had left valves open connecting this tank to two adjacent storage tanks, and the contents of those also flowed into the ocean.

Offshore winds kept the oil at sea for several days, but then it came ashore. Approximately 14 miles of beaches were closed for a period of up to 34 days from Alamitos Bay in Los Angeles County to Crystal Cove State Beach in Orange County (see Figure 15.1). The affected beaches were reopened in stages as the clean-up progressed, with the last beaches reopening on 14 March. To protect fragile wetland areas, Newport Harbor, Huntington Harbor, Alamitos Bay and the mouth of the Santa Ana river were boomed off to prevent oil from entering the harbours. In addition, a large portion of the Huntington Flats fishing area, off the coast of Huntington Beach, was closed to boating and fishing for about two weeks.

On 8 February the State of California contacted Hanemann and asked him to conduct an economic analysis of the natural resource damages caused by the spill.[7] On 9 February Chapman, who had been born and raised in the Los Angeles area and was then a graduate student in the Department of Agricultural and Resource Economics at the University of California at Berkeley, went down to Huntington Beach to start collecting data. By the time of trial, the state's economic team had grown to include Paul Ruud,[8] Roger Tourangeau,[9] Stanley Presser[10] and Michael Ward.[11] Pierre Du Vair, staff economist in the Office of Oil Spill Prevention and Response (OSPR) of the California Department of Fish and Game (DFG) served as that agency's project manager for the economic component of the damage assessment.

This chapter is organized as follows. The next section provides an overview of the case and the events preceding the trial. The economic research performed for the state can be divided into two phases. The first phase of the research was performed with the expectation of a negotiated settlement; this work is described in the third section. The defendants' responses to it are described in the fourth section. The second phase of our work, which is next described, began when it became apparent that the case would go to trial, a description of which is in the following section. The final section offers some concluding observations about presenting economic analysis in court.

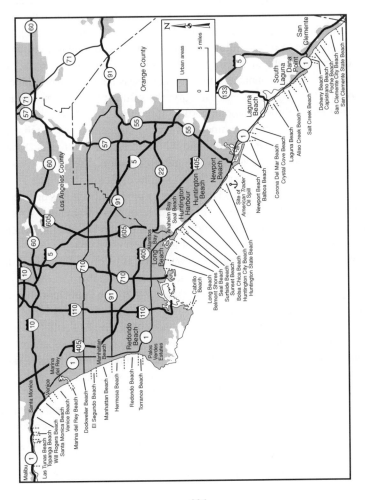

Figure 15.1 Beaches in Los Angeles and Orange Counties, California

OVERVIEW OF THE CASE

At the time of the spill, there existed various state and federal statutes allowing for natural resource trustees to make damage claims for injury to, loss of or loss of use of natural resources. The main federal statutes were the Comprehensive Environmental Response, Compensation, and Liability Act of 1980 (CERCLA), the Federal Water Pollution Control Act (Clean Water Act), and the Trans-Alaska Pipeline Authorization Act (TAPAA). The Oil Pollution Act of 1990 (OPA), written in part as a response to the *Exxon Valdez* oil spill, was not signed into law until August of 1990. For the State of California, the primary authorizing statute at the time of the spill was section 294 of the Harbors and Navigation Code. Subsequent to the spill, the State of California enacted the Lempert–Keane Act, which is now the primary oil spill legislation in the state.

Under all of these statutes, a damage claim consists of three components: the cost of projects to restore injured natural resources; compensation for the loss of services from the affected resources during the period when they are injured; and the cost of conducting the damage assessment. The work done by the authors focused on the second category: the value of lost recreational use. This was the focus of the economic portion of the trial.

The state's strategy was determined early in the assessment process through discussion between the NRDA team and the Trustees: the California Departments of Fish and Game and Parks and Recreation, the State Coastal Conservancy, the Regional Water Quality Control Board, the State Lands Commission, NOAA, and the US Department of the Interior. It was decided to separate the assessment of injuries to biological resources[12] from the lost recreational use. Also, to keep the costs down, it was decided to use the benefits transfer approach to obtain an estimate of recreation use damages.

As with many other natural resource damage cases, multiple responsible parties were involved in the *American Trader* case. The tanker was owned and operated by ATTRANSCO, and was under charter to British Petroleum Shipping Company. BP Oil Supply Company was the title owner of the oil cargo, and Golden West Refining was the owner and operator of the sea berth. Since the oil came from Alaska, another entity involved as a defendant in a separate legal proceeding in federal court was the Trans-Alaska Pipeline Liability Fund, created by Congress to provide compensation for any losses sustained as a result of a spill of oil from the Trans-Alaska Pipeline system (TAPS).

The initial presumption was that the case would be settled through negotiation, without going to trial. This had happened with previous natural resource damage suits brought by the State of California. For example, litigation following an oil spill in San Francisco Bay in March 1988 at the Shell Oil refinery at Martinez had been settled within less than a year.[13] Trials are expensive and fraught with uncertainty. As one of the attorneys said to us: 'You only go to trial when there is a breakdown in rationality'.

Negotiations with the various parties commenced very soon after the spill. At the same time, work proceeded on a preliminary damage assessment. The first settlement was with British Petroleum in 1993; BP agreed to pay a total $3 894 247 for bird restoration, fish hatchery projects, coastal pollution mitigation projects, agency revenue losses and response costs. In 1994, faced with a lack of progress in negotiations with the other parties, it was decided to revise and expand the damage assessment, and Paul Ruud was added to the state's economic team. Ruud and Hanemann produced written expert reports in December 1994. At about this time, following a presentation by the state's team to the TAPS economic consultants, a $3 million settlement was reached with the TAPS Fund to be applied towards clean-up costs and loss of use damages.

This left Golden West and ATTRANSCO as the remaining defendants. Golden West's economic experts were Professors Robert Deacon and Charles Kolstad from the Economics Department at UC Santa Barbara, and they issued a written review of the state's economic analysis in March 1995.[14] ATTRANSCO's economic experts were Triangle Economic Research (TER) – economists formerly employed by the Research Triangle Institute (RTI) – led by Dr Richard Dunford. TER brought in Professor Walter Thurman from the Department of Agricultural and Resource Economics at North Carolina State University to review and rebut Paul Ruud's analysis; TER and Thurman issued written reports in May 1995.[15]

By the end of 1995, it appeared likely that, while there would be a settlement with Golden West, ATTRANSCO would not settle. In January 1996, therefore, the state began preparing for a trial on the economic issues. The settlement with Golden West was finalized in July 1996, in the amount of $4.15 million. This left ATTRANSCO as the only defendant in the case.[16] The sole remaining claims at the trial were the Trustee's claims for lost recreational use and civil liabilities under the California Water Code. In preparation for the trial, Hanemann, Ruud, and Thurman issued supplementary written reports, and depositions of economic experts were held in September, November and December 1996. Another round of depositions was held in August 1997, and Hanemann issued a final expert report. Overall, between 1996 and 1997, there were more than 20 days of deposition and a filing cabinet's worth of documents exchanged among the parties. The trial commenced on 30 September 1997 and ended with the jury's verdict on 8 December 1997.

At the trial, losses to six recreational activities were presented:

1. general beach use;
2. surfing;
3. private boating;

4. party/charter boat fishing;
5. whale watching; and
6. excursions to Catalina Island off the coast of Los Angeles.

From discussions with local officials and user groups, we knew that other recreational activities occur in the area and were likely to have been affected by the spill, including wildlife viewing, running, rollerblading, hiking and bicycling. But lack of readily available data led to a decision to exclude those activities from the state's claim. Also, there was no claim for losses of non-use value associated with the spill.

This chapter focuses on our assessment of the impacts on general beach recreation and surfing, which constituted the bulk of the state's recreation claim. The economic issues that arose in that analysis are the subject of the sections that follow.

THE FIRST ROUND OF ECONOMIC ANALYSIS

The beaches affected by the spill provide a high-quality recreational experience to users from many parts of the Southern California Basin. For the population of Orange County and the southern part of Los Angeles County these are the beaches and harbours of choice. Other beaches in Santa Monica Bay would generally be considered too far to drive to. In addition, many of the affected beaches are excellent surfing locations; in fact, Huntington Beach is known as 'Surf City' and is enshrined in popular culture as the centre of the Southern California beach lifestyle. While only a fraction of the population engages in surfing, this adds an aura of glamour which many visitors find attractive. Besides surfing, many of the beaches in the area affected by the spill offer a wider and more attractive mix of recreational opportunities than some of the beaches in Santa Monica Bay. Beaches in Santa Monica Bay tend to offer open expanses of sand but few other facilities. By contrast, at the beaches affected by the spill, in addition to large expanses of sand, there are boardwalks, piers, shops and other attractions for visitors and tourists, combined with excellent access and ample parking.

The use of the affected beaches is highly seasonal: it climbs as the weather grows warmer and summer arrives, and falls as winter approaches. But even in the winter there is still a considerable attendance. At the time of the spill, for example, Newport Beach, the largest of the affected beaches, had an average daily attendance of about 5000 persons/day in January, 10 000 in February, 15 000 in March, 22 000 in April and May, 40 000 in June, 65 000 in July and August, 22 000 in September and 5000 in October, November and December. The spill kept parts of Newport Beach closed from 8 February through 9 March.

Had it occurred during the summer, the loss of beach recreation would have been tremendous.

From the beginning, the state decided to rely primarily on existing data. Because of lack of time and personnel (there were only two of us, working part-time, with only one of us on the scene in Orange County), because of the limited budget, and because of the expectation of a negotiated settlement, it was decided not to attempt any large-scale collection of original data such as a travel cost survey.[17] The other factor that entered into this decision was our knowledge that there existed unusually extensive data on daily attendance at most of the affected beaches covering a period of years prior to the spill. We decided to rely on these data to develop an estimate of the lost beach recreation attributable to the spill, and to use benefits transfer for an estimate of the lost consumers' surplus per trip.

With refinements, this remained our strategy from the initial assessment after the spill up to the trial. In implementing it, we had to deal with six major issues: compiling and verifying the attendance data; developing a statistical model to forecast attendance in the absence of the spill; adjusting for attendance recorded at beaches while they were closed; dealing with the issue of substitution to other beaches that remained open; allowing for the possible impact on attendance after reopening; and selecting an estimate of consumers' surplus from the literature.

Compiling Attendance Data

The attendance data were the backbone of our analysis. At each of the main affected beaches, the lifeguards make a serious effort to record daily attendance. In our experience, these data are more extensive than is usually found in most other parts of the United Sates, including in Northern California. However, since they are collected for administrative and management purposes, including scheduling lifeguard staffing and budgetary planning, they are estimates and not a scientific census of beach attendance.

Different procedures are used at different beaches. Three of the affected beaches – Bolsa Chica, Huntington State and Crystal Cove – are state beaches run by the California Department of Parks and Recreation. These beaches have paid parking lots at the beach and are designed so that people coming to the beach are funnelled through a small number of checkpoints. Typically, there are three or four pedestrian and vehicle entrances, roughly one per mile of beach length. During the winter, however, all but one of these entrances is usually closed to vehicle traffic. The remaining entrance is manned during most of the daylight hours for the purpose of collecting the entrance fee.[18] However, vehicles on official business do not have to pay the entrance fee. All vehicles entering the park, whether or not they pay the fee, are counted and these counts form the basis for the official estimate of daily beach attendance. Two conversion factors are used in this calculation: an estimate of the number of people per vehicle, and an estimate of the ratio of 'walk-on' beach users to users entering in a vehicle. These factors are based on observations by the lifeguards and are periodically revised. They can vary seasonally and, sometimes, from one month to another; they also can vary across beaches. Typically, the DPR lifeguards might use 3.5 or 4 persons per paid vehicle, and a ratio of 1:1 for walk-ons versus drive-ins. There are also separate calculations for organized groups and, at Bolsa Chica, for overnight parking by campers.

The other two main affected beaches are operated by the cities of Huntington Beach and Newport Beach. The Huntington Beach lifeguards base their estimate of beach attendance on monitored parking at two parking lots by the beach, extrapolated to cover other, unmonitored, city-operated parking, and then adjusted by a factor to account for night-time beach attendance and daytime beach attendance at two more distant parts of the beach. At Newport Beach, the reports are based on estimates of attendance by the lifeguards at various points along the beach, updated several times during the day; these estimates generally are rounded numbers (for example, 1000, 2500, 25 000).

In addition to the affected beaches, we also collected daily attendance data for Laguna Beach, a beach four miles south of Crystal Cove that remained open throughout the spill. This beach is operated by the city of Laguna Beach, and the lifeguards there make estimates of attendance in a manner similar to Newport Beach.[19]

In addition to compiling the data, we made a concerted effort to understand how they were collected. This was rather like peeling the layers off an onion. At the state beaches, it turned out that there are several levels of reporting. First, the lifeguards at the parking booth keep a contemporaneous handwritten record of receipts and a count of free vehicles. Then, every few days, they fill out a typed Report of Collections form, detailing receipts from paid vehicles. The information on daily paying and free vehicles is also entered on a handwritten Monthly Visitor Attendance Report, which has a row for each day of the month and columns for the number of paying and free vehicles and campers. At the end of the month, this form is forwarded to DPR Headquarters in Sacramento, where the data are keypunched to generate a computerized version of the Monthly Visitor Attendance Report. It is the monthly total attendance figures that appear in publicly available reports issued by DPR. To get at the daily data, we obtained photocopies of the handwritten Monthly Visitor Attendance Reports from the local DPR office. In 1990, what was available of these forms went back to around 1985. The appropriate multipliers for that month were not usually listed in the form and, while the forms contained the elements that go into the calculation of total daily attendance, the total itself was usually not filled in. The computer-generated version of the Monthly Visitor Attendance

Reports at DPR headquarters does contain the multipliers and the calculated total daily attendance, but we did not learn of the existence of microfiche copies of these reports in DPR headquarters until August 1994. For our analysis prior to that time, we had been compelled to figure out for ourselves the calculations that were supposed to be performed, keypunch all the raw data, program the calculations, and then compare the results with the published monthly attendance data. When there were occasional discrepancies, we had to try to guess the cause; sometimes, for example, this was due to data being entered in the wrong column on the handwritten form. Once we obtained the microfiches of the computer-generated forms, we switched to using the daily attendance totals recorded in those forms as the official DPR estimate of attendance.

Because of the pronounced difference between winter and summer beach attendance, we decided at a very early stage to focus our efforts on modelling daily attendance at the affected beaches during winter months only: we felt that it would only confound the analysis if we were to combine summer with winter months. This also reduced the amount of data that we would need to collect. Beach attendance generally begins to pick up around the Easter break at local schools. We therefore decided to focus on daily attendance during the period December–March. To have a comparable data set for all beaches, we started our analysis with the winter of 1986 (December 1985–March 1986). Our data set eventually covered eight winters, four months per winter, from 1986 through 1993.[20]

Modelling Attendance

Paul Ruud estimated a vector-autoregressive model consisting of separate equations for daily attendance at each of the six beaches for which we had collected data (Ruud 1994).[21] The explanatory variables included rain at the beaches, maximum and minimum daily temperature inland, dummy variables for holidays and weekends, annual dummies, linear and non-linear time trends within the winter season, and lagged values of attendance of the beach in question and at neighbouring beaches. The lagged variables captured the empirical fact that high attendance at a beach one day is usually followed by high attendance there on the next day; but, because of some substitution among beaches, high attendance at one beach might be followed by low attendance the next day at a neighbouring beach. Because of the clear presence of heteroscedasticity, the model was formulated as an exponential regression equation with an additive normal error, fitted by non-linear least squares. This allowed the explanatory variables to influence the variance as well as the mean of the logarithm of daily attendance. The model fitted the data well and closely tracked fluctuations in attendance on both normal weather days and unusually cold or wet days.

The fitted model was used to predict the daily attendance that would have occurred during the period 8 February–31 March 1990 in the absence of an oil spill at each of the beaches that were closed. This prediction is summarized in the first two rows of Table 15.1, in the column labelled 'predicted attendance'.[22]

Table 15.1   Estimates of the loss of beach recreation trips

	Recorded attendance	Adjusted attendance	Predicted attendance	Estimated loss
Plaintiff's analysis[a]				
Hanemann (1994):				
During the closure period	225 915	75 984	530 265	454 281
Outside the closure period	683 033	629 537	908 523	278 986
Additional surfing loss				30 485
Total beach loss				763 752
Trial estimate:[a]				
During the closure period		119 135	565 154	446 019
Outside the closure period		575 347	748 213	172 866
Total beach loss				618 885
Defendant's analysis				
Dunford *et al.* (1995):				
During the closure period	225 915	116 622	297 992	181 370
Outside the closure period				0
Adjustment for children				−19 946
Adjustment for foreigners				−2 744
Total beach loss				158 680
Trial estimate:[b]				
During the closure period	226 000	76 000	340 000	264 000
Outside the closure period				0
Total beach loss				264 000

Notes:
[a]   Hanemann exhibit 937, November 1996.
[b]   Dunford exhibit 2224, November 1997.

Adjustments to Attendance Recorded During the Closure Period

The loss of beach recreation was taken to be the difference between the number of beach recreation trips that *would have* occurred at a site from 8 February

1990 onward, as predicted by our model, and the number of beach recreation trips that *did* occur there.

Determining the latter was non-trivial, however, because even when the beaches were closed, some cars were parked in places that lifeguards normally counted, and these were counted in the usual manner regardless of whether or not the occupants were engaged in anything resembling normal beach recreation. The lifeguards continued to count in the usual manner when beaches partially reopened, with clean-up operations continuing in closed-off portions of the beach. From what lifeguards subsequently told us, it was evident that some of the people being counted were working on the spill or were coming as onlookers to view the clean-up. Vehicles recorded as free vehicles at the state beaches included volunteers coming to work on bird rescue, people delivering supplies for bird rescue and oil spill clean-up, and state and local agency personnel working on spill response and clean-up. At Huntington State Beach, for example, 12 858 free vehicles were recorded in March 1990, compared to an average of 2062 free vehicles in March of 1986, 1987, 1988, 1989 and 1991. We assumed that people associated with the unusual increase in free vehicles were not engaged in beach recreation. There was also an unusually large number of paid vehicles using annual passes. From our conversations with lifeguards, we believe that some of these were volunteers coming to work on bird rescue and others were locals coming to the parking area to check things out, but not necessarily to engage in beach recreation.[23] At Huntington State, annual passes accounted for 65 per cent of paid vehicles in March 1990, compared to 22 per cent in February 1990 before the spill, and 25 per cent in March 1991.[24] We assumed that the excess over 25 per cent of paid vehicles represented people not engaged in beach recreation. We made similar adjustments at Bolsa Chica for excess free vehicles and paid vehicles using annual passes.

At Newport Beach, a different adjustment was required. Unlike state beaches where public access is restricted to three or four entry points, there is public access to the city beaches from anywhere along the boardwalk running parallel to the beach. In their attendance estimates, the lifeguards at Newport Beach aim to record the number of people they are responsible for guarding and protecting, not just beach recreation *per se*; therefore, they count anybody in the general vicinity of the beach. Normally these are people engaged in beach recreation; during the spill, this also included clean-up workers, local officials, members of the press, and onlookers standing around the boardwalk watching the clean-up. Hence the Newport Beach attendance data after 7 February include many people who were not engaged in beach recreation, but there was no way of telling how many from the data itself. We knew what fraction of the beach was open each day, and we decided to use this fraction multiplied by our prediction of what beach recreation would have been in the absence of the spill as our estimate of the beach recreation that did occur during the period of beach closure.[25]

Our modifications of the officially recorded attendance are reflected in the first two rows of Table 15.1 in the column labelled 'Adjusted attendance'. The lifeguards reviewed these estimates and concurred with them. We felt that, while they were based on rough judgement and were not precise estimates, they reflected the best information available to us.

Substitution

An issue to which we paid particular attention was the possibility of substitution that could offset the loss of recreation at the beaches affected by the oil spill. This could take the form of *spatial* substitution, whereby trips were diverted from beaches that were closed to other beaches in the Los Angeles area, or *temporal* substitution, whereby trips lost at the time of the spill were merely postponed to a later date. However, after carefully examining the available information, we reached the conclusion that there was probably *no* overall substitution, in the sense of a net increase in aggregate attendance either at other beaches outside the spill area or at the spill area beaches after they reopened.

This conclusion was based on several pieces of evidence. If there had been any substantial spatial substitution, Laguna Beach was an obvious candidate since it was the closest unaffected beach to the south. However, the data there showed an overall *decline* in visitation of approximately 23 per cent compared to what we predicted in the absence of an oil spill. We also found no evidence of an increase in attendance when we looked at other beaches further south, including Aliso Creek Beach, Salt Creek Beach and Doheny State Beach. Similarly, when we looked at four beaches to the north of the spill areas in Santa Monica Bay – Redondo, Hermosa, Manhattan and Dockweiler Beaches – and compared monthly attendance at these beaches in February and March 1990 with attendance in February and March of 1988 and 1989, we found that, if anything, there was a decrease in 1990. This was consistent with something we had been told by lifeguards at one of these beaches, namely that they had received phone calls at the time of the spill from people asking whether it was safe to go to these beaches because of the oil spill. There certainly may have been spatial substitution by some people who used beaches closed due to the spill. But it was apparent that the oil spill had cast a pall over beach recreation through the entire region. Extra visitation of the beaches that remained open by people substituting away from the closed beaches could have been more than offset by a reduction in visitation by people who normally used these other beaches but were staying away because of concerns fuelled by the extensive media coverage of the spill.

With regard to temporal substitution, the data do show a net increase in visitation at two beaches, Bolsa Chica State Beach and Huntington State Beach, after they had reopened (14–31 March 1990).[26] At the other three beaches, however, while there were unusually large crowds on the weekend after the reopening, attendance after that was depressed through to the end of the month compared with what our model predicted in the absence of a spill. This was consistent with the lifeguards' impression that the initial turnout after reopening represented widespread curiosity about the state of the beaches, but then lingering concerns kept some people away. Even including the unusually large attendance immediately following reopening, there was an overall *reduction* in aggregate visitation at the five beaches combined between reopening and 31 March 1990. We suspected that attendance at some of the affected beaches remained depressed into April, but we were not in a position to measure this since Ruud's model was not designed to predict beach attendance in April.

Estimated Loss of Beach Recreation

Using the assumptions described above, our estimate of lost beach recreation in the oil spill area during the period of beach closure amounted to 454 281 lost trips. Overall, we estimated a net loss of 278 986 trips outside the beach closure period through 31 March1990. While we believed there may have been some net loss of beach recreation in April, we could not measure this and did not include it in our estimate.

In addition, we believed that this estimate of lost beach recreation omitted some loss to surfing recreation that was not being captured in the official reports of beach attendance. Surfers often go to the beach very early in the morning and they generally try to avoid paid parking. On both grounds, they are likely to be undercounted when reported beach attendance is based on counts of cars using paid parking lots. By interviewing surfers, surfshop operators and lifeguards, we developed estimates of the number of surfers per week day and weekend day at various surfing locations in the affected area who might be excluded from the official reports of beach attendance. Applying this to the beach closure period (but not the period after reopening), we estimated an additional loss of about 30 485 surfing trips, producing an estimated total loss of 763 752 beach recreation trips, as indicated in the top panel of Table 15.1.

Unit Values

To convert this estimated loss of recreation into a monetary value, we reviewed the existing literature to find an appropriate unit value of beach recreation. When performing this analysis in 1994, we were aware of only a few travel cost studies that provided estimates of consumers' surplus for beach recreation. Of the studies listed in Table 15.2, we were aware at the time of Binkley and

Table 15.2 Unit values for general beach recreation

Study	Beach area	Method	Per trip Value ($1990)	Study cited by:					
				Hanemann (1994)	Dunford et al. (1995)	Deacon & Kolstad (1995)	DOI French et al. (1996)	Hanemann (1997b)	Kolstad & Deacon (2000)
Bell & Leeworthy (1986)	Florida	TC	13.19	×		×	×	×	×
Bell & Leeworthy (1986)	Florida	CV	1.63			×			×
Binkley & Hanemann (1978)	Boston	CV	4.88			×	×		×
Bockstael, McConnell & Strand (1988)	Maryland	TC	1.53–12.55			×			×
Curtis & Shows (1982)	Florida	CV	3.00			×	×	×	
Curtis & Shows (1984)	Florida	CV	5.73			×	×	×	
Dornbusch (1987)	So. California	TC	9.94–10.58			×	×	×	
Leeworthy & Wiley (1991)	New Jersey	TC	21.05				×		
Leeworthy, Schruefer and Wiley (1991)	San Diego	CV	1.00		×	×			
Leeworthy (1995)	San Diego	TC	60.79					×	
Leeworthy, Schruefer and Wiley (1990)	San Onofre	CV	4.33		×	×			
Leeworthy (1995)	San Onofre	TC	57.31					×	
Leeworthy, Schruefer and Wiley (1990)	Cabrillo-Long Beach	CV	1.95–2.17		×	×			
Leeworthy & Wiley (1993)	Cabrillo-Long Beach	TC	8.16					×	
Leeworthy, Schruefer and Wiley (1990)	Santa Monica	CV	1.15–2.33		×	×			

			Value	13.19	2.30	<5.00	11.00	15.00	1.00–4.00
Leeworthy & Wiley (1993)	Santa Monica	TC	18.36					X	
Leeworthy, Schruefer and Wiley (1990)	Leo Carillo	CV	5.38		X				
Leeworthy & Wiley (1993)	Leo Carillo	TC	51.94					X	
Leeworthy (1995)	Pismo Beach	TC	26.20					X	
McConnell (1977)	Rhode Island	CV	0.95–4.30			X			X
McConnell (1992)	Massachusetts	TC	0.70–1.14			X			X
Meta Systems (1985)	Boston	TC	13.60				X		
Moncur (1975)	Hawaii	TC	1.07–4.18			X			X
Silberman and Klock (1988)	New Jersey	CV	4.25			X			
Tyrrell (1982)	Rhode Island	TC & CV	12.82				X		
US Army Corps of Engineers (1981)	Florida	TC	2.47			X			
US Army Corps of Engineers (1993)	Florida	TC	2.17			X			
Recommended unit value ($1990)				13.19	2.30	<5.00	11.00	15.00	1.00–4.00

Hanemann (1978), Meta Systems (1985), Bockstael *et al.* (1988), and McConnell (1977, 1992). However, those studies all valued beach recreation in the Northeast, which we felt was likely to be different from beach recreation in Orange County because:

> both the economic and social situation are different. Orange County offers high quality beaches close to – even immediately adjacent to – where people live. In the Boston area, there are beaches in Boston Harbor which are located close to where people live, but these are decidedly not high quality beaches. The high quality beaches tend to be quite distant, around Cape Cod. In economic terms, the price associated with high quality beach recreation is very different in Orange County than Boston. Partly because of this, and partly because of the climate, beaches play a different role in social life in the two regions. There are good reasons why the phrase 'beach boy' is associated with California rather than Massachusetts. (Hanemann 1994)

Aside from the Northeast beach studies, we were aware of two travel cost studies on beach recreation, one for California by Dornbusch (1987) and the other for Florida by Bell and Leeworthy (1986). Both were well known and often cited in the literature.[27] Although the study by Dornbusch would seem an excellent candidate for a benefits transfer exercise, since it provides estimates of the consumers' surplus associated with water-dependent and water-enhanced recreation at beaches along the entire California coast, including Orange County, we felt that it had a serious flaw which rendered it unreliable. The Dornbusch model was estimated from survey data on beach trips by California residents. Although this was not widely appreciated at the time, the survey only asked respondents how many beach trips they took; it did not ask where they went. Analysts in DPR subsequently used a gravity model to allocate the trips among alternative destinations, and these 'home-made' origin–destination data were then provided to Dornbusch to analyse, as though these were real observations on destination choice behaviour. We felt this was, at best, a circular exercise.

No such problems were apparent in the study by Bell and Leeworthy (1986), based on a statewide survey of Florida residents in March 1984 covering their beach use during the previous 12 months. Bell and Leeworthy estimated a demand function for days at Florida beaches, from which they derived an estimate of consumers' surplus of $10.23 per person-day, in 1984 dollars.[28] We felt that beach recreation plays a similar role in people's lives in Southern California as in Florida. The average household income of the respondents to the Florida residents survey in 1984 was $26 871, compared to a median income of about $37 600 in Orange County in 1985; if anything, this should make Bell and Leeworthy's figure a conservative estimate of the consumers' surplus for beach recreation in Orange County. We used the Consumer Price Index for urban consumers in the Los Angeles–Anaheim–Riverside area to convert their estimate to February 1990 dollars, the time of the spill, which raised it to $13.19 per trip.

While surfing is a specialized recreation activity which would generally be considered to have a higher unit value than general beach recreation – see, for example, Walsh *et al.* (1998) – we knew of no valuation study that dealt specifically with surfing. We decided to use a unit value of $16.95 per surfing trip. This corresponded to the entrance fee at an inland water park in Southern California; the amount was suggested to us by an official of the Surfrider Foundation, who thought most surfers experienced a consumers' surplus at least equal to this, and it represented a premium of about 30 per cent over our estimate of the unit value of general beach recreation.[29]

Our resulting estimate of the value of the lost beach and surfing trips totalled $10 188 500, in 1990 dollars, as indicated in Table 15.3.

Besides beach recreation and surfing, our 1994 analysis covered private boating and party/charter boating for sport fishing, whale watching, and excursions to Catalina Island. Combined, these amounted to about 31 000 trips.[30] Using benefits transfer estimates of consumers' surplus for boating and sport fishing, we estimated a total loss of $1 231 609 for these categories of recreation. Thus, the total estimate in our 1994 report for lost recreation use value amounted to $11 420 108, as indicated in the top panel of Table 15.3.

THE RESPONSE FROM THE DEFENDANTS

In response to our 1994 reports, economists for two of the defendants produced reports critiquing our analysis: Professors Deacon and Kolstad wrote a report in March 1995 on behalf of the Golden West refinery, and Professor Thurman and Dr Dunford wrote reports in May 1995 on behalf of ATTRANSCO.[31] These reports covered fairly similar ground, disputing both our estimate of lost recreation trips and the consumers' surplus estimates we used for benefits transfer.

Disputing the Estimate of Lost Beach Use

With respect to the estimate of the number of beach trips lost as a result of the oil spill, the defendants raised five issues. First, there were criticisms of our data: the lifeguards' reports of beach attendance seemed unreliable. The defendants questioned both the methods by which attendance was estimated and the specific conversion factors used for passengers per vehicle, and walk-ons as a proportion of drive-ins.[32] Professors Deacon and Kolstad indicated that they intended to conduct overflights of beaches to verify the lifeguards' reports of attendance.

Table 15.3   Estimates of the overall recreation loss

	No. of trips	Per trip loss (1990$)	Total loss (1990$)
Plaintiff's analysis			
Hanemann (1994):			
(A) Loss during beach closure period			
General beach recreation trips lost	454 280	13.19	5 991 953
Surfing trips lost	30 485	16.95	516 721
Private boating trips lost	22 074	34.00	750 516
Sport fishing trips lost	1 860	87.12	162 043
Whale watching and excursion trips lost	7 090	45.00	319 050
(B) Outside closure period			
General beach recreation trips lost	278 986	13.19	3 679 825
Total loss			11 420 108
Hanemann (1997b):			
(A) Loss during beach closure period			
General beach recreation trips lost	389 580	15.00	5 843 700
Surfing trips lost	28 290	18.75	530 438
Surfing trips diverted to substitute sites	28 148	12.00	337 776
General beach recreation and surfing trips under adverse conditions	119 135	3.00	357 405
Private boating trips lost	13 074	40.00	522 960
Sport fishing trips lost	1 860	83.00	154 380
Whale watching and excursion trips diverted	7 090	12.00	85 080
(B) Net loss after reopening, in March			
General beach recreation trips lost	147 064	15.00	2 205 960
Surfing trips lost	12 901	18.75	241 894
Surfing trips diverted to substitute sites	12 901	12.00	154 812
General beach recreation and surfing trips under adverse conditions	212 878	3.00	638 635
(C) Net loss in April			
General beach recreation and surfing trips under adverse conditions	370 000	3.00	1 110 000
Total loss			12 183 039
Defendant's analysis			
Dunford *et al.* (1995):			
Loss during beach closure period			
General beach recreation trips lost	158 680	2.30	365 403
Credit for rubbernecker trips	109 164	0.95	(103 257)
Total loss			262 146
Dunford exhibit 2224:			
Loss during beach closure period			
General beach recreation trips lost	264 000	2.30	607 200
Total loss			607 200

Second, the defendants criticized the adjustments we made to reported attendance during the period when beaches were partially reopened and clean-up was still proceeding. Without offering any estimates of their own, they asserted that our adjustments lacked foundation. Moreover, Dr Dunford argued that the oil spill and clean-up activities provided a positive consumers' surplus to 'rubberneckers' which should be counted as an offset to some of the lost consumers' surplus from beach recreation.[33] He also proposed two other adjustments. First, he noted that some of the beach recreation in Southern California was made by foreigners and/or illegal immigrants. On legal grounds, ATTRANSCO's attorney held that this should not be counted in a damage assessment; Dunford felt we should have made an effort to estimate this beach use and omit it from our calculation of lost recreation. Second, he took the position that 'children should be excluded from estimates of forgone user days when calculating natural resource damages' on the grounds that they 'do not understand the concepts of prices and income constraints'.

Third, the defendants challenged our conclusion that there was no net substitution of recreation to beaches elsewhere in the region. They found our lack of evidence for an increase in attendance at Laguna Beach and at beaches in Santa Monica Bay unpersuasive. On theoretical grounds they felt that substitution must have occurred since there were many other beaches in Orange County and Los Angeles County that remained open during the spill and could have been used as substitutes 'given southern Californians' well-known penchant for driving long distances to work and recreate'.[34] Beyond the general argument, however, they presented no specific empirical evidence that significant substitution had occurred.

Fourth, they took the position that there could be no loss of recreation once the affected beaches had fully reopened; their estimate of loss was confined to the closure period.[35]

Fifth, Professor Thurman and Dr Dunford criticized Ruud's (1994) econometric model of beach attendance. They suggested that different weather variables should have been used, such as temperature at the beach as opposed to temperature inland. They claimed that the weather during the closure period in 1990 was unusually cold and that of 'Ruud's model does not produce predictions that are consistent with the low temperatures'. They also objected to his use of lagged dependent variables because actual lagged attendance could not be known when forecasting attendance during the spill period, and the use of a prediction of lagged attendance would lead to a compounding of the errors in attendance predictions. Using our data on attendance, which we had turned over along with the expert reports in 1994, Thurman (1995) estimated his own model of attendance at the five beaches affected by the spill, and he obtained a much lower prediction of what attendance would have been during the closure period in the absence of a spill: 297 992 trips in aggregate, as compared to Ruud's prediction of 530 265 trips for the same beaches during the same period.

Thurman's model differed from Ruud's in three main ways: he used different temperature variables and made minor changes to some of the other variables; he omitted the lagged dependent variables; and he adopted a different stochastic specification. Ruud (1994) had conducted a preliminary analysis using a log-linear model of the form:

$$\ln(y) = X\beta + \varepsilon, \tag{15.1}$$

in which the natural logarithm of beach attendance, y, was explained by a linear function of exogenous explanatory variables and lagged dependent variables plus a normal random error term, ε, with zero mean. After estimating a system of equations like (15.1), Ruud had performed diagnostic tests for first-order autocorrelation and heteroscedasticity in the residuals. The score test statistics unambiguously indicated the absence of autocorrelation, but gave a strong indication of heteroscedasticity. To deal with the heteroscedasticity, Ruud adopted an alternative specification with an additive error:

$$y = \exp(X\beta) + \nu, \tag{15.2}$$

where ν is a normal error with zero mean, which he estimated by non-linear least squares. This was the model that he used for predicting beach attendance. Thurman (1995) first estimated an ordinary least-squares model like (15.1), omitting the lagged dependent variables and making changes to the temperature variables and some other variables. Observing evidence of autocorrelation and heteroscedasticity in the residuals, he then estimated a generalized least-squares (GLS) version of (15.1) incorporating an autocorrelated and heteroscedastic error structure for ε. To estimate predicted attendance, Thurman used the anti-log of the predicted dependent variable in (15.1), namely $\exp(Xb)$, where b was his GLS estimator of β. This, of course, generates an estimate of the *median* of y which, for the lognormal distribution, is lower than the mean. This oversight accounted for some of the difference in attendance predictions; it was subsequently corrected in Thurman (1996), produced at his deposition.[36] However, we believe that most of the difference in attendance predictions is due to Thurman's use of specification (15.1) instead of (15.2), combined with the omission of the lagged dependent variables.

Our own view was that the vector autoregression model is a standard procedure for making forecasts in economics and business, and is entirely appropriate for forecasting beach attendance. We felt that Ruud's inclusion of lagged variables accurately captured the complex pattern of autocorrelation that one observes in daily beach attendance. Ruud's goal was to find the best prediction of daily attendance. He used weather variables and other exogenous variables that he found produced the best fit.[37] On inspecting the day-to-day predictions, we found no indication that Ruud's model performed poorly on unusually cold days.[38] We noted that Professor Thurman's model without the lagged dependent variables did not fit the data as well as Ruud's model based on adjusted R^2 statistics. At his deposition, Professor Thurman testified that he had not investigated whether his model fitted the data as well as Ruud's, and he had not performed a non-nested specification test of (15.1) versus (15.2) that had been suggested to him by a peer reviewer for TER.[39]

Disputing the Estimate of Consumers' Surplus

The defendants also criticized the estimates of consumers' surplus that we used to value the recreational losses. In the case of beach recreation, they both criticized various aspects of Bell and Leeworthy's (1986) study and also proposed alternative studies that yielded considerably lower estimates of consumers' surplus.

With regard to Bell and Leeworthy, they objected that this survey involved the recall of beach trips over the preceding year, which was likely to be unreliable, and they criticized the specification of the price variable, the poor fit of the demand equation, the absence of attributes of individual beaches as factors influencing demand, and the sensitivity of the estimates of consumers' surplus to functional form. In addition, Dunford *et al.* (1995) claimed that the Bell and Leeworthy study violated the necessary criterion of similarity for a benefits transfer exercise because 'the beaches in the Bell and Leeworthy study are not similar to the injured beaches' and 'there are substantial differences ... with respect to racial composition, gender, age and household income' between Bell and Leeworthy's respondents and the users of the injured beaches.[40] While we were aware of the shortcomings of the Bell and Leeworthy study, the study had been widely cited in the literature, and it was not obvious to us in which direction its potential shortcomings would affect the estimate of consumers' surplus.

The defendants also made the point that Bell and Leeworthy were valuing beach recreation during the summer while the oil spill occurred in the winter when, they claimed, beach recreation should have a lower value. They cited a contingent valuation (CV) survey of beach users by McConnell (1977) which found that beach users gave a lower value for beach recreation on days when the temperature was lower: 'for example, reported values when temperatures are 65°F were less than half of values when temperatures were 75°F'. But McConnell's study was conducted during ten days in August 1974 at Rhode Island beaches, and we felt it shed no light on the difference between summer and winter beach recreation in Los Angeles or Florida.[41] It seemed entirely possible to us that, in Los Angeles, the average consumers' surplus *for those people who go to the beach during the winter* could be at least as high as the average consumers' surplus for those who go to the beach in the summer.

Another argument offered against our analysis was that the loss of beach trips during February and March amounted to only about 8 per cent of the total number of trips to these beaches over the year as a whole. Therefore, it was claimed that there should only be a small marginal loss of consumers' surplus. This argument was emphasized by Randy Moss and Dr Bruce Owen of Economists, Inc., consultants to the TAPS fund, who applied it to the Bell and Leeworthy data and measured the consumers' surplus loss per trip associated with the least valuable 8 per cent of beach trips, which they calculated at around $1 per trip as opposed to the average consumers' surplus of $13.19 per trip. We disagreed because we felt that, in the circumstances of the beach closure, it was the average consumers' surplus per trip and not the marginal consumers' surplus per trip that was relevant. While the marginal consumers' surplus per trip would be appropriate if the authorities had used prices to allocate the reduction in beach use, the actual circumstances created by the oil spill were more akin to non-price rationing, where it was agreed in the literature on peak load pricing that the average consumers' surplus was the relevant measure of the welfare loss due to outages.[42]

The defendants also criticized us for not using other sources of information on the consumers' surplus from beach recreation, most especially surveys of beach users in Los Angeles and San Diego counties conducted in the summers of 1989 and 1990 by Dr Vernon R. Leeworthy, the co-author of Bell and Leeworthy (1986) and now on the staff on NOAA's Strategic Assessment Branch. These surveys were part of a larger multiyear intergovernmental cooperative research project to develop estimates of the economic value of recreational activities on the public lands known as Public Area Recreation Visitors Survey (PARVS).[43] The questionnaire contained a large number of travel cost type questions for beach goers interviewed on site. Dr Leeworthy and his colleagues had estimated a variety of travel cost models to these data. Using what they considered their most conservative judgements with respect to price definition and specification of functional form, and truncating consumers' surplus at the highest observed price in the data, they obtained the following estimates of average consumers' surplus per trip (in 1990 dollars) for beaches in Southern California: $8.16 at Cabrillo-Long Beach, $18.36 at Santa Monica, $26.20 at Pismo State Beach, $51.94 at Leo Carillo State Beach, located at the northern end of Los Angeles County, $57.31 at San Onofre State Beach in San Diego County, and $60.79 at beaches in San Diego.[44]

At the end of the survey, after all the travel cost questions, there was a closed-ended contingent valuation (CV) question: 'Suppose the agency that manages this site started charging a *daily* admission fee of $X *per person*. The money from the admission fee will be used to maintain the site in the present condition, but there would be *no* improvements. Would you continue to use this site?'. The daily admission fee was one of 10 randomly assigned amounts between $1 and $75. Most of those who responded said 'no'. Leeworthy *et al.* (1990, 1991) tabulated these responses, but did not analyse them further for an estimate of willingness to pay (WTP) because they felt that the payment vehicle was flawed. These were public beaches which people already supported through their tax dollars. Leeworthy felt that beach users might have resented the notion of paying a charge just to walk onto the beach (which is virtually unheard of in California) as opposed to paying a fee for some specific service such as parking; and they might have especially resented the notion that the revenues would not be used to improve the beach in any way.

The defendants rejected the travel cost component of the PARVS survey, but they embraced the CV data with enthusiasm. Dunford *et al.* (1995) obtained the PARVS data from Leeworthy and fitted a WTP model to the CV responses. They obtained estimates for the mean WTP per trip of $2.17 for Cabrillo-Long Beach, $2.33 for Santa Monica, and $3.38 for all California sites combined. Based on this, they decided to use $2.30/trip as their best estimate of the value per trip for the lost beach recreation.

Several aspects of their analysis struck us as questionable, including the fact that they analysed the CV responses without any reference to the respondent's actual travel cost, they selected the two least-valued Southern California beaches to represent the beaches affected by the oil spill,[45] and their welfare calculation implied that beach users' WTP to go to the beach is *negative* in the left tail of the distribution.[46] Beyond this, there were two fundamental reasons why we considered the PARVS CV data unsuited to the purpose for which Dunford *et al.* were using them. The first is 'protest zeroes': that is, respondents who say 'no' to a CV survey, not because the item is not worth that much to them but rather because they feel that *they* should not have to pay for it in the manner proposed. In our view, the form of the payment vehicle made this likely. There were data from the PARVS survey itself to substantiate this concern.[47] At the end of the on-site interview, respondents were asked to supply a mailing address so that they could be sent a short questionnaire covering additional information on their expenses during the trip. The closed-ended CV question was repeated in this mail survey. In the mail survey, but not the on-site survey, there was also a follow-up question for people who answered 'no' which asked them to check the reason for their response. We subsequently examined the mail survey responses for the Southern California beaches and concluded that a minimum of *one-third* of the negative responses to these CV questions were likely to be protest zeroes because the respondent either checked 'I do not believe fees should be charged' or gave another reason such as 'they shouldn't charge pedestrians' or 'taxes should be used to maintain and improve the facility'. The proportion of protest zeroes among the responses to the on-site survey is likely to have been higher because the protest zeroes are more likely than others to have been non-respondents to the mail survey.[48]

Second, even with protest zeroes properly accounted for, we do not believe that the PARVS CV can provide an estimate of use value applicable to the loss of beach recreation caused by the *American Trader* oil spill. The CV question values a single beach taken by itself, with no change or interruption in the availability of any other beach in the area.[49] However, the essence of what happened in February and March 1990 is that multiple beaches were closed simultaneously: almost all beach recreation in that part of Orange County was effectively shut down for a period of time. If the beaches in that area are substitutes for one another, Carson *et al.* (1998) show that the loss of consumers' surplus from the closure of one beach is *raised* by the simultaneous closure of another substitute beach. Even if there were no other problems the PARVS CV questions would not capture this, leading to an underestimate of the welfare loss per trip during the closure period.

With respect to the PARVS travel cost data, Dunford *et al.* had nothing to say about this data and did not mention the estimates of consumers' surplus that Leeworthy and Wiley's (1993) derived from it.[50] Deacon and Kolstad (1995) did mention the PARVS travel cost data but they rejected it as unreliable, and focused instead on the CV results.[51] Unlike Dunford *et al.* (1995), Deacon and Kolstad (1995) went to some lengths to review the literature on valuation of beach recreation, as indicated in Table 15.2. They identified a number of relatively obscure studies, including Silberman and Klock (1988) and Curtis and Shows (1982, 1984) which used an open-ended CV to value beach recreation. Their citations from the valuation literature were distinctly weighted towards CV. In addition to not citing the analysis of PARVS travel cost data by Leeworthy and Wiley (1991, 1993), they cited Binkley and Hanemann's analysis of the CV data collected in the 1974 Boston area beach recreation survey, but not the analysis by Hanemann (1978) or Meta Systems (1985) of the travel cost data collected in that survey. On the basis of the studies they had cited, they concluded that 'the value of a winter beach day in California ... is likely to be in the under-$5 per day range'.[52]

PREPARATION FOR THE TRIAL

During 1996 and 1997, as prospects for a settlement with ATTRANSCO faded, we prepared for trial. Our work proceeded in four phases. The first phase was conducting a beach count survey in February and March 1996 to investigate the accuracy of the lifeguards' reports of attendance during that time of year at the beaches affected by the spill; the findings were reported in Hanemann (1996). This was followed by preparation for the depositions of Chapman,

Ruud, Thurman, Hanemann and Dunford in September, November and December 1996. Subsequently there was a legal fight over documents which Dr Dunford had brought to his deposition but which were withheld by ATTRANSCO's attorney. This ended in February 1997 when the court ordered that the documents be turned over to us. The third phase was conducting a boating and surfing survey in Orange County in February and March 1997, the findings of which were reported in Hanemann (1997a). The fourth phase was preparation for the depositions of Hanemann and Dunford in August 1997, including the production of a final report on our conclusions (Hanemann 1997b). This work had three main goals: to improve our estimate of the number of beach trips lost due to the spill; to break out surfing from general beach recreation; and to refine our estimates of unit value for surfing and general beach recreation.[53] As we obtained information and data from Dr Dunford through the deposition process, we modified and refined our analysis.

Verifying the lifeguards' reports of attendance in a reliable and systematic manner through some form of survey had long been on our minds. But we estimated that to do this right would cost $50 000 or more. As long as the Trustees thought that the case would settle, they were reluctant to authorize spending on that scale. Now that a trial seemed imminent, they allowed us to go ahead, with the full understanding that they would have to live with whatever we found.

An important factor in their decision was information they received that Professors Deacon and Kolstad had conducted an aerial survey of some of the affected beaches in February and March 1995. When they compared the results with the lifeguards' reports of attendance for those days, Deacon and Kolstad concluded that the lifeguards' reports significantly overstate actual attendance.[54]

Overflights are a relatively inexpensive way to measure beach attendance at a particular point in time: the beach is photographed from a low-flying plane, and then a count is made of all the people in the photograph. By itself, however, this is not conclusive: the number of people on the beach during the rest of the day is not known; neither is it known whether the people seen on the beach on different overflights are the same or different – it depends on beach visit duration. To deal with this Deacon and Kolstad had stationed interviewers at the beach on the day of the overflights who stopped people and asked them when they had arrived at the beach that day and when they expected to leave. From the survey responses, Deacon and Kolstad produced an estimate of mean visit duration. The overflights were conducted at 11 a.m., 1:30 p.m. and 4 p.m. on two weekdays and three weekend days. At Huntington City Beach on Friday 17 February 1995, for example, 345 people were counted on the beach from the aerial photographs at 11 a.m., 700 people at 1:30 p.m., and 555 people at 4 p.m. Deacon and Kolstad estimated the mean visit duration at 1.91 hours that day. They assumed that there were no people on the beach before 6 a.m., and that instantaneous attendance then rose linearly from zero to 345 at 11 a.m.; for instantaneous beach attendance between 11 a.m. and 4 p.m. they extrapolated between the three aerial counts. To extrapolate after 4 p.m., Deacon and Kolstad used an estimate of the number of people on the beach at 6 p.m. developed by the interviewers on the ground. They summed their estimates of instantaneous attendance from 6 a.m. to 6 p.m., and then divided this total by the estimate of mean visit duration to obtain their estimate of the total number of visits to the beach. Their estimate for Huntington City Beach on 17 February was 2676; this was well below half the total attendance reported by the Huntington City Beach lifeguards that day, which was 6242. At Newport Beach, the discrepancy between their estimate of attendance and the lifeguards' report was even greater.

However, their estimate depends on some assumptions which are open to question: that there is nobody on the beach before 6 a.m. or after 6 p.m. (both of which are inconsistent with data from the on-site interviews), that attendance grows linearly from 6 a.m. to 11 a.m. (the evidence is that there is an initial pulse of early-morning surfers and beach-goers), and the estimate of mean visit duration.[55] Moreover, when converting from aggregate instantaneous visitation to the number of separate visits, they assumed that one over the mean of visit duration is a good estimate of the expectation of the reciprocal of visit duration, which is incorrect: for a positive random variable x, $1/E\{x\}$ is *not* a good estimate of $E\{1/x\}$.[56] The failure to allow for this may have reduced their attendance estimate by 40–60 per cent, given the distribution of trip durations in their survey. When all these factors are considered, the conclusion regarding the accuracy of the lifeguards' reports of attendance was less clear-cut.

The best way to resolve this, in our view, was a careful, ground-based count of beach attendance using observers on the beach to count people as they arrived. We conducted this beach count survey at the beaches affected by the spill on randomly selected days during the period from 10 February to 17 March 1996.[57] To implement the count, we hired interviewers from a local survey company to serve as enumerators, we selected sampling locations, we trained the enumerators, and we designed a sampling plan that provided coverage of the beaches for 12 hours per day, with each team of enumerators working half-an-hour on and half-an-hour off from 6:30 a.m. to 6:30 p.m.[58] In all, there were 57 individual beach count days, randomly assigned over the five-week survey period, with oversampling of weekend days and Fridays relative to the other weekdays.[59] To deal with beach users who leave the beach during their visit and then return, we designed a separate repeat visitor survey. This was conducted by a separate interviewer on two weekdays and two weekend days at each beach. The interviewer sampled every tenth person entering the beach and asked them: 'Is this the first time that you have come onto the sand at a beach today?'.

If the answer was 'no', the interviewer asked: 'Where did you come onto the sand at a beach earlier today?'.[60] The results were used to adjust the attendance estimates from the main beach count survey.[61]

When we compared the results of our counts with the lifeguards' reports of attendance for those same days we found that, on any given day, there usually was some discrepancy, but the discrepancy could be in either direction: some days, the lifeguards reported a larger attendance than we had counted, and some days a smaller attendance. On Saturday 9 March for example, the lifeguards at Newport Beach reported an attendance of 45 000 while our count from the beach survey was 19 699. However, on Saturday 24 February the lifeguards at Newport reported an attendance of 22 000 while we counted 22 767, and on Saturday 10 February the lifeguards at Newport reported an attendance of 3500 while we counted 10 958. At the state beaches, while we observed fewer people per vehicle than the conversion factors used by lifeguards, we also observed a higher ratio of walk-ons to drive-ins than they assumed. Extrapolating from the survey days to the entire five-week survey period, the attendance reported by the lifeguards at the three state beaches combined understated our count of beach attendance by 4.2 per cent, while the attendance reported by the lifeguards at the two city beaches combined overstated our count of beach attendance by 13.3 per cent.[62] For all five beaches combined, the attendance reported by the lifeguards over the five-week period exceeded our count of attendance by just 9.4 per cent.

The comparison revealed a distinct pattern in the reporting errors. The lifeguards cover attendance for only part of the day, and they tend to miss out on early morning and late afternoon attendance. On the other hand, while their estimates are fairly accurate for normal attendance, they tend to overstate attendance when large crowds show up.[63] The result is a tendency to understate attendance on days with low attendance and overstate it on days with high attendance. If our count of daily attendance (on the vertical axis) is plotted against the lifeguards' report of daily attendance (on the horizontal axis), the shape of the graph looks something like a logarithmic function for both the city and the state beaches. We ran logarithmic, exponential and Gomperz regressions of our counts versus the lifeguards' reports and found that the exponential model – similar to (15.2) above – fitted the data best. We could not reject the hypothesis that the regression equations are the same across the city and state beaches, and therefore used a single equation for all beaches pooled.[64] We used the pooled exponential regression equation to correct both the *predictions* of beach attendance in the absence of a spill during the period 8 February–31 March 1990 from Ruud's model, and also our estimates of the beach recreation that *did* occur during this period.[65] Our revised estimate of lost beach use during this period was about 618 000 trips, as shown in the second panel of Table 15.1.

Following the reports on the 1996 beach count survey, the next major event was the depositions in September, November and December 1996. From our perspective, an important aspect of the depositions was the opportunity it afforded us to see for the first time the information that had been collected by RTI/TER. Since Dr Dunford's public position had been that he was unfamiliar with the lifeguards' attendance data and had no estimate of his own for the loss of recreation, we were interested to learn that, in 1990 and 1991, RTI had contacted the same lifeguards and had collected the same data from them as we did, and had used this to estimate a similar model of beach attendance. We were also interested in an extensive collection of clippings from the *Orange County Register* that Dr Dunford turned over. In particular, we noted a story about some surfers going to other sites because their usual sites were closed as a result of the spill; we had not seen a story to this effect in the *Los Angeles Times*, which we had monitored on-line for the duration of the spill.[66]

We therefore decided to make an attempt to collect some more information about the effect of the spill on surfers, and to break surfing out from general beach recreation. To accomplish the latter, we conducted a second beach count survey in February and March 1997, designed to collect information on the proportion of surfers using each beach. We employed the same methodology as in our 1996 survey but on a smaller scale, involving only 22 individual beach survey days spread over the four main beaches, excluding Crystal Cove. At each beach, we counted the number of surfers and non-surfers entering the beach. We found that the proportion of beach trips accounted for by surfers was 9.9 per cent at Newport Beach, 13.9 per cent at Huntington City Beach, 14.9 per cent at Bolsa Chica and 17.5 per cent at Huntington State Beach (Hanemann 1997a).

We also collected the official reports of beach attendance for the survey days, and compared them with our counts. We obtained the same results as in 1996 – extrapolating to the full five-week period of the survey, in aggregate the official reports exceeded our counts by about 9.4 per cent, and the same regression equation was consistent with both years' data. We saw no reason, therefore, to revise our estimate of 618 000 lost beach trips between 8 February and 31 March 1990, but we now subdivided these into lost surfing trips and lost general beach recreation trips using the proportions of surfers from the 1997 beach count survey.[67]

To prepare for the 1997 beach count survey we conducted two focus groups with surfers, in the course of which we asked if anyone remembered the 1990 oil spill and how had they been affected.[68] Everyone who was an active surfer and lived in the area in 1990 remembered the spill and had been affected by it. On weekends, they had been able to go to other locations outside the spill area but, on weekdays, they could not manage the extra time needed to travel outside the area and they generally gave up their surfing.[69] Overall, for this group, about 50 per cent of their surfing trips were lost, and 50 per cent were made to substitute sites outside the spill area. We therefore decided to assume that only half of the surfing trips lost at beaches affected by the spill between 8 February and 31 March 1990 were ultimately lost, and the other half were offset by trips made to other, substitute sites.

With regard to general beach recreation, however, we still found no evidence of spatial substitution by the general public; the information available indicated no net increase, or perhaps a net decrease, in attendance at beaches outside the spill area during February and March 1990. Therefore, we saw no reason to revise our assumption of no net substitution for non-surfing trips lost at the affected beaches between 8 February and 31 March 1990.

In addition to refining our estimate of lost beach and surfing recreation, we also worked to improve our estimate of lost consumers' surplus per trip. We had two new pieces of information since completing our 1994 report. First, we had received a copy of the Department of Interior's (DOI) revised Type A Natural Resource Damage Assessment Model for Coastal and Marine Environments, which included a value for beach recreation (French *et al.* 1996, section 10.3.3). The DOI report contained a literature review that selected seven studies for consideration, as indicated in Table 15.2. The report used the average value from these studies – about $11 in February 1990 dollars – as 'representative of the available empirical results of the value of a day at the beach. ... This average net value represents a best estimate for the baseline value of a general beach recreational opportunity'.

Second, once we knew of the availability of the PARVS data for Southern California beaches we obtained a copy and conducted our own statistical analysis of the travel cost data. To be conservative, we restricted our analysis to one-day beach trips by residents of Southern California. In order to avoid sensitivity to functional form, we estimated the recreation demand functions non-parametrically using a kernel estimator.[70] In our estimation, we corrected for the sampling bias that is associated with an intercept survey by weighting the data proportionally to the inverse of the number of beach trips.[71] Non-parametric estimation is necessarily limited to the range of prices covered in the data; with a sample of beach users, therefore, it provides no information on the part of the demand function in the vicinity of the cut-off price, which determines the upper corner of the Marshallian triangle. To handle this, we made a conservative assumption about the cutoff price based on an assessment of the spatial extent of the market for each site, and then calculated the upper part of the Marshallian triangle using a linear interpolation to the upper end of the non-parametrically estimated demand function. We tried several treatments including using log price instead of price and travel cost at 13 versus 21 cents per mile (the latter was the cost reported by respondents in the PARVS surveys). We focused on Cabrillo Beach and Long Beach (broken down separately) and

Santa Monica and San Diego Beaches, both separately and pooled. We estimated the predicted consumers' surplus per trip at approximately$35–40 for Long Beach and San Diego, and $20–25 for Cabrillo, Santa Monica and all four beaches pooled.

We believed that the beaches affected by the *American Trader* oil spill are better than an average beach in the US. Therefore, we considered that the consumers' surplus associated with the use of these beaches was some amount higher than DOI's estimate of $11 for a generic beach trip. Our own non-parametric analysis of the PARVS travel cost data supported Leeworthy's parametric estimate of $23/trip for Southern California beaches pooled. Based on this, our final conclusion was that a reasonable range for the consumers' surplus from general beach recreation at the beaches affected by the spill would be $11–23/trip, in 1990 dollars. Our specific point estimate, intended to be conservative, was $15/trip.

We believed that a different value should be used for surfing, since it is a more specialized activity that requires a higher degree of skill, knowledge and appreciation, and draws a very loyal following. Based on the travel cost literature, we believed that the consumers' surplus for surfing in Orange County was likely to be at least 25 per cent higher than the consumers' surplus for general beach recreation, and we therefore used a value of $18.75/trip in 1990 dollars for surfing trips lost.

As noted above, we assumed that half of the affected surfing trips were offset by substitution to beaches outside the area. This still entailed some loss of consumers' surplus, due to the increased cost of travel. For a surfer who lived in Huntington Beach and went instead to San Clemente, there would be an extra 74 miles of round-trip travel and an extra 90 minutes of travel time. For one who lived in Anaheim, the second most common city of origin for visitors to Huntington Beach, and went to San Clemente instead, there would be an extra 38 miles in round-trip travel and an extra 38 minutes in travel time. To reflect this cost, we used $12/trip as our estimate of the average loss of consumers' surplus for surfing trips diverted to substitute sites.

At Dr Dunford's deposition in December 1996, ATTRANSCO's attorney withheld some of the documents that he had brought along to comply with a document production request. In February 1997, the Court directed that these be turned over. Among them were a number of documents containing portions that had been redacted. In May, the Court directed ATTRANSCO to turn over unredacted versions of the documents. Among the documents we then obtained were various materials relating to a survey that RTI had conducted at the affected beaches in Orange County immediately after the beaches reopened, comprising on-site interviews with about 560 beach users during March and April 1990. The interviewer asked about the travel time, distance and mode of transportation for the current trip, what activities they engaged in and how long they had been there, and then continued: 'Now I'd like to ask several questions about your use of beaches earlier this year. About how many trips to the beach did you make in February? Which beaches did you visit? Would you also describe your typical recreational activity and the approximate number of hours you stayed on a typical visit?'. The same questions were then asked for beach trips in January. At the end, the interviewer asked about the respondent's education, occupation, race and income. The survey was designed to collect information 'that will allow us to estimate the value which surfers and other users give to a trip to the beach' (Morton *et al.* 1991). It was apparent, however, that RTI subsequently did not perform this analysis. We decided to try to obtain the data with a view to doing this. Since the documents we had received did not include the data from the survey or the sampling plan, we asked the state's attorneys to press ATTRANSCO further. This resulted in the production, in June, of 35 floppy diskettes that ATTRANSCO's attorney had inadvertently overlooked. These contained about 700 electronic files which RTI staffers took with them when they moved to TER in October 1994. There was no documentation for the contents of these files. On searching through them, we found no master copy of the survey data, no codebook, and no account of the sampling design or the sample weights.[72, 73] In the absence of this information, we were unable to proceed with using the RTI survey data to estimate a travel cost model.[74, 75]

Nevertheless, we did find some information from the survey that was of interest. After the travel cost questions, the interviewer asked: 'Do you think the condition of the beach is better, worse, or about the same as it was before the spill?'. These questions had been added at the insistence of BP, which was co-funding the survey along with ATTRANSCO. The responses were perhaps not what the survey's sponsors had wished to hear, and we suspect that this is why the survey had been placed, as it were, in a deep freeze. Even eight weeks after the beaches had reopened, 50 per cent of the respondents at Huntington City and Bolsa Chica State Beach and 43 per cent at Newport Beach felt that the condition of the beach was worse than before the spill.[76] When asked in what way, 56 per cent of respondents cited oil or tar balls, 54 per cent cited appearance or odour, and 26 per cent cited lower-quality recreation.[77] It was also noteworthy that 37.5 per cent of the beach users intercepted in the survey reported that they were engaged in surfing, since this was far more than the 10–18 per cent of beach users we had observed to be surfers in our 1997 beach count survey.[78] The unusually high proportion of surfers would be consistent with the hypothesis that non-surfers were tending to stay away from the beaches after they reopened while surfers, being more avid, went back as soon as possible. It would explain the overall lack of spatial and temporal substitution that we were finding. It would also imply that there had been some loss of beach recreation in April as well as March 1990.[79]

In the light of this new information, we decided to add a component to our estimate of beach recreation loss that would account for the reduction in consumers' surplus that we believe occurred when people went to the beach but found that the quality of their recreational experience was impaired due to the abnormal circumstances created by the spill. This diminution of utility enjoyment applied to people who used the affected beaches in February, March and April 1990, both while the clean-up was still progressing and immediately after reopening. We felt that a rough but reasonable estimate for the loss of utility when recreation was occurring under adverse conditions was 20 per cent of the consumers' surplus for a normal general beach recreation trip, or $3/trip in 1990 dollars. We applied this loss to all the beach and surfing trips that did occur at the affected beaches between 8 February and 31 March 1990; we also applied it to 37 per cent of approximately one million beach and surfing trips that were made to these beaches in April 1990.[80]

As indicated in Table 15.3, our overall estimate for the value of lost beach recreation, including both surfing and general beach recreation was $11 420 619 in 1990 dollars. In addition, we estimated the loss of boating recreation at $762 420 in 1990 dollars.[81] These two losses, totalling $12 183 039, were what the state presented to the jury at trial. At the trial, we also testified that, if the loss were adjusted by the increase in the Consumer Price Index between the time of the spill and the time of the trial, this would raise the damage estimate to about $14.5 million.

THE TRIAL

The argumentation in the economic portion of the trial focused largely on the concept of consumers' surplus, the quality of the lifeguards' data and the estimates of the number of beach trips lost as a result of the spill, and the value that should be applied to these trips.

The objectives of the state's attorneys in this phase of the trial were: (a) to demonstrate to the jury the painstaking nature of our efforts to collect the best possible information about beach-related recreation in Orange County and the effect on this of the oil spill; and (b) to demystify for the jury the economic concept of consumers' surplus and make it a matter of common sense to them that they should award damages to the state for the public's loss of the use and enjoyment of public beaches. They were successful in both objectives. Part of their success was due to a skilful strategy for managing the exposition of the state's case. The case rested on a mass of tedious detail conjoined with poten-tially impenetrable economic and statistical argumentation. To render this both transparent and credible, without overloading the jury, they presented the state's case in successive iterations, through the successive testimony of Chapman,

Ruud and Hanemann. Each gave a more detailed explanation of the state's approach, building on what had been said before and paving the way for what would be said next. While formally entering documents into evidence, the attorneys took Chapman through all the data that we had assembled, filling a large box with papers and reports. 'That box' became something of a running gag during our direct examinations; at the same time, it was a tangible symbol of our research-oriented approach to analysing the effects of the spill.

As the judge stated in his directions to the jury, the plaintiffs were entitled to receive 'damages for the loss of use and enjoyment of public beaches and other public resources or facilities'.[82] What was at issue was the measurement of this loss of use and enjoyment. The state's attorney argued that these were real economic damages, they could be measured, and the appropriate measure was the loss of consumers' surplus from beach recreation, which was a well-known and accepted concept in economics. While Dr Dunford was on record as agreeing with those statements, ATTRANSCO's attorney challenged them vigorously. 'This is the very first trial for consumer surplus in the United States', he told the jury.[83] He employed three main lines of attack. First, he argued that consumers' surplus was 'totally speculative' and not something real: 'If you intended to go to the store and buy a pair of dockers and you've budgeted $80 ... and if you find those dockers for $40, you have made a consumers' surplus of $40. Now, whether that is real money is for you [the jury] to determine'.[84] Moreover, he argued, there was no direct evidence that anybody *had* a consumers' surplus of $15 for beach recreation. 'Did you interview anybody and ask them what their consumers' surplus would be for a day at the beach?' he then asked Hanemann. Second, he argued that there could not have been any real loss of consumers' surplus when the beaches were closed because '618,000 people didn't sit home, drinking their beer and crying they couldn't go to the beach. They did something else. They went to the mall'.[85] Third, he objected that the value we were using was an average, which made it unreliable. 'Professor Hanemann also says that a babe in arms suffers the same loss of consumers' surplus as the parents. You simply will have to judge whether that kind of mathematical calculation is credible'.[86] He also challenged the use of an average on legal grounds because 'we do not have a plaintiff, we have an average man, and there is no legal authority for awarding average damages to an average man'.[87] The judge called this 'an interesting issue' but rejected the argument.[88]

A second issue that was much debated was the matter of spatial substitution. ATTRANSCO's attorney raised this as a legal matter of the plaintiff's obligation to mitigate damages: 'A person who has been damaged by the wrongful act of another is bound to exercise reasonable care and diligence to avoid loss and minimize damages and may not recover for damages that could have been prevented by reasonable efforts ... The issue we have here is substitution, and substitution is mitigation. If someone does not go to the beach, but could go to the beach, there's been a failure to mitigate'. The judge called this 'an interesting concept' but rejected it.[89] Dr Dunford raised the issue of substitution as a matter of economics, and argued that substitution was very likely to have occurred because, in Orange County alone, there were many very good substitutes for the closed beaches. On cross-examination, however, he conceded that he did not have 'a factual analysis or any sort of attendance analysis to support that [conclusion about substitution]'.[90] He also argued that an absence of substitution must mean that the consumers' surplus from beach recreation was lower than the incremental cost of going to a substitute site, thereby supporting his estimate of a low consumers' surplus from beach recreation.[91,92]

With regard to the amount of recreation, Dr Dunford's estimate was a loss of 264 000 beach recreation trips during the beach closure period.[93] He decided to 'stay with' the figure of $2.30 per trip to value them, resulting in an estimate of a total recreational loss amounting to $607 200, as shown in Tables 15.1 and 15.3.[94]

The new element in Dr Dunford's testimony dealt with an analysis by his staff of the PARVS travel cost data – as opposed to the CV data – for Southern California beaches. Dr Dunford testified that his staff had recently analysed our data set on one-day recreation trips by Southern California residents;[95] using OLS, Poisson regression and quantile regression and specific parametric functional forms (a different functional form with each estimation method), they had come up with estimates of consumers' surplus of about $5 per trip, compared to our estimates of $20–40 per trip. These conclusions were delivered with no advance notice to the state's attorneys and with no details of the estimation. Without these details, we could not exactly replicate the TER analysis. However, we believe that most of the difference between their estimates and ours are due to three factors: (a) TER staff used a different functional form with each estimation method, and we believe that some selection bias was taking place; (b) our estimate was based on averaging the predicted consumers' surplus per trip for each individual in the data set, while their estimate was based on the ratio of average predicted total consumers' surplus for each individual in the data set divided by the average predicted total number of trips per individual; (c) similarly, to account for multiple people in a party, we calculated the average of predicted consumers' surplus per person-trip, while they divided the average of total consumers' surplus by the average number of household trips *and* the average number of people per party. In both cases, we believe they had fallen into the error of estimating the mean of a ratio by taking the ratio of the means.

One of the more memorable experiences in life is to sit in the witness box before a jury and have the other side's attorney confront you with an embarrassing error in your data. Hanemann had the pleasure of this experience during his cross-examination when ATTRANSCO's attorney confronted him with errors in five of the handwritten State Beach Monthly Visitor Attendance Reports. The total attendance data had been wrongly entered in the paid vehicle counts column and erroneously multiplied by the conversion factors that applied to paid vehicles; the effect was an eightfold error in each day's reported attendance during these particular months.[96] We had actually noticed and corrected this and other errors when we keypunched the data ourselves, prior to August 1994. Unfortunately, it had not been noticed when the data were keypunched at the Sacramento headquarters of DP&R, and we had not noticed DP&R's oversight when we used the microfiche versions of the Monthly Visitor Attendance Reports that we obtained from DP&R headquarters. This was certainly an error, for which Hanemann took full responsibility. ATTRANSCO's lawyer hammered away at the fact that this could affect our entire analysis. Hanemann pointed out that it involved only five out of 160 months of beach data used in our statistical model, and would probably have only a small effect.

Following Hanemann's testimony, we immediately corrected the keypunch errors, together with some other minor errors that we found when rechecking the data. Paul Ruud re-estimated his models with the corrected data and produced new predictions of beach attendance during the period 8 February–31 March 1990. We then revised our estimates of lost surfing and general beach recreation. We found that the net effect of the correction to the data was to *increase* the estimated loss of beach recreation by about 1 per cent. The data errors had occurred during December and January, not the spill months of February and March (which partly explains why we had not detected them). Correcting the data errors had the effect of *lowering* predicted attendance in December and January, and *raising* it in February and March. The errors involved two state beaches; but, because our statistical model included lagged attendance at neighbouring beaches with generally negative coefficients, prediction errors tended to be self-cancelling in the aggregate. Overprediction of attendance at one beach tended to induce a lower prediction of attendance at the neighbouring beaches, and conversely. The overall effect was to minimize the bias that had been created by the data errors.

After some deliberation, the state's attorneys decided *not* to present this as rebuttal testimony at the end of the trial. While we deferred to the attorneys' judgment, it was a painful decision for us. They felt that, when the defence rested its case, the jury would be eager to wrap up the trial and would resent the days of additional testimony and cross-examination it could take to put on this evidence. They were also confident that there already was enough evidence in the record to show the jury what little difference the data errors made to our estimate of beach recreation loss. In addition, both Dr Dunford and Professor

Thurman had testified that they could not say whether the errors in the data would affect the amount of predicted attendance one way or the other.[97]

The jury deliberated for two and a half days before returning a verdict awarding the Trustees recreation damages in the amount of $12 753 071 plus a civil liability of $5 311 624.50 under the California Water Code, for a total of $18 064 695.[98] The next day, the *Los Angeles Times* quoted some jurors as saying that the jury had reached this figure by applying a 10 per cent reduction to our estimate of lost beach recreation, to allow for the keypunch errors in our data; as an added caution, they had gone back to the Bell and Leeworthy (1986) estimate of $13.19 for consumers' surplus per beach trip, and then updated this to 1997 dollars. Essentially, they gave the state most of what it had asked for.[99]

Following the verdict, the judge awarded the Trustees an additional $4.37 million dollars in costs, expert fees and attorneys fees. ATTRANSCO filed a motion for a new trial, which the judge denied. ATTRANSCO next filed an appeal of the verdict. Some months later, ATTRANSCO brought in a new attorney. On 31 August 1999 ATTRANSCO and the state agreed to a settlement in which ATTRANSCO paid to the plaintiffs a total of $16 million and the plaintiffs released ATTRANSCO from any and all claims. With that, the case was finally closed.

SOME LESSONS

The *American Trader* case illustrates several issues that can arise in the course of implementing the liability approach to the control of pollution which are sometimes overlooked in the environmental economics literature.

Unlike, say, the Microsoft case, this case did *not* involve a disagreement about economic theory. Here the experts on both sides agreed that consumers' surplus is the theoretically correct measure of the loss and that both the travel cost method and CV can be used to measure this. However, there was substantial divergence on the economic facts of the case. At trial, the plaintiff, the victim of the pollution, argued that there had been a loss of at least 618 000 trips, and probably a couple of hundred thousand more. The defendant, the polluter, argued that there had been a loss of at most 264 000 recreational trips, and up to 100 000 less. The victim argued that the lost trips should be valued at $15 per trip, and possibly as much as $23. The polluter argued that the lost trips should be valued at no more than $2.30 per trip, and probably some amount less. On both sides, these were sincerely held views, not just strategic positions adopted for purposes of bargaining. Nor were these differences peculiar to the trial. Except for the fact that we had additional information in 1997, our position at the trial was similar to what we had advised the state when it began settlement negotiations in 1991. And, while TER adopted a different position on several aspects of the benefits transfer in this case than in other cases in which it was engaged during the same period, we felt this was at the behest of its client, ATTRANSCO's attorney, whose position at the trial was similar to what it had been throughout settlement negotiations. The two parties saw basic facts regarding the damages very differently. This is not always recognized in economic models of bargaining and pollution control.

It is sometimes claimed that the benefits transfer approach provides a convenient solution when the requisite data are lacking. But in this case there was considerable disagreement over basic issues such as whether or not beaches in Florida are 'substantially dissimilar' from beaches in Southern California. If this benefits transfer is problematical, how much more so others! It is striking that, although both parties initially decided to use benefits transfer, as the trial approached they each felt compelled to undertake original research to re-analyse the data and re-estimate the models used in the benefits transfer studies – both the Florida data from Bell and Leeworthy (1986), which was re-analysed by TER, and the PARVS data, which both we and TER re-analysed.

The case also illustrates how alternative analyses of data can produce quite different results. An example is the alternative models of daily beach attendance estimated by Ruud and Thurman; using exactly the same data, one model predicts an attendance of 530 00 trips and the other an attendance of around 300 000 trips. Some of the difference can be explained by professional judgements of statistical issues of the sort most economists are used to. However, we also believe that the daily attendance data we collected are genuinely difficult to model as time series. In the winter, beach attendance can switch very suddenly from many days of very low turnout to a bonanza day when crowds show up at the beach. The effects of changes in temperature may be quite non-linear, and there are also complex lag effects. Most consumer demand analysis in economics deals with monthly, quarterly or annual data; disaggregation to daily or weekly data can pose challenges which have not been widely experienced.

One might think that this case was just about using economic valuation in the courts. But we would argue it was about something more general, namely using economic analysis in the courts. A significant part of the argumentation was about measuring the quantity of a commodity: how many trips do people take to the beach in February? This is hardly different from measuring the consumption of any other commodity at a micro level, such as how many eggs are consumed in Orange County in February; anybody who has attempted it will know how difficult the measurement can be. Moreover, in our view the other main issue at stake in the trial – what is the consumers' surplus per trip to the beach? – is not substantially different from measuring other economic parameters such as the price elasticity of demand for eggs. Both measurements rely on models and involve judgements about matters of model specification and estimation that are inevitably open to dispute.

Looking back, it is striking to us how much of the case revolved around surveys and issues of data collection. Dunford *et al.* (1995) and Deacon and Kolstad (1995) criticized the PARVS and Florida survey data in Leeworthy and Wiley (1993) and Bell and Leeworthy (1986) because these involved the recall of trips over a 12-month period. Dr Dunford criticized the 1990 RTI survey as being unreliable. And we criticized the PARVS CV survey for the poor design of the payment scenario. Morever, the quality of the lifeguards' attendance data was a central issue from the very beginning, prompting Deacon and Kolstad to conduct an aerial survey of beaches in 1995 and RTI and us to conduct our ground-level beach count surveys in 1990 and 1996–97, respectively. In an adversarial setting one acquires an even greater respect for data than is common when writing papers for academic journals. A noteworthy example in this case is the errors in the Monthly Visitor Attendance Reports. We described these forms in mind-numbing detail at the beginning of this chapter. In the end, keypunch errors in five of those forms may have cost the state 10 per cent of its claim, about $1.4 million, according to the account in the *Los Angeles Times*; under other circumstances, we believe the loss could have been significantly larger.

We draw two final conclusions from our experience in this case. First, details matter! Second, although the case was played out in an entirely non-academic setting, we found that it required a distinctly research-oriented approach in order to be credible with the judge and the jury. Issues of data collection and analysis played a central role in the four weeks of trial testimony, and these were as challenging as any academic research we have conducted.

NOTES

1. This is a revised and substantially expanded version of Chapman *et al.* (1998). We are grateful to the State of California's attorneys, Sylvia Cano Hale, Deputy Attorney General, and Michael Leslie, Mary Newcombe and David Pettit of Caldwell, Leslie, Newcombe and Pettit, for their assistance in providing information; it was a pleasure to work with them throughout the course of this litigation.
2. *People of the State of California ex rel. Department of Fish and Game, et al.* v. *BP America, Inc., et al.*, Orange County Superior Court Case Number 64 63 39; the authors were testifying experts for the plaintiffs.
3. Dunford (1999) and Deacon and Kolstad (2000) discuss this same case from a defendant's perspective. Some other natural resource damage cases have been discussed in Mead and Sorenson (1970), Brown *et al.* (1983), Kopp and Smith (1993), and Ward and Duffield (1992).
4. In the case of the *Exxon Valdez* oil spill, the state and federal governments negotiated a settlement with Exxon in 1991 before they had completed their natural resource damage assessments. The cases that did go to trial involved claims by commercial fishermen for private economic losses. Cases by Alaskan natives for loss of subsistence use of fish and

wildlife were settled just prior to trial; the court refused to allow other private claims for economic loss and for loss of recreational use and enjoyment (Duffield 1997).

5. ATTRANSCO, the sole defendant in the 1997 trial, had already accepted responsibility for the spill. The other issues being tried were the amount of oil (the state is allowed to impose a civil liability not to exceed $20 per gallon spilled) and whether or not the defendant was negligent because its employees had not taken sufficient steps to avert the accident, which would expose ATTRANSCO to claims from the other defendants who had already settled.

6. Testimony revealed that the ship's pilot thought he was in 56 feet of water, when he was actually in 50 feet.

7. Also on 8 February, ATTRANSCO signed a contract with RTI to conduct an economic damage assessment.

8. Paul Ruud is a Professor in the Department of Economics at the University of California, Berkeley.

9. At the time of the assessment, Roger Tourangeau was a survey research expert at the National Opinion Research Center; he has since joined the University of Michigan's Survey Research Center where he is a Senior Scientist.

10. Stanley Presser is Director of the Survey Research Center and Professor of Sociology at the University of Maryland, College Park.

11. Michael Ward is an Assistant Professor in the Department of Agricultural and Resource Economics at the University of California, Berkeley.

12. After the spill, 595 oiled birds were recovered dead or died at cleaning centres, including 79 brown pelicans, an endangered species. Allowing for unobserved bird injuries and deaths, it is estimated that a total of 5390 birds were oiled, of which 2544 died. In addition there was some death of finfish and shoreline organisms, but no marine mammal deaths.

13. For an account of this case, see Hanemann (1992).

14. Their analysis was subsequently described in Deacon and Kolstad (2000).

15. Their analysis was subsequently described in Dunford (1999).

16. Before the trial, ATTRANSCO offered to settle for $2.5 million; the state asked for $5.5 million, and the negotiations were inconclusive.

17. The National Marine Fishery Service (NMFS) had just decided in January 1990 to discontinue its bi-monthly telephone survey of households in coastal counties along the West Coast to measure participation in saltwater fishing. The state agreed to fund one more wave of this survey, covering January–February 1990, with a slightly expanded questionnaire that covered saltwater boating as well as fishing. However, the NMFS survey did not contain valuation questions.

18. At the time of the spill, this was $4 per vehicle or $50 for an annual pass.

19. It was not possible to obtain data on daily attendance at other beaches near the spill area. The next two beaches south of Laguna Beach, Aliso Creek Beach and Salt Creek Beach, are both operated by the Orange County Recreation Department, which reports attendance on a monthly but not a daily basis. At Doheny State Beach, daily attendance data might have been available but we thought this would not be useful because the main parking lot at Doheny was closed for repair at the time of the spill, which significantly affected recorded attendance. The two closest beaches to the north of Bolsa Chica are Sunset Beach and Surfside Beach; both are small beaches and no attendance records are kept for them. Part of Seal Beach was closed for two days following the spill. The lifeguards at Seal Beach had kept a record of daily attendance from 1985 through 1987, but had discontinued this from 1988 onwards. The next beaches to the north are in Los Angeles County, starting with Belmont Shores; there were monthly but not daily attendance data for the beaches in Los Angeles County.

20. When estimating his model, Ruud did not use the data from 7 February through 31 March 1990.

21. These are the five beaches closed due to the spill: Bolsa Chica, Huntington and Crystal Cove state beaches, and the city beaches of Huntington Beach and Newport Beach – together with Laguna Beach.

22. In Table 15.1, the 'closure period' refers to the dates when the beaches were partially or completely closed. At Newport Beach, the first part of the beach reopened on 19 and 20 February, other parts reopened on 28 February, and the remainder reopened on 10 March. At

Huntington City Beach, part reopened on 1 March, and the remainder on 14 March. Part of Bolsa Chica and Huntington State Beaches reopened on 2 March and 3 March, the remainder reopening on 14 March. 'Outside the closure period' refers to any days during the period 8 February–31 March 1990 when the particular beach was fully open.

23.   A story in the *Los Angeles Times* on 3 March 1990 noted the 'throngs of curiosity-seekers who flocked to the area to see the effects of the spill'.

24.   This breakdown comes from the Report of Collection forms; these forms were no longer available for the years prior to 1990.

25.   Even when the whole beach was roped off, there was access to a small portion immediately adjacent to the boardwalk, representing about 5 per cent of the beach area.

26.   At both of these beaches we adjusted the attendance reported after reopening to correct for an excess number of free vehicles but we did not correct for an excess number of paid vehicles with annual passes. Some of the latter were coming just to see what the beach looked like after reopening rather than to engage in beach recreation, but we included them in the total of beach users anyway.

27.   In a natural resource damage assessment for another Southern California oil spill, at Avila Beach in 1992, Dunford had used the corresponding regional value of beach recreation from Dornbusch (1987) amounting to $12.08 per trip in March 1993 dollars (Dunford *et al.* 1993).

28.   Bell and Leeworthy (1986) also collected data on recreation by non-residents at Florida beaches, from which they estimated a non-resident demand function and calculated consumers' surplus for a non-resident trip. We had no data which would allow us to break down lost beach recreation by residents versus non-residents of Southern California.

29.   In his Avila Beach analysis, Dunford had used a premium of 20 per cent to value nude beach use, viewed as a specialized activity, and he had valued windsurfing at $16.91 in March 1993 dollars.

30.   These boating and fishing trips were lost when harbour entrances were blocked by booms to keep the oil out.

31.   Deacon and Kolstad (1995); Thurman (1995); Dunford *et al.* (1995).

32.   Dunford *et al.* (1995) made no reference to the fact that RTI had interviewed the very same lifeguards and collected the same attendance data from them in 1990 and 1991. Instead, the report professed to be baffled by the lifeguards' data and to have no independent knowledge of this beyond what was contained in our 1994 report.

33.   To implement this, he assumed that the consumers' surplus from rubbernecking lay between one-third and one-half of the consumers' surplus from beach recreation. See Dunford *et al.* (1997) for an elaboration of his arguments and Randall (1997) for an opposite view.

34.   Dunford *et al.* (1995). In our experience, this exaggerates the ease of getting around Los Angeles and ignores the fact that during most hours of the day there is significant congestion on both the Pacific Coast Highway and the inland freeways which most visitors of the beaches closed by the spill would have had to use to reach beaches south of Laguna Beach or to the north in Santa Monica Bay. We checked this out by driving the routes that beach users would take and timing the trips (Hanemann Exhibit 909).

35.   In 1991, RTI had estimated preliminary models of attendance for the five affected beaches using monthly attendance data from the lifeguards' reports covering the period January 1981 through December 1990. The RTI models showed a loss of 145 518 beach trips in February and March 1990, without any adjustment to reported attendance during the closure period, and an additional loss of 288 613 trips in April 1990.

36.   The error was noted in Hanemann (1996). Adjusting the predicted median of *y* to obtain the predicted mean is non-trivial. Goldberger (1968) and Bradu and Mundlak (1970) discuss some of the complexities involved in the homoscedastic case. Thurman did not provide enough details of his GLS estimation for us to tell whether he had fully adjusted for the predicted mean in his GLS model.

37.   The lifeguards confirmed that, in their experience, the temperature inland usually had more impact on beach attendance than the temperature at the beach. They had also said this to RTI staff in February 1991 (Trial transcript, p. 4506).

38.   To convey the impression that the spill period was unusually cold, Dunford used a graph, reproduced as Figure 1 in Dunford (1999), which showed that 1990 had the lowest average

maximum daily temperature over the period 8 February–9 March of any year between 1986 and 1993. But the conclusion did *not* hold if one used other time periods such as the month of February or the month of March. In February 1990 there had been six days with a maximum daily temperature of 60°F. But in February 1993 there had been five days when the maximum daily temperature ranged from 58 to 61°F and in February 1992, there had been six days when the maximum daily temperature ranged from 58 to 61°F. In 1989 there had been eight days when the maximum daily temperature ranged from 52 to 59°F.

39. Thurman deposition 11/7/96, pp. 32, 106; 11/8/96, pp. 159, 175. The reviewer was Professor Matthew Holt, his colleague in the Department of Agricultural and Resource Economics at North Carolina State University.

40. Dunford *et al.* (1995). In support of this assertion, they compared Bell and Leeworthy's respondents with the respondents to a NOAA survey of beach users in Los Angeles County, to be mentioned further below. The NOAA respondents were richer (46 per cent had an income over \$40 000, versus 20 per cent for Bell and Leeworthy), younger (mean age of 33.4, versus 43.5 for Bell and Leeworthy), more masculine (57 per cent male, versus 50 per cent for Bell and Leeworthy), and fewer white (79 per cent white, versus 92 per cent for Bell and Leeworthy). We felt that, if anything, these demographics implied a higher beach value in Los Angeles than Florida, and we were unconvinced that Bell and Leeworthy's Florida study was too different from Los Angeles to be considered for use in a benefits transfer.

41. In Florida, the summer, though the hottest time of the year, is *not* the high season for beach use; the winter is the high season.

42. With this type of outage, *everybody's* consumption is shut down, both those with high consumers' surplus and those with low consumers' surplus. The error of using marginal consumers' surplus in these circumstances was first pointed out by Seneca (1970) and Visscher (1973).

43. When we wrote our 1994 report we were aware that Dr Leeworthy had conducted surveys of beach users in Southern California, but we had not seen any results of the surveys or any of Leeworthy's analysis. The data are summarized in Leeworthy *et al.* (1990, 1991). Leeworthy's first report on his analysis of PARVS data, using data from a 1988 survey at Island Beach State Park in New Jersey in the summer of 1988, was published in Leeworthy and Wiley (1991).

44. The results for Cabrillo-Long Beach, Santa Monica and Leo Carillo are reported in Leeworthy and Wiley (1993); the other three results were in a personal communication, Leeworthy (1995). All of these results are based on single-site models. Leeworthy (1995) wrote that he also estimated a pooled cross-section model for the Southern California Region: 'The data were weighted by total site visitation when pooling across sites. A count data model, using the Poisson regression (both untruncated and truncated models) was estimated. Results here on a per person per day basis for the consumers' surplus were \$44.52 for the untruncated model, and \$23.58 for the truncated model'.

45. These are Cabrillo-Long Beach, where there is a heavily urban setting unlike that at the beaches affected by the spill, and Santa Monica Beach. In February 1991, RTI staff had been told by lifeguards there that 'Long Beach is too filthy to swim in usually' and had concluded that it 'may not be a good control beach'. Dr Dunford assumed that Santa Monica referred to Santa Monica City Beach, which is fairly comparable to the affected beaches in several respects other than surfing – the surfing is much better at the Orange County beaches. However, we researched this and found out from Dr Leeworthy that Santa Monica referred to certain *other* beaches in Santa Monica Bay – Dockweiler, Manhattan, Hermosa and Redondo Beaches – which are less attractive and have less convenient parking than either Santa Monica City Beach or the Orange County beaches.

46. In a subsequent paper for an academic conference, Dr Dunford modified his analysis to assume that WTP for beach recreation is non-negative; this raised his estimate of mean WTP per trip for all California beaches combined to \$4.74 (Dunford and Fowler 1996).

47. Other evidence of public opposition to this payment vehicle in Southern California comes from an incident in March 1992 when the Santa Barbara County Board of Supervisors permitted the Nature Conservancy to introduce an entrance fee to walk on to Guadalupe Beach. There was a public uproar because, in the words of an outraged citizen, 'a free beach is a God-given and American right'. Under intense pressure, the Supervisors rescinded their

approval of the entrance fee in June 1992 (*Santa Maria Times* 14 April 1992/12 November 1992). Twenty years earlier, in 1972, California voters had approved a proposition guaranteeing the public right of access to the shoreline.

48. There was only a 23 per cent response rate for the mail surveys at the Southern California beaches, and 11 per cent of these respondents did not answer the CV question.

49. The mail survey responses confirm that this is how respondents interpreted the question.

50. We found their position curious. They expressed the opinion that 'the random utility model (RUM) approach, a sophisticated variation of the travel cost method, provides better use-value estimates than any other non-market valuation method ... It is ideally suited for measuring recreation use damages resulting from oil spills'. Absent such data in the PARVS survey, for unexplained reasons they preferred what they called 'a high-quality CV study' over the travel cost data that *was* collected in the PARVS survey. Ironically, in 1990 RTI *had* collected data suitable for estimating a RUM model at beaches affected by the spill, but Dunford *et al.* never made any reference to it and never used it to estimate a RUM model.

51. They objected that the PARVS travel cost data included not just local residents but also respondents who were from out of state and even abroad, which made the price variable unreliable. They did not address the fact that the same respondents were also in the CV data. In fact, the travel cost model selected by Leeworthy and Wiley (1993) excluded outliers, which is likely to have eliminated many non-residents.

52. Their recent paper, Deacon and Kolstad (2000), reviews the same literature and, as indicated in Table 15.2, now drops several of these studies 'due to limitations with the data or methodology used', but does not add any new ones. They conclude by recommending a value for saltwater beach recreation in the range of $1–4 (1990 dollars).

53. A fourth goal was to refine our estimate of boating trips lost due to the spill.

54. They have described the survey and their findings in Deacon and Kolstad (2000).

55. While they were careful to correct for the oversampling of longer trips, they made no adjustment for the uncertainty when somebody who arrived at the beach at, say, 1 p.m. and is interviewed at 1:45 p.m. says he is going to stay at the beach until 10 p.m.

56. The relevance of this for the estimation of beach attendance from aerial photographs is pointed out by Tourangeau and Ruser (1999).

57. The lifeguards informed us that there had been no changes since 1990 in the patterns of beach attendance, or their methods of reporting attendance, which would render it inappropriate for us to develop a correction factor for estimates of beach attendance in 1990 based on a comparison between their reports of attendance and our more comprehensive count of beach use in 1996.

58. For our attendance estimate, we doubled the half-hour counts. The sampling design is described in Tourangeau (1996).

59. The survey schedule at the city beaches called for six weekend survey days, three Fridays, and once each for the other days of the week, for a total of 13 survey days per beach. There was a similar schedule at the two main state beaches, involving 12 survey days at Bolsa Chica and 11 survey days at Huntington State; at Crystal Cove, which is much smaller than the other two state beaches, we had eight survey days. On two survey days there was no official report of attendance because parking booths at state beaches were not being manned on those days. This left 55 survey days for making the comparison between our counts and the official reports of beach attendance.

60. This is the wording used at city beaches. At the state beaches, the wording was modified to fit the different logistics of entry to state beaches.

61. Another special survey was the count verification survey, in which two interviewers made independent counts of the number of people entering a specific segment of beach during a particular time slot. Afterwards, the two counts were compared to see if they matched. In 20 such tests there was never any disagreement in counting cars, but there was a minor disagreement in counting people in four of the 20 tests. For all tests combined, the overall accuracy rate for counting beach attendance was 98.9 per cent.

62. Note that our count was deliberately conservative since, to simplify the sampling design, we excluded people using piers or the boardwalk at the city beaches, but not stepping on the

sand. The lifeguards did count these people, and some of them would undoubtedly have lost recreation because of the spill.

63. Two factors may account for this tendency. First, the number of people per vehicle may decline when there is a large turnout. Second, it is known from the literature on the sociology of crowds that, when there is a large crowd, while a greater fraction of the meeting space is filled, the average density of people per square foot may be lower with a larger crowd; the variation in density can cause visual estimates made from ground level to overstate the size of large crowds (McPhail *et al.* 1997).

64. Hanemann (1996). We found that the day of the week and the weather had no effect on the reporting error once one controls for actual attendance.

65. In the course of conducting the beach count survey, we collected the lifeguards' reports of daily attendance for all the days in February and March 1996. Paul Ruud compared these actual reported attendances with his predictions of attendance for each day at each beach, using his model from Ruud (1994). He found that the 1996 data were substantially consistent with his original model, except that the original model somewhat underpredicted 1996 attendance at Bolsa Chica and Huntington City Beaches. He therefore saw no reason to modify his model in the light of the 1996 data (Ruud 1996). Thus, the change in 'adjusted attendance' and 'predicted attendance' numbers in the first and second panels of Table 15.1 is due not to any change in Ruud's model but solely to the correction we made based on the 1996 survey to adjust actual and predicted lifeguards' reports of daily attendance to the counts that we would have observed if we had conducted a beach count survey.

66. The *Orange County Register* was not available online, and we had not seen its full coverage of the spill.

67. For Crystal Cove, we assumed that surfers were 9.9 per cent of total beach users.

68. A separate component of the 1997 survey dealt with counts of boating activity at harbours affected by the oil spill. In preparing for these counts, we planned to conduct two focus groups of boaters, one dealing with people who launched their boats from public boat ramps in these harbours. That focus group turned into a natural experiment on the value of boating. We had recruited 14 users of boat launches who had agreed to attend a focus group in Irvine at 1 p.m. on Sunday 2 February 1997 in return for a payment of $50. That morning, however, 11 people phoned in to say that they would not be coming because it was such a nice day for boating. In the end, only one person out of the 14 recruited showed up. We inferred that the median value of boating to these people exceeded $50/trip. In Hanemann (1994) we had used a value of $34/trip for boating based on studies of boating in the Sacramento Delta and at Sierra reservoirs by Spectrum Economics (1991) and Mannesto (1989).

69. One of the beaches in the area, Seal Beach, a surfing beach, was open for most of the spill period. However, the surfers in the focus group considered it an unattractive substitute due to its relatively small size and wave congestion, combined with extreme territoriality by the regular surfers there; it also had a reputation for poor water quality due to storm water runoff. Most of the surfers in the focus group said that on weekends during the spill they went south to surf at San Clemente or at San Onofre Beach in San Diego County. This is highly consistent with the responses by the surfers whom RTI interviewed when the beaches reopened in March 1990 (see below).

70. The non-parametric analysis was conducted by Michael Ward. He chose the narrowest bandwidth that was consistent with a monotone downward-sloping demand function for each site.

71. Chapman *et al.* (1998) prove that this also corrects for the truncation bias associated with sampling limited to beach users. The oversampling of more frequent beach users had not been taken into account by Leeworthy and Wiley (1993) or, indeed, by Dunford *et al.* (1995) when they analysed the CV data.

72. There were multiple files with the same name but different contents, including seven separate files containing what appeared to be the survey data but with differing numbers of observations and of variables, and no explanation for the differences. There was a similar experience in the State of Montana's suit for natural resource damages in the Upper Clark Fork Basin, where RTI had conducted a travel cost survey for the defendants in 1992–3. With the Montana survey, too, TER turned over a huge mass of files in 1995 lacking documentation, including

multiple files with the same name but different contents, and without a master copy of the survey data or a codebook.

73. The state's attorneys filed a request for the original questionnaires from the survey. It was then learned that, when Dr Dunford moved from RTI to TER in October 1994, he left these and other materials relating to the survey behind at RTI. Following its usual policy for materials from inactive cases, RTI waited for a period and then destroyed them, probably towards the end of 1996. When the Court learnt of this, it sanctioned ATTRANSCO for the destruction of evidence.

74. When asked at his deposition on 10 December 1996: 'Have you or any members of your team ever done any beach surveys in connection with any aspect of the *American Trader* incident?' Dr Dunford answered 'No'. On 13 December 1996, he was again asked: 'and you have not performed any original studies, correct?' and he answered: 'I have not ... I was not asked by my client to do such a study' (Dunford depositions, pp. 35–6, 538). Sara Hudson, a co-author of the 1991 report on the RTI survey, was working on the case for Dr Dunford at the time of these depositions. Dr Dunford subsequently testified that he had reviewed the report on the survey when taking over as manager of the case. He did not mention the survey at his deposition because: 'I did not rely on any of this survey information for my opinion and my report'. He told ATTRANSCO's attorney: 'I did not feel that any of that information was relevant and met the terms of the request for document production. And therefore, I don't think that I need to produce these. And he said, well, if that's the way you feel, that's fine' (Dunford deposition 23 July 1997, pp. 30–31). Dr Dunford said that he felt that the attendance estimates from the survey were 'not all reliable and accurate estimates' and 'I dismissed [the survey] from the very beginning when I started working on the case' (Trial transcript, pp. 4594, 4597). In Dunford (1999) he elaborated that 'two of the main oiled beaches were excluded from the sample frame. Furthermore, too few interviews were completed at some of the included beaches to produce statistically meaningful results. Thus, the chance that the RTI survey would yield reliable results was very low'. It should be noted that one of the designers of the RTI survey was Ronaldo Iachan, a sampling statistician and expert on recreational surveys (Iachan and Kemp 1995). The report he co-authored, Morton *et al.* (1991), expresses a different view from Dunford's with regard to the meaningfulness of the survey results. The sample sizes – 151 interviews at Huntington City Beach, 116 at Newport Beach, and 119 at Salt Creek Beach – would not usually be considered too small to be reliable for a travel cost study, especially since the respondents may each have taken several trips to various beaches over the two months covered by the survey.

75. The 1990 RTI survey had also included a boat count at harbours and launch ramps affected by the oil spill, similar to the boating count survey we conducted in 1997. However, the boat count data had not been used by Dr Dunford, and none of it appeared to have survived.

76. When Sunset, Surfside and Seal Beaches are included, the overall percentage of respondents over the eight weeks of the RTI survey stating that the beach was in a worse condition than before the spill was 37 per cent.

77. Morton *et al.* (1991, figs 6-1, 7-1 and 7-2).

78. Ibid.: fig. 4–2.

79. In fact, the RTI report on the survey gives an estimate of the total attendance at Huntington City and Newport Beaches during April 1990 and compares this with the lifeguards' attendance data for the same period in 1986–9, suggesting a loss of several hundred thousand trips in April 1990 (ibid.: figs 3-1, 3-2 and 3-3). In the absence of the survey data and information on the sampling plan and the survey weights, we were not in a position to verify this figure.

80. Apart from the diminution in utility, we did not assume any actual loss of beach trips in April 1990.

81. Party/charter boat sport fishing trips lost were valued at $83/trip in 1990 dollars, using the value from Walsh *et al.* (1988) for all saltwater fishing modes combined. This was slightly more conservative than the value of $87.12 /trip from a Southern California fishing study by Jones & Stokes (1989), which had been used in Hanemann (1994). Private boating trips were valued at $40/trip, a figure we considered conservative in the light of our experience with the cancelled focus group mentioned in note 68.

82. Trial transcript, pp. 5458–9.

83. Ibid. He also tried to introduce a form of guilt by association, asking Hanemann: 'You've told us about the theory of consumer surplus and you referred to Alfred Marshall. The theory of surplus value itself was invented by Karl Marx, wasn't it? ... Did [Marshall] borrow the theory of surplus value from Karl Marx?' (ibid., pp. 3123–4).
84. Ibid., p. 547.
85. Ibid., pp. 5344–5. On cross-examination, our response was 'the consumers' surplus builds in an assumption that you will be doing something else with your time and your money, just not this activity' (ibid., p. 3174).
86. Ibid., p. 553. Our response in cross-examination was that this was an average over the different people using the beach and the different trips they took there. Consequently, 'if the babe in arms did engage in beach recreation ... I'd apply the average to the babe in arms' (ibid., p. 3140).
87. Ibid., pp. 3994, 4016–19.
88. Ibid., p. 4020.
89. Ibid., pp. 5117, 5120.
90. Ibid., p. 4498.
91. Ibid., pp. 4187–9. Dunford used Seal Beach and Doheny Beach as substitute sites in calculating the cost of diverted trips, and he assumed that the diverted trips largely avoided travel along Pacific Coast Highway. These assumptions, which we found implausible, made his estimate of the extra cost of diverted trips about half of ours.
92. Hanemann pointed to some empirical evidence that we felt refuted this inference. On 4 September 1990 the parking charge at Bolsa Chica and Huntington State Beaches had been raised from $4 to $6. There was no change at that time in the parking fees at other beaches in the area. If beach users' mean WTP was only $2.30, as Dunford argued, the $2 increase would have greatly reduced the number of visits to the two state beaches. However, the attendance at these beaches showed no evidence of any reduction due to the increase.
93. This was based on a prediction by Thurman (1996) of 340 000 trips during the closure period in the absence of an oil spill, using Ruud's non-linear specification (15.2) but with the lagged dependent variables omitted. For the number of recreation trips that did take place during the closure period, Dr Dunford used the figure of 76 000 from Hanemann (1994). He did not use the higher figure from Hanemann's Exhibit 937, which would have been more favourable to his client, because of concerns he had with our 1996 beach count survey: 'I felt it had flaws in it such that you could not get an accurate or reliable estimate of the actual number of people on the beach'(trial transcript, p. 4171). He did not elaborate on what these flaws were.
94. He explained this as follows: 'If this spill closed all the beaches in California for a year, I would say $2.30 is too low. But, in fact, this spill closed a few beaches for a few weeks in the winter, and I don't think that $2.30 is particularly low' (ibid., p. 4219).
95. This analysis was conducted after Dr Dunford's final deposition in August. He said then that between December and then his staff had worked mainly on re-analysing Bell and Leeworthy's (1986) Florida travel cost data.
96. The error was detected by ATTRANSCO's attorney on the eve of trial.
97. Trial transcript, p. 4081.
98. *California Law Business* (23 March 1998) listed this as the tenth largest jury award in California in 1997. The jury also found that ATTRANSCO had been negligent.
99. After the trial, the judge complimented the attorneys on both sides for what he had found 'a very pleasant and enjoyable trial ... It was very well prepared, very professionally presented' (trial transcript, pp. 5472–3).

REFERENCES

Bell, Frederick W. and Vernon R. Leeworthy (1986), 'An economic analysis of the importance of saltwater beaches in Florida', Florida State Sea Grant College Report SGR-82, Florida State University, February.

Binkley, Clark S. and W. Michael Hanemann (1978), *The Recreation Benefits of Water Quality Improvement: Analysis of Day Trips in an Urban Setting*, US Environmental Protection Agency, Office of Health and Ecological Effects, Office of Research and Development Report, Contract no. 68–01–2282, June.

Bockstael, Nancy E., Kenneth E. McConnell and Ivar E. Strand (1988), 'Benefits from improvements in Chesapeake Bay water quality', EPA Report, Final Draft, April.

Bradu, Dan and Yair Mundlak (1970), 'Estimation in lognormal models', *Journal of the American Statistical Association* 65(329): 198–211, March.

Brown, Gardner M., Jr, Richard Congar and Elizabeth A. Wilman (1983), 'Recreation: tourists and residents', in US National Ocean Service, *Assessing the Social Costs of Oil Spills: The* Amoco Cadiz *Case Study*, Washington, DC: National Oceanic and Atmospheric Administration Report NTIS PB84–100536, ch. 4.

Carson, Richard, Nicholas E. Flores and W. Michael Hanemann (1998), 'Sequencing and valuing public goods', *Journal of Environmental Economics and Management* 36(3): 314–23.

Chapman, David J., W. Michael Hanemann and Paul Ruud (1998a), 'The *American Trader* oil spill: a view from the beaches', *Association of Environmental and Resource Economists Newsletter* 18(2): 1–6.

Chapman, David J., W. Michael Hanemann and Michael Ward (1998b), 'Nonparametric modeling of travel cost data', paper presented at the First World Congress of Environmental and Resource Economists, Venice, Italy, 25–27 June.

Curtis, T.D. and E.W. Shows (1982), 'Economic and social benefits of artificial beach nourishment civil works at Delray Beach', Department of Economics, University of South Florida, September.

Curtis, T.D. and E.W. Shows (1984), 'A comparative study of social economic benefits of artificial beach nourishment – civil works in Northeast Florida', Prepared for Florida Department of Natural Resources, Division of Beaches and Shores, Department of Economics, University of South Florida.

Deacon, Robert T. and Charles D. Kolstad (1995), 'A review of the damage estimates provided by the plaintiff's experts in the case of the *American Trader* oil spill', 7 March.

Deacon, Robert T. and Charles D. Kolstad (2000), 'Valuing beach recreation lost in environmental accidents', *Journal of Water Resources Planning and Management* 126(6): 374–81.

Dornbusch, David M. and Co., Inc. (1987), *Impacts of Outer Continental Shelf (OCS) Development on Recreation and Tourism*, Minerals Management Service Report MMS 87–0066, San Francisco, CA, April.

Duffield, John (1997), 'Nonmarket valuation and the courts: the case of the *Exxon Valdez*', *Contemporary Economic Policy* xv: 98–110.

Dunford, Richard W. (1999), 'The *American Trader* oil spill: an alternative view of recreation use damages', *Association of Environmental and Resource Economists Newsletter* 19(1): 12–20, May.

Dunford, Richard W. and Robert B. Fowler (1996), 'An analysis of intrastate and interstate differences in beach-use values', Triangle Economic Research, paper presented at the Agricultural Economics Association meeting, San Antonio, Texas, July.

Dunford, Richard W., H. Spencer Banzhaf and Kristy E. Mathews (1993), 'Damage estimates for selected recreation activities from Avila Beach oil spill', Center for Economics Research, Research Triangle Institute, RTI Project Number 5390–3, May.

Dunford, Richard W., F. Reed Johnson and Emily West (1997), 'Whose losses count in natural resource damages?', *Contemporary Economic Policy* xv: 77–87, October.

Dunford, W.D., E.S. West, R.B. Fowler, L.A. Sturtevant and S.E. Holden (1995), 'A review of the Trustees' use damage estimates for the *American Trader* oil spill', Report submitted to Williams, Woolley, Cogswell, Nakazawa and Russell, Triangle Economic Research, 30 May.

French, Deborah P., et al. (1996), *The CERCLA Type A Natural Resource Damage Assessment Model for Coastal and Marine Environments (NRDAM/CME)*. Technical Documentation Volume I, Part 1: *Model Description*, prepared for Office of Environmental Policy and Compliance, US Department of Interior, April.

Goldberger, Arthur S. (1968), 'The interpretation and estimation of Cobb–Douglas functions', *Econometrica* 35 (3–4): 464–72.

Hanemann, W.M. (1978), 'A theoretical and empirical study of the recreation benefits from improving water quality in the Boston area', PhD dissertation, Department of Economics, Harvard University.

Hanemann, W.M. (1992), 'Natural resource damages for oil spills in California', in Kevin M. Ward and John W. Duffield (eds), *Natural Resource Damages: Law and Economics*, New York: John Wiley, pp. 555–80.

Hanemann, W.M. (1994), 'Expert report of Professor Michael Hanemann regarding the *American Trader* oil spill', report submitted to the State of California Attorney General's Office, 4 December.

Hanemann, W.M. (1996), 'A report on the Orange County beach survey', report submitted to the State of California Attorney General's Office, 16 September.

Hanemann, W.M. (1997a), 'A report on the 1997 Orange County boating and surfing survey', report submitted to the State of California Attorney General's Office, 6 June.

Hanemann, W.M. (1997b), 'Final conclusions of Professor Michael Hanemann regarding lost recreational damages resulting from the *American Trader* oil spill', report submitted to the State of California Attorney General's Office, 15 August.

Iachan, Ronaldo and Suzanne Kemp (1995), 'Visitor sample surveys', *Survey Methodology* 21(1): 89–96.

Jones & Stokes, Inc. (1989), *Final Report: Development and Application of a Predictive Model to Analyze the Economic Effects of Species Availability* (JSA 85–099), Sacramento, CA. Prepared for National Coalition for Marine Conservation, San Diego, CA and National Marine Fisheries Service, Southwest Region, Terminal Island, CA, June.

Kopp, Raymond J. and V.K. Smith (eds) (1993), *Valuing Natural Assets*, Washington, DC: Resources for the Future.

Leeworthy, Vernon R. (1995), 'Transferability of Bell and Leeworthy beach study to Southern California beaches', memo to David Chapman, 22 June (Exhibit 939).

Leeworthy, Vernon R., Daniel S. Schruefer and Peter C. Wiley (1990), *A Socioeconomic Profile of Recreationists at Public Outdoor Recreation Sites in Coastal Areas*, vol. 5,' Rockville, MD: National Oceanic and Atmospheric Administration.

Leeworthy, Vernon R., Daniel S. Schruefer and Peter C. Wiley (1991), *A Socioeconomic Profile of Recreationists at Public Outdoor Recreation Sites in Coastal Areas*, vol. 6, Rockville, MD: National Oceanic and Atmospheric Administration.

Leeworthy, Vernon R. and Peter C. Wiley (1991), *Recreational Use Value for Island Beach State Park*, Rockville, MD: NOAA Strategic Environmental Assessments Division, Office of Ocean Resources and Conservation, November.

Leeworthy, Vernon R. and Peter C. Wiley (1993), *Recreational Use Value for Three Southern California Beaches*, Rockville, MD: NOAA Strategic Environmental Assessments Division, Office of Ocean Resources and Conservation, March.

Mannesto, G.M. (1989), 'Comparative evaluation of respondent behavior in mail and in-person contingent valuation method surveys', PhD dissertation, Department of Agricultural and Resource Economics, University of California, Davis.

McConnell, Kenneth E. (1977), 'Congestion and willingness to pay: a study of beach use', *Land Economics* 53(2): 1–28.

McConnell, Kenneth E. (1992), 'On-site time in the demand for recreation', *American Journal of Agricultural Economics* 74(4): 918–25.

McPhail, Clark, David Schweingruber and Nancy Bern (1997), *The Collective Action Observation Prime*r, 3rd edn, Urbana, IL: Department of Sociology, University of Illinois at Urbana-Champaign.

Mead, Walter J. and Philip E. Sorenson (1970), 'The economic cost of the Santa Barbara oil spill', in *Proceedings of the Santa Barbara Oil Symposium*, University of California, Santa Barbara, 16–18 December, pp. 183–226.

Meta Systems, Inc. (1985), *A Methodological Approach to an Economic Analysis of the Beneficial Outcomes of Water Quality Improvements from Sewage Treatment Plant Upgrading and Combined Sewer Overflow Controls*, prepared for the US Environmental Protection Agency, Office of Policy Analysis, Washington, DC.

Moncur, James E.T. (1975), 'Estimating the value of alternative outdoor recreation facilities within a small area', *Journal of Leisure Research* 7: 301–11.

Morton, Brian J., Sara P. Hudson and Ronaldo Iachan (1991), *The 1990 Beach Recreation Survey and Boat Count*, Research Triangle Park, NC: Research Triangle Institute, August.

Randall, Alan (1997), 'Whose losses count? Examining some claims about aggregation rules for natural resource damages', *Contemporary Economic Policy* xv: 88–97, October.

Ruud, P.A. (1994), 'Beach attendance in the vicinity of the *American Trader* oil spill', report submitted to the State of California Attorney General's Office.

Ruud, Paul A. (1996), 'Beach attendance in the vicinity of the *American Trader* oil spill', report submitted to the State of California Attorney General's Office, 12 September.

Seneca, Joseph J. (1970), 'The welfare effects of zero pricing on public goods', *Public Choice* 8: 101–10.

Silberman, Jonathan and Mark Klock (1988), 'The recreation benefits of beach renourishment', *Ocean and Shoreline Management* 11: 73–80.

Spectrum Economics, Inc. (1991), *Recreation Forecasts and Benefit Estimates for California Reservoirs: Recalibrating the California Travel Cost Model*, report to Joint Agency Recreation Committee, July.

Thurman, Walter N. (1995, 1996), 'Simulating attendance during closures resulting from the *American Trader* oil spill', 15 May 1995; revised, October 1996.

Tourangeau, Roger (1996), 'Survey design for the Orange County beach survey', report to Professor W. Michael Hanemann, 27 August.

Tourangeau R. and J. Ruser (1999), 'Discrepancies between beach counts and survey results', report submitted to the National Oceanic and Atmospheric Administration, August.

Tyrrell, T.J. (1982), 'Estimating the demand for public recreation areas: a combined travel cost-hypothetical valuation approach', Working Paper no. 11, University of Rhode Island, Department of Resource Economics, Kingston, RI.

US Army Corps of Engineers (1981), *Beach Erosion Control and Hurricane Protection Study for Dade County North of Haulover Beach Park, Florida*, Appendix 4, Survey Report and EIS Supplement.

US Army Corps of Engineers (1993), *Martin County, Florida, Shore Protection Project, General Design Memorandum*, Jacksonville District, South Atlantic Division, December (revised June 1994).

Visscher, Michael L. (1973), 'Welfare-maximizing price and output with stochastic demand: comment', *American Economic Review* 63(1): 224–9.

Walsh, R., D.M. Johnson and J.R. McKean (1988), *Review of Outdoor Recreation Economic Demand Studies with Nonmarket Benefit Estimates: 1968–1988*, Colorado State University, Colorado Water Resources Research Institute Technical Report no. 54.

Ward, Kevin M. and John W. Duffield (1992), *Natural Resource Damages: Law and Economics*, New York: John Wiley.

16. Protest, property rights and hazardous waste: a reassessment

**Robert Cameron Mitchell and
Richard T. Carson**

INTRODUCTION

In 1986 we published an article on the hazardous waste siting dilemma in which we identified the ambiguity of property rights as an important factor underlying the failure of siting proposals to get a considered hearing. We proposed that if government clarified who holds the property right to a hazardous waste site by granting prospective host communities veto power, this would create the context for a meaningful decision process. A key part of our proposal was that the community decision should be based on the outcome of a referendum rather than a vote by elected officials. In this chapter we assess the contemporary relevance of our proposal by reviewing the siting experience of the last 15 years. The first section presents the text of our 1986 *American Economics Review Papers and Proceedings* paper. In the second section we discuss two examples of *de facto* property right shifts to an affected public along the lines of our proposal. We also present the economic rationale for discrepancies between the willingness-to-pay measure of economic welfare change and the large willingness-to-accept amounts demanded by the public in these cases. In the following section we review the subsequent siting experience as presented in the literature. Although this literature has largely ignored our property rights analysis, we find that referendums have played a significant role in the few successes in siting hazardous waste facilities during this period. We consider the implications of this finding in our conclusion.

PROTEST, PROPERTY RIGHTS AND HAZARDOUS WASTE

The ambiguity of existing property rights that govern the siting of hazardous waste facilities[1] is an important cause of the stalemate in siting these facilities. What is called for is a new approach to siting. We suggest a political market, via a referendum mechanism that recognizes the *de facto* property rights assumed by local communities. The referendum, supervised by the state, would be held at the request of the firm wishing to site the facility. The developer, in effect, would offer a comprehensive package of incentives to the community in exchange for a yes vote.

Protest is Effective

To understand the rationale of our approach, it is necessary first to examine the evolving nature of the property rights in question, an evolution driven by changing perceptions of the risks associated with toxic waste disposal and a social movement of considerable power that has raised the cry of 'not in my backyard'. Of course, citizens as individuals have much to gain by opposing hazardous waste facilities near them, but their resistance imposes large costs on society as a whole. After all, blocking new waste facilities does not make the waste itself disappear. Quite the contrary: growing quantities of toxic chemicals held in temporary and deteriorating storage conditions as they await destruction or a permanent home create strong incentives for illegal 'midnight dumping'.

Hazardous wastes are a byproduct of the chemical revolution that followed World War II. Until recently waste disposal was not considered a social problem. Dumps containing hazardous materials were treated by the public and planners as minor extensions of garbage dumps and sanitary landfills; and opposition, if any, was based on the dumps' nuisance characteristics, not on their perceived safety risks. As for property rights, the developer's entitlement to engage in waste handling was pre-eminent as long as the facility was located in an industrial area.

Passage in the US of the Resource Conservation and Recovery Act (RCRA) in 1976 marked official recognition that these wastes, many of them disposed of improperly in the past, posed a potentially serious threat to health. Three years later, the Superfund legislation targeted existing toxic waste dumps for clean-up. In between, the issue exploded into public awareness when the problems at New York's Love Canal reached the national news media. Subsequently the entire town of Times Beach, Missouri, was abandoned after authorities found dioxin contamination there in 1982, and news reports of contaminated drinking water wells now are commonplace.

Proposed hazardous waste facilities quickly became the subject of widespread and effective protest, despite stringent federal design and operation safety standards imposed by RCRA and augmented by state regulations. For example, four years of work and $1.5 million were spent on a comprehensive treatment and land disposal facility in Los Angeles County before its corporate owner withdrew in the face of seemingly insurmountable public opposition. In Texas, a regional authority proposed a high-temperature incinerator for toxic wastes from the area (a solution favoured by environmentalists). Notwithstanding a well-demonstrated need for such a facility and initial support from local governments, citizen opposition caused the developer to give up after a three-year battle when it became apparent that political approval was not forthcoming.

Aversion Profiles

'Not-in-my-backyard' aptly captures the views of those who resist facility siting. The syndrome itself is not new: homeowners have long resisted having undesirable facilities in their neighbourhoods. What is new is the scale and intensity of protests provoked by facilities perceived to be a risk: Figure 16.1 shows the percentage of the public in a national survey[2] who were willing to accept (without protesting or moving) each of five hypothetical facilities.

Three distinct 'siting aversion profiles' emerge, with corresponding 'backyards' and protest constituencies. Reactions to a ten-storey office building represent a useful baseline. Over half say they would accept one if it were at least a mile from their homes. Majority acceptance of an industrial plant or a coal-fired electric power plant, both likely to be perceived as dirty and potentially obnoxious neighbours, occurs at about nine miles. High contrast is provided by the two facilities posing potentially catastrophic but extremely low probability risks. Both a nuclear power plant and a new, well-regulated disposal site for hazardous wastes reach majority acceptance only at the 50-mile mark, a 'distance premium' of 49 miles from the office building baseline. This suggests a crucial difference between an ordinary industrial facility and one involving hazardous wastes: the neighbours affected by the latter involve entire communities. Another difference is the number of people who feel strongly about the issue. Whereas only 9 per cent expressed the extreme view that they did not want the two industrial facilities as neighbours 'at any distance', 29 per cent took this stance about the two 'risky' facilities.

Protest Mobilization

At the local level, the aversion to hazardous waste facilities is translated into active protest whenever new facilities are proposed. Why do local residents protest? Mobilization is facilitated by: (a) the high cost perceived to be imposed on the local community by the facility; (b) the low cost of protesting; and (c) the high probability of success.

First, hazardous waste facilities are a prime example of a regulated entity whose costs and benefits are so distributed that the former are concentrated, while the latter are distributed far beyond the local area. The principal costs believed to be posed by these facilities are the health risks posed by groundwater and soil contamination in the case of landfills and contamination of the air by

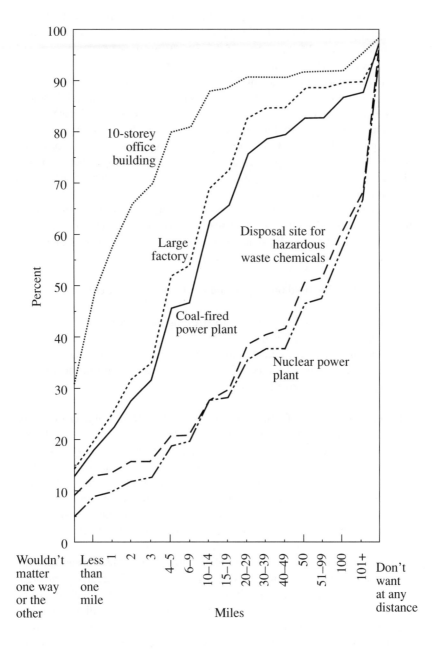

Figure 16.1   Cumulative percentage of people willing to accept new industrial installations at various distances from their homes

cancer-causing substances in the case of incineration facilities. The high level of perceived risks may be attributed both to the institutional context in which these risks occur and to the nature of the risks themselves.

The news media have highlighted past failures to handle toxic wastes properly and scientific uncertainties about the risks they pose to the public. At the local level, the siting issue appears as an abrupt threat that involves a visible source (the site) for which clear responsibility can be ascribed (the developer) – characteristics that heighten public awareness of the perceived risk. In contrast to nuclear power plants or industrial plants, for which there is usually a local constituency, a hazardous waste facility provides few offsetting benefits such as jobs or tax revenues (Tarlock 1984). Finally, residents may fear the decline of local property values.

The degree of concern about the risk externality posed by the facilities is strongly influenced by the nature of the perceived risk, which includes characteristics that have been shown in other contexts to be strongly associated with risk aversion (Slovic *et al.* 1980). They are perceived as:

1. involuntary (imposed on the community without its consent);
2. lethal;
3. memorable (due to being subject to arresting media coverage);
4. not susceptible to personal control;
5. persistent (having the potential to affect future generations); and
6. unfair (since most of the benefits accrue to those living far beyond the geographic area subject to risk).

Two characteristics of siting controversies help lower mobilization costs. First, the local character of the controversy makes it easy to identify and communicate with potential protesters. Geographic concentration also allows use of pre-existing social networks and institutions (such as churches and neighbourhood organizations). This reduces organizational costs and makes free-riding easier to manage through informal social control in the form of pressure to participate.[3] Second, public participation procedures used in many siting processes, such as hearings, offer a focal point both for organizing and for news media coverage, and easy access to decision-makers.

For individual participants, the cost of mobilization involves time and money. This includes time spent in activities such as recruitment, fund raising and organizational maintenance, as well as time spent in protest activities such as writing letters, working on lawsuits, and organizing and attending rallies. The time commitments necessary for a successful local protest movement are lumpy; only a relatively small number of activists need to commit substantial amounts of time to the effort. Siting efforts easily mobilize the necessary number of local residents who are concerned enough to become activists. For most participants, only occasional participation is necessary, because much is demanded of only a few.

The third factor affecting mobilization is the perceived likelihood that the protest activity will benefit the participant. Some people, usually highly committed activists, derive utility from the act of protest itself, which confirms their values and sense of self-worth. The efficacy calculus for ordinary participants normally involves a belief that their cause has some chance of achieving its goals. Factors that contribute to a sense of efficacy in siting protests include the widespread support for the protest in the affected community, the frequent sympathy or even support for the protest on the part of local elected officials, the availability of proven tactics (ranging from sit-ins and demonstrations to lobbying and legal interventions), expertise (from national organizations), and arenas in which to contest and delay the siting (such as local hearings, the courts and, of particular importance, local zoning and permitting processes).

Evolving Property Rights

Property rights specify how persons may benefit or be harmed and, therefore, who must pay whom to modify the actions taken by affected parties. In a now-famous article, 'The problem of social costs', Ronald Coase (1960) argued that the assignment of property rights to one party or another does not, in the absence of transaction costs, affect economic efficiency, although it does affect the distribution of wealth. Coase's insight was deep: resources are put to their most efficient use regardless of how the political system initially chooses to allocate property rights. The problem with the hazardous waste situation is that currently no one really has clear title to site a hazardous waste facility: not the firm, not the community, and not community residents as individuals.

Harold Demsetz (1967) correctly saw that property rights were subject to change over time to 'accommodate externalities associated with important changes in technology or market values'. As noted, firms wishing to site a hazardous waste facility have lost their unfettered right to locate where they wished as the public and government officials became alarmed over the possible risks posed by the technology. Local residents increasingly have been able to delay (and thus effectively block) siting efforts in administrative and judicial hearings, and communities have taken a leading role in stopping the construction of new hazardous waste facilities through the use of their extensive police powers to regulate zoning and safety. With a few exceptions, however, communities do not have the legal right to ask for sizeable payments in exchange for issuing the necessary licences and permits.

The recent establishment of state siting boards with the power to pre-empt local governments is an attempt to reassert the former property rights regime. The concurrent establishment of schemes for compensating communities for the presence of a hazardous waste facility represents a movement in the opposite direction – towards giving the property right to the community. The innovative Massachusetts siting law (O'Hare *et al.* 1993) has both features, going further in the direction of bargaining for compensation and less in the direction of pre-emption (calling for binding arbitration only in the case of irreconcilable differences) than any law in the country. No facilities yet have been sited under this law, suggesting that compensation without ultimate local veto power over a facility may not be a successful strategy.

Community Rights: A Proposal

If local residents were individually to hold the property right, developers could not bargain efficiently with the large number of potentially affected residents and one holdout could block a well-conceived project. We suggest, therefore, that a *collective property right* be established by having states pass a law specifying the use of referendums to determine local approval or rejection of a proposed facility. Such a law would require the relevant political authorities to hold a referendum when requested by a qualified developer meeting state requirements. Specific plans for the facility and for compensation to the community for its perceived drawbacks would be proposed by the developer and incorporated into the ballot proposal. Developers obviously would aim at selecting potential sites where voters would be more likely to agree to the least expensive package of measures designed to compensate a community for accepting the facility. Designing the package and promoting it would neces-sarily involve the equivalent of a public participation programme. Naturally the costs of the package would be passed on to enterprises that wished to use the facility. In order for such a proposal to be viable, there would have to be enough technically acceptable sites available so that the political market could be sustained, and no single community would have a siting monopoly.

A number of possible compensatory measures have been suggested in recent years, and the contents of a developer's particular package probably would vary according to the nature of the facility, the characteristics of the site, and the community's concerns. The types of measures that might be offered include guarantees against declines in property value, incentive payments to the community (which could be earmarked to reduce property taxes or for other purposes), outside monitoring,[4] accident insurance, credible guarantees of non-abandonment, donation of land for use as parks, and in-kind services like free waste disposal for community residents and businesses.

Should the decision rule be a simple majority, or something larger, such as the often-used two-thirds majority? Although a two-thirds majority requires a more expensive package, we argue that it is more likely to result in a Pareto-improving outcome and greater community harmony.

Who would administer and enforce the contract established by the referendum? This undoubtedly would fall first to the local political authorities and ultimately to the state. This must be made clear beforehand, because doubts about enforcement would increase the payments required to pass the referendum. In addition, there must be sufficient administrative flexibility to respond to new EPA regulations and to technological change. The boundaries defining who should be allowed to vote on the proposal is a difficult political question that the state legislature would have to decide.

The advantages of a referendum law are several. The developer and the state have strong incentives to address the issues of most concern to the community. The community's incentive to be intransigent is minimized because it has the power to say no, and it is protected from unwittingly accepting too great a risk because the facility would have to meet strict federal and state safety regulations. Moreover, the debate occasioned by the referendum should ensure close scrutiny of the developer's proposal. Paying for the compensation package transforms the costs – hitherto concentrated on the local community – into altogether more equitably shared burdens, borne by the ultimate beneficiaries of the facility. Finally, to the extent that this plan increases the costs of handling hazardous wastes, those who produce the wastes will have an incentive to engage in in-plant waste stream modifications and resource recovery.

FURTHER REFLECTIONS

From Theory to (Almost) Practice

Almost simultaneously with the publication of our paper, and quite by coincidence, the *New York Times* (6 May 1986) reported that something which illustrates some important components of our proposal was in the works in rural Lisbon, Connecticut.

According to the *Times*, Philip Armetta had proposed to locate in 3400-resident Lisbon a modern incinerator that would generate both energy from waste and $1 million in tax revenues. Despite the financial incentive and assurances that the incinerator would be equipped with the latest antipollution devices, Armetta was rebuffed. Indeed, the issue so galvanized the electorate that in November 1985 forces opposed to the incinerator captured control of Lisbon's Planning and Zoning Commission. In January 1986 the Commission majority delivered on its campaign promise and voted to prohibit the siting of waste plants in Lisbon.

At this point Armetta put a new spin on his proposal. In place of saying it would bring the town $1 million a year in new tax revenues – a solid-enough figure but one lacking appeal to individual voters – he promised to pay the 1986 property taxes of every landowner in Lisbon and to continue paying the same amount for the next 25 years. At an average of $900 per homeowner, Armetta had shrewdly calculated, his promise came to a rough annual total of $1 million. The dollars involved may have remained constant, but political winds shifted, minds changed, the local newspaper modified its editorial stance, and a referendum was scheduled. In a turnaround from the November election, Lisbon voted 680 to 590 to rezone the town to allow incinerators.

Had our proposal been law, Armetta would have his incinerator and Lisbon's property owners would have their $900 per year for 25 years. But Connecticut does not permit binding referendums in such matters and the vote thus was only advisory. In a meeting on 25 August 1986 the town Planning and Zoning Commission again voted against the incinerator by a 5 to 4 vote. Was the issue then dead? 'Nothing's dead when a substantial number of people still want it', said Lisbon First Selectman in a prescient post-vote telephone interview with the editor of *Resources* in 1986. In 1993, the Wheelabrator Company began construction of the incinerator and it is now in operation.[5]

From our property rights perspective, the negative vote by the newly elected Commission reassured property owners that the incinerator would not be forced on them and therefore that the property right was theirs, and this was confirmed by the developer's championing the non-binding referendum on his proposal. With their intransigency level disarmed they apparently were more willing to listen to Armetta's proposal. His new way of framing it highlighted the compensation in a manner that helped voters make the risk–benefit calculation.

Developers Adaptation to Property Right Shift

In some instances, the shift in the property right rules of the game can occur by a new legislative mandate. An interesting case of this occurred in San Diego, California, in 1985 when a voter-initiated proposition passed that required voter approval of any proposal to increase the zoning density in a large block of agricultural and undeveloped land within the city. Previously the City Council, whose members were heavily dependent upon developer contributions, upgraded zoning in the block in a piecemeal fashion by approving zoning variances for a sequence of small projects that many voters found objectionable on environmental and city planning grounds.

What was the effect of giving the property right to the public in this way? It eventually resulted in a situation where developers developed winning compensation packages, but this did not happen right away. For the first ten years of the new regime, 1985–95, the voters passed only one of the three developer proposals the City Council placed on the ballot, and the one that passed was a fairly small and non-controversial project. The stalemate between the voters and the developers was suddenly broken in 1996. Over the three-year period from 1996 to1998 nine proposals for changing the zoning on large parcels of land appeared on the ballot and seven passed. The winning proposals conveyed much larger benefits to the public than would have been conceived of during the days when the San Diego City Council held the decision-making power. They included a lane on Interstate 15, large amounts of land dedicated to open space, parks and other public facilities. What happened? Each of the seven winning proposals received an endorsement by the Sierra Club while those the Club did not endorse failed. It appears that by 1996 the developers discovered that obtaining an endorsement from a trusted organization that had closely examined a proposal – in this case the Sierra Club – was an effective means of reducing the informational related transactions costs to voters. The Sierra Club apparently understood which types of compensation packages voters would approve and it successfully bargained with the developers on the public's behalf for a larger fraction of the surplus associated with the zoning upgrades.

The Willingness-to-accept–Willingness-to-pay Distinction

A consequence of giving the property right to the voters is that the appropriate welfare measure is willingness to accept (WTA). In our two examples above, the WTA amounts that bought citizen approval are much larger than the amounts the citizens would presumably personally be willing to pay (WTP) to prevent the loss they would suffer from having an incinerator as a neighbour or living in an overdeveloped community if the developer held the property right. According to the typical consideration of the relationship between maximum willingness to pay (WTP) and minimum willingness to accept (WTA) for a good, the dollar amounts of the two compensation measures of economic welfare change should be quite close together. This belief stems largely from Willig's (1976) seminal work on price changes. If this is the case, it should not make much difference, either in terms of welfare calculations or actual behaviour, who holds a property right.

Recent research shows that WTA commonly exceeds WTP and that this difference is consistent with welfare theory. Large differences between willingness to pay and willingness to accept compensation measures were first observed in contingent valuation surveys (Hammack and Brown 1974). At first, this difference was seen as a survey artefact (Bishop and Heberlein 1979). Later work (for example, Knetsch *et al.* 1990) found substantial differences between the two measures even for everyday goods such as coffee mugs. A recent extensive review of the literature by Horowitz and McConnell (1999) suggests that the ratio of WTA to WTP estimates found in surveys is roughly the same as the ratio for actual transactions.

Two competing explanations have been put forth to explain the divergence. The first is prospect theory (Kahneman and Tversky 1979) which replaces utility theory's emphasis on final asset positions with a descriptive framework for analysing preferences based on gains or losses from a neutral reference position. According to prospect theory, the value function is steeper for losses than for gains. The second is Hanemann's (1991) extension of Willig's neoclassical framework to consider imposed quantity changes. Hanemann's work shows that the difference between the WTP and WTA measure is a function of the ratio of a Hicksian income elasticity term to a Hicksian gross substitution term. For changes involving large income effects or fairly unique commodities, the difference between a WTP and a WTA measure can be quite large. In the case of imposing an incinerator or a hazardous waste facility on existing residents, the good in question is typically quite unique and as such there is little to distinguish between standard neoclassical theory and prospect since both predict that there may be substantial differences between WTP and WTA measures. As Knetsch (1990) notes, the common practice of substituting a WTP estimate for the correct WTP measure can substantially underestimate the amount of compensation necessary to gain voluntary acceptance of the proposal.

Recent models that incorporate bargaining, information effects, transactions cost/experience, and uncertainty show considerable promise in being able to explain the magnitude of the divergence between WTP and WTA amounts (see, for example, Kolstad and Guzman 1999; Zhao and Kling 1999; List 2000). This work suggests factors such as knowledge of the magnitude of the potential gain to the facility operator; reversibility of the activity; trust in the operator, government regulatory authority, and non-governmental organizations (NGOs) actively involved in the issue; information-related transactions costs, and experience in making similar transactions may influence the amount of compensation required to gain voluntary acceptance of the facility. Groothuis *et al.* (1998) show that it is possible to do a WTA contingent valuation survey to obtain an estimate of the required compensation for a given case.

SITING EXPERIENCE IN THE 1980s AND 1990s

We now turn to the siting experience of the past two decades to see if there have been any successful sitings[6] of hazardous facilities since 1980 and, if so, whether the property rights were clarified along the lines of our original proposal. We were able to find descriptions of seven successful sitings of hazardous facilities. In six of the seven cases the procedures effectively granted the property right to the community, most commonly by requiring a favourable vote in a local referendum.

The continued failure to site hazardous facilities in the late 1970s and early 1980s owing to not-in-my-backyard (NIMBY)[7] protests (Murdock *et al.* 1999) and the perceived dearth of alternative ways to dispose of hazardous chemical and nuclear wastes led government agencies to redouble their exertions to solve this problem. During the 1980s 'directed siting' procedures that use a top-down approach began to be replaced in a number of states and countries by the 'voluntary' or 'willing host' approach.[8] Today, according to Puschchak and Rocha (1998), the voluntary approach 'is the preferred method of siting risk-generating facilities'. As its name suggests, this approach's key feature is the proviso that a prospective host can terminate the siting process at any time, a proviso that clarifies the property right ownership along the lines that we advocated in 1986.

Table 16.1 lists the seven successful sitings we were able to identify in the scholarly literature;[9] five are hazardous waste and two are nuclear waste facilities. The facility located at Last Chance, Colorado in the early 1980s represents, fittingly enough, the last case of a siting authority – in this case the State of Colorado – imposing a comprehensive hazardous facility on an unwilling community. In the wake of vigorous protests by local ranchers in this largely unpopulated rural area, the Adams County[10] commissioners voted to reject the Last Chance siting proposal, whereupon the State of Colorado promptly amended its siting law to enable the state ultimately to force the county to accept the facility. Making the best of a suddenly altered hand, the commissioners negotiated with Browning-Ferris Industries, then the owner of the site, to obtain the best possible benefits package (Gerrard 1994).

Of the remaining six siting successes, the Swan Hills, Alberta comprehensive hazardous waste facility is particularly noteworthy because it was the first *major* siting success in the 1980s and pioneered the use of the voluntary approach. Swan Hills,[11] an economically depressed community of fewer than 3000 residents located northwest of Edmonton in the Canadian province of Alberta, now hosts 'the most comprehensive waste treatment and disposal facility in North America' (Rabe 1994: 61).[12] The process of siting this facility, which opened in 1987, began in 1980 when the Alberta legislature approved a radical change in the Province's siting process proposed by a special Hazardous Waste Management Committee. The new voluntary strategy emphasized openness and public participation throughout the siting process, including the early stages when the geological criteria were being established and applied through constraint mapping. To be seriously considered, an aspiring host community was required to win the approval of a majority of its voters in a referendum.

Fifty-two Albertan communities voluntarily expressed a preliminary interest in the possibility of hosting the facility. Intensive efforts were made by the provincial officials to meet with groups in each of these communities. Despite some early problems with the quality of a workshop contractor's efforts which alienated some of the potential hosts, five communities remained whose leaders were sufficiently interested in hosting the facility to seek their residents'

Table 16.1 Successful sitings in 1980–1995 of hazardous facilities described in the literature

Type of Facility and Location	Decision Mechanism and Vote	Compensation – Benefit Package	Special Factors	Sources
1. Hazardous waste landfill and treatment facility. Last Chance, Colorado, USA	Approved in 1983 by Adams County commissioners after state threatened to use pre-emption.	Among benefits negotiated by the county were specified engineering techniques and truck routes, payment of 2 per cent of gross revenues to county, right to review construction and inspect the facility.	Rural, little populated, ranchland.	Gerrard (1994)
2. Hazardous waste solidification and disposal facility. Does not include an incinerator nor does it handle organic wastes such as PCBs. Blainville Quebec, Canada	Explicit declaration that siting would proceed only if a community formally agreed to participate. No mention of referendum on the facility *per se* but siting proponents won a contested 1981 referendum to fund an exit to a major highway needed for the facility.	No direct economic benefit. However the community secured a cloverleaf exit needed for commuting and economic development and the transfer of land from Canadian military to the city for an industrial park.	Small working-class suburb of Montreal. The siting effort lacked the institutional framework of the other Canadian sitings.	Rabe (1994)
3. Hazardous waste storage, treatment and disposal facility. Does not include an incinerator nor does it handle PC13s, dioxins, or cyanide. Greensboro, NC, USA	In 1983–84 developer sought 'broad community consensus'. Actual decision mechanism unspecified in sources.	According to Rabe (1994) economic compensation was minimal. Procedural compensation, such as a number of 'explicit guarantees against exploitation' were of critical importance.	Individual developer, a resident of Greensboro, convinced the community that the facility was needed and would be safe. Gained early support of environmental leaders.	Committee on Risk Perception and Communication (1989); Rabe (1994)

4. Comprehensive hazardous waste facility. Swan Hills, Alberta, Canada	1984 local referendum, 79 per cent in favour.	Local jobs (amounted to 90 jobs in 1991); 35 subsidized housing units; other government and corporation support such as a golf course, new fire equipment; commitment to restrict waste imports; special facility safety measures.	Small (pop. = 2400), economically depressed oil town. Model for the voluntary approach. Exceptionally strong public participation effort.	Schmeidler (1993); Rabe (1994)
5. Integrated hazardous waste facility. No incinerator. Montcalm, Manitoba, Canada	1991 local referendum with about 67 per cent in favour.	Prospect of economic diversification attractive but not crucial. Community received tax revenues from facility; corporation contributed funds for community facilities. Guarantees to recompense any loss in property values. Strong co-management agreement.	Rural municipality consisting of three villages. Small (pop. = 1700), relatively prosperous French speaking community. Siting process emulated Alberta's.	Rabe (1994)
6. Low–mid-level nuclear waste. Wolfenschiessen, Switzerland	1993 vote in town meeting by raising hands with approximately 60 per cent in favour.	$3 million a year for 40 years (amounts to $4687 per family).	The facility also required approval in a cantonal referendum.	Frey et al. (1996a, 1996b); Frey and Oberholzer-Gee (1997); Richardson (1998)
7. Low-level nuclear waste facility. Deep River, Ontario, Canada Site withdrawn in 1997.	1995, local referendum, 72 per cent in favour.	Agreement to maintain 1995 employment levels at AECL's nearby Chalk River Nuclear Labs, 8.75 million dollars in economic diversification funds.	Majority of Deep River workers are employed by Canada's equivalent of the Department of Energy, the AECL. Negotiated package was subsequently rejected by the federal government which led to the withdrawal of the site.	Latonis (1996); Richardson (1998); Gunderson and Rabe(1999)

Note: Includes landfill, incineration and various treatment technologies unless otherwise specified.

approval, which they received in every case and in three by large margins. Swan Hills, with 79 per cent voting in favour, was judged to be technically superior to its rivals. Despite determined efforts by a competitor community that 'storm[ed] the Alberta legislature in a futile protest' (Rabe 1994: 68), Swan Hills won the right to host the facility.

It should be noted that when Swan Hill officials first began to consider the siting prospect many residents reacted negatively and immediately formed anti-facility citizen groups. Pre-emptive level protests were avoided once residents realized that they would be able to vote the siting proposal up or down. Scholars who have examined the Swan Hill case identify a number of other factors which contributed importantly to this siting success. One was the institutional framework for siting and operating the facility. The province established a crown corporation which assumed 'a number of important responsibilities delegated to either private firms or regulatory agencies in most states and provinces' (Rabe 1994: 72). The corporation's independence, and the fact that it would oversee whichever contractor was chosen to build and operate the facility, helped it win the residents' trust. A second was the herculean effort made by local and provincial officials to meet with as many residents as possible in small group settings in order to hear and address their concerns. This was an extension of the extensive public participation effort that marked this siting process from the very beginning. The third factor was the compensation package that provided tangible economic benefits and safety assurances. The basic elements of the package were made known early in the siting process before the selection of Swan Hill, and additional features were negotiated prior to the referendum. The overall package included the promise of jobs, subsidized housing units, money for local facilities such as a golf course and new fire equipment. It also contained specified measures to take to ensure the facility's safe operation.

Manitoba emulated the Alberta voluntary process and succeeded in siting an integrated hazardous waste facility in the small rural municipality of Montcalm (Rabe 1994). The province began its siting process in 1988 and the Montcalm facility was approved four years later in 1992. Again a vigorous public partic-ipation effort combined with the assurance that the residents could veto the project enabled the proponents to overcome initial resistance. Because Montcalm was relatively prosperous, its compensation package focused on safety assurance and included institutional mechanisms whereby the community could play an active role in the facility's governance. The Montcalm Council was given the power to appoint an independent Community Liaison Committee and to nominate community representatives to a Plant Co-management Committee and the board of directors of the Manitoba Hazardous Waste Management Corporation. Sixty-seven per cent of the voters approved the siting proposal.

The two remaining successful hazardous waste facility sitings occurred earlier in the decade. Although neither involved a binding referendum on the siting issue, in both the proponents clearly signalled that they would not proceed without local approval. In the Blainville, Quebec case, the developer declared he would not go ahead unless the community formally agreed to accept the facility. Although there was no referendum directly on the issue, siting proponents won a contested referendum in 1981 which approved the construction of a highway exit from a major highway required by the facility (Rabe 1994). The second instance of a successful siting in the United States during our period occurred in 1984 when the Greensboro, North Carolina City Council accepted a hazardous waste storage, treatment and disposal facility. Again, there was no referendum, but the developer, a local resident respected in the community, assiduously sought a 'broad community consensus' (Committee on Risk Perception and Communication 1989) by holding many meetings with community leaders and citizens. Importantly, he succeeded in winning the support of local environmental leaders. In his search for consensus, he modified the proposal during the public participation period in order to address public safety concerns.[13]

Because they require secure storage for very long time periods, it is even more difficult to site facilities that handle nuclear waste. In the 1990s two governments, Switzerland and Canada, succeeded in siting new low-level nuclear waste facilites. The Swiss case, which involved a low–mid-level nuclear waste facility, is described in a series of articles by Oberholzer-Gee and Frey and colleagues. Originally the federal government and the developer were opposed to granting veto power to local communities, but the canton of Nidwalden successfully challenged this in court, with the result that *both* the canton and the selected town gained veto power (Oberholzer-Gee *et al.* 1997). The authors do not describe the public participation procedures the authorities used to convince the population of the town of Wolfenschiessen of the siting proposal's merits but presumably they were extensive. The developer offered compensation in the form of a generous annual monetary payment to the community.[14] In 1993 Wolfenschiessen voters approved the plan by a 60 per cent vote in a town meeting.

Several years later a similar facility was sited in Ontario after an arduous effort. Again the siting procedures followed the Alberta model including the requirement of a binding referendum. The authorities found the low-level nuclear waste facility a hard sell and the siting effort nearly became unrailed due to bureaucratic problems (Gunderson and Rabe 1999), but eventually the residents of Deep River voted for it by a large margin (72 per cent). One factor that made the facility less threatening to the community was that many residents were employed by the nearby Chalk River Nuclear Labs. Another was the very generous compensation package that the community negotiated with the siting agency, which committed the government to maintain the 1995 employment levels at the local nuclear labs and to provide a generous amount of money in economic diversification funds.[15] We regard this as a successful siting from our perspective even though the provincial government ultimately refused to accept the negotiated compensation package.

Our review of these siting successes confirms the importance of establishing a clear property right as the basis for negotiation between developers and agencies who wish to site a hazardous facility and prospective host communities. Every case but one granted this right to the community. Without this, pre-emptive protests would likely have prevented the siting process in many, perhaps all, of the communities described above, and in other communities which ultimately voted against hosting the facility, from reaching the voting stage. When the property right is granted 'the community's incentive to be intransigent is minimized because it has the power to say no' (Mitchell and Carson 1986: 289). For example, Denis Hall, a member of the Low-level Radioactive Wastes Siting Task Force stated: 'We got acceptance through a large majority of the voters in Deep River whereas earlier attempts through straw polls and other petitions that had been run around town indicated a strong rejection of a siting proposal' (Hall 1996). According to Armour (1999), a close observer of hazardous facility siting during our period: 'When a community is not forced into a corner and made to defend itself against an unwelcome intrusion, it is more likely to explore the possible positive as well as negative consequences of a facility siting decision'.

Also supportive of our argument that only community approval (preferably in the form of a referendum) clarifies property rights in a way that makes it possible for a community to meaningfully consider an offer to host a hazardous facility is what happens when this element is missing from an otherwise enlightened set of siting procedures. Massachusetts is one example. In our original article (Mitchell and Carson 1986) we were sceptical that the carefully devised and public-oriented Massachusetts siting procedures (O'Hare *et al.* 1993) would succeed. It did not; Massachusetts failed to site a single facility (O'Hare and Sanderson 1993).[16] California is another example. In 1986, frustrated with its inability to site new hazardous facilities, the state passed the Tanner Act (McCarthy 1999) which mandated the use of citizen review panels in the hopes that they would encourage 'meaningful dialogue' and negotiation during the siting process. If its elaborate system of public participation failed to sway a target community to favour the siting of a proposed facility, the Act ultimately allowed for state pre-emption. The outcome? None of the various attempts to site hazardous waste facilities in new locations[17] under the Tanner Act has succeeded.

We believe the cases of successful and unsuccessful sitings described in this chapter support the use of binding referendums as the best way to reassure citizens that a proposed facility will not be forced on them against their will. Our cases show that binding votes by local residents have been successfully used in three countries and there is now widespread support for binding referendums in the siting literature (Sandman 1992; Kunreuther *et al.* 1993; Rabe 1994; Gerrard 1994; Kuhn and Ballard 1998). The rationale for referendums rather than approval by town authorities is that town authorities do not always represent citizen interests. Oberholzer-Gee *et al.* (1997) observe that: 'Politicians have a large number of private incentives (career opportunities, national recognition, etc.) to agree to siting proposals'. Moreover mistrust of public officials is very widespread (Armour 1999; Pharr and Putnam 2000). Other decision mechanisms, such as the devices proposed by some economists to use a lottery- or auction-based approach (Kunreuther and Portney 1991; Swallow *et al.* 1992; Quah and Tan 1998) are shown by Frey and Oberholzer-Gee to fail the tests, which referendums pass, of fairness and competence (Frey and Oberholzer-Gee 1997; Oberholzer-Gee *et al.* 1997).

CONCLUSION

There is no question that hazardous facilities are difficult, very difficult, to site in modern societies because the risks they pose are unacceptable to many people (Slovic 1999). Our examination of the siting successes since 1980 supports our view that clearly assigning the property right to potential host communities is a necessary condition for siting this type of facility. Of course the agency that attempts to site a facility must conduct a comprehensive and credible public participation programme, another necessary condition. Even so, many attempts to employ the voluntary approach to siting hazardous waste or nuclear waste facilities fail to win majority votes in some or all of the communities they approach. This is as one would expect; some proposed facilities are flawed, some proposed locations are inappropriate and some public participation programmes are insufficient or insensitively administered. But, to those familiar with the siting wars of the 1970s and 1980s, it may come as a surprise that some communities actually volunteer to host risky facilities and that referendums on siting proposals sometimes can win majority and even super-majority votes.

The purpose of this chapter is to reiterate the *central* importance of property right clarification as a condition for successful negotiation. We have noted above the growing acceptance of the voluntary approach and the number of scholars who recommend the use of referendums as a desirable decision mechanism. Few of these scholars, however, acknowledge that the essence of a voluntary siting approach is the clarification of the property right. Instead, they treat it as just one of a number of important siting procedures which they regard as necessary for a successful siting process. For example, Kunreuther *et al.*, in their article proposing the 'Facility siting credo', approve of the voluntary approach and declare that: 'Subjecting the final decision to a binding referendum will help establish its legitimacy' (Kunreuther *et al.* 1993: 304). But referendums are considered optional and the voluntary approach is included in a list of seven recommended procedural steps that are given equal weight. In his list of the 'four design characteristics of successful siting demonstrated in the Alberta case', Barry Rabe (1994) does not include the importance of clarifying the property right by giving communities veto power. Other discussions of hazardous waste siting policy don't even consider the property right issue (Lowry 1998; Kuhn and Ballard 1998) including discussions that treat the issue from the economic point of view (Swallow *et al.* 1992; Wagner 1998).

We believe that the siting of new hazardous facilities, an inherently difficult task in modern democracies, is close to impossible unless property rights are clarified in the way we have suggested. Clarification, by recognizing that the local community holds the property right and can vote the project up or down in a referendum, reduces the incentives for residents to mobilize for a pre-emptive protest movement. On the other hand clarification creates incentives for state authorities to engage in an intensive public participation process and the developer to negotiate an acceptable compensation and reassurance package.

NOTES

1. These include waste treatment facilities, landfills and incinerators.
2. These data are from a survey conducted by Resources for the Future (Mitchell 1980). The general shape of the profiles has been found to be robust against alternative question wordings and the addition of other types of facilities.
3. We use social movements theory here, specifically the resource mobilization approach (Zald and McCarthy 1979).
4. If the developer or government is not trusted by the community to monitor the facility, the cost of a winning compensation package may be drastically increased. Monitoring by an outside agent, such as an environmental organization, might reduce the cost of the package's other elements.
5. http://www.workonwaste.org/wastenots/wn255.htm. The same source reported that Armetta will be paid about $3 million for his role in linking up another waste incinerator company with Briston-area communities.
6. We consider only facilities sited at new locations, not those sited at an existing hazardous waste site.
7. The acronym stands for Not In My Backyard and is used to refer to the knee-jerk opposition by communities proposed as sites for risky facilities.
8. At the time we wrote our paper we were unaware of the early movement towards a voluntary approach in Canada.
9. We do not include in our list any sitings that have occurred in places with existing hazardous facilities; our focus is on new sites. We have not examined the various trade journals and other primary sources of information on this subject.
10. The area is home to only a few people and there is no community located near the proposed site.

11. Our description of the Swan Hills case is based on Rabe (1994).
12. This small, isolated community was hard hit by a permanent downturn in the local oil industry, which had been its economic base.
13. Our source (Committee on Risk Perception and Communication 1989) does not mention any economic compensation.
14. On the basis of a survey they conducted in communities facing the prospect of hosting the nuclear waste site, Frey and Oberholzer-Gee (1997) conclude that compensation *reduces* people's likelihood to vote in favour of the facility because they resent the offer as a 'bribe'. We believe this finding is an artefact of their asking respondents how they would vote if $x compensation is offered *after* they have already said how they would vote with no mention of compensation. If the compensation had been included in the scenario for the original vote we believe few if any respondents would express moral objections and that the vote for the facility would have been as high or higher.
15. Indeed the compensation was too generous for the federal government, who rejected the package, leading Deep River to withdraw its siting permission.
16. In their post-mortem two authors of the plan blame its failure on 'design defects of the law itself and general characteristics of the Massachusetts public decisionmaking process' (O'Hare and Sanderson 1993). Although the defects they identify are many, they fail to recognize the key importance of clarifying the property right.
17. Two sitings occurred in at existing oil company facilities.

REFERENCES

Armour, Audrey (1999), 'Social trust: new challenges and opportunities', unpublished paper presented at E7 Seminar on Electric Utilities and Social Trust in a Changing World, Tokyo, Japan, February.

Bishop, Richard C. and Thomas A. Heberlein (1979), 'Measuring values of extra-market goods: are indirect measures biased?', *American Journal of Agricultural Economics* 61: 926–30.

Coase, R.H. (1960), 'The problem of social cost', *Journal of Law and Economics* 3: 1–44.

Committee on Risk Perception and Communication, National Research Council (1989), *Improving Risk Communication*, Washington, DC: National Research Council.

Demsetz, Harold (1967), 'Toward a theory of property rights', *American Economic Review Proceedings* 57: 347–59.

Frey, Bruno S. and Felix Oberholzer-Gee (1996a), 'Fair siting procedures: an empirical analysis of their important and characteristics', *Journal of Policy Analysis and Management*, 15(3): 353–76.

Frey, Bruno S. and Felix Oberholzer-Gee (1996b), 'The old lady visits your backyard: a tale of morals and markets', *Journal of Political Economy*, 104(6): 770–99.

Frey, Bruno S. and Felix Oberholzer-Gee (1997), 'The cost of price incentives: an empirical analysis of motivation crowding-out', *American Economic Review* 87: 746–55.

Gerrard, Michael (1994), *Whose Backyard: Fear and Fairness in Toxic and Nuclear Waste Siting*, Cambridge, MA: MIT Press.

Groothuis, Peter A., George Van Houtven and John C. Whitehead (1998), 'Using contingent valuation to measure the compensation required to gain community acceptance of a LULU: the case of a hazardous waste disposal facility', *Public Finance Review* 26: 231–49.

Gunderson, William C. and Barry G. Rabe (1999), 'Voluntarism and its limits: Canada's search for radioactive waste-siting candidates', *Canadian Public Administration* 42: 193–214.

Hall, Denis (1996), Presentation before Canadian Environmental Assessment Review Agency, Nuclear Fuel Waste Management and Disposal Concept Public Hearings. Canadian Environmental Assessment Review Agency. On Internet http://www/ceaa.gc.ca/panels/nuclear/transcripts/earav6/s5.htm, Canadian Environmental Assessment Review Agency.

Hammack, Judd and Gardner M. Brown Jr (1974), *Waterfowl and Wetlands: Toward Bioeconomic Analysis*, Baltimore, MD: Johns Hopkins University Press.

Hanemann, Michael (1991), 'Willingness-to-pay versus willingness-to-accept: how much can they differ?', *American Economic Review* 81(3): 635–47.

Hazardous Waste Consultant (1985), 'The outlook for commercial hazardous waste management facilities: a nationwide perspective', *Hazardous Waste Consultant* 4 (March–April): 1–49.

Horowitz, John and Kenneth E. McConnell (1999), 'A review of WTA/WTP studies', working paper, Department of Agricultural and Resource Economics, University of Maryland.

Kahneman, Daniel and Amos Tversky (1979), 'Prospect theory: an analysis of decisions under risk', *Econometrica* 47: 263–91.

Knetsch, Jack L. (1990), 'Environmental policy implications of disparities between willingness to pay and compensation demanded measures of values', *Journal of Environmental Economics and Management* 18: 227–37.

Knetsch, Jack L., Richard H. Thaler and Daniel Kahneman (1990), 'Experimental tests of the endowment effect and the Coase theorem', *Journal of Political Economy* 98: 1325–49.

Kolstad, Charles D. and R.M. Guzman (1999), 'Information and the divergence between willingness to accept and willingness to pay', *Journal of Environmental Economics and Management* 38: 66–80.

Kuhn, Richard G. and Kevin R. Ballard (1998), 'Canadian innovations in siting hazardous waste management facilities', *Environmental Management* 22: 533–45.

Kunreuther, Howard C., Kevin Fitzgerald and Thomas D. Aarts (1993), 'Siting noxious facilities: a test of the facility siting credo', *Risk Analysis* 13: 301–15.

Kunreuther, Howard C. and Paul Portney (1991), 'Wheel of fortune: a lottery/auction mechanism for siting of noxious facilities', *Journal of Energy Engineering* 117: 125–32.

Latonis, Graham (1996), 'Presentation to the Canadian Environmental Assessment Review Agency, Nuclear Fuel Waste Management and Disposal Concept Public Hearings, March 25, 1996', URL: http://www.ceaa.gc.ca/panels/nuclear/transcripts/earav6/s10.htm.

List, J. (2000), 'The incredible disappearing act: the effect of market experience on the WTP/WTA disparity', paper presented at the European Association of Environmental and Resource Economists Meeting, Rythymnon, Greece.

Lowry, Robert C. (1998), 'All hazardous waste politics is local: grass-roots advocacy and public participation in siting and cleanup decisions', *Policy Studies Journal* 26: 748–59.

McCarthy, Catherine (1999), 'Testing the Tanner Act: public participation and the reduction of local opposition in siting hazardous waste facilities in California', dissertation, University of California, Davis.

Mitchell, Robert Cameron (1980), *Public Opinion on Environmental Issues: Results of a National Public Opinion Survey*, Washington, DC: White House Council on Environmental Quality.

Mitchell, Robert Cameron and Richard T. Carson (1986), 'Property rights, protest, and the siting of hazardous waste facilities', *American Economic Review Papers and Proceedings* 76(2): 285–90.

Murdock, Steven H., Richard S. Krannich and F. Larry Leistritz (eds) (1999), *Hazardous Wastes in Rural America: Impacts, Implications and Options for Rural Communities* Lanham, MD: Rowman & Littlefield.

Oberholzer-Gee, Felix, Iris Bohnet and Bruno S. Frey (1997), 'Fairness and competence in democratic decisions', *Public Choice* 91: 89–105.

O'Hare, Michael, Lawrence S. Bacow and Debra Sanderson (1999), *Facility Siting and Public Opposition*, New York: Van Nostrand Reinhold.

O'Hare, Michael and Debra Sanderson (1993), 'Facility siting and compensation: lessons from the Massachusetts experience', *Journal of Policy Analysis and Management* 12: 364–76.

Pharr, Susan J. and Robert Putnam (2000), *Disaffected Democracies: What's Troubling the Trilateral Countries?*, Princeton, NJ: Princeton University Press.

Puschak, Ron and Cecilia Rocha (1998), 'Failing to site hazardous waste facilities voluntarily: implications for the production of sustainable goods', *Journal of Environmental Planning and Management* 41: 23–43.

Quah, E. and K.C. Tan (1998), 'The siting problem of NIMBY facilities: cost–benefit analysis and auction mechanisms', *Environment and Planning C: Government and Policy* 16: 255–64.

Rabe, Barry George (1994), *Beyond NIMBY: Hazardous Waste Siting in Canada and the United States*, Washington, DC: Brookings Institution and MIT Press.

Richardson, Peter J. (1998), 'A review of benefits offered to volunteer communities for siting nuclear waste facilities', URL: http://www.radgiv-karnavf.gov.se/publikat/incitame.htm.

Sandman, Peter M. (1992), 'If coercion doesn't work, what does? Siting controversial facilities: some principles, paradoxes, and heresies', *Consensus* July: 2.

Slovic, Paul, Baruch Fischhoff and Sarah Lichtenstein (1980), 'Facts versus fears: understanding perceived risk', in R.C. Schwing and W.A. Albers, Jr (eds), *Societal Risk Assessment: How Safe is Safe Enough?*, New York: Plenum.

Swallow, Stephen K., James J. Opaluch and Thomas F. Weaver (1992), 'Siting noxious facilities: an approach that integrates technical, economic, and political considerations', *Land Economics* 68: 283–301.

Tarlock, A.D. (1984), 'Siting new or expanded treatment, storage, or disposal facilities: the pigs in the parlors of the 1980s', *Natural Resources Lawyer* 17: 429–61.

US Environmental Protection Agency (1980), *Hazardous Waste Facility Siting: A Critical Problem*, Washington, DC: US Environmental Protection Agency.

Wagner, J. (1998), 'That was then and this is now: an economist's wish list for the LLRW siting paradigm', *Natural Resources Journal* 38: 635–49.

Willig, Robert D. (1976), 'Consumer's surplus without apology', *American Economic Review* 66: 587–97.

Zald, Mayer N. and John D. McCarthy (1979), *The Dynamics of Social Movements: Resource Mobilization, Social Control, and Tactics*, Cambridge, MA: Winthrop Publishers.

Zhao, J. and C.L. Kling (1999), 'Real options and the WTP/WTA disparity', working paper, Department of Economics, Iowa State University.

Index